The Pennsylvania Weather Book

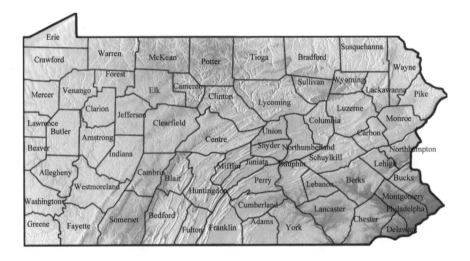

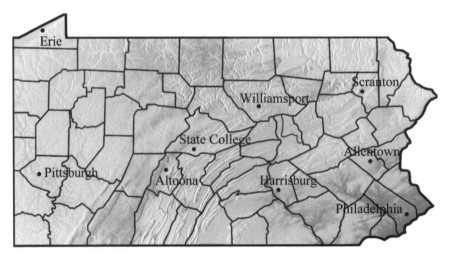

The Pennsylvania Weather Book

BEN GELBER

Rutgers University Press
New Brunswick, New Jersey

Frontis 1. Pennsylvania counties
Frontis 2. Pennsylvania cities

Library of Congress Cataloging-in-Publication Data
Gelber, Ben.
  The Pennsylvania weather book / Ben Gelber.
    p. cm.
  Includes index.
  ISBN 0-8135-3056-3 (alk. paper)
  1. Pennsylvania—Climate—History. I. Title.
QC984.P4 G45 2002
551.69748—dc21   2001048612

British Cataloging-in-Publication information for this book is available from the British
Library.

Photos from American Philosophical Association, *Easton Express-Times,* Monroe
County Historical Association, Pennsylvania State Archives, *Pittsburgh Post-Gazette*
Photo Archives, Michael Pontrelli, and Elizabeth (Korb) Schuman reprinted with
permission.

Manufactured in the United States of America

To Justin,
Joshua,
and Jordan,
my parents,
and my loving family

Contents

Figures

Figures

x

Tables

Preface and Acknowledgments

The weather has always been a favorite topic of conversation since the dawn of civilization. Undoubtedly, someone must have said to Noah, "I thought they said it was supposed to let up Tuesday."

Although you hear this refrain everywhere, New Englanders have been generally credited with the popular notion "If you don't like the weather, wait a few moments." Over a century ago, American essayist Charles Dudley Warner (1890) wrote in the *Hartford Courant*, "Everybody talks about the weather but nobody does anything about it." Warner merely echoed the comments of Samuel Johnson in 1758, who observed, "When two Englishmen meet, their first talk is of the weather." The great American author Mark Twain was always offering his two cents on the weather, commenting on the "sumptuous variety" of New England atmospherics.

As early as February 1735, Benjamin Franklin asserted in his publication *Poor Richard's Almanac*, "Some are weather-wise, some are otherwise." These days almost everyone is weather-wise, thanks to the Weather Channel, local television, and newspaper weather reports, which blend local forecasts with national maps and coverage of severe weather. A spate of popular books and videos cover a wide range of weather subjects, ranging from great hurricanes and storm-chasers to almanacs and climate histories.

Television newscasts dazzle us with an array of three-dimensional graphics depicting falling precipitation from the perspective of an airplane ride, moving jet streams, and animated clouds. Not that many years ago (early 1980s), local television meteorologists, I among them, drew weather fronts on a shiny weather wall with a magic marker, complete with stick-on symbols and letters.

Nowadays, radar and satellite imagery capture incipient storms thousands of miles away. Doppler radar provides us with an analytical view of the inside of a thunderstorm, highlighting areas of wind shear with the potential for rotation and damaging winds before a storm strikes.

Medium-range weather forecasts (three days out) today are now considered as accurate as the short-range predictions of little more than twenty years ago, hitting the mark an average of 70 percent of the time. Long-range forecasting is still speculative, but a better understanding of the complex interactions between the ocean, land, and atmosphere will ensure even more reliable extended weather predictions in the near future.

Until now, there was no up-to-date, comprehensive source of historical weather events in Pennsylvania, and I hope this project will provide a chronological database with sufficient information and sources for others to follow up on past weather events in their communities. The inspiration for this book was the seminal work of Dr. David M. Ludlum (1910–1997), the prolific author of many historical weather books and articles that laid the groundwork for the rest of us.

I wish to thank the editors at Rutgers University Press for their helpful guidance and desire to see this project through to completion, especially Helen Hsu and Suzanne Kellam. Graphical credits belong to Rick Smeltzer of Weather Detection Systems, Inc., Columbus, Ohio. Karie Kirkpatrick compiled the index.

I wish to thank the following persons for offering helpful manuscript suggestions: Michael Hanson, Ohio Geological Survey; Ian Ackroyd-Kelly, East Stroudsburg University; Jay Hobgood, Ohio State University; and Jym Ganahl, WCMH-TV, Columbus, Ohio. I also wish to thank Michael Pontrelli, Murad Dervish, and Kelly Frank for additional comments and data.

I sincerely appreciate the enthusiastic support of NBC 4 (WCMH-TV) president and general manager Michael Jack, and my friends and colleagues throughout this process. Many others provided key assistance with pictures and links to documents essential to the completion of this project: Sherry Whittaker, Upper Arlington (Ohio) Public Library; Michael Sherbon, Pennsylvania State Archives, Harrisburg; Alva Wallis, National Climatic Data Center, Asheville, North Carolina; Robert Cox, American Philosophical Society, Philadelphia; Maria Carpico, *Pittsburgh Post-Gazette*; Carol King, *Express-Times*, Easton; Patricia Jersey, East Stroudsburg University; Nancy Amspacher, York County Historical Trust; Candace McGreevy, Monroe County Historical Association; Jacalyn Mignogna, Carnegie Department of Pittsburgh; Betty Schuman, Hilliard, Ohio; Paul Knight, Pennsylvania state climatologist, University Park; Jeff Rogers, Ohio state climatologist, Columbus; Bradley Rehak, National Weather Service, Pittsburgh; Keith Eggleston, Northeast Regional Climate Center, Ithaca, New York; and Daniel McCarthy, Storm Prediction Center, Norman, Oklahoma.

Most of all, I owe a great deal of gratitude to my parents, Norman and Judith Gelber, for their cheerful assistance in gathering historical meteorological data at local libraries that I could not reach.

The Pennsylvania Weather Book

Nay, oft so quick the change,—so great its pow'r—
As summer's heat and winter in an hour!
Sometimes the ice so strong and firm, we know
That loaded wagons on the river go.
But yet so temp'rate are some winters here,
That in the streams no bars of ice appear!

—Thomas Makin Latin on Pennsylvania, 1729

Pennsylvania Landscape and Climate

The beauty of the countryside in Pennsylvania is distinct from that of other regions.

—Wallace Nutting, *Pennsylvania Beautiful*

The state of Pennsylvania encompasses 46,059 square miles, including a small part of Lake Erie. The widest portion of the Keystone State extends 306 miles from west to east and 175 miles from north to south. The geographical midpoint of Pennsylvania is located 2.5 miles southwest of Bellefonte in Centre County, which places the heart of the state near latitude 40.5 degrees North and longitude 77.5 degrees West.

Pennsylvania features a visually impressive array of landforms, subject to a wide variety of climatic patterns, depending on latitude, elevation, and proximity to the Great Lakes to the northwest and the Atlantic Ocean to the east. The highest point in Pennsylvania is Mount Davis in Somerset County, which rises to 3,213 feet near the Maryland border. The lowlands along the Delaware River in the southeast corner of the state are near sea level.

Climate and Weather

Weather is what we experience when we step outside—wind, rain, snow, sleet, sunshine—sometimes all in the course of an hour or two.

Climate represents a more statistical and descriptive treatment of the weather, grounded in an understanding of how the landscape, large bodies of water, and urban development influence local and regional weather patterns. Most climatological statistics are based on the recent thirty-year period. For example, the 1990s, as a decade, averaged about 1.4 degrees warmer in Pennsylvania than the 1960s and featured generally wetter conditions, which is reflected in shifting the climate means from the years 1961–1990 to the period of 1971–2000.

Pennsylvania experiences an interesting variety of weather and climate patterns by virtue of latitude and geography. The eastern portion of North America sits squarely in the middle latitudes beneath a belt of meandering westerly winds that girdle the globe. These winds are often visible on satellite imagery by the pattern of clouds and weather systems that follow the serpentine upper-air circulation. Subsequently, air masses that reach Pennsylvania may have originated thousands of miles away and are usually significantly modified by passing over bodies of water, mountains, and other surface features.

The climate of Pennsylvania is influenced a great deal by topography. The Appalachian Mountains that bisect the state are high enough to affect Pennsylvania weather on a daily basis. Air is frequently forced to rise over the high plateaus and taller ridges in northern and western Pennsylvania. Rising air cools by expansion and may reach the condensation point if the air is relatively moist, resulting in greater cloud cover and more frequent showers over the higher elevations. The air warms by compression as it sinks crossing the eastern slopes of the mountains, which is why southeastern Pennsylvania experiences more hours of sunshine and fewer rainy and snowy days compared with other parts of the state.

The climate of Pennsylvania is marked by four distinct seasons, because the earth is tilted 23.7 degrees from a perpendicular to the orbital plane. Pennsylvania receives an average of 15 hours of daylight at the summer solstice around June 21, which is a time when the sun is at its highest point in the sky at solar noon. The daylight period shortens to about 9.5 hours in late December at the beginning of astronomical winter around December 21. The spring (vernal) and fall (autumnal) equinoxes (Latin for "equal nights") mark the passing of the direct rays of the sun over the equator at solar noon on or about March 20 and September 21, respectively, when Pennsylvania has 12 hours of daylight.

Physiographic Regions and Climatic Patterns

The landscape of Pennsylvania is distinguished by a seemingly endless pattern of parallel ridges and verdant valleys trending northeast to southwest through the middle of the state. Northwestern Pennsylvania is comprised of high, rugged plateaus that are separated by deep river valleys. The southwestern portion of the state blends into a low plateau with rolling hills. Southeastern Pennsylvania features gently rolling farmland bounded in the east by the heavily urbanized Delaware River valley.

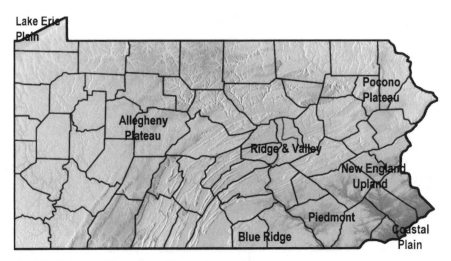

Fig. 1.1. Physiographic regions of Pennsylvania

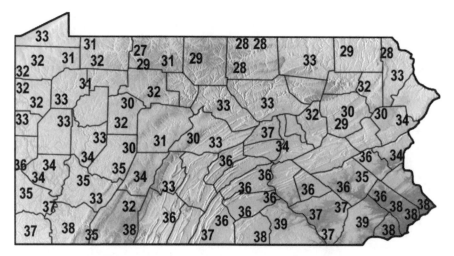

Fig. 1.2. Average January maximum temperatures in degrees Fahrenheit

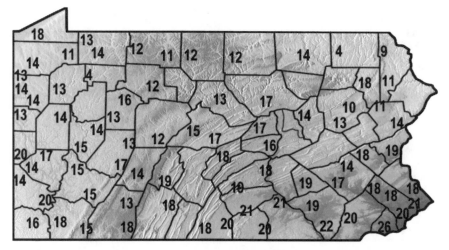

Fig. 1.3. Average January minimum temperatures in degrees Fahrenheit

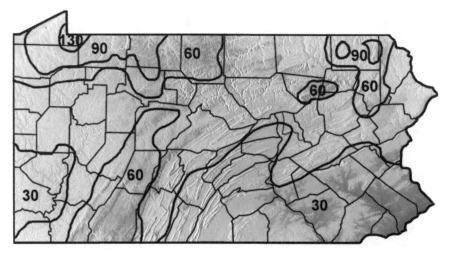

Fig. 1.4. Average annual snowfall in inches

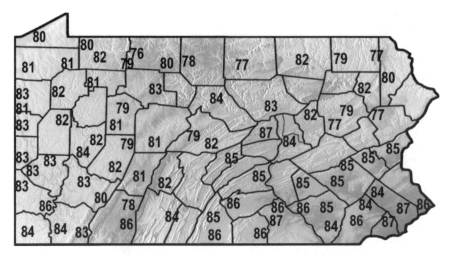

Fig. 1.5. Average July maximum temperatures in degrees Fahrenheit

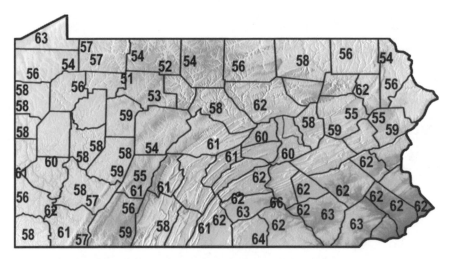

Fig. 1.6. Average July minimum temperatures in degrees Fahrenheit

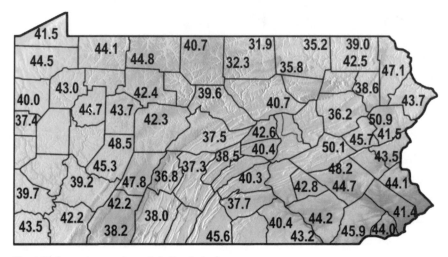

Fig. 1.7. Average annual precipitation in inches

There are seven distinct physiographic regions of Pennsylvania: the (1) Atlantic Coastal Plain; (2) Piedmont; (3) New England Upland; (4) Ridge and Valley; (5) Blue Ridge; (6) Appalachian Plateaus; and the (7) Central Lowland.

Atlantic Coastal Plain. The Atlantic Coastal Plain is narrow strip of mostly urban land about ten miles wide and fifty miles long that lies adjacent to the Delaware River, which includes all but the northwestern part of Philadelphia.

The average annual precipitation at Philadelphia is 41.41 inches, and moisture is fairly evenly distributed over the course of the year. The greatest precipitation totals normally occur in the early summer, with a maximum of 4.30 inches in July. The infrequent passage of a tropical storm in the late summer or early autumn may bring exceptionally high rainfall totals in August and September.

Winters in the Atlantic Coastal Plain are much less severe compared with those in northwestern Pennsylvania. The average January maximum/minimum temperatures at Philadelphia are 38/23 degrees, and the mean annual snowfall is about 20 inches. Most winter storms are accompanied by a mixture of snow, sleet, and rain in the Philadelphia area, due to the modifying effects of mild Atlantic air.

Summers are notoriously hot and humid in the Atlantic Coastal Plain, with minimal breezes to stir the heat and humidity. Summer nights are often warm and sticky, made more uncomfortable by the urban heat island effect of buildings and pavement absorbing and retaining heat. The mean July maximum/minimum temperatures at Philadelphia are 86/67 degrees, and readings of 90 degrees or higher occur on average about twenty-three days in a year.

Piedmont. The Piedmont province of southeastern Pennsylvania stretches from the edge of the Atlantic Coastal Plain to the Blue Ridge Mountains in the south-central portion of the state. The topography comprises rolling hills and extensive farmland, with elevations ranging from 100 to 600 feet above mean sea level.

The Piedmont begins in the northwestern part of Philadelphia and continues westward just beyond Gettysburg to the foothills of the Appalachians. Once part of a tall, majestic mountain range, the Piedmont plateau has been eroded over millions of years by the ceaseless movements of air and water.

The climate of southeastern Pennsylvania is beneficial for farming, and fruit trees and vegetables generally enjoy a frost-free season of about 170 to 180 days. Southeastern Pennsylvania enjoys far less rigorous weather conditions compared with northern and western parts of the state, with considerably more sunshine throughout the year and comparatively mild winters.

Winters are usually moderate, with infrequent subzero temperatures. The average January maximum temperature in southeastern Pennsylvania ranges from 36 to 39 degrees, and minimum readings vary from 18 to 22 degrees. Winter snowfall in southeastern Pennsylvania is relatively light—25 to 35 inches—compared to northern and western parts of the state, because the majority of winter storms are accompanied by a mixture of snow and rain.

Summers are generally warm and rather humid in southeastern Pennsylvania. The mean July maximum temperature ranges from 84 to 87 degrees, and typical nighttime lows fall between 62 and 67 degrees. Precipitation is ample through the year in the southeastern counties, varying from 40.00 inches along the foothills of the Blue Ridge Mountains to 46.00 inches west of Philadelphia.

New England Upland. The New England Upland province is a discontinuous rectangular section of east-central Pennsylvania composed of resistant rock worn down by erosion into rounded hills. The region known as the Reading Prong begins at Mount Penn in Reading and includes a portion of southern Northhampton and Lehigh Counties, and parts of northern Berks and Bucks Counties. The climate of the New England Upland province of Pennsylvania is quite similar to that of the northern Piedmont.

Ridge and Valley. The distinctive feature of the Appalachian Ridge and Valley province is a series of parallel ridges that arc from southwest to northeast. The Appalachian Mountains extend all the way from southeastern Canada to northern Alabama. The tall ridges are largely composed of resilient sedimentary rock (sandstones, hard shales, conglomerates) that formed hundreds of millions of years ago. Sediments laid down by ancient rivers were compressed over millions of years into prominent layered rock formations.

A great geologic uplifting caused by the collision of lithospheric plates that ride along the semi-molten mantle of the earth diverted streams between the folded ridges, carving out the picturesque valleys of central and northeastern Pennsylvania. Scenic river valleys are fairly narrow, about two to five miles wide, and about one hundred miles long, reflecting the erosional power of water working through softer limestones and shales.

The Great Valley, which marks the southern margin of the Ridge and Valley province in east-central Pennsylvania, contains fertile farmland in Lehigh, Lebanon, and Cumberland Valleys. Prominent ridges in the northeast (Poconos), east-central (Blue Mountain) and south-central (Tuscarora and Jacks Mountains) sections rise to elevations of 1,500 to 2,000 feet, with visually striking local relief of about 400 to 800 feet through heavily wooded areas.

The western boundary of the Ridge and Valley province is determined by the Allegheny Front bordering the Allegheny Plateau. The climate is more rigorous compared with that of the valley floors, featuring stronger winds and lower temperatures, which normally drop about 4 degrees for every rise in elevation of 1,000 feet. Cloud cover is more persistent because moist air cools when forced to ascend over higher terrain. In contrast, valleys receive more sunshine when northwesterly winds cross the northeast-southwest trending ridges at right angles, because air sinking downslope warms and becomes drier.

Winters in the Ridge and Valley province are sometimes severe, but generally alternate between periods of cold weather and milder days. Maximum readings in January average 32 to 36 degrees, with the lower readings in the northeastern highlands. Mean minimum temperatures in January fall between 14 and 18 degrees, and even lower values are recorded in the high elevations. Most sections of the Ridge and Valley province receive about 40 to 50 inches of snow annually, though higher totals are often observed in the northeast.

Summers are warm and moderately humid in northern and central Pennsylvania. Cooling breezes are a redeeming summer feature in the upper elevations, offering relief from the sweltering summer heat. The average July maximum temperature ranges from 82 to 86 degrees, and early morning minimums average 58 to 62 degrees. Maximum temperatures seldom rise above 90 degrees in the higher elevations of northern and central Pennsylvania, while valley cities typically see five to ten days of 90-degree heat in the north and closer to twenty 90-degree days in the south-central valleys.

Normal precipitation ranges from 36.00 to 42.00 inches across the Ridge and Valley province, but it increases to 44.00 to 50.00 inches in the northeastern and east-central hills, which are more often affected by weather systems moving northward along the Atlantic coast. The highest annual average precipitation is observed on the Pocono Plateau in western Monroe County. The mean monthly rainfall in the warm season is generally 3.00 to 4.00 inches but exceeds 4.50 inches on the Pocono Front and over the east-central hills in the late spring.

The growing season in the Ridge and Valley province varies significantly with elevation. The deeper valleys are susceptible to early and late frosts on calm nights as heavier cold air drains off the hillsides like water running downhill, collecting in the valley floors on clear, windless nights. The average frost-free season is 140 to 170 days.

Blue Ridge. A small portion of south-central Pennsylvania, known locally as South Mountain, is part of the Blue Ridge province, which is composed of highly resistant bedrock dating back about 500 million years. The Blue Ridge province extends from Cumberland County in Pennsylvania southwestward to Virginia. The climate of the Blue Ridge is typical of the higher elevations of the Appalachian Ridge and Valley province.

Appalachian Plateaus. The northern fringe of the Appalachian Plateaus province includes more than half of Pennsylvania. The Allegheny Plateaus section comprises a large portion of western and northern Pennsylvania west of the Allegheny Front. The high plateau region experienced considerably less folding and compression compared with areas farther east. The ridges rise above 2,000 feet, while lower plateaus in the northeastern and southwestern counties lie about 1,000 feet above mean sea level.

The topography of the Appalachian Plateaus province is quite rugged, featuring broad, relatively level plateaus that are abruptly cut by narrow river valleys. Lakes, swamps, and peat bogs in the northern part of Pennsylvania are filled with deposits of sedimentary materials where glaciers once invaded the state.

The high elevation of the Appalachian Plateaus affords pleasantly cool weather at times during the summer, but winters may be harsh, with little sunshine and lengthy periods of snow cover. Typical January maximum/minimum readings in this broad region of Pennsylvania range from the upper twenties in the northern mountains to the upper thirties in the southwestern corner of the state. High elevation stations report average January maximum readings of 27 to 32 degrees, while the temperatures in the southwestern hills are milder, ranging from 33 to 37 degrees. Mean minimum readings in January average from 10 to 15 degrees in the northern mountains and 15 to 20 degrees in the southwestern counties.

Average maximum/minimum readings in July at Bradford (el. 2,142 feet) in the northwest are delightful (76/54 degrees), substantially cooler than those in the southwestern portion of the state, where average maximum/minimum readings at Donora (el. 762 feet) are nearly 10 degrees warmer (86/62 degrees).

The average annual rainfall over the Appalachian Plateaus province varies from about 32.00 inches at Covington and Wellsboro in the north-central highlands to more than 50.00 inches on the Pocono Plateau. The wettest months are those in the summer season, when the average rainfall is about 3.50 to 4.50 inches. A few spots in the north-central part of the state have mean monthly rainfall figures slightly below 3.00 inches in August.

Seasonal snowfall averages a little less than 40 inches in southwestern Pennsylvania, but more than 90 inches in western Venango County and nearly 130 inches in eastern Erie County, in the northwest corner of the state. On the opposite end of the state, the seasonal snowfall averages between 60 and 80 inches over the higher ridges of western Monroe and Pike Counties and the Endless Mountains. The greatest average snowfall is recorded in Susquehanna and Bradford Counties near the New York border. The weather site at Montrose in Susquehanna County receives an average of nearly 90 inches of snow annually.

The average frost-free period ranges from barely 100 days at Kane (el. 1,750 feet), on the high plateau in the northwest, to 170 days in the southwestern corner of Pennsylvania. Most locations in the Appalachian Plateaus province of Pennsylvania have a period of 140 to 160 frost-free days.

Central Lowland. Adjacent to Lake Erie lies a forty-mile-wide strip of fertile land marked by gently sloping terrain and low hills called the Central Lowland province, or locally the Lake Erie Lowland. Sand and gravel make up the low ridges that were formerly beaches when the lake was higher during the Ice Age.

Lake Erie retains enough warmth from the summer months to provide a measure of protection against autumn frosts up to several miles inland. The growing season near the shoreline is several weeks longer than that of interior portions of the northwestern corner of Pennsylvania. The modifying influence of the water creates a favorable zone for the cultivation of grapes and other fruits.

On the other hand, moisture picked up by cold air masses crossing the relatively mild water promotes considerable cloudiness during the cooler months. Rain and snow squalls are common when cold, dry air crosses the warmer waters. Moistened air is forced to rise over higher terrain east of Lake Erie, resulting in condensation and squally precipitation. Snowfall rates of 3 inches per hour are not unusual in a lake-effect snow event. The average annual snowfall in the city of Erie is 86 inches, and January maximum/minimum readings average 33/18 degrees.

Summers are quite pleasant in the Lake Erie Lowland section of Pennsylvania. Lake water temperatures usually peak in the middle seventies, which is reflected in a comfortable average July maximum figure of 80 degrees at Erie and a relatively mild mean minimum reading of 63.

Climate merely suggests the average weather conditions at certain times of the year, but the anomalies usually draw the most attention. Although fair-weather days widely outnumber the stormy ones, the outstanding and extreme weather events have the greatest impact on our daily lives. There is no shortage of material contained in various county histories, newspapers, journals, and local diaries to chronicle these extraordinary weather occurrences, which will be explored in historical detail with the help of a network of mostly volunteer weather observers, who tracked these events for posterity.

Pennsylvania Weathers Many Climates

We do not pretend even to conjecture as to the duration of the causes that produce this weather; our present business is to inquire what change has taken place, what are its present effects, and what will be the probable consequence of its continuances.

—*Niles' Weekly Register,* August 10, 1816

The landscape of Pennsylvania has been shaped by endless cycles of erosion and deposition, finely sculpted by the movements of air, water, and vast continental ice sheets. A visually striking series of parallel ridges and narrow valleys trending southwest to northeast bisects the state, separating forested high plateaus in the west and low rolling hills in the southeast.

Pennsylvania Journeys through Time

A trip back in time some 500 million years ago would find the land that is now Pennsylvania about 20 degrees south of the Equator. An ancient North America was oriented differently, with today's East Coast facing south. Convective currents driven by the earth's red-hot, partially molten mantle caused vast chunks of the crust to shift gradually over time, eventually altering the position of North America to its present orientation.

The area of Pennsylvania was a shallow marine basin situated on the eastern edge of a large the continent and bordered by the Iapetus Ocean (proto-Atlantic) east of the present location of Pittsburgh. Sand, mud, and carbonates carried off by rivers and streams draining the interior landmass were deposited on the margin of the continent, forming layers of sedimentary rock.

Under intense heat and pressure, molten material (magma) blasted through the ocean floor to form volcanic island arcs that would eventually run into the eastern coastline. A collision between eastern North America and an island arc forced material from the Iapetus Ocean onto the continental margin about 440 million years ago, creating an ancient mountain chain northeast of Pennsylvania (Taconic orogeny).

Around 400 million years ago, a series of collisions occurred between North America (Laurentia) and northern Europe (Avalonia and Baltica), forming a much larger landmass (Laurasia) and thrusting up the ancient Acadian Mountain range east of Pennsylvania. Eroded materials from the Acadian Mountains were carried westward by rivers that forged a path to the shoreline of the Appalachian Sea.

Layers of sediments piled up in the elongate Appalachian basin, which extended from Newfoundland southwest to Alabama, leading to a cycle of deposition, subsidence, and more deposition evident in the rock formations in Pennsylvania. The abundance of sediments accumulating in the Appalachian basin would eventually drive the shoreline west to near the Ohio border (Barnes and Sevon 1996).

Around 350 million years ago, most of Pennsylvania east of Pittsburgh was immersed in shallow tropical waters. The northwestern part of the state remained a little above sea level, covered by swampy forests teeming with shrubs and ferns. The lush vegetation reflected a tropical climate at a time when Pennsylvania was about 5 to 10 degrees south of the equator. The eastern part of the state remained on the edge of the Appalachian Sea, also covered by swamps and marshes.

The last time Pennsylvania would be submerged beneath shallow tropical seas was during the Carboniferous Period about 365 to 290 million years ago. The Appalachian Sea sloshed back and forth across Pennsylvania, reaching as far east as Wilkes-Barre about 310 million years ago. The climate of Pennsylvania remained warm and moist, and tropical vegetation flourished along the swampy shoreline.

During the latter part of the Carboniferous time, referred to as the Pennsylvanian Period, plants and trees decayed in shallow waters that contained little oxygen. Peatlike layers with a high carbon content were buried by sediments and compressed under great heat and pressure, forming the coal beds that underlie western and northern Pennsylvania.

A pattern of uplifting and folding along the margin of the North American plate thrust up in fits and spurts a towering Appalachian Mountain range that extends from southern New York to northern Alabama. Layers of coarser sediments proved more resistant to wind and water erosion and stand out as a series of nearly parallel ridges composed of sandstone and conglomerates.

The uplifting process diverted running water between the ridges, which more easily wore down softer layers of limestone, shale, sandstone, and marine siltstone, creating the spectacular Appalachian valleys. Farther west, the more level high plateaus composed of coarser shale and sandstone and conglomerates were subjected to less compressional force and upheaval.

The Iapetus Ocean closed in scissorlike fashion from north to south during the Paleozoic Era, culminating in a series of collisions involving eastern North America, Europe, and the northwestern part of Africa. The eventual merger of these ancient landmasses about 250 million years ago led to the formation of a supercontinent called Pangaea.

The once formidable Appalachian Mountains were 150 miles wide and reached an altitude of more than ten thousand feet, but erosional forces had substantially lowered the height of the Alleghenian Mountains in eastern Pennsylvania by the conclusion of the Permian Period. The climate in Pennsylvania around the beginning of the Mesozoic Era, the age of the dinosaurs, had become drier and a little cooler. The great swamps disappeared as rainfall patterns changed, altering the type of vegetation and marking the end of many marine organisms.

North America continued to drift northward into the northern hemisphere, moving farther away from the Equator, and eventually split off from western Africa around 220 million years ago. The Atlantic Ocean opened up as North America and Africa parted company. Incidentally, the timeless process of seafloor spreading continues today at the rate of about an inch per year.

Pennsylvania Drifts into the Temperate Zone

An extended period of erosion over the succeeding 200 million years resulted in the landscape features we recognize today in Pennsylvania. North America would finally break away from Europe, only to collide with the North Pacific plate about 70 million years ago that initiated the building of the Rocky Mountains.

A cataclysmic event occurred around 66 million years ago, resulting in a mass extinction that wiped out about 70 percent of the existing plant and animal life on earth. This event marked the end of the dinosaurs that had reigned the earth for more than 150 million years.

One plausible explanation for this mass extinction of life forms was a massive collision between Earth and a giant asteroid. Evidence comes from chemical samples of ancient soil, and the discovery of a 112-mile-wide crater below the Gulf of Mexico near the tip of the Yucatan Peninsula. In one scenario, the atmosphere probably filled with a poisonous haze of sulfuric acid and blast debris that blotted out the sun. Temperatures may have dropped nearly 10 degrees, and forest fires and acidic rains destroyed much of the lush vegetation covering North America.

Around 55 million years ago during the Eocene Epoch, the climate warmed up and species of mammals that had remained obscure during the Mesozoic suddenly proliferated around the world. Tropical vegetation grew at the latitudes of the Arctic and Antarctic, where there was a considerable amount of water and even jungles, according to fossil records buried in layers of ancient sediments. Crocodiles lived as far north as Minnesota, basking in the hot sun surrounded by groves of palm trees in the upper Midwest.

Of course, the climatic pendulum would swing again, and Earth slowly cooled over tens of millions of years, culminating in the most recent ice age, which left plenty of telltale reminders in the form of grooves, scratches, and stony soils.

Ice Ages

A hike through the woods in northern Pennsylvania will occasionally turn up a large boulder seemingly misplaced by the forces of nature. Chances are the obtrusive stone is an erratic left over from the scouring and plucking powers of a moving ice sheet.

Warmer climatic conditions are suggested by fossil evidence of tropical organisms, or trees without annual rings. The presence of desert sandstones and evaporites in a region where there is ample rainfall today suggests that an arid climate once prevailed.

Another way to study past climates is to extract sediments from the bottom of lakes and oceans. Deep-sea cores are analyzed to ascertain the relative water temperature at the time the small-shelled animals were alive. The depth and rate of accumulation of sediments confirm patterns of colder or warmer climates. Fossil spores and pollen grains extracted from the bottom of lake beds similarly provide evidence of past ice ages.

The ratios between different oxygen isotopes found in the shells of small marine animals called foraminifera offer scientists important clues about ancient climates. Chemical analysis of calcium carbonate shells of marine invertebrates shows a higher concentration of heavier oxygen during glacial times. The reason is that more of the lighter oxygen (O-16) in the glaciers evaporates, leaving behind heavier oxygen (O-18) in the oceans.

Geologic evidence suggests there was a glacial period about 600 million years ago that covered at least six of the seven continents, and another around 300 million years ago. However, when we talk about *the* Ice Age we are referring to the most recent extensive glaciation in North America and Eurasia during the Pleistocene Epoch, beginning about 2 million years ago.

Earth Grows Colder

Air and water erosion continued to reshape Pennsylvania, reducing the elevation of the land by hundreds of feet 10 to 15 million years ago, sharpening the differences in topography. New drainage patterns were created by rivers carving new pathways to the sea.

About 16 million years ago, ice and snow began to accumulate in the Arctic. Fresh snow and ice reflect more than 90 percent of incoming sunlight, preserving the ice through the short, chilly polar summers. Around 2.3 million years ago, the glaciers advanced from northeastern Canada, eventually reaching a thickness of nearly two miles around Hudson Bay. Sea levels lowered 300 feet because so much water became locked up in the vast continental ice sheets. During the period of maximum glacial expansion, the Atlantic coastline was about 60 miles farther east than it is now.

The most extensive glacial coverage in Pennsylvania occurred about 750,000 years ago. Ice sheets covered northern Pennsylvania again during the late Illinoisan glaciation, about 196,000 to 128,000 years ago. Oxygen-isotope ratios confirm that the climate was distinctly colder at the time, and conducive to the expansion of the continental glaciers. A relatively brief interglacial period 120,000 years ago lasted 10,000 years as the climate warmed, but colder conditions would initiate another glaciation (Wisconsinan) about 25,000 years ago.

Radiocarbon dating places the peak of the most recent glacial advance in Pennsylvania between 22,000 and 17,000 years ago. The western lobe (Erie Lobe) traveled from northwest to southeast, while the eastern lobe (Champlain Lobe) came from the northeast. The ice acted as a bulldozer, planing softer hills and scouring deeper valleys in the direction of the ice movement. Glaciers plucked out large boulders, which were deposited in unusual settings in northern Pennsylvania.

Frozen material beneath the ice sheets scratched rock surfaces parallel with the ice flow, creating telltale striations. The end point of the ice (*terminal moraine*) in northern Pennsylvania was marked in places by an assortment of glacial debris (*till*) that piled up at nearly right angles to the ice sheets.

During glacial times, the Pennsylvania landscape almost certainly resembled a Siberian tundra, bordered on the southern edge by a boreal forest. The depth of the ice in northern Pennsylvania about 18,000 to 20,000 years ago was at least several hundred feet (Sevon and Fleeger 1999).

Glaciers Retreat

Around 17,000 years ago the ice began a fairly steady retreat, and most of the ice was gone from Pennsylvania, except over the highest elevations, by about 14,000 years ago. Melting glaciers deposited a great deal of gravel, clay, silt, and sand, which collected in low spots. Scenic lakes dotting portions of northern Pennsylvania are also the work of the glaciers, forming in depressions scoured out by the ice sheets that later filled with meltwater as the climate warmed up.

A cooling trend around 12,000 years ago (Younger Dryas) allowed some mountain glaciers to survive for a while longer. Another cool spell 8,200 years ago was probably caused by the dumping of fresh water into the oceans as the ice melted, temporarily halting the flow of warmer water from the equatorial regions.

Over time the landscape in Pennsylvania changed with the departure of the ice sheets. The crust rebounded after being relieved of the frozen mass. Great channels of meltwater created new waterways in search of an outlet to the sea. Sea levels rose more than 250 feet by around 10,000 years ago, when coastlines began to resemble their present shapes.

The downcutting force of water from melting ice carved out the majestic Delaware Water Gap in eastern Pennsylvania, where the Delaware River cuts through Kittatinny Mountain. The local relief rises to 1,400 to 1,600 feet, offering spectacular views of the countryside. In other places, the erosional power of water was later offset by uplifting forces, which diverted mountain streams and left behind prominent dry gaps in the Blue Ridge, such as the Lehigh Gap and Wind Gap in east-central Pennsylvania.

The Last Ten Thousand Years

The climate of the earth continued to warm up, coinciding with the blossoming of agriculture societies in the Middle and Near East almost 10,000 years ago. Global temperatures averaged about two degrees higher than present times 7,000 to 4,000 years ago during a period known as the Climatic Optimum, which is regarded as the warmest time of the past 10,000 years.

Agriculture flourished in many parts of the world during the Climatic Optimum, which peaked about 6,000 years ago. Inevitably, the climatic pendulum would swing back and forth many times, bringing periods of cooler and drier conditions. Long-term regional droughts may have been responsible for the demise of some ancient civilizations, such as Akkadian (Mesopotamia), Mayan, and pre-Inca societies, which would have had experienced severe agricultural losses.

The Last One Thousand Years

A significantly warmer pattern, known as the Medieval Warm Period, lasted from around A.D. 950 until about 1270. Global temperatures were probably a degree warmer than they are today. Vineyards flourished in northern Europe under more benign weather conditions.

However, around 1300 the weather turned colder and stormier. Crops withered on the vines and in the fields. Only a few hundred years earlier, shrinking sea ice had encouraged the Vikings to settle Greenland and explore areas as far east as Newfoundland. As the climate cooled dramatically by the early fourteenth century, the Greenland outposts were isolated by expanding sea ice.

Overextended and overgrazed farmlands generally fared poorly when shorter growing seasons brought low crop yields. Deteriorating weather conditions in Europe contributed to stress, starvation, and disease, culminating in the rampant Black Death that swept the region from 1347 to 1352.

The weather in Europe settled down a bit in the fifteenth century, but a sharp dip in average temperatures between 1550 and 1850, known as the Little Ice Age, brought even more hardships to farmers. Global temperatures were at least two degrees lower than those of today, and periods of cold, stormy weather lasted for decades with few mild intervals.

Mountain glaciers expanded and slid into farming valleys in the highlands of northern Europe. Crops were ruined by bouts of cold, damp weather. Cold winters and wet, cool summers spelled poor harvests and subsequent food shortages. The Little Ice Age ended around 1850, and since then the Northern Hemisphere has warmed about 1.5 degrees.

The warming rate accelerated after 1980, lengthening the period between the last killing frost in spring and the first autumn freeze by several weeks in parts of Canada and Europe. Sea-surface temperatures along the Pacific coast of the United States warmed about 2 degrees since 1950, a trend that has been mirrored by a rising tropical ocean temperatures in the northern hemisphere in the past two decades.

Climate of the Past Two Hundred Years: A Philadelphia Perspective

Philadelphia temperature records spanning the past two centuries show the cold conditions near the end of the Little Ice Age. The 1830s brought the lowest average annual temperatures at Philadelphia since records began in 1825. Three of Philadelphia's four coldest years occurred in succession—1836, 1837, and 1838.

A gradual rise in average annual temperatures through the Civil War years was followed by a slight cooling in the 1870s, when three very chilly years in Philadelphia records (1872, 1873, and 1875) were observed, along with a series of cold, snowy winters. A warming trend in the late 1880s and 1890s gave way to cooler and wetter weather in the early part of the twentieth century at Philadelphia.

Another warming trend prevailed through the 1910s and 1920s, though 1917 was a very cold year. A series of notoriously hot, muggy summers and warm autumn seasons prevailed in the late 1940s and 1950s in Pennsylvania despite a hint of a cooling trend.

A well-defined pattern of colder, drier conditions took hold by the early 1960s in the Northeast as a predominantly northwesterly flow from Canada directed chilly, dry air southward across the eastern United States. Anomalously cool sea-surface temperatures in the eastern North Pacific Ocean promoted a persistent ridge of high pressure in the western states through the early 1960s, causing the jet stream to buckle southward over the East and Midwest. Philadelphia had its coldest decade since the 1830s, and a protracted drought (1962–1966) created serious water shortages for years in the Northeast.

Pennsylvania winters were generally cold and snowy from the late 1950s through the early 1970s, which explains why some of us remember deep snows in our childhood. As far as the validity of stories passed down by family members who recalled walking five miles to school through high drifts and bitter cold, the data suggest boomers growing up in the 1960s and early 1970s trudged through every bit as much snow as our parents and grandparents. In fact, the winters of the 1960s averaged a substantial 4 degrees colder than the winters of the 1990s.

The chilly pattern moderated in the early 1970s, when winters were milder in Pennsylvania, and heavier precipitation replenished lakes and reservoirs. The late 1970s brought a memorable series of cold, snowy winters and chilly summers in the Northeast. The first half of the 1980s offered greater variability but still included some bitterly cold Januarys (1981, 1982, 1984, and 1985). The latter part of the 1980s featured milder winters and hot summers.

The 1990s turned out to be the mildest decade in Philadelphia, surpassing the warmth of the 1930s by a narrow margin. Many summers were hot and humid, and winters were usually quite mild with relatively little snow. Yet, there were notable exceptions. Very cool summers were observed in 1992, 1996, and 2000 in Pennsylvania, and two extreme winters in 1993–94 and 1995–96 featured record cold and historic snowfalls.

A very warm year in 1998 (58.1 degrees) matched the record warmth in Philadelphia in 1991 and back in 1931, followed by 1990 (57.5 degrees). The contemporary average annual temperature at Philadelphia is 54.3 degrees.

Global Warming

During the past century, global temperatures have warmed 1.1 degree Fahrenheit, and the ten warmest years have occurred since 1983. In the 1990s, exceptional warmth led to successive heat records in the Northern Hemisphere in 1990, 1995, 1997, and 1998.

The National Oceanic and Atmospheric Administration (NOAA) reported that 1998 was the hottest year on record in the Northern Hemisphere, only slightly warmer than 1997 and 1999. However, NOAA satellites equipped with microwave-sounding units that measure temperatures up to an altitude of eight kilometers sometimes show contradictory data. The year 2000, regarded as quite warm, was actually the eighth coolest in the past twenty-two years, according to the records of John Christy, director of the Earth Science Center at Huntsville, Alabama, and NASA scientist Roy Spencer.

In the United States, 1998 (54.94 degrees) narrowly edged out 1934 for the title of the warmest year on record since at least 1895. (The average annual temperature in the United States is 52.8 degrees.) The following year—1999—also finished near the top of the charts (54.5 degrees). Temperatures in the United States warmed 0.9 degree during the past century, but rose at the rate of 3 degrees per century after 1980.

In the past fifty years, parts of the Arctic have warmed as much as 11 degrees, causing the permafrost to retreat, and open water was recently discovered at the

North Pole. Satellite imagery revealed that 7.5 cubic miles of the West Antarctica Ice Sheet had melted between 1992 and 2000. In the lower latitudes, bleached corals and other changes to marine ecosystems reflect the impact of warming tropical seas.

Another consequence of global warming is a heightened risk of coastal flooding as glaciers and sea ice melt. Some scientists feel that stronger storms would develop in a warmer atmosphere, though others have challenged this as an oversimplification of the water vapor budget. Crop forecasting models suggest reduced agricultural yields in parts of the Midwest resulting from more frequent droughts and higher summer temperatures.

Whether the recent global warming is due primarily to human activity or is part of a natural cycle has sparked a heated debate in the meteorological community. The answer may be a little of both, because the output of carbon dioxide, chlorofluorocarbons (CFCs), methane, and other heat-trapping gases may have accentuated a natural warming trend at the conclusion of the Little Ice Age in the middle of the nineteenth century.

The burning of fossil fuels (coal, oil, and natural gas) have increased the amount of carbon dioxide in the atmosphere by more than 25 percent since the early nineteenth century. The molecular structure of carbon dioxide and other so-called greenhouse gases traps heat in the lower atmosphere that would otherwise escape to space.

On the other hand, sulfate particles emitted from smokestacks filter sunlight, countering the effects of global warming. Sulfur-rich volcanoes have been associated with short-term global cooling. A veil of sulfuric acid droplets reduces the amount of energy that reaches the earth's surface. Large eruptions eject a considerable amount of ash, dust, and gases into the upper atmosphere, where reflective particles have a longer residence time in the stable lower stratosphere.

Many natural factors play a role in climate change. Subtle variations in the total energy output of the sun, the distribution of clouds and water vapor, and the planetary *albedo* (reflectivity) must be incorporated into climate models. In regional studies, the effects of overgrazing, deforestation, and urban development are known to alter the hydrologic (water) cycle by influencing evaporation rates, and thereby local temperature regimes.

Pennsylvania Weather-Watchers

The weather often changeth without notice, and is constant almost in inconstancy!

—William Penn, 1683

Pennsylvania was sparsely settled at the time William Penn (1644–1718) arrived on October 27, 1682, in pursuit of his "Holy Experiment" to develop a prosperous Quaker community. Penn wrote a glowing letter home in the spring of 1683 addressed to Lord North, wherein he offered up the timeless observation that the only predictable aspect of the weather was its "inconstancy."

Penn took a keen interest in the climate of the Delaware Valley. In a lengthy letter to the Society of the Free Traders in London dated August 1683, Penn wrote that the weather from late October until early December resembled "an English mild spring." Penn's first southeastern Pennsylvania winter "had sharp frosts with a clear sky as in summer, and the air dry, cold and piercing." The summer of 1683 was a typical Delaware Valley summer, bringing "extraordinary heats" (Watson 1868, 347–348).

The first thermometer in America to be "employed for meteorological purposes, according to evidence now at hand" belonged to Dr. Cadwallader Colden of Philadelphia. Preeminent weather historian Dr. David M. Ludlum documented the background of Dr. Colden in his distinguished *Early American Winters, 1604–1820* (1966). Colden, who first came to America in 1710, returned to his Pennsylvania home from a trip to England with a combination barometer-thermometer, commencing the first Pennsylvania instrumental weather records in the winter of 1717–18.

For an early climate study of Pennsylvania, we turn to a Swedish traveler, Professor Peter Kalm, who visited Philadelphia in 1748–1749. Kalm consulted "aged Swedes" about the local weather and, after conducting extensive interviews, asserted that winters were more severe in the early eighteenth century but that spring seemed to be coming later around the time of his sojourn.

A scientifically valid explanation was put forth for the apparent climate change, suggesting that the "lessening of vapours by cultivation, &c., was supposed to have changed the seasons" (Watson 1868, 349). The notion that land use could somehow affect local climate patterns reflected an early understanding of the hydrologic cycle. Natural vegetation releases more moisture into the atmosphere than plowed fields, potentially influencing regional temperature and precipitation patterns.

Benjamin Franklin (1706–1790)

Benjamin Franklin was a polymath and a student of the early science of meteorology. Franklin was born in Boston in 1706 but spent much of his life in Philadelphia, where in October 1752 he conducted his famous kite experiment to prove his hypothesis that lightning is a form of electricity. Franklin owned a thermometer at least as early as 1749, when he recorded a temperature of 100 degrees on "Hot Sunday," June 29 (Ludlum 1984, 21).

Several years before taking an active interest in lightning, Franklin had made another important contribution to the fledgling science of meteorology. On the evening of November 2, 1743 (October 21, Old Style), he had intended to observe a lunar eclipse in Philadelphia, but clouds rolled in from the northeast, obscuring his view.

After corresponding with his brother in Boston, Franklin learned that the eclipse had been visible at exactly the same hour some three hundred miles northeast of Philadelphia (Laskin 1996, 69–70). The source of the clouds and heavy rain, which would reach Boston four hours later, was an offshore hurricane (Ludlum 1984, 20).

The autumn hurricane in 1743 proved costly in southeastern New England, churning up the highest tide in twenty years, causing extensive damage to wharves and shipping interests. Franklin pursued information on the storm's northward progress, checking articles and notes from travelers all the way from Georgia to New England.

His studied review of all available storm accounts illuminated an important meteorological truth about East Coast storms originating over the southeastern United States. Northeasters traveling up the Atlantic coast usually reach the Middle Atlantic states from a southwesterly direction, though surface winds blow out of the northeast. However, his notion of straight winds blowing into the storm was too simple, despite an accurate perception of the rotary nature of smaller whirls, which are a small-scale model for low-pressure areas.

In August 1755, Franklin witnessed a "whirlwind" in the Maryland countryside while traveling with his son and a group of gentlemen. Franklin's notes on the subject of vortices caught the attention of natural philosophers in Europe after letters written to members of the Royal Society of London were eventually published.

Franklin had another vocation: investigating the properties of lightning. Franklin took an avid interest in the nature of electricity around 1747, and he would write down his ideas over the next couple of years in letters to friends in the science community and his own observational notes (Ludlum 1970, 138).

In June 1752 (probably June 10 [Ludlum 1982, 129]), with his son James in tow, Franklin conducted the famous kite experiment in a field on the edge of Philadelphia (Laskin 1996, 66). He was clearly fortunate to survive with only a mild shock, though several others attempting to duplicate the experiment would suffer fatal consequences. An outgrowth of Franklin's thunderstorm experiment was his invention of the lightning rod, which was introduced in Philadelphia in 1752 (Rosenfeld 1999, 38–40). Franklin had successfully challenged the ingrained belief that lightning bolts aimed at church steeples (and other tall objects) were an example of the wrath of God rather than a preventable tragedy.

Franklin was also among the first to propose a link between volcanoes and the weather. He wondered if a persistent dry fog over Europe in 1783–1784 was somehow linked to the severe winter that gripped northern Europe and North America. Franklin astutely speculated that the mammoth eruption of the Laki volcano in Iceland was responsible for the dry fog by filtering out a portion of the sun's incoming energy, cooling the climate.

Early Pennsylvania Weather Observers

The American Philosophical Society, founded in 1743 in Philadelphia, was an organization devoted to providing a forum for scientific discourse. The first three presidents of the society were Benjamin Franklin, David Rittenhouse, and Thomas Jefferson—all renowned inventors and distinguished men of science who shared an interest in meteorological observations.

Associates of the American Philosophical Society were active in recording and exchanging weather data. In the 1790s, the society started to solicit historical weather manuscripts, and by about 1820 a considerable number of weather records were deposited in the library for further study.

The earliest continuous weather observations in Philadelphia appear to date back to 1758 (Ludlum 1983, 10). A longer historical record of the weather belongs to Thomas Coombe, a resident of West Philadelphia who maintained weather observations at least as far back as 1767 (Ludlum 1966, 101). Coombe noted the condition of the sky, the barometric pressure, and the temperature at inside and outside exposures around 8:00 A.M. and 3:00 P.M. Phineas (Israel) Pemberton, also of Philadelphia, kept a fine record of the weather from 1775 to May 1778.

Weather diaries have provided historians with a rich source of information on the weather conditions during colonial times and the War of American Independence. The Reverend Henry Melchoir Muhlenberg made highly detailed notes of the weather during the period from 1742 to 1787 at several locations in southeastern Pennsylvania. His weather records are included in a three-volume publication entitled *The Journals of Henry M. Muhlenberg* (1945).

David Rittenhouse, a renowned astronomer and inventor and the first director of the United States Mint (1792–1795), kept a record of the weather in Philadelphia as early as the Hard Winter of 1779–1780. Rittenhouse continued to provide data through the second inauguration of President George Washington in Philadelphia on March 4, 1793. Rittenhouse family members maintained the weather observations for several years after David's death in 1796. An entry on March 4, 1797, when John Adams took the oath of office in Federal Hall in Philadelphia in the chamber of the House of Representatives, noted, "Cloudy, some rain A.M, fair P.M." The early afternoon temperature of 53 degrees on March 4, 1797, was accompanied by a southwesterly wind (Ludlum 1984, 112–113).

A detailed analysis of the climate of Philadelphia in 1789 was undertaken by Dr. Benjamin Rush, a local physician, and was later revised in 1805. His studies appeared in *Hazard's Register of Pennsylvania* (1828, 1:151). Rush believed that the climate in the late eighteenth century was less extreme than that of the early part of the century, except that the spring weather seemed colder. Rush cited Native

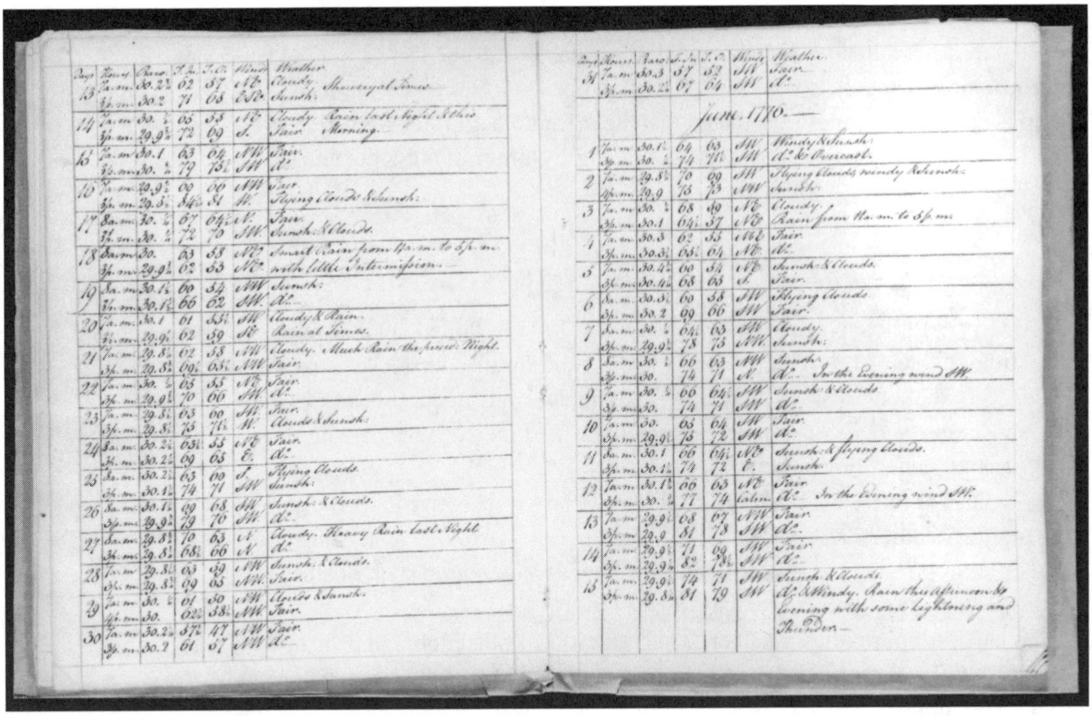

Fig. 3.1. Weather observations of Phineas (Israel) Pemberton, May–June 1776, Philadelphia. (Courtesy American Philosophical Society)

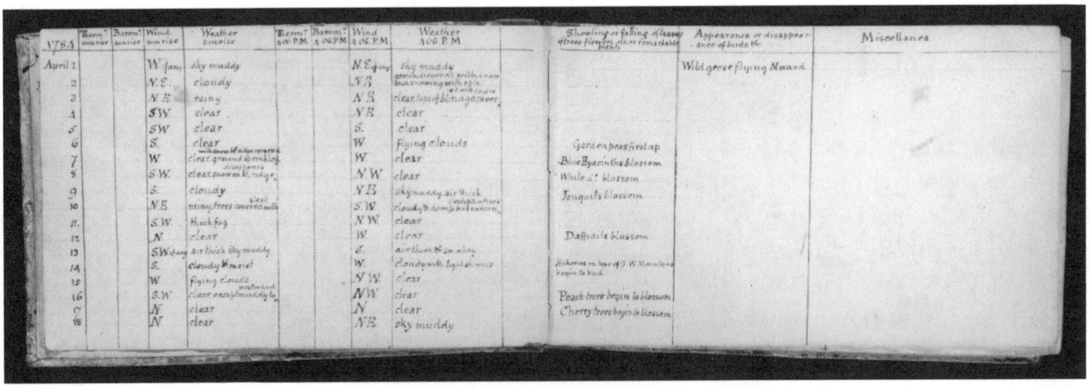

Fig. 3.2. Weather observations of President James Madison in April 1784, which were donated by his wife, Dolley. (Courtesy American Philosophical Society)

American lore that October rains determine the degree of cold weather in the coming winter season. He concluded, "We have no two successive years alike. . . . There is but one steady trait, and that is, it is uniformly variable."

Several other notable early Pennsylvania weather observers with long records included David Schultze of Goshenhoppen (near Philadelphia), Peter Legaux, who maintained weather observations near Norristown for the Pennsylvania Vine Company (1786–1828), and Robert Cathcart of York (1801–1808).

Charles Peirce summarized the weather in *A Meteorological Account of the Weather in Philadelphia, January 1, 1790, to January 1, 1847* (1847). Historian John F. Watson, author of the *Annals of Philadelphia and Pennsylvania, in the Olden Time* (1868, 347–369), gathered a considerable amount of information on historical weather events.

Some of Watson's information was gleaned from correspondence with Samuel Hazard, editor of the *Register of Pennsylvania*. Hazard compiled notices on winter weather in "Effects of Climate on Navigation" (Delaware River, 1681–1828) in his weekly publication (July and December 1828).

An interesting story arises about a local weather observer by the name of Stodgell Stokes, who was born into a Quaker family in Bucks County in 1788 and would later settle in Stroudsburg, in the foothills of the Pocono Mountains, around 1815. Stokes ran a general store and became a local judge. An early opponent of slavery, he joined the Society of Friends, assisting in the operation of the Underground Railroad, which helped secure safe passage of former slaves to Canada.

In later life, Stokes rejoined his family in Moorestown, New Jersey, not far from his roots in Bucks County. At the age of ninety-nine, Stodgell Stokes purportedly invented a new type of rain gauge, an event that was described in a paper presented at the Monroe County Historical Society in 1928: "He [Stodgell Stokes] then conceived that the ordinary rain gauge was wrong in principle, and invented a new one which he thought was better. No storm was too severe for him to go out in and experiment with this gauge, and he soon took a severe bronchitis from which he died. I fully believe had it not been for this rain gauge he would have lived to well over a century."

Stodgell Stokes had a son, John N. Stokes (1826–1875), who would also take an interest in the weather. A biographical index prepared by the curator of the Monroe County Historical Society, Mrs. Horace G. Walters (1965), stated that John N. Stokes did not possess the keen business acumen of his father, though for a short time he would be a partner in the family general store.

John N. Stokes was generally regarded as "a good horseman, a splendid swimmer, and an inveterate practical joker. His kindly disposition and his inability to say 'no' led to his listening to many a hard-luck tale and to his endorsement of many a note which he afterward had to pay."

Until his accidental drowning at Lamberts Rock on McMichaels Creek in July 1875, Stokes occasionally supplied weather information to the local newspaper, Stroudsburg's *Jeffersonian,* chiefly during the harsh winters in the early 1870s. Interestingly, another member of Stokes's clan, Anna Maria (1819–1878), daughter of Dr. Samuel Stokes, was the earliest "official" weather observer in Stroudsburg, using instruments supplied by the Franklin Institute in Philadelphia.

Another longtime weather observer resided in the northeastern highlands of Pennsylvania. Theodore Day was born in 1837 in Elizabeth-town (now Elizabeth), New Jersey, and later settled in Dyberry Township in Wayne County, north of Honesdale, where his grandfather, Stephen Day, had set down roots around the autumn of 1816.

Early in his career Theodore Day was a schoolteacher, and he would later provide research for the United States Department of Agriculture in the area of "grafting and pruning trees" (Haines 1902, 107). Day's outdoor work bred a studious fascination and genuine love for the state of the weather and climate.

Theodore Day kept some general weather records as early as April 1854, though none of his early readings have been located. Day would commence a series of temperature observations in 1860, and he eventually hooked up with the national network of voluntary observers affiliated with the Smithsonian Institution. Day's detailed records are among the best ever kept in the state, and they are currently on file at the National Archives (1865–1892) and the National Climatic Data Center (1893–1903).

Pennsylvania academic institutions have often served as the center of local weather records throughout the past two hundred years. Professor Michael Jacobs spent more than thirty years (1832–1866) as a professor of mathematics and science at the Pennsylvania College (now Gettysburg College), where he maintained a lengthy set of records for the Franklin Institute and the Smithsonian Institution (Ludlum 1984, 90). Professor Jacobs's entry in early July 1863 simply stated, "Great battles of Gettysburg fought," as he watched his beloved natural paradise become a slaughtering ground in the infamous Civil War battle of attrition.

The weather at Gettysburg in the first few days of July 1863 was moderately warm and humid with light winds and no rain. However, rain began falling late on July 3, and Professor Jacobs would measure 1.39 inches by 4:00 P.M. on the fourth. A British correspondent wrote, "The night [of July 4–5] was very bad—thunder and lightning, torrents of rain, the road knee-deep in mud and water." The soggy conditions slowed the movement of General Robert E. Lee's Confederate Army southward across Maryland. More heavy rain on July 8–9 caused the Potomac River to rise, delaying further troop withdrawal until the thirteenth (Ludlum 1960, 101–105).

During the 1880s, Professor Selden J. Coffin at Lafayette College in Easton was involved in the chore of taking daily weather readings, and observations had commenced at Bethlehem's Lehigh University.

In 1971, the Pennsylvania state climatologist Paul W. Daily Jr. determined that the sixty-five-year span of weather records maintained by Dr. Jesse C. Green (1855–1920) of West Chester constituted the longest period of record for a single Pennsylvania weather observer up until that time. Green took daily readings until he passed away at the age of 102 in July 1920. The earliest records taken in West Chester date back to the period of 1823–1827 and were maintained by William Darlington.

A few months before the death of Dr. Green in 1920, J. Clyde LaBar, proprietor of LaBar's Drug Store on Main Street in Stroudsburg, ended his tenure as the official weather-watcher, which had begun in December 1910. LaBar had provided weather data to the local press for many years prior to becoming a local observer. The press took note of his retirement in February 1920, taking the opportunity to editorialize on the state volunteerism:

> For ten years he [LaBar] has been very faithful in making the reports of the weather to the bureau during which time his only compensation has been the thanks of the department. . . . It is unfortunate that the government cannot see its way clear to offer a reasonable compensation for a service which requires considerable time of the

observer as well as requiring the service of a person who has patience to be very exacting in manner of keeping records, for the weather records are worthless if they are not letter perfect. (*Daily Record* [Stroudsburg], March 4, 1920)

Historical Meteorological Studies

In 1822, Dr. Robert Hare (1781–1858), a chemistry professor at the University of Pennsylvania and a lifelong resident of Philadelphia, published a paper describing in some detail the surface flow of northeasterly winds attending a coastal storm. His research grew out of studies tracing the passage of a great hurricane that wreaked havoc from Norfolk, Virginia, to Long Island in September 1821. Hare later pursued the intriguing relationship between electricity and the formation of tornadoes inside a thunderstorm.

In September 1834, Philadelphia was the seat of the first true joint conference of meteorologists when committees of the American Philosophical Society and the Franklin Institute convened in order to "confer together on the best means of promoting the advancement of meteorology." This illustrious gathering marked "the first effort of meteorologically-minded men in the United States to advance the science by cooperation" (Ludlum 1970, 162).

The Joint Committee on Meteorology was chaired by native Pennsylvanian James Pollard Espy (1785–1860), who was born in Westmoreland County in the southwestern corner of the state on the edge of the western frontier. After a period of time in the Ohio Valley, Espy moved to Philadelphia in 1817 and would join the Franklin Institute in Philadelphia as an instructor in 1824.

Espy, along with a group of notable early American meteorologists, studied the storm damage in Connecticut caused by a powerful hurricane in the autumn of 1821. Ten years later, he established a committee to collect weather data. Espy visited the scene of a number of American tornadoes between 1834 and 1839. His observations helped refine his notion of storms as a region of low pressure marked by an inward circulation caused by centrifugal forces. He later put down his ideas in a *Philosophy of Storms* (1841), which was widely read and debated in its day (Monmonier 1999, 34–36).

Espy tackled a wide range of physical science subjects—astronomy, barometric pressure, dew point, and latent heat—in a slew of academic papers. In 1836–1837, he refined his centripetal storm theory to include the life cycle of a thunderstorm, and he fairly accurately portrayed the convective processes in the atmosphere. Espy advanced the notion that clouds and storms were formed by rising currents of warm air that cool by expansion in a lighter environment. He was likely the first scientist to recognize the concept of storms fueled by a low-level inflow of moist air sustained by an upper-level outflow, often likened to a chimney circulation.

Through Espy's efforts and with the backing of the American Philosophical Society, the state legislature of Pennsylvania authorized a sum of $4,000 to procure and distribute weather instruments to each county to be overseen by the Franklin Institute, which Espy outlined in a report to the institute.

Espy is credited with the first attempt to plot weather data in the United States, which was based on reports from forty correspondents taken during the rain- and snowstorm of March 16–18, 1838. Meanwhile, Espy raised the possibility of artificial rainmaking in 1838 to ease drought conditions by "setting fires to the woodlands in the western country." However, his weather modification proposals, which were reinforced in papers he wrote in the 1840s, "greatly damaged his standing in the scientific community" (Ludlum 1970, 164–165).

Espy later worked in various capacities for the navy and war department from 1842 to 1857. He continued to push for the formation of a national team of weather observers, an idea that would finally be realized in 1848 under the auspices of the Smithsonian Institution.

Lorin Blodget (1823–1901), who was born in Jamestown, New York, served as volunteer weather observer in his hometown before moving to Philadelphia. In 1857, then a "youthful statistician," Blodget wrote a masterly 536-page volume entitled *Climatology of the United States and of the Temperate Latitudes of the North American Continent.* His seminal work, using meteorological data obtained from a national network of Smithsonian observers, was the best early description of climatic patterns of the United States (Ludlum 1970, 151–152).

Weather-Watching in the Nineteenth Century

After the War of 1812, the Medical Corps of the United States Army was instructed to maintain weather records at outposts on the edge of settlements. A directive handed down on May 2, 1814, by Dr. James Tilton, surgeon general of the Army, instructed the local surgeon or chief medical officer to record the temperature and wind direction at daily intervals at their posts (Ludlum 1966, 178–180). These early weather records were spotty, but provided important information about the climate of the Northwest Territory. Data collected by the Medical Corps, along with observations taken by the Corps of Topographical Engineers, were then forwarded to Washington, D.C.

Weather observations were taken at the Allegheny Arsenal at Pittsburgh as early as 1835, under the direction of the surgeon general's office of the United States Army. The following year rain gauges were supplied to midwestern posts, and in 1843 some stations received barometers and sling psychrometers to measure the air pressure and calculate the relative humidity.

The first attempt to organize weather records in Pennsylvania was in the late 1830s. Weather summaries from volunteer observers appeared in the *Journal of the Franklin Institute* in 1839. In the 1840s, several leading scientists in the field of meteorology pursued the notion of a systematic nationwide weather-observing system, which received a major boost with the opening of the first public telegraph line in 1845. In 1848, the Smithsonian Institution in Washington set aside a sum of $1,000 for the procurement of instruments, and congressmen were advised to put out requests for volunteer observers (Ludlum 1983, 11).

Under the direction of Professor Joseph Henry, the Smithsonian network thrived in the 1850s until the Civil War intervened. Volunteer observers were issued a thermometer and a rain gauge and were asked to take three (later four) observations each day. Observers were directed to note any interesting weather phenomena, such as lightning, auroras, and other atmospheric events. At the end of the month, the records were sent to Washington by franked mail.

National Weather Bureau

Congress authorized President Ulysses S. Grant to establish a storm-warning system in February 1870. The operation was handed over to the Army Signal Service, shifting the voluntary weather-gathering apparatus from the Smithsonian Institute to the military by 1873.

Weather observations appeared in the government *Monthly Weather Review,* first published in 1872, which included accounts of unusual weather phenomena, climate studies, and articles on physics and mathematics that support the field of modern meteorology. At the time, the Franklin Institute in Philadelphia collected much of the Pennsylvania data that appeared in the national weather publication, and the renowned science center remains active in the field of weather observations to this day.

In 1891, the national weather-observing network was transferred to the Department of Agriculture, marking the official beginning of the United States Weather Bureau. The State Weather Service in Philadelphia published Pennsylvania weather data in *Climate and Crop Service* beginning in March 1896. Pennsylvania weather records appeared in the monthly publications *Climatological Data—Pennsylvania Section* (1914–1948) and *Climatological Data—Pennsylvania* (1948–present).

Official responsibility for government weather observations and forecasting shifted in the early 1940s from the weather bureau to the Department of Commerce. In 1965, the weather bureau became part of the Environmental Science Services Administration (ESSA). The National Oceanic and Atmospheric Administration (NOAA) took over administrative duties in 1970, and is now known as the National Weather Service (NWS).

Cooperative Weather Observer Program

In March 1891 the *Monthly Weather Review* proudly announced that 2,406 volunteer weather observers were currently involved in the government data-collection program. In 1970 the number of volunteer weather-watchers in the United States peaked at 13,500, though that figure has dropped off to about 11,700 observers currently participating in the Cooperative Weather Observer Program.

Local weather observers take daily observations across the United States to maintain a fairly continuous record of the weather and climate for communities across the country. The record for the longest record of voluntary observations belongs to Earl Stuart of Cottage Grove, Oregon, who took daily weather readings for seventy-seven years from 1917 to 1994 (Johnson 2000).

In Pennsylvania there are currently about two hundred cooperative weather stations, where observers record daily measurements and submit the data to a local National Weather Service office. All climatological data is then sent on to the National Climatic Data Center in Asheville, North Carolina.

All sections of Pennsylvania are fairly well represented by weather stations, with the greatest concentration of observers in the eastern and southwestern areas of the state, where the population is most dense. The elevation of the weather sites in Pennsylvania ranges from near sea level at the Philadelphia International

Airport (el. 5 feet), to an elevation of 2,760 feet at Laurel Mountain in Somerset County.

Volunteer observers are folks from various walks of life who simply enjoy taking weather readings in their backyards, or perhaps at a local school or university. Over the past two centuries, countless weather enthusiasts have loyally braved the elements to keep a careful log of the state of the atmosphere in their hometown. Many, though not all, local observers have been affiliated with the government network. These diligent people record daily and even hourly records of the temperature, precipitation, snowfall, and snow depth.

Many private observers have purchased weather stations from instrument catalogs that allow the observer to plot and analyze local weather data. The unstinting efforts of tens of thousands of individuals, along with a cadre of scientists, historians, diarists, and journalists, have made it possible to reconstruct more than two centuries of historical weather events.

The task of assembling, analyzing, and editing a large volume of historical data for the purpose of presenting an organized record of Pennsylvania weather is an ongoing project, because, as we all know, in weather tomorrow is another day with the potential for record-breaking or noteworthy events.

Longest Pennsylvania Observer

Recognition for dedication for length of service in keeping track of the weather in Pennsylvania goes to Dixon R. Miller of Blakeslee, a small town atop the high Pocono Plateau in western Monroe County. Miller was born on March 3, 1911, in Summerdale, west of Harrisburg. As a youth in about 1920, he commenced a series of rainfall reports for the government.

After passing a civil service examination in 1940, Miller was responsible for airways observations at the Harrisburg Airport for six months, before assuming the same duties in East Waterford, Perry County, in 1941. Miller moved to Long Pond in 1948, where he resumed his observations and forwarded data to the Swiftwater office of the Division of Forest and Water (now the Department of Forestry).

Dixon Miller still spends afternoons and evenings scanning the horizon at the fire tower on Pimple Hill, two miles southwest of Long Pond, near his residence. His weather station (el. 2,212 feet) is at one of the highest points in Monroe County. Miller published an article on the severe winter of 1957–1958 in the June 1958 issue of *Weatherwise* magazine, which inspired me to begin my own local observations. It was a great personal thrill to finally meet Dixon Miller in June 1999 in Long Pond at a Nature Conservancy gathering.

The rich history of weather-watching in Pennsylvania, beginning with William Penn's early climate narrative, has provided modern historians with a panoramic view of weather events in the Keystone State. How Pennsylvanians coped with the vagaries of Mother Nature is evident in the literary and scientific records.

Great Winter Storms

The weather-wise decide that we shall having a rousing winter of it; we put great faith in this prediction, and advise our friends abroad to put in a good stock of anthracite coal.

—*Miners' Journal* (Pottsville), October 22, 1842

The most famous winter weather forecaster in North America resides in a small western Pennsylvania town about ninety miles northeast of Pittsburgh. Every year on February 2, thousands of eager spectators and media personnel gather on Gobbler's Knob to witness the peerless prognostication of Punxsutawney Phil.

The predictive powers of a furry animal in the early days of February are rooted in medieval European folklore and the association of Candlemas Day with the midpoint of winter. Clymer Freas, editor of the *Punxsutawney Spirit,* is credited with the formal conception of Groundhog Day in 1886, though the initial trip up Gobbler's Knob would not occur until February 2, 1887.

According to popular tradition, if Punxsutawney Phil sees his shadow, we can expect six more weeks of wintry weather. Local records show that Phil (or one of his ancestors) has seen his shadow on all but thirteen occasions since 1898, which merely proves that winter is usually still alive and kicking after the opening days of February, at least in the mountains of Pennsylvania.

The familiar exclamation "It's raining cats and dogs!" comes from Pennsylvania German farmers. The expression "It is raining to keep in the cats and bring out the ducks" was a mistranslation of "It is snowing for cats and ducks," which meant there was enough snow for animal tracking (Sloane 1963, 18).

Pennsylvania Winters

Winter weather patterns in Pennsylvania vary considerably from one season to the next. In recent years, the prodigiously snowy winter of 1995–96 was sandwiched between two very mild winters. A similar reversal of fortune occurred in 1918–19, when a very mild winter with little snow followed the bitterly cold "War Winter" of 1917–18.

A review of snowfall seasons in eastern Pennsylvania over the past 150 years, where lengthy records exist, revealed two exceptionally snowy fifteen-year winter periods—1859–60 to 1874–75 and 1957–58 to 1970–71—as shown in Table 4.1 (Gelber 1998, 115, 125). These "old-fashioned" winters, much like the recent outstanding winters in 1993–94 and 1995–96, featured a parade of coastal storms

Table 4.1. Snowiest Winters in Eastern Pennsylvania (October–May)

	1862–63	1867–68	1872–73	1873–74	1874–75
North Whitehall (el. 350)	77.3	78.2	—	—	—
Egypt (el. 450)	—	—	87.5	—	—
Blooming Grove (el. 1000)	—	92.0	93.0	86.4	100.0
Dyberry (el. 1,100)	—	115.4	113.2	112.2	98.0

	1957–58	1960–61	1962–63	1963–64	1966–67	1969–70	1970–71
Stroudsburgs (el. 480)	109.5	98.6	67.8	75.9	100.6	63.9	56.1
Hawley (el. 890)	104.6	86.3	70.2	68.6	96.5	76.1	68.8
Gouldsboro (el. 1,875)	147.1	126.0	100.0	101.0	104.0	113.0	94.6

Table 4.2. Warmest Winter Months in Pennsylvania

	Winter of 1889–90	Warmest Months (after 1890)
December	39.0	38.4 (1923)
January	36.9	39.1 (1932)
February	36.4	35.5 (1998)
Average	37.4	36.7 (1931–32)

that brought frequent heavy snowfalls to the Keystone State, sometimes as late as April.

At the opposite extreme, persistently mild winters with little snow are a bonus for homeowners but a bane to skiers. The winter of 1889–90 (see Table 4.2) was the warmest Pennsylvania winter on record (Karl et al. 1983) since statewide records commenced in 1888. Pittsburgh enjoyed a record warm December (45.6 degrees) without snow and witnessed only a trace in January 1890, which was followed by the city's second warmest February (42 degrees) with nary a cold snap.

The warmest winter of the twentieth century in Pennsylvania was 1931–32, averaging 9.7 degrees above the modern normal. January 1932 (39.2 degrees) was warmer than any other winter month in state weather history at 14.6 degrees above average. In recent years, the winter of 1997–98 was consistently warmer than normal. Unusually mild winter seasons seem to come in clusters in the region: 1927–28 to 1932–33, 1936–37 to 1938–39, 1951–52 to 1954–55, 1971–72 to 1975–76, 1988–89 to 1991–92, and 1996–97 to 1999–2000.

Snowfall Season

The average annual snowfall in Pennsylvania (October–May) ranges from about 20 inches in the southeastern tip of the state at Philadelphia to nearly 130 inches about twenty-five miles east of the Lake Erie shoreline in the northwestern corner. Most of the state receives an average of 30 to 60 inches of snow per year.

Seasonal snowfall extremes in Pennsylvania have ranged from a trace at the Philadelphia International Airport (el. 5 feet) in 1972–73 to 225 inches at Blue Knob in 1890–91. Blue Knob, a ski resort situated about fifteen miles southwest of Altoona in the southwestern mountains, is billed as the "highest ski-able mountain" in Pennsylvania (el. 3,146 feet). The post office, which is presently located at an elevation of around 2,500 feet, is probably representative of the weather station in December 1890. Another popular ski resort, located in the Laurel Highlands at Seven Springs (el. 2,800 feet), received 222.5 inches of snow in the winter of 1992–93.

Winter Storms

The first heavy snowfall of the season is normally greeted with mixed feelings. Youngsters and winter weather enthusiasts generally delight in the rapid fall of swirling snowflakes that gradually pile up in powdery heaps. Motorists navigating snow-covered roads and icy bridges, however, usually take exception to the unabashed joy of snow-lovers on the day of a big snowfall.

In the wintertime, snowflakes typically form at fairly low altitudes (below 10,000 feet) in a subfreezing environment that contains both water and ice. Ice particles grow as water droplets come in contact with tiny ice crystals. Soon, larger ice particles collide with falling ice crystals, and they stick together to form snowflakes.

Snowflakes take on myriad shapes and patterns depending on the humidity and temperature, though the most common shape is that of a fluffy star (dendrite), forming in very cold clouds where the temperature is slightly below 10 degrees. Ice crystals may also fall as hexagonal plates, columns, or needles. Snowflakes passing through a cold, dry environment are powdery and fine in texture. Ice crystals falling through warmer air begin to melt, and the thin layer of water acts as glue, causing flakes to clump together.

The ingredients for a major winter storm include a requisite amount of cold air and a stream of warm, moist air brought together by a developing low-pressure system. A favored zone for winter storm formation is along the northeast coast of

Table 4.3. Snowiest Months in Pennsylvania (1890–2000)

Month	Total (inches)	Location	Year
September	1.0	Strongstown	1993
October	19.0	Corry	1962
November	60.5	Corry	1933
December	96.0	Blue Knob	1890
January	84.4	Ebensburg	1978
February	88.0	Seven Springs	1993
March	79.5	Seven Springs	1993
April	38.5	Somerset	1928
May	16.0	Monroeton	1945
June	Trace	Ten stations	1902, 1907, 1918, 1945

North Carolina, where cold continental air draining down the Appalachians encounters the tropical currents of the Gulf Stream a short distance offshore.

The heaviest snows typically fall in a band about 75 to 150 miles northwest of the storm track. The greatest accumulations may occur in a narrow stripe little more than 25 miles wide and 100 miles long. Meteorologists rely on as many as six computer models of the atmosphere to project where converging airstreams will produce the largest snow totals. However, mathematical simulations of the atmosphere lack the resolution to precisely forecast the eventual storm path that ultimately determines where the heaviest snow will occur or whether the precipitation will come in the form of a "mixed bag" of sleet, freezing rain, and rain.

Heavy snowfalls in the northeastern United States are frequently augmented by the presence of a blocking ridge of high pressure over Quebec-Labrador that prolongs a snow event. As easterly winds strengthen, a conveyor belt of mild, damp Atlantic air is forced to rise over the shallow wedge of cold air, resulting in condensation and the accretion of snowflakes.

The difference between a moderate snowfall and a major snowstorm in Pennsylvania often depends on where two branches of the polar jet stream converge near the East Coast. The arrival of a potent upper-level disturbance associated with an intrusion of arctic air energizes coastal storms. The "phasing" process uniting arctic and subtropical airstreams provides favorable dynamics for the evacuation of air aloft that requires a compensating inward flow of warm, moist Atlantic air toward the center of an intensifying disturbance.

Lake-Effect Snowfalls

Lake Erie is the only lake that freezes over in severe winters due the shallowness of the lake bed. During the late autumn, dense chilly water sinks and is replaced by warmer water rising to the surface. Because water reaches a maximum density at 39 degrees, further mixing ends at that point, and the surface gradually chills toward the freezing point, forming a layer of ice.

Cold northwesterly winds sweeping southward pick up considerable heat and moisture in transit over the relatively warm lake waters. The temperature difference between the lake surface and the air aloft (5,000 feet) is sometimes 30 degrees, making the lower atmosphere highly unstable. Snow squalls in northwestern Pennsylvania are sometimes accompanied by thunder and lightning.

Lake-effect snow events are enhanced when moistened air is forced to rise over hilly terrain in northwestern Pennsylvania. Plumes of lake-effect snow showers tend to dissipate east of the mountains as the air sinks and subsequently becomes drier (*downsloping*). However, snow showers often redevelop over the Poconos in the northeast, as cold, unstable air is lifted again (*upsloping*).

The town of Corry, about thirty miles east of the Lake Erie shoreline, has the highest average annual snowfall in Pennsylvania at nearly 130 inches. Even a mild Pennsylvania winter like 1998–99 brought generous snow totals in Erie County, where the maximum seasonal snowfall was 172.3 inches.

The greatest modern lake-effect snowfall in northwestern Pennsylvania and northeastern Ohio occurred in early November 1996. From November 9 to 15, 1996, bands of heavy snow developed over the lake, borne on the wings of northwesterly winds that poured across the relatively warm water.

In Erie County, Pennsylvania, a weather service spotter measured 54.8 inches of snow at Edinboro. The official snowfall at the airport in Erie was 26.8 inches, with a maximum daily fall of 11.7 inches on November 10. The Erie city weather site reported 41 inches. In nearby Crawford County, 21 inches fell at Conneaut-ville, and similarly large totals were observed in Warren and McKean Counties, with up to 21 inches piling up at Lottsville. The lake-effect snow bands extended as far east as Lycoming County.

The earliest recorded major lake-effect snowfall in Pennsylvania deposited 3 feet of snow at Erie on November 27–30, 1831, preceding a record cold December (*Hazard's Register of Pennsylvania,* December 17, 1831).

Ice Storms

When snow falls through a shallow layer of above-freezing temperatures aloft and begins to melt, the result at the surface is often a mixture of *ice pellets* (sleet) and rain. Ice pellets are usually quite small (0.16 inch in diameter), occasionally accumulating to the depth of a few inches in a heavy fall. A mixture of sleet and rain at near-freezing temperatures creates very slippery conditions as smaller drops freeze on contact with the cold ground.

The most treacherous form of winter precipitation is *freezing rain,* which glazes roadways, sidewalks, and exposed surfaces. Freezing rain occurs when a layer of mild air overrides a wedge of subfreezing air near the surface. The air a few thousand feet overhead may be warm enough to melt snowflakes into rain, but a pocket of cold, dense air trapped in the deeper valleys of the Appalachians sets the stage for a prolonged interior ice storm, referred to by meteorologists as *cold air damming.*

The buildup of ice on tree limbs and power lines can cause breakage and widespread power outages, affecting thousands of residents. An especially dangerous situation is the formation of *black ice* that appears wet to a motorist, but actually cloaks a thin patch of ice. Black ice forms when water droplets rupture upon impact with the pavement, releasing trapped air bubbles that normally make ice film shiny. Bridges, overpasses, and ramps are especially susceptible to icing, because heat is lost more readily by evaporation in the open air compared with surface features.

At least one or two glaze storms can be expected in a Pennsylvania winter. Ice storms rarely occur before the middle of December, because the ground is still relatively warm. Ice storms are also unlikely after the middle of February, because the increasing sun angle allows more diffuse solar radiation to filter through leaden skies.

Severe ice storms have affected large portions of Pennsylvania on January 5, 1873, February 21–22, 1902, December 29–30, 1942, January 1, 1948, January 8–11, 1953, and December 16–17, 1973. One of the earliest widespread ice storms occurred on the morning of November 14, 1997. Nearly an inch of mixed precipitation fell over east-central and northeastern Pennsylvania in subfreezing nighttime conditions, resulting in an unprecedented mid-November ice storm as far south as the Lehigh Valley.

Ice storms rarely occur after the middle of March, when the sun is higher in the sky and increasing solar energy warms the ground. Yet, a damaging spring ice storm struck the northern mountains of Pennsylvania on April 15–16, 1929, while a chilly rain fell in the valleys. On April 7, 1972, a thin layer of ice glazed roads in the Delaware Valley, southern New Jersey, and the nation's capital.

Early Pennsylvania Winters

William Penn arrived in Pennsylvania on October 27, 1682, settling in the fertile Delaware Valley. The following summer he wrote a letter to the Free Society of Traders in London, comparing the previous mild winter experienced by early settlers that brought "scarce any ice at all" to the winter of 1682–83, which "for a few days froze up our great River Delaware" (Ludlum 1966, 31).

Penn displayed the instinct of a climatologist, offering an explanation for the harsh winter chill: "The reason of this cold is given from the Great Lakes that are fed by the fountains of Canada." He added, "The wind that ruleth the summer season, is the southwest; but spring, fall, and winter, 'tis rare to want the wholesome northwester seven days together: and whatever mists, fogs or vapours foul the heavens by easterly or southerly winds, in two hours time are blown away; the one is always followed by the other: a remedy that seems to have a peculiar providence in it to the inhabitants."

The Delaware Valley had another severe winter in 1697–98, which was described by Peter Kalm, a Swedish professor who visited in Philadelphia in 1748–49 (Watson 1868, 348). Kalm interviewed a ninety-one-year-old resident who recalled crossing the frozen Delaware River on wagons loaded with hay during that winter.

A notice on the cold winter of 1704–5 appeared in John F. Watson's superb chronicle *Annals of Philadelphia and Pennsylvania, in the Olden Time*. Norris described the rigorous conditions that beset Philadelphia: "We have had the deepest snow this winter, that has been known by the longest English liver here. No traveling; all avenues shut; the post has not gone these six weeks; the river fast; and the people bring loads over it as they did seven years ago—[as in 1697–98, aforementioned]. Many creatures are like to perish."

The most rigorous winter of the early eighteenth century in Pennsylvania occurred in 1740–41. The depth of the snow in eastern Pennsylvania was "in general more than three feet deep," forcing settlers to subsist on the remains of animals found frozen in the woods as the severe cold persisted through February. A longtime inhabitant, Mrs. Shoemaker, recalled that "all the tops of the fences were so covered, that sleighs and sleds passed over them in every direction." In a letter penned in 1748, James Logan also remembered "the hard winter of 1741" as "one of remarkable severity," lasting from the third of week of December 1740 through the middle of March 1741 (Watson 1868, 349–350).

1764–65

The winter of 1764–65 was widely judged to be "the snowiest since 1748 and the coldest since 1741" (Ludlum 1966, 20). A holiday snowstorm lashed Philadelphia on December 25–26, 1764, and was followed by another heavy snowfall on January 5–6, 1765. In early January 1765, the snow cover was a respectable 2 feet, according to the Reverend Henry M. Muhlenberg (1945, 2:163) of Germantown.

The weather during the last week of January 1765 was intensely cold. Samuel Hazard, who collected notices on winters in the Delaware Valley from 1681 to 1800, wrote that the Delaware River was closed to navigation due to ice from December 24, 1764, until February 28, 1765 (Watson 1868, 356–357). On February 7, 1765, "an ox was roasted whole on the river Delaware, which, from the novelty of the thing drew together a great number of people."

After the advent of spring, a great snowstorm buried Philadelphia and vicinity on March 24, 1765, which was "said to lie 2, or 2½ feet on the level, and in some places deeper." Trees were uprooted by the weight of the snow, and roads were impassable for days. Snow had fallen on and off in southeastern Pennsylvania for a few days, but the major blow came during the night of March 23–24, 1765. The furious nor'easter caused numerous shipwrecks from North Carolina to Maine (Ludlum 1966, 62).

The *Pennsylvania Gazette* in Philadelphia declared that the March 1765 storm brought "the greatest quantity of snow that had been known (considering the advanced season) for many years past; it being generally held to be two feet." Surveyors Charles Mason and Jeremiah Dixon measured the snow on the Maryland-Pennsylvania border in March 1765. Shortly after daybreak on March 24, 1765, the "snow was near 3 feet deep." Such snow depths have been witnessed in Pennsylvania only after great snowstorms in January 14–16, 1831, February 11–13, 1899, March 19–21, 1958, and January 7–8, 1996.

Revolutionary War Winters

An enduring image of the Revolutionary War is the portrait of George Washington crossing the Delaware River at Coryell's Ferry on Christmas night 1776 in a driving snow and sleet storm, with the aim of surprising the Hessian forces encamped just to the south at Trenton. The Reverend Henry M. Muhlenberg, who was then living at Trappe, thirty-five miles west of Trenton, stated in his journal that the snow was "a foot deep and it's bitter cold" (1945, 2:767). Monitoring the weather in December 1776 at his Monticello, Virginia, home, Thomas Jefferson variously mentioned an accumulation of 22 or 24 inches, suggesting a storm track that passed south of Pennsylvania (Ludlum 1966, 98–100).

A larger snowfall hit southeastern Pennsylvania later that winter—on February 24, 1777, which Muhlenberg (1945, 3:16) called "an extraordinary snow storm," adding, "Perhaps as much as two feet fell." The observations of Phineas Pemberton, on file at the American Philosophical Society, listed an 18-inch snowfall in Philadelphia.

The winter of 1777–78 was immortalized by the harsh conditions faced by George Washington's troops housed at Valley Forge, northwest of Philadelphia. The Continental Army arrived on a cold, stormy day, December 19, 1777, which was a harbinger of a terrible ordeal awaiting American soldiers, who would suffer through a miserable winter with few rations and tattered clothing (Ludlum 1982, 264).

The winter of 1778–79 was noteworthy for the Hessian Storm of December 25–26, so named for the battering sustained by British mercenaries harbored at New York City and Newport, Rhode Island (Ludlum 1966, 107–111). Snow, high winds, and low temperatures on Christmas Day afternoon buffeted the Hessian soldiers at New York City, where many died from exposure to the harsh conditions.

The "Hard Winter" of 1779–80 was the worst winter in the region since 1740–41. The Delaware River at Philadelphia froze around December 1, 1779, and retained a layer of ice two or three feet thick at times until March 14, 1780 (Garriott 1906, 9). Thomas Jefferson recalled that "in 1780 the Chesapeake Bay was frozen solid from its head to the mouth of the Potomac." Weather historian David M. Ludlum (1988, 334) wrote, "The Hard Winter of 1780 is the only winter in American history when the waters surrounding New York City have frozen over and remained closed to all navigation for five consecutive weeks."

The onset of the Hard Winter could be traced back to late November 1779, when a cold pattern settled in for a long stay and two heavy snowfalls left a substantial snow cover. Henry M. Muhlenberg entered in his journal "a dreadful wind and snow-storm" on November 26. Another heavy snowfall on December 5 hit southeastern Pennsylvania after several days of rain, after which time the snow "lay a foot and a half deep and there was no going out of doors" (Ludlum 1966, 121–123).

A heavy rainstorm on December 12–13, 1779, ended with the passage of an arctic cold front on the fourteenth, described as "such a terrible and bitterly cold windstorm as we have not had in a long time. Men and beasts tremble." Several days later, a heavy snowfall changed to rain at Trappe on December 17–18, washing away much of the snow, while a deep blanket of snow covered areas to the north.

The first in a series of three major snowstorms during a ten-day period, noted in Muhlenberg's journals (1945, 3:282–286), arrived on December 28, 1779, which began as a heavy snowstorm and ended as a chilly rain at Trappe. A second powerful winter storm struck on January 2–3, 1780, accompanied by gusty winds. Reverend Muhlenberg commented on January 3, "the house and yard are so circumvallated that one can scarcely get out or in, and the snow is still falling."

The third snowstorm in ten days hit Pennsylvania on the night of January 4–5, 1780. Wind-blown snow continued to fall periodically on the sixth and seventh. Muhlenberg wrote on January 6, 1780: "Violent storm from the northwest the whole day with intermittent snow." A few weeks later, on January 23, Muhlenberg noted that the snow was "over three feet deep" in Lancaster County.

During the Hard Winter of 1779–80, American troops were encamped in Morristown, New Jersey, about twenty-five miles west of New York City, keeping a watchful eye on the British, who enjoyed more comfortable quarters in Manhattan. American troops would eventually cross from New Jersey to Staten Island on foot over the frozen bay to do battle with the British.

General George Washington, in addition to his duties as commander in chief of the Revolutionary Army, found the time to keep a record of the weather, noting the 18-inch snowfall in northern New Jersey on January 5–6, 1780, in his diary.

The best source of historical weather information in 1779–80 in northeastern Pennsylvania comes from Oscar J. Harvey's two-volume series *A History of Wilkes-Barre* (1909, 2:1225–1226): "By the middle of December [1779] the snow was about two feet deep in central and northern New Jersey and eastern Pennsylvania. . . . In the woods and other sheltered places it lay for many weeks at least four feet deep upon the level. The weather was intensely cold during a greater part of that period, and harbors, rivers and creeks and brooks were all frozen over."

A diary entry written by Revolutionary War officer John Jenkins Jr. on January 11, 1780, stated: "A party of men set out to go through the swamp—across the Pocono range—on snow-shoes; the snow about three feet deep."

The brutally cold weather froze inland bays and harbors as far south as the Virginia–North Carolina border (Ludlum 1982, 211). In central New Jersey, the Somerset militia tried to create a road between Hackettstown and Princeton, New Jersey, but encountered impossible conditions. An observer on the scene, Andrew Mellick Jr., vividly described the snowy landscape: "The whole face of the country lay buried from three to five feet deep; roads, fences, and frozen streams were obliterated . . . in places the drifts were piled ten to twelve feet high" (Ludlum 1966, 114).

A Philadelphia physician, Dr. Benjamin Rush, reviewed the extreme conditions in January 1780. In 1789 he wrote: "During the whole of that month [January 1780]—except one day—it never rose, in the city of Philadelphia, to the freezing point." The records of David Rittenhouse of Philadelphia indicated that temperatures edged above freezing on January 31, 1780, when the eaves of the houses were reported to be dripping from melting snow and ice.

A sunrise observation of −16 degrees at British headquarters on Manhattan Island on January 29, 1780, if accurate, would be comparable to the modern record minimum at Central Park of −15 degrees set on February 15, 1934. The location and exposure where the −16 reading was obtained is not known, which Ludlum (1966, 115) attributed to a notice in the *New York Packet* of Fishkill, New York.

A great tragedy occurred near Lancaster on February 5, 1780, which was related in the diary of Thomas Hughes (Ludlum 1984, 58): "Forty people crossing the Susquehanna in sleighs—being on their return from a wedding—the ice broke, and six and thirty were drowned—amongst the unfortunates the new married couple."

In western Pennsylvania, at the present site of Pittsburgh, a February 11, 1780, letter from Colonel Daniel Brodhead at Fort Pitt forwarded to General George Washington declared: "Such a deep snow and such ice has not been known at this place in the memory of the eldest natives; Deer & Turkies die by hundreds for want of food, the snow on the Alleghany & Laurel hills is four feet deep."

The weather finally thawed on February 11, 1780, after an interminable period of cold, though the Delaware River, which had frozen over on December 21, would not open up for navigation until March 4. Bouts of wintry weather prevailed during the second half of March, culminating in a heavy snowfall in northern New Jersey (9 inches at Morristown) and eastern Pennsylvania on March 31–April 1, 1780.

The opening days of April 1780 brought more cold winds and snow showers.

Flurries were noticed in northern New England as late as May 1, 1780, and frost was observed in some low places on June 5–6, and 9. A rare summer frost was observed in some of the cold hollows on July 12, 1780 (Ludlum 1966, 117).

1783–84

Only four years after the Hard Winter of 1779–80, along came the Long Winter of 1783–84. On December 26, 1783, navigation ceased on the Delaware River, which would freeze a few days later and not open up until March 12, 1784 (Hazard 1828, 380).

The most comprehensive record of snowfall for the region comes from the diary of Joseph Lewis in Morristown, New Jersey, twenty-five miles west of New York City. The first snowfall of the season blanketed the eastern seaboard from New Jersey to Maine on November 12–13, 1783, depositing 2.5 inches at Morristown. A major winter storm followed on November 27–28, leaving a hefty 11 inches (Ludlum 1966, 65).

The weather in December 1783 was marked by "periods of alternate cold and warmth" with frequent snows. The Morristown records indicate snowfalls on December 2–3 (2 inches), 4 (3 inches), 18 (5 inches), 24 (2 inches), 25–26 (1 inch), and 29 (1 inch). The heaviest snowfall of the winter arrived on December 30–31, accompanied by much drifting. The snow began falling at Morristown around 3:00 A.M. and continued for twenty-five hours, accumulating "about 20 inches."

The snow reached a considerable depth in northern New Jersey and Pennsylvania in January 1784. Significant snow fell at Morristown on January 11 (5 inches), 18–19 (10 inches), and 20 (3 inches). The biggest fall of the month arrived on January 26–27, when 18 inches piled up in twenty-four hours, commencing at 9:00 P.M. on the January 26.

Adding the January 1784 snowfalls (36 inches) to those of November and December 1783 at Morristown gives an accumulation of 83.5 inches for the three-month period. This partial total is comparable to the snowiest winters on record in northern New Jersey (1867–68, 1960–61, and 1995–96) over an entire season.

There was a sudden thaw on January 13, 1784, "so that within a few hours, we have experienced a transition from heat to cold, of at least 53 degrees" (Watson 1868, 358). Bitter cold returned in February, and a deep freeze prevailed from the tenth through the seventeenth. Garriott (1906, 10) listed a low temperature of −12 degrees recorded somewhere near the city of Philadelphia, probably observed in a mid-February deep freeze. This value is comparable to the modern Philadelphia record minimum temperature of −11 degrees on February 9, 1934.

At Hartford, Connecticut, the mercury dipped below −10 degrees on eight consecutive mornings from February 10 to 17, 1784, with minimum readings of −20 (fourteenth) and −19 degrees (Webster 1835, 186). Another late-winter cold snap brought three consecutive subzero mornings at Philadelphia (February 29–March 2, 1784), and February 29 was an especially bitter Leap Day.

Two "moderate falls" of snow in early March 1784 were followed by a thaw during the second half of the month (Ludlum 1966, 66). However, snow would cover the ground several times in April 1784 in parts of Pennsylvania. Ludlum (1966, 223) uncovered the records John Fitch, a surveyor who recorded bits of weather information in the "western country" in the middle 1780s. Fitch observed the final breakup of ice along the Monongahela River on March 10, 1784, and on the Youghiogheny River the day after. Fitch's records (1784–91) have been preserved in the Library of Congress in Washington.

1798–99

The Long Winter of 1798–99 began with an early snowstorm that started as rain at New York City on November 19, 1798, which changed to a heavy snow shortly before midnight. Local observer Hugh Gaine, who maintained a weather journal, measured 18 inches at New York City, which easily exceeds all modern November snowfalls in the city. Up to three feet of snow fell over interior New England (Ludlum 1966, 74–75).

Four significant snowfalls in the Northeast followed during the first nineteen days of December 1798. At Philadelphia the accumulation of snow was thought to be the greatest ever known up to the first of January (Hazard 1828, 2:382). Bouts of bitterly cold weather accompanied by light to moderate snowfalls contributed to an extended period of rough, wintry weather in the Northeast through March 1799. Subzero temperatures were recorded as late as March 5, 1799, along the Connecticut coast.

A substantial snow cover lingered as late as March 12, 1799, at Philadelphia, attesting to the prolonged chill. Two local histories recounted an exceptionally deep snow cover in sparsely settled western Pennsylvania during the second week of March 1799: Alfred Creigh (1870, 349) mentioned a snow depth of 3 feet in Washington County southwest of Pittsburgh, and W. J. McKnight (1905, 375) wrote that as much as 5 feet of snow covered the ground near Lake Erie. Snowflakes were frequently flying over the highlands of New England in April and early May 1799, earning 1798–99 the title of the Long Winter.

Historic Pennsylvania Snowstorms

December 1786: Triple Storms I

A barrage of three major snowstorms in early December 1786 brought unprecedented early-season snow depths to northern New Jersey, though less is known about the snowfalls in eastern Pennsylvania. The Morristown, New Jersey, records of Joseph Lewis spanning the years of 1783 to 1795 provide the best perspective on snowfall totals during the meteorological triple play in early December 1786 (Ludlum 1983, 87).

The first of three major snowstorms dropped 18 inches at Morristown on December 4–5, 1786. We learn from the diary of David Shultze of Goshenhoppen, near Philadelphia, that there was "a very deep snow" (Berky 1953, 2:198–199). Three days later, another 8 inches of snow fell at Morristown. A third storm added 15 inches on December 9–10, for an incredible total of 41 inches in one week!

Winthrop Sargent was in Philadelphia in December 1786 before taking an active role in the Ohio Company and settling in Marietta, Ohio. Sargent left us with a good description of the Triple Storms of that December, which he recorded while traveling from Philadelphia to New York City (Ludlum 1966, 72):

December 4–5: At 10 oClock [December 4] some light snow, & by 12 we had a severe storm which continued through the day. . . . This morng [December 5] at 10 oClock it abated & the wind backened in to N W from which quarter it blew in force all Day—it ceased to snow after noon but here are drifts of more than four feet in Height which very much impedes our travelling.

December 7–8: In the last night there fell five or six inches of snow at very least, which may make tolerable sleigh'g.

December 9–10: A N East wind last night, which was this morng [December 9] increased to a violent gale attended with a great fall of snow—A continuation of the storm through the Day. . . . Full two feet of snow on a level over the whole country.

By December 14, 1786, Sargent noted, "snow dissolving fast." The lowest temperature in his diary was 12 degrees on December 6 after the first snowfall. The weather moderated in Philadelphia by the middle of December, dissolving much of the deep snow cover, which was nearly all gone by early January 1787.

March 30–April 1, 1807: Deep Northern Snowfall

A massive late-season snowstorm traveled from the Tennessee Valley to southeastern Pennsylvania on March 30–April 1, 1807. The disturbance undoubtedly drew considerable moisture from the Atlantic Ocean, resulting in a spectacular snowfall over the mountains of central and northern Pennsylvania.

Heavy wet snow began falling over Pennsylvania on the evening of March 30, piling up to historic depths by the next morning. The *Democratic Press* in Philadelphia reported a fall of 36 inches at Huntingdon, in the south-central hills, and 36 to 42 inches in the Nittany Valley, near the present site of Pennsylvania State University. Twenty-nine years later, after another huge snowstorm, the editor of the Montrose *Independent Volunteer* recalled a snowfall of 54 inches in 1807 in the *United States Gazette* (January 20, 1836).

In Bradford County, near the New York border, "snow fell continuously three days and was between four and five feet deep" (Heverling 1926, 72). Despite "cold, blustery weather" over the next few days, April sunshine caused the massive snow accumulation to melt rapidly, resulting in "a great flood, one of the most notable in the Susquehanna river."

January 6–7, 1821: Great January Coastal Storm

A major coastal disturbance brought rain and sleet to Charleston, South Carolina, on January 5, 1821, which became mostly snow over eastern Virginia. Secretary of State John Quincy Adams described a snowfall of 12 to 18 inches around Washington, D.C. At Philadelphia the snow began at dusk on the sixth, piling up to a depth of 18 inches, according to the *Franklin Gazette*.

March 30–31, 1823: Great Easter Blizzard

A powerful spring blizzard on the closing days of March 1823 wreaked havoc along the eastern seaboard with a combination of rain, snow, and high winds. In south-central Pennsylvania 2 feet of snow piled up at Carlisle. The Stroudsburg

Jeffersonian (April 20, 1854) recalled a fall of 24 inches. High winds toppled trees in eastern Pennsylvania and New Jersey, and 10 inches fell at Fort Columbus, New York City (Ludlum 1968, 8–9).

January 14–16, 1831: Great Snowstorm

The winter of 1830–31 in northern Pennsylvania was deemed "very severe, hardest experienced since that of 1779–80," according to Clement Heverling (1926, 569) in a *History and Geography of Bradford County, Pennsylvania.*

January 1831 provided all the elements of a harsh winter month, starting with heavy rain that led to an "unprecedented freshet" inundating lower sections of Kingston and Wilkes-Barre in the Wyoming Valley on New Year's Day. Two weeks later a massive winter storm formed over the Gulf of Mexico that would become a great nor'easter.

The storm center churned northeast across Georgia early on Friday, January 14, before turning up the East Coast. Several inches of snow blanketed interior sections of Georgia and the Carolinas northward to coastal Virginia. Snow began falling in the morning hours of January 14 just south of the Mason-Dixon line, piling up to a depth of 13 inches at Washington and 18 inches at Baltimore. The snow spread north very slowly and would not reach Philadelphia until 8:00 P.M. (Ludlum 1968, 99–100).

The snow became heavier over Pennsylvania on the Saturday, January 15, and did not let up until midday on Sunday. The slow movement would contribute to very large snow totals as low pressure encountered resistance from a dome of cold air. Samuel Hazard, editor of the *Register of Pennsylvania,* took it upon himself to provide a thorough account of the "Great Snowstorm of January 14–16, 1831."

The geographical extent of deep snow cover laid down by the Great Snowstorm of January 1831 may have been surpassed only by the East Coast blizzards of February 1899 and March 1993. A storm summary in *Hazard's Register of Pennsylvania* on April 16, 1831, revealed the breadth of the huge winter storm. The West Chester *Republican* reported that the "average depth of three feet" was the greatest since the winter of 1804–5. In the Susquehanna Valley, the snow depth at Lewistown reached 3 feet and was reportedly 3.5 feet deep in the countryside, which "exceeds that of any period," according to the recollection of the oldest inhabitants.

In the lower Susquehanna Valley the *Columbia Spy* reported "about three feet, and the drifts to be twelve feet high." At Harrisburg the snow was thought to be "upwards of two feet," and together with strong winds blocked all mail deliveries from Philadelphia and Baltimore. The librarian at the State Library at Harrisburg said the snow was the deepest since the winter of 1783–84.

The *Lancaster Journal* stated that the average depth of the snow was "variously estimated at from two to two-and-a-half feet," including what remained of the "nine to twelve inches" on the ground at the end of a recent snowstorm on January 11. Drifts were 5 to 6 feet, "rendering the main roads impassable for several days." A Gettysburg observer measured 30 inches (Ludlum 1968, 11–15).

In the east-central Pennsylvania hills, the Pottsville *Miners' Journal* reported a snow depth of 3 feet, probably including a portion of a 10-inch snowfall that had occurred on January 10–11. After a lighter 1-inch snowfall on January 18, the editor declared, "The oldest inhabitants declare that the quantity of snow on the ground exceeds that for any period within their recollection."

The *Easton Argus* reported that the snow was "at least three feet on the level," presumably including what remained from a recent storm. The snow accumulation at Easton was probably about 30 inches. About sixty miles farther north along the Delaware River the snowfall at Milford was given as 20 inches.

In western Pennsylvania the *Pittsburg Gazette* reported a 22-inch snowfall during these days. Such a massive storm total has been exceeded only in December 1890, November 1950, and March 1993 in the Pittsburgh area. However, the heavy snowfall of January 14–16, 1831, apparently did not extend to the shores of Lake Erie. The *Erie Observer* remarked that it was "scarcely enough to make good sleighing."

Near the coast, the snowfall in the New York City area averaged 15 to 20 inches, based on the observations of local weather-watcher Henry Laight, who watched the New York weather scene from 1786 to 1836. His fine records have been preserved in the National Archives and the New York Historical Society.

A dispatch from the *Boston Gazette* noted that the Great Snowstorm of January 1831 continued to vent its fury well to the northeast of Pennsylvania. The snow began to fall in the Boston area around sunrise on Saturday, January 15, and would continue in full force until late in the day on the sixteenth, with an accumulation of "two feet on the level." The account added, "For thirty hours or more the wind blew with great violence, a part of the time a perfect hurricane."

A Lewistown correspondent noted that three significant snowfalls followed the Great Snowstorm of January 14–16, 1831, all ranging in depth from 6 to 12 inches, which certainly amounted to a massive snow cover.

January 8–10, 1836: Big Snow

The winter of 1835–36 would be long remembered for the duration of cold weather and the single largest snowstorm in the history of eastern Pennsylvania. This winter was probably the coldest on record in Philadelphia, based on data extending back to 1825. The mean temperature in 1835–36 for December, January, and February averaged 27.7 degrees at Philadelphia at the Pennsylvania Hospital, compared with the contemporary mean temperature for these months of 33.1 degrees.

On January 18, 1918, in the grip of another historically severe Pennsylvania winter, the *Stroudsburg Times* brought out their historical files. Stroudsburg resident Henry R. Biesecker, then over ninety years old, recalled the winter of 1835–36, reporting, "There was a fall of four feet of snow that lay for days and people would find deer floundering in it, unable to escape."

Monroe County historian Luther S. Hoffman was interviewed by the press in 1928 about the winter of 1835–36: "There had been a very mild fall until during November, when a storm brought several inches of snow while freezing set in. Piles of corn in the ear were on the ground, unhusked, and were frozen fast . . . remaining there until spring. In the early part of December, snow started to fall . . . traffic was tied up for many weeks. . . . Rural roads were blocked practically all winter. Farmers afoot and on horseback went to the boroughs to have grist around or to secure food" (*Morning Sun* [East Stroudsburg], April 28, 1928).

A moderating trend in the weather in early January 1836 following a cold December featured a moist easterly flow of maritime air, bringing periods of light rain to eastern Pennsylvania and light snow over the crest of the Appalachians (Ludlum 1968, 29).

On January 7–8, 1836, a low-pressure wave moved northward along a trough of low pressure anchored a short distance offshore. Arctic air eventually met up with a moist flow of subtropical air, changing rain to heavy, wet snow along the coastal plain early on January 9.

The amount of moisture associated with the storm was remarkable. The catch at Pennsylvania General Hospital in downtown Philadelphia over a four-day period, beginning Thursday, January 7, 1836, and continuing through the tenth, totaled 4.50 inches. As temperatures dipped to freezing, 1 to 2 feet of wet snow piled up across the southeastern Pennsylvania and southern New Jersey to New York City. The *United States Gazette* reported a slushy 15-inch accumulation in Philadelphia, adding that the figure would have been closer to 36 inches if temperatures had been a few degrees colder.

The *New York Herald* stated, "The quantity of snow lying on our streets is beyond anything that ever appeared in our time. About four or five years ago [January 1831], we had a tolerable snowstorm, which afforded fine sleighing for six weeks in succession. But the quantity then was only half what it is at present." Snowfall measurements around New York City averaged about 15 inches, though the *Herald* account suggested a heavier fall, since the January 1831 storm deposited 18 inches at Erasmus Hall in Brooklyn.

The storm apparently stalled near the southeastern tip of New England, prolonging the period of heavy snow. Spectacular depths averaging from 3 to 5 feet were observed over the highlands of northern Pennsylvania northward into central New York (Ludlum 1968, 29–32). The greatest falls approached 5 feet at Ithaca and Rome, New York.

The editor of the *Independent Volunteer* in Montrose observed: "We are literally surrounded on all sides by mountains of snow, which peer through their snow-capped peaks above one another in a style quite magnificent." The Big Snow (42 inches) was compared with another huge storm that dropped 54 inches on Montrose on March 30–April 1, 1807, and it was noted that the 1807 storm left "a trifling greater depth."

In his unpublished historical notes, Luther Hoffman stated, "In January [1836], snow fell continuously for three days to a depth of about four feet in what is known as the Big Snow." The *Easton Argus* reported a fall of 34 inches. Both totals exceed all modern single snowfall records by a substantial margin.

A moderate snowstorm brushed the Northeast on January 24–25, 1836, depositing up to 6 inches in central New Jersey, reported the *New Jersey Journal*. Waves of bitterly cold air reached the Northeast in late January and early February. The press noted that snow depths ranged from 4 to 8 feet over interior portions of eastern Pennsylvania. Philadelphia endured the third coldest February (24 degrees) in 1836.

Heavy snow fell again on February 28, marking the sixteenth snowstorm of the winter, according to the *United States Gazette*. Substantial negative temperature departures in March and April preserved some of the snow cover well into spring, and snow fell at Philadelphia and New York City as late as April 13, 1836.

December 1839: Triple Storms II

Three major snowstorms lashed the Northeastern states in December 1839, accompanied by powerful winds that caused great destruction in coastal New England (Ludlum 1968, 33). As much as 20 inches of snow fell at New Haven, Connecticut, and 24 inches in Westchester County, New York, north of New York City, on December 14–15. However, an inland storm track brought mostly rain to Pennsylvania.

A second disturbance traveled farther south across North Carolina on December 22–23 before sliding up the Atlantic coast. This path took the heaviest swath of snow over northeastern Maryland and southeastern Pennsylvania (Ludlum 1968, 38). Snow reached the nation's capital about 3:00 A.M. on the twenty-second, quickly spreading northward into southeastern Pennsylvania by morning. Totals were reported to be 10 inches of snow at Washington and 16 inches of snow (and sleet) at Baltimore.

The *Gettysburg Sentinel* reported "at least 24 or 25 inches on the level" with much drifting. At Chambersburg a fall of 2 feet was also measured, completely blocking roads in all directions. The *Easton Sentinel* reported the "average depth of the snow to be two feet." Various press accounts mentioned accumulations of 18 inches at Lancaster and in Chester County. The fall at Philadelphia was put at 10 inches.

A third great snowstorm struck the Northeast on December 27–28, but an interior storm path over Virginia caused the snow to quickly change to rain over the Middle Atlantic states. Farther north in the colder air, 2 feet of snow fell in a band from Hartford, Connecticut, to Worcester, Massachusetts, and whole gales caused numerous shipwrecks along the New England coastline (Ludlum 1982, 265).

January 18–19, 1857: Great Cold Storm

The Cold Storm of January 1857 stands out for a combination of heavy snow, driving winds, and near-zero temperatures. A frigid mass of arctic air settled over the northeast and Middle Atlantic states on January 17–18.

A clash of arctic air pushing south along the spine of the Appalachians and a tropical air streaming northward set the stage for low pressure to intensify over the Gulf of Mexico. The storm moved quickly north along the Atlantic coast, spreading heavy snow from the mountains of northern Georgia to the interior Carolinas late on the seventeenth, leaving 8 inches on the ground at Athens, Georgia.

The leading edge of the snow arrived in southern Virginia shortly after midnight on the eighteenth. Heavy snow broke out over Pennsylvania by early afternoon. Accumulations over interior sections of eastern North Carolina and Virginia exceeded 12 inches. A dispatch from Raleigh, North Carolina, in the *Washington Post* (February 14, 1899) recalled a 24-inch snowfall at Raleigh in January 1857. The Cold Storm of January 1857 is still Raleigh/Durham's heaviest recorded snowstorm and has been approached only by the modern record fall of 20.3 inches on January 24–25, 2000.

The Philadelphia *Evening Bulletin* reported 18 and 24 inches of snow from

Washington northeastward to Baltimore and Philadelphia. At Baltimore the depth of the snow was reportedly "on the level about two feet," piling up in drifts as high as 6 to 10 feet.

Professor Michael Jacobs at Gettysburg recorded a temperature of zero at 9:00 A.M. when the snow commenced to fall. The temperature continued to drift downward, reaching −3 degrees at night, an unprecedented degree of cold during a nor'easter. Powerful north-northeast winds piled the estimated 9-inch snowfall into large drifts.

The observer at Norristown, northwest of Philadelphia, estimated a little more than 12 inches of snow accumulated from 1.20 inches of melted precipitation, adding, "The snow lies in drifts from 6 to 12 feet." At Lafayette College in Easton 17 inches fell in twenty-three hours, commencing at 3:00 P.M. on January 18 and ending around 2:00 P.M. on the nineteenth. Temperatures hovered near or slightly above zero throughout the day.

Thirty miles north of Easton, the Stroudsburg *Jeffersonian* (December 29, 1887) would later mention a snowfall of 18 inches on January 18–19. About sixty miles west of Stroudsburg, the observer at Berwick reported 17 inches. A poetic postscript to the storm appeared in the *Belvidere Intelligencer* in northwest New Jersey: "The very sunbeams froze, or whatever of them found their way through the clouds. The wind blew furiously, driving the snow through every nook and cranny."

December 25–27, 1872: Post-Christmas Blizzard

A severe arctic outbreak gripped the Northeast beginning on December 22, 1872, with temperatures tumbling far below zero. Christmas morning dawned bitterly cold and dry over Pennsylvania, as temperatures hovered near or below zero. Far to the south, a mighty winter storm was gathering strength along the southeast Atlantic coast. At Columbia, South Carolina, a dispatch called it "the heaviest storm of snow and sleet ever known in this section."

The canopy of heavy snow spread rapidly north up the eastern seaboard, reaching Washington around noon on Christmas Day in 1872. The snow began at Philadelphia a little after sunset, coming down furiously within hours. The *Public Ledger* reported a fall of at least 10 inches, continuing, "The most terrific snowstorm prevails here today that we have had for many years. The snow is two feet deep and is still falling rapidly. The wind blows a fearful gale, drifting so as to render travel almost impossible. The mercury is 6 degrees above zero" (December 27, 1872). West of the city, a Chester County observer measured 15 inches before the storm diminished to flurries on the afternoon of the twenty-sixth.

The weather observer at Egypt, northwest of Allentown, gave a measurement of 22 inches. The *Easton Express* reported a snow depth of 30 inches on December 27, probably including what remained of a heavy snowfall on December 18–20 that averaged 6 inches in the region. The Stroudsburg press reported a snow depth of "a little over two feet," at the end of the storm on December 27, but later clarified that the actual measurement was 18 inches. There apparently was a sharp cutoff to the north and west, because only 10 inches fell at Blooming Grove and 7.5 inches at Dyberry in the northern Poconos.

The snowfall of December 25–27, 1872, averaged 18 inches along a line from

Trenton to New York City. The *New York Times* commented, "The most remarkable feature of the storm was found in the darkness, for so dense was the fall of snowflakes that the atmosphere was absolutely darkened all day," calling the storm "one of the most severe snowstorms on record in this latitude."

The cold, snowy winter of 1872–73 lingered into the lap of spring. Snow fell frequently in March 1873, with light to moderate falls during the second week of the month and a heavy fall of 10 inches at Dyberry in the northeast on March 21–22. More snow fell on March 24–25, prompting the mercury to plunge to another late-season mark (−5 degrees) on the twenty-eighth at Dyberry. Local observer Theodore Day noted on March 31, 1873, "Snow from 1 to 3 feet deep." In Bradford County the snow was "so deep in the woods that sugar-makers were unable to gather sap" (Heverling 1926, 577).

Snow fell again across much of Pennsylvania on April 1, 5–6, 12, 17, 21–22, and 25, 1873. Blooming Grove had a 9-inch fall on the twelfth, and snow "fell to the depth of two feet" in Bradford County on April 21–22, 1873. The unseasonably cold and backward spring pattern continued in May, with an inch of snow at Dyberry on May 3.

The season snowfall total at Dyberry (113.2 inches) was only 2.4 inches shy of that of the snowy winter of 1867–68 (115.6 inches). The weather observer at Egypt, near Allentown, logged a total of 87.5 inches in 1872–73. No winter during the past 150 years brought more than 80 inches of snow to the Allentown/Bethlehem area.

January 8–9, 1884: Big Pittsburgh Snowstorm

On January 8, 1884, snow began falling in Pittsburgh around 1:00 A.M. at the rate of 1 to 2 inches an hour, as measured by the Signal Service. By the time the storm ended around 12:30 A.M. on the ninth, the official accumulation reached 18 inches, with outlying districts reporting 2 feet.

The January 1884 storm at Pittsburgh was called the "greatest on record in this section." At Titusville the storm brought "heaviest fall of snow in a single day ever known here." Streetcars were halted in their tracks, and wagons and sleds did not fare any better. In the eastern part of the state, snow eventually changed to sleet and rain over the southeast early on the eighth, but a heavy snowfall occurred in the central and northeastern mountains before the precipitation gradually became mixed with sleet and freezing rain.

The central pressure of the storm deepened below 29.00 inches along the coast, strong enough to draw mild Atlantic air inland, bringing a soaking rain to Philadelphia. High winds lashed northeastern Pennsylvania through the day and night of January 8–9. A Shenendoah dispatch relayed, "Telegraph and telephone wires were blown down, colliery stacks and breaker roofs destroyed, and plate-glass windows in this place and Shamokin were blown in."

The January 1884 blizzard extended far and wide, with reports of heavy snow from Atlanta to Harrisonburg, Virginia. A dispatch from Wheeling, West Virginia, mentioned a fall of 20 inches, and another from Richmond, Kentucky, reported 14 inches. The greatest fall noted was 36 inches in western New York at Lockport.

Curiously, two years later to the date, on January 8, 1886, another heavy snowstorm set in at Pittsburgh around 10:00 A.M., and by noon on the ninth had deposited 18.5 inches of snow on Pittsburgh—slightly more than the January 1884 fall.

March 11–14, 1888: Blizzard of '88

The winter of 1887–88 in Pennsylvania is most famous for a great March blizzard, but this was actually not the heaviest snowfall of the season. An early snowstorm on December 17–18, 1887, deposited 6 to 10 inches of snow from Washington to New York City but dumped nearly 2 feet of snow on east-central Pennsylvania.

The Stroudsburg *Jeffersonian* reported a spectacular snowfall of 26 inches in less than twenty-four hours, which exceeds the modern December record of 18.8 inches (1966). A Reading dispatch reported 18 inches with snow still falling. The weather observer at Lafayette College in Easton measured a respectable 22 inches of snow in eighteen hours, starting at 5:00 P.M. on December 17 and ending at 11:00 A.M. on the eighteenth. This total equaled the December 1872 snowfall record at nearby Egypt.

Farther southeast, amounts tapered off to 7 inches at Philadelphia and 10.6 inches at Baltimore in the December 1887 storm. Over in northern New Jersey, 13.5 inches fell at Dover, with amounts falling off to 6 inches at New York City. The *New York Times* reported heavier falls of 12 inches at Poughkeepsie and 16 inches at Albany.

A blizzard in the Great Plains in January 1888 caught the attention of the press, though no one anticipated a Western-style blizzard would strike the Northeast in the middle of March 1888. Weather historian David Ludlum (1983, 41) wrote, "Nothing in the folklore traditions of colonial America or the formally recorded meteorological history of the northeastern United States equals the storm that enveloped the area from Virginia to Maine on March 11–14, 1888."

The weather map on Saturday, March 10, revealed an innocuous-looking trough of low pressure over the Great Lakes. Over the next twenty-four hours, a secondary storm developed on the southern end of the trough and was centered over eastern Georgia on Sunday morning, March 11.

Two distinct low-pressure areas of equal intensity were now evident near Wilmington, North Carolina (29.68 inches), and north of the Lake Ontario (29.70 inches) in the afternoon. The coastal disturbance quickly became the main center of energy, tapping warm, moist Atlantic air and at the same time drawing bitterly cold arctic air southward into the Northeast. The clash of air masses caused rapid intensification of the storm, accounting for the violent winds.

The system churned northward along the Atlantic coast, reaching a position off the tip of southern New Jersey early on March 12 (Ludlum 1983, 120). Twenty-four hours later, the center of the storm had drifted to a position near Block Island, Rhode Island (28.92 inches).

Light rain fell much of the day over eastern Pennsylvania on March 11, 1888, in advance of an arctic cold front. The switchover from rain to snow occurred around 3:00 P.M. at Washington on the eleventh, and by midnight 6 inches of snow had fallen on the nation's capital. The change from rain to snow did not occur at Philadelphia until 11:15 P.M., and not until after midnight (12:10 A.M.) at New York City.

The Signal Service observer in Philadelphia called the storm "the most disastrous that has ever visited this locality." Twenty-seven of forty vessels in the harbor along the Delaware River near the mouth of the bay were damaged, and total marine losses were put at $500,000 (*Monthly Weather Review*). The snowfall at Washington and Philadelphia totaled 10 inches, though the snow was difficult to measure because of the high winds.

The Stroudsburg *Jeffersonian* recorded the storm timeline for the area about ninety miles north of Philadelphia: "Between 9 and 10 o'clock [March 11] it began a very gentle drizzle, and this kept on until 2 o'clock in the afternoon when the rain had turned into sleet, and continued until about 5 o'clock when it began to snow. On Monday [March 12] we had a full twelve inches of snow. . . . The wind from Monday morning until Tuesday [March 12–13] morning blowing great guns."

The slow movement of the storm added many hours of blinding snow to the Northeast, from New York City northward, that continued on March 13, 1888. A blocking ridge of high pressure to the north caused the system to stall for many hours off the southeastern tip of New England. The large pressure difference brought sustained gale-force winds that drove the powdery snow into mountainous drifts as high as 25 feet, as temperatures plunged to near zero across eastern Pennsylvania and northern New Jersey.

The weather records of Luther S. Hoffman, a local historian, gave a total snowfall of 18 inches in the Stroudsburg area. North of Honesdale in Wayne County, a longtime Dyberry observer Theodore Day also measured 18 inches. The NOAA *Climate Narrative* for Scranton listed a snowfall of 15 inches, driven into huge drifts by winds gusting to 50 miles per hour, correcting for the employment of four-cup anemometers beginning in 1928, which requires a reduction in the velocity of 20 percent (Ludlum 1983, 99).

The *Bethlehem Daily Times* detailed the great storm of March 1888 in the Lehigh Valley: "The blizzard was terrific for nearly 48 hours, not abating until about 9 o'clock last evening [March 13] and the temperature still hovering about freezing point this morning and snow falling lightly." After the storm had been raging for only twenty-four hours, communications were cut off from rural sections after the snow drifted as high as 20 feet.

In contrast, western Pennsylvania was largely spared from the storm's fury because the storm tracked well offshore was fairly compact. The monthly snowfall at Pittsburgh in March 1888 was only 2 inches.

Spectacular snow totals were recorded over western New England and eastern New York as the storm looped over the southeastern tip of New England. Storm totals mounted to 20.9 inches at New York City, 44.7 inches at New Haven, Connecticut, 46.7 inches at Albany, and 58 inches at Saratoga, New York. Communications were lost all along the eastern seaboard from Virginia to Maine, as snowbound communities struggled to cope with huge drifts and downed power lines.

The death toll from the Blizzard of '88 was estimated at around four hundred persons, including two hundred in the New York City alone. Many lost their lives attempting to travel to or from work during the height of the storm, perishing in deep snow banks after wandering in the numbing cold.

December 1890: Snowiest Month in Southwest

Several big snowfalls made weather history in an otherwise mild winter in 1890–91 in Pennsylvania. A huge snowfall buried extreme western and northern Pennsylvania on December 16–18, depositing 25.7 inches at Pittsburgh. The storm was called by the *Pittsburgh Commercial Gazette* "the most destructive of the kind that has ever been experienced in this city," taking a heavy toll on "operations of railroad, telegraph, and street-car companies."

Press dispatches indicated a broad canopy of heavy snow that accumulated more than a foot along the Ohio River from Wheeling to Parkersburg, West Virginia. More than 2 feet of snow fell in the northwestern mountains of Pennsylvania at Bradford. In the northeast, a press notice from Wilkes-Barre reported about 18 inches, and the Dyberry observer farther east measured 12 inches.

A second heavy snowfall developed on December 25–27, leaving fairly uniform totals of 10 to 15 inches from the nation's capital northward through much of Pennsylvania. Dyberry added another 15 inches to the monthly total, and Pittsburgh received 13.2 inches, helping to set an all-time monthly snowfall record of 41.3 inches.

The resort community of Blue Knob, about fifteen miles southwest of Altoona at an elevation of about 2,500 feet, recorded 96 inches in December 1890, establishing a state record for a single month! In the north-central highlands, Nisbet in Lycoming County tallied 31 inches of snow in December 1890.

The winter of 1890–91 ended with another massive snowfall on March 27–28. Heavy accumulations extended from Baltimore (9.5 inches) to Harrisburg (18.1 inches) and north to Dyberry (14 inches). The *Washington Post* reported tremendous falls to the west over the Appalachians on March 27–28, including "two and a half feet" at Winchester, Virginia, and 30 inches at Martinsburg, West Virginia.

The *Philadelphia Inquirer* reported impressive totals in interior southeastern Pennsylvania at Huntingdon (28 inches), Lancaster (19 inches), and Norristown and Collegeville (12 inches). The *New York Times* mentioned 15 inches at Reading and 20 inches at Charleston, West Virginia.

February 11–13, 1899: Great Eastern Blizzard

The winter of 1898–99 brought a record accumulation of snow at Philadelphia (55.4 inches) that stood until 1995–96 (65.5 inches).

A moderate snowfall on November 24, 1898, brought a fresh blast of cold air, helping to energize a tremendous coastal storm that followed on November 26–27. The barometric pressure reading at Boston dipped to 28.38 inches during what became known as the "*Portland* Storm" after the passenger ship the SS *Portland* sank west of Cape Cod, taking 120 lives. At least 50 more persons died, and perhaps as many as 200, mostly at sea, as the storm battered the East Coast from Virginia to New England.

The greatest snowfall (27 inches) occurred at New London, Connecticut. New York City (10 inches) and Philadelphia (9.2 inches) had record November snowfalls. In the upper Delaware Valley, the Stroudsburg *Jeffersonian* reported 10 inches of snow with a "terrific gale of wind." Record November snowfalls of

12 inches were reported at South Bethlehem, and 10 inches fell at Belvidere, New Jersey.

Moderate snowfalls in eastern Pennsylvania on November 24 and 30 contributed to record November snow totals at South Bethlehem (21 inches), New York City (19 inches), Belvidere, New Jersey (19 inches), and Philadelphia (9.2 inches).

The month of February 1899 would bring more havoc to the Northeast. Back-to-back coastal storms on February 5 and 7–8 deposited 6 to 14 inches of snow on much of Pennsylvania. An arctic outbreak of historic proportions arrived in the Northeast on the ninth and tenth. Minimum temperatures ranged from −6 degrees at Philadelphia in the southeast to −39 at Lawrenceburg in the north-central highlands.

The meteorological setting on February 10 featured a vast high-pressure system (31.15 inches) over the Great Plains and a low-pressure wave developing over the Gulf of Mexico along an old frontal boundary that brought snow to the Gulf coast. Another wave off the coast of northern Florida was spreading a mixture of snow, sleet, and rain as far north as the Carolinas.

The eventual merger of these disturbances brought snow to southeastern Pennsylvania by the evening on February 11. The storm rumbled up the eastern seaboard to a position off the Virginia Capes on the twelfth and would follow a familiar course parallel to the New Jersey coast, slowing down long enough to drop copious amounts of snow on the mid-Atlantic region.

Washington and Baltimore each recorded snowfalls of 20.5 inches, with record depths of 34.2 and 30 inches, respectively. The storm snowfall total at Philadelphia was 18.9, raising the depth to 26 inches—the largest on record until January 1996 (28 inches). Cape May, New Jersey, reported 34 inches, heavy enough to establish a state snowfall record and record depth of 40 inches. Several stations in eastern Maryland and northern Delaware also recorded historic 30-inch falls. Farther north, the official snowfall at New York City totaled 15.6 inches (24-inch depth), and 16 inches of snow fell at Boston.

The greatest snowfall occurred over interior southeastern Pennsylvania. The Kennett Square observer, about fifteen miles west of Philadelphia, reported 32 inches. Farther west, at York, the measurement was 29.5 inches. The snow depth at both locations reached 36 inches. (A daily measurement of 35 inches at Coatesville was deemed highly questionable, in light of an excessively high water equivalent measurement, perhaps reflecting a buried rain gauge.)

Amounts increased dramatically from west to east, ranging from 10 inches at Wilkes-Barre to 24 inches at Hawley on the eastern side of the Poconos. North of Hawley, the snowfall was 18 inches at Dyberry. The *Stroudsburg Daily Times* reported 25 inches, with drifts as high as 18 feet, whipped up by winds in excess of 35 miles per hour. At Stroudsburg, temperatures on February 12, 1899, during the height of the storm at noontime hovered a little above zero. The estimated fall at Easton's Lafayette College, thirty miles south of Stroudsburg, was listed as 16.5 inches.

The *Philadelphia Inquirer* chronicled the misery brought on by the Eastern Blizzard: "There is no way of adequately describing the storm which raged in and through and over and around Philadelphia yesterday, and drove to the woods that class of 'oldest inhabitants' who are fond of indulging in the reminiscences of winters we used to have. Not since the city was a baby has such an avalanche of congealed moisture descended upon it." The storm center was far enough off-shore to keep snow totals down over western Pennsylvania. Only a dusting of snow fell in the northwest, and 3 to 9 inches covered an area from Pittsburgh to Williamsport.

The Great Eastern Blizzard of February 1899 was noteworthy for the greatest longitudinal snowfall along the eastern seaboard. A trace of snow was seen at Fort Myers, Florida, the most southerly occurrence of snow in the United States until January 1977. In central Florida, Tampa had 0.1 inch, and 1.9 inches fell at Jacksonville. Charleston, South Carolina, reported 3.9 inches, which is the second heaviest of record. Eighteen inches of snow fell at Raleigh, North Carolina, which was the heaviest snowfall there since· January 1857, according an item in the *Washington Post.*

The heaviest monthly snowfalls in February 1899 in Pennsylvania were recorded at York (47.1 inches) and Hamlinton, Wayne County (46.2 inches). (A total snowfall of 69.8 inches at Coatesville is suspect and should be disregarded because of questionable liquid-equivalent measurements, as noted earlier.)

February 1902: Back-to-Back Snowstorms

Two heavy snowfalls hit Pennsylvania in less than a week in February 1902. The first storm lashed the eastern counties on February 16–17, dumping 11.4 inches at Philadelphia and a record 18 inches at Atlantic City, New Jersey. Amounts tapered off to 8 inches at Dyberry in the northeast, with less falling in the west. High winds piled the snow into drifts as high as 15 feet at Pen Argyl in the hills north of Easton. Along the coast winds gusted to nearly 50 miles an hour (corrected) at New York City.

A second storm on February 21–23 started as heavy snow but soon turned into a major ice storm in southeastern Pennsylvania. Philadelphia received 3 inches of snow and sleet, followed by many hours of freezing rain into the night of the twenty-second. The storm was described as "the most destructive to telegraph and telephone lines ever experienced" in the monthly *Climatological Data* report. Broken tree limbs encased in ice littered city streets and brought down electrical lines throughout the city and neighboring communities in southeastern Pennsylvania. Communications were severely disrupted and transportation was paralyzed for several days after the storm.

In the northeast, Dyberry received 11 inches, while the interior was generally buried under up to 2 feet of snow. Williamsport received 23 inches in twenty-four hours ending on February 23, along with a record snow depth of 29 inches. (The only greater twenty-four-hour snowfall in Williamsport was 24.1 inches in January 1964. The modern February record snowfall is 22.8 inches on February 19–20, 1972.)

The *Stroudsburg Daily Times* reported: "The snow lays between two and three feet deep on the Pocono." The depth at Tamaqua was estimated to be "about two feet" on February 23, 1902, with light snow still falling. A press dispatch from Altoona stated: "All Friday night [February 21–22] the white flakes dropped in great profusion. The railroad and telegraph companies are the most seriously crippled."

A thaw several days after the snowy onslaught resulted in damaging floods in eastern Pennsylvania, which were made much worse by the breakup of ice and snow, releasing a large volume of pent-up water all at one time. Yet another major snowstorm blasted Pennsylvania on March 5, 1902, leaving an additional 8 to 18 inches of snow on much of the state, including 17.5 inches at State College.

January 24–25, 1905: Massive January Snow in East

The winter of 1904–5 was exceptionally cold and snowy in Pennsylvania. Scranton received 88.6 inches of snow, setting a longtime record. A heavy November snowfall (November 13–14) and a frigid December 1904 with frequent snows set the pace for the winter.

A heavy snowstorm on January 3–4 deposited an average of 6 to 12 inches in the east, but the major storm of the winter would not arrive until later in the month.

A blizzard on January 24–25 dumped 1 to 2 feet of snow on the Delaware Valley. The *Stroudsburg Daily Times* reported 20 inches. Milford observer Alla K. Doughty, who measured 26.6 inches, wrote in her report: "The woods were so blocked with snow drifts . . . that no mail was received for two days in the county." The January snow total at Milford (43 inches) was remarkable for a valley location (el. 500 feet).

December 25–27, 1909: Post-Christmas Blizzard in East

In 1909, a great post-Christmas blizzard swept over eastern Pennsylvania and the Middle Atlantic region that paralleled a similar storm in 1872, though the cold was not as severe in 1909. The *Philadelphia Inquirer* described the storm as "hampering railroads and trolley traffic, breaking down wires, blocking navigation on the river . . . and sending scores to the hospitals, victims of falls on the ice."

When the snow that began Christmas Day finally ceased overnight on December 26–27, the tally in Philadelphia set a longtime record (21 inches). The snowfall at Reading was 22 inches, and the *Morning Call* in Allentown reported 20 inches. The *Stroudsburg Times* measured 15 inches of snow, followed by a chilly reading of −4 degrees on the twenty-eighth. The largest snowfalls were in Delaware, ranging as high as 25 inches at Milford, Delaware, 23 inches at Wilmington.

Less than three weeks after the post-Christmas storm in 1909, a second great snowfall buried a large portion of the state on January 13–14, 1910. The press and local observers reported accumulations of 10 inches at Milford, 16 inches at Bethlehem, and 18 inches at Stroudsburg.

The month ended with another storm on January 29–30 in the northern part of the state that brought howling winds. Twelve inches fell of snow at Pocono Lake, pushing the monthly total to 38 inches, a figure not exceeded in the region in January until 1987 (48 inches at Tobyhanna).

January 2–3, 1925: Big East-Central Snowfall

A deep snowfall kicked off the snowiest January on record in east-central Pennsylvania. Heavy snow began falling before dawn over eastern Pennsylvania on January 2, 1925, and would reach historic depths at Pottsville (25.8 inches), Freeland (21 inches), and Allentown (20.2 inches). The *Pike County Press* mentioned

20 inches at Stroudsburg, though only 10 inches fell at Milford thirty miles to the northeast. New York City had a snowfall of 11.1 inches before the precipitation mixed with sleet and rain.

Heavy snow fell frequently during the closing days of the month on January 20, 27, and 28–29. Accumulations in each storm averaged 4 to 8 inches or more. In northwestern New Jersey, Belvidere had a 50-inch total that nearly overtook the state record of 51.2 inches at Freehold (December 1880). In eastern Pennsylvania, all-time monthly snowfall records were established at Freeland (56.5 inches), Phoenixville (48 inches), Allentown (43.2 inches), and Carlisle (41.5 inches).

Surprisingly, Allentown did not have any measurable snow over the remainder of the winter of 1924–25 after the record-breaking January snowfall. February 1925 was exceptionally warm at Philadelphia (42.2 degrees), averaging 9.2 degrees above the contemporary normal, and is the warmest second month in city records.

The following winter (1925–26) brought another massive snowstorm on February 3–4, 1926. The heaviest accumulation was reported at Freeland (31 inches —station record). In the Poconos, 20 inches fell at Gouldsboro, and the Stroudsburg press reported 17 inches.

March 28–30, 1942: Deep Central Snowfall

Rain gradually changed to snow west of the Atlantic coast from Virginia to Pennsylvania on March 28–30, 1942, as an undercurrent of polar air wedged in from the northwest beneath a mild easterly flow of moisture-laden maritime air. Eastern Pennsylvania received a rain and snow mix on March 28–30, with only minor accumulations, and the western portion of the state got off lightly, as well.

However, the central portion of the state was not so lucky. In the early evening of March 28, rain changed to heavy wet snow on the Pennsylvania State University campus at State College, and by morning a total of 13 inches had fallen. Over the next twenty-four hours, another 17.5 inches were measured, plus an additional 0.5-inch, for a record storm total of 31 inches. The monthly tally for March 1942 also set a record at State College (47.5 inches).

The heaviest official snowfall in Pennsylvania was 34 inches at the weather site six miles south of Renovo in the north-central mountains. In the south-central part of the state, the Shippensburg observer caught 26 inches. In western Maryland, a twenty-four-hour total of 31 inches at Clear Spring and a storm total of 36 inches at Edgemont both established state snowfall records.

At Washington, D.C., the official snowfall was 11.5 inches on March 28–29, 1942, nearly matching the March record fall of 12 inches (March 16–18, 1892), but the northwest suburbs received up to 18 inches of sloppy wet snow. A record March snowfall of 22 inches at Baltimore is among the greatest in city weather history.

November 24–27, 1950: Great Appalachian Wind Storm

The Great Appalachian Wind Storm of November 24–27, 1950, brought record-breaking snowfalls to western Pennsylvania at the same time that hurricane-force winds and torrential rains pounded the eastern portion of the state. Low pressure developed over the hilly regions of western North Carolina on Friday, November 24, as arctic air edged across western Pennsylvania. A chilly Thanksgiving Day rain on the twenty-third soon turned to light snow, while a unique weather situation took shape farther southeast.

On Friday, November 24, a storm of vast proportions would organize, driven by a tremendous thermal contrast across the central Appalachians. An upper-level storm over Wisconsin drifting southeast eventually closed off into a circular pattern over eastern Ohio, causing an arctic front to stall over western Pennsylvania. Meanwhile, warm, moist air was funneled northward on the eastern flank of the mountains by a developing storm over the southeastern states.

Two high-pressure centers, one over eastern Canada and the other in Texas, pinned the circulation to a narrow corridor in the East, effectively halting the east–west progression of a powerful storm lying astride polar air just to the west. Upper-air charts revealed a potent jet stream disturbance diving around the base of the trough and interacting with a the deepening low-pressure system over eastern North Carolina.

The storm moved north into southern Virginia Saturday morning, November 25, eventually passing over Washington, D.C., into central Pennsylvania the next day. Torrential rains totaling 3.00 to 5.00 inches pelted eastern Pennsylvania all day long on November 25, while blizzard conditions prevailed west of the Appalachian crest.

On the eastern side of the storm path, destructive hurricane-force winds battered eastern Pennsylvania and New Jersey. Winds gusted to 76 miles per hour at Stroudsburg, according to the records of local weather-watcher William Hagerty, and 88 miles per hour at Allentown/Bethlehem. Near the coast, a tremendous gust of 108 miles per hour was registered at Newark. In sheltered Central Park, New York City, peak winds measured 76 miles per hour. Enormous wind damage was reported throughout the region. Homes, businesses, and resorts took a pounding, resulting in considerable property damage in eastern Pennsylvania.

As the snow decreased in intensity over the western counties, rain later changed to snow in the northeastern part of the state. On November 26, the huge storm turned northwest underneath a vast upper-level cold trough and would eventually stall over Lake Erie on the twenty-seventh, prolonging a pattern of light snow for several more days over the western and northern mountains.

A look at the daily snow totals in western Pennsylvania showed that on November 24, 14 inches of snow fell at Pittsburgh's Allegheny County Airport, seven miles southeast of Pittsburgh, followed by 10.1 inches on the twenty-fifth and 2.3 inches on the twenty-sixth. A record storm total of 27.4 inches of snow fell at Pittsburgh in three days. By the end of November 1950, some 32.3 inches of snow had accumulated at the airport site, with all but an inch coming during the last eight days.

Light snow continued to fall for several more days across northern and western Pennsylvania as the storm gradually filled over the lower Lakes. The greatest snowfalls measured between November 23 and 28, 1950, were 37 inches at New Castle (33-inch depth) and 35.3 inches at Meadville. Erie received 19.5 inches on the twenty-fourth, and a storm total of 28.4 inches through the twenty-seventh, which was the second greatest snowfall (30.2 inches fell on December 11–14, 1944). The monthly tally for November 1950 at Erie was a record 46.9 inches.

Fig. 4.1. November 29, 1950, snowstorm. Cars buried on Reifert Street, Pittsburgh, several days following the Thanksgiving weekend blizzard. (Photo by Morris Berman; *Pittsburgh Post-Gazette* Photo Archives, copyright 1950, all rights reserved)

Spectacular snowfall totals were also reported in the mountains of northern West Virginia westward across eastern Ohio. Pickens, West Virginia, measured a state record snowfall of 57 inches. In eastern Ohio, Steubenville logged 36 inches during November 24–26, 1950, and a total of 44 inches through the twenty-eighth, establishing a state snowfall mark. Drifts in eastern Ohio and southwestern Pennsylvania reportedly reached 25 feet!

January 8–11, 1953: Glaze Storm

Freezing rain coated the eastern ridges of the Appalachians in Pennsylvania and neighboring states for more than forty hours on January 8–11, 1953. Ice accumulated to a depth of 1.00 to 2.50 inches in central and northeastern Pennsylvania, and 4.00 to 4.75 inches across the upper elevations of Carbon and Monroe Counties.

An upper-level trough over the eastern states drew warm, moist Gulf air over a shallow dome of arctic air wedged against the eastern slopes of the mountains. Light mixed precipitation fell in some sections from the afternoon of January 8, until the evening of the January 10. Tens of thousands of trees were bent to the ground by the weight of the ice, and breakage increased as winds accelerated from January 10 to 12.

The higher elevations of east-central and south-central Pennsylvania reported severe damage to utility lines where downed trees and wires blocked roads and highways for days. Power-line damage in the Reading area alone totaled $22,000. The Pennsylvania Power and Light Company reported that 50,000 residents of eastern Pennsylvania were without power at one time or another during the storm, and 2,500 phones were out of service from Stroudsburg area to Allentown.

A 33,000-volt substation atop North Bangor Mountain, south of Stroudsburg, was disabled when the steel support towers collapsed under the load of ice. More than 2.00 inches of mostly liquid precipitation fell in about fifty hours at near-freezing temperatures.

March 16–19, 1956: One-Two Punch

A cold, wintry March 1956 brought back-to-back snowstorms that plastered the northeastern United States with deep snows on the eve of spring. The first storm traveled quickly from Alabama to Nantucket, Massachusetts, on March 16–17, bringing moderate snows to eastern Pennsylvania.

A trough of low pressure remained in the East as a second disturbance dove farther south across the Midwest to West Virginia on the eighteenth, spreading a fresh canopy of snow eastward across Pennsylvania. Secondary storm formation off the Virginia coast brought another round of heavy snow that continued into the afternoon of the nineteenth.

Ten inches of snow fell at Allentown/Bethlehem, and 18.2 inches accumulated at Newark, New Jersey. The four-day snow totals (March 16–19, 1956) were substantial for so late in the season at Newark (23.9 inches), Stroudsburg (17.4 inches), Harrisburg (15.8 inches), and Allentown/Bethlehem (15 inches).

February 15–17, 1958: Great Mid-February Blizzard

The months of February and March 1958 are the two snowiest consecutive months in weather records over eastern sections of northeastern Pennsylvania. A total of four major snowstorms deposited 88.5 inches of snow on Stroudsburg (el. 480 feet) and 92.1 inches at Gouldsboro (el. 1,890 feet) during February and March 1958. An inch or more of snow remained on the ground at Gouldsboro through April 14.

The winter of 1957–58 was largely uneventful through January 1958 before a heavy snowfall on February 7–8 dropped up to a foot of snow on northeastern Pennsylvania. This would be just the first volley in a series of heavy snowfalls that would leave a blanket of snow from 2 to 5 feet deep over the next six weeks.

Weather historian David Ludlum (1985, 172–73) placed the Great Mid-February Blizzard of 1958 in historical perspective: "No other snow even of the twentieth century can match the huge dimensions displayed by the Great Mid-February Storm of 1958, extending as it did along the entire Atlantic seaboard and inland to the Appalachians. In the nineteenth century, only three snow storms rate as equals: The Great Snowstorm of January 1831, the Cold Storm of January 1857, and the Great Eastern Blizzard of February 1899. Even the Blizzard of '88 did not meet the above requirements since its geographical extent was limited to the Northeast."

Eastern Pennsylvania was blanketed with snow on February 7–8, 1958, which began as rain in the southeast but accumulated to 12.6 inches at Stroudsburg in the northeast. One week later, the seeds of a great blizzard were already evident on February 14, as a wave developed along the Gulf coast.

The storm quickly followed a classic path across the northern Gulf states on February 15, picking up abundant moisture before "turning the corner" and heading northeast up the Atlantic coast. A deep mantle of snow blanketed the interior Southeast from Alabama to Virginia on February 14–15.

The winter storm assumed blizzard proportions on February 16 as it churned past the New Jersey coast, piling fluffy snow into huge drifts over the interior Northeast. The largest falls were reported in northeastern Pennsylvania, where roads were impassable, stranding hundreds of travelers. Rescue teams from the Tobyhanna Army Depot on the Pocono Plateau were dispatched to dig out trapped motorists.

The *Stroudsburg Daily Record* reported huge snowfalls of 36 inches at Buck Hill Falls and 30 inches at Mount Pocono. Official snowfall totals in the region were 24.3 inches at Stroudsburg (snow depth of 33 inches), 30 inches at Gouldsboro (snow depth of 48 inches), and 35 inches at Hawley (snow depth of 48 inches). The greatest snowfall (42.5 inches) in the February 1958 blizzard was measured at a site four miles southwest of Hawley. The *Wayne Independent* in Honesdale reported wind gusts of 40 to 60 miles per hour, creating massive drifts that shut down transportation countywide for days. The depth at Lakeville was 55 inches.

The eastern urban centers received 10 to 15 inches of snow, from Washington, D.C. (14.4 inches), to Baltimore (15.5 inches), northeast to New York City/La Guardia (10.4 inches). Heavier falls occurred over eastern New York and southern New England, ranging from 17.2 inches at New Haven, Connecticut, to 26.5 inches at Syracuse and 38.7 inches at Calicoon, New York. Boston was buried under 19.4 inches, one of the city's heaviest snowfalls.

Accumulations in southeastern Pennsylvania varied from 13 inches at Philadelphia to 17 inches at West Chester, and 20 inches at Lancaster. In the Lehigh

Fig. 4.2. February 17, 1958. Two-day blizzard deposited 3 feet of snow on Honesdale, raising the depth to 4 feet on Tryon Street. (Courtesy Elizabeth [Korb] Schuman)

Valley, 15.8 inches fell at Allentown/Bethlehem, tapering off to 11.2 inches at Scranton/Wilkes-Barre, and only 2 to 8 inches across central and western Pennsylvania. The Mid-February Blizzard of 1958 claimed forty-three lives and caused $50 million in property damage.

March 19–21, 1958: Great March Snowstorm in the Southeast

The stormy pattern in February and early March 1958 left a huge amount of snow on the ground in the northeast. A third heavy snowfall dropped another 10.7 inches at Stroudsburg and 16 inches at Gouldsboro on March 13–14, raising the snow cover to 30 inches on the high Pocono Plateau. In the southeast, a lighter fall (3 inches) was measured at York.

Blocking high pressure to the north of the storm slowed the system down long enough to amass great snow depths, with water equivalent precipitation totals in excess of 3.00 inches. Residents of eastern Pennsylvania were finally looking forward to spring after being battered by a succession of winter storms since Groundhog Day.

Instead of a break from the late-winter siege, a fourth storm would bring heavy wet snow to Pennsylvania beginning early on March 19. Near-freezing temperatures combined with a slow-moving storm brought a prolonged snow event with large, sticky flakes piling up to massive depths over interior sections of eastern Pennsylvania. Trees and power lines snapped under the weight of the heavy snow, putting millions in the dark. Traffic accidents and heart attacks claimed twenty-seven lives in Pennsylvania.

A corridor of exceptionally heavy accumulations developed west of the major metropolitan areas along the East Coast, from the northwest suburbs of Washington and Baltimore northward through southeastern Pennsylvania. The greatest snowfall occurred at Morgantown in Berks County, about ten miles south of Reading, and just forty miles northwest of Philadelphia. A state record 50 inches fell during the three-day storm period, including 38 inches in twenty-four hours on March 20, 1958.

In southeastern Pennsylvania near the Maryland border, York had a record snowfall (33 inches) and snow depth (36 inches tied February 1899). Holtwood, near Lancaster, also reported a storm total of 33 inches. The snowfall at West Chester, twenty-five miles west of Philadelphia, totaled 32 inches for a local record. At Allentown/Bethlehem, 20.3 inches of snow set a March storm record.

In the northeast the Stroudsburg observer logged a record snowfall of 35.4 inches (32-inch depth), including 29 inches in twenty-four hours on the twentieth and a record intensity fall of 6.8 inches in one hour. On the Pocono Plateau in southern Wayne County, Gouldsboro had an almost identical storm total of 35.3 inches, which raised the snow depth to an all-time record of 60 inches! The Hawley observer caught 28 inches. In northwestern New Jersey, the greatest snowfall was 30 inches at Branchville.

Near the coast temperatures hovered a little above freezing, limiting accumulations to about 5 to 10 inches of slushy snow. The fall at Philadelphia was 11.4 inches, which was typical of all the major metropolitan areas from Washington, D.C. (5 inches), to New York City (11.8 inches). Northeast of New York City,

22.5 inches fell at Eastchester, New York. Record snowfalls occurred across northern Delaware at Middletown (27 inches) and Wilmington (17.9 inches).

The winter of 1957–58 was historic in northeastern Pennsylvania for the sheer volume of snow. In a valley setting four miles west of the Delaware River, 109.5 inches were tallied at Stroudsburg from November to April. The seasonal snowfall at West Chester was a record 73.5 inches. The Philadelphia total for the winter of 1957–58 (41.8 inches) was the greatest since 1904–5 (43.8 inches).

March 3–5, 1960: March Blizzard

A great nor'easter was in its formative stage over the northwestern Gulf of Mexico early on March 2, 1960, while the East was in the grasp of a remarkable late-season cold wave. A new storm developed off the South Carolina coastline during the predawn hours of March 3, spreading a canopy of heavy snow northward over the Middle Atlantic states and the eastern half of Pennsylvania by mid-morning.

Snow began falling over southeastern Pennsylvania shortly before daybreak on the third, becoming heavy by late morning. The storm moved rapidly northeast to a position about 150 miles off the New Jersey coast by early evening. The system slowed as the storm intensified, generating strong easterly winds that brought blizzard conditions near the coast.

Heavy accumulations developed over interior sections of Virginia (Roanoke, 17.4 inches), with more than 20 inches falling in the mountains of eastern West Virginia. Six to 12 inches of snow blanketed all but the extreme southwestern and northwestern corners of Pennsylvania, but a band of much heavier totals occurred to the east.

A total of 21 inches fell at Stroudsburg in twenty-eight hours on March 3–4, 1960. Farther northwest, 18 inches fell at Scranton/Wilkes-Barre through the morning of the fifth. In the southeast, Allentown/Bethlehem recorded 14.4 inches, and Philadelphia received 8.4 inches. Ten to 15 inches of snow covered the Susquehanna Valley, and a substantial fall of 12.8 inches covered Pittsburgh.

Along the coastal plain, Baltimore (10.4 inches) and New York City (14.2 inches) received heavy falls. Southeastern New England had to dig out from under 1 to 2 feet accompanied by fierce northeasterly winds that created blizzard conditions for many hours. The top snowfall was 31.3 inches at Nantucket, Massachusetts. At Boston, 19.8 inches were measured at Logan Airport near sea level, rising to 30.3 inches inland at Milton and 22.1 inches at Worcester, Massachusetts. Providence, Rhode Island, received 17.7 inches.

Winter of 1960–61: Three Deep Snowfalls

The winter of 1960–61 brought three noteworthy East Coast snowstorms: December 11–12, 1960; January 19–20, 1961; and February 3–4, 1961. The December storm hit the coastal sections hardest with winds gusting to 55 miles per hour. Snowfall amounts ranged from 10 to 15 inches over extreme eastern Pennsylvania. A total of 14.6 inches piled up at Philadelphia, and 20.4 inches fell at Newark, New Jersey.

Bouts of arctic chill mixed with brief thaws prevailed through the middle of

January 1961. On the eve of President John F. Kennedy's inauguration on January 19, heavy snow and strong winds accompanied a coastal disturbance that deposited 7.7 inches of snow on the nation's capital. The snow cleared by daybreak on Inauguration Day, January 20, but conditions were bitter for outdoor festivities.

Farther north, the snow totals increased to 1 to 2 feet. Winds topping 30 miles per hour whipped the snow into deep drifts. Snowfall totals included 9.9 inches at New York City, 13.2 inches at Philadelphia, 16 inches at Allentown/Bethlehem, 18.7 inches at Harrisburg, and 23 inches at Stroudsburg, mostly accumulating in about twenty-four hours.

By the end of January 1961, Harrisburg had established a new monthly record snowfall of 34 inches that would last until 1996 (38.9 inches at Harrisburg/Middletown), already surpassing the previous record for an entire season set in 1892–93.

Low pressure traveling east from the southern Plains to the Ohio Valley on February 1–2, 1961, eventually yielded to a coastal system that formed along the southeastern Georgia coast on the third. Heavy snow broke out on February 3, 1961, across the Keystone State, dropping a band of snow 10 to 20 inches deep that crippled the eastern counties, while light falls were reported in the extreme western counties.

Snowfalls on February 3–4 increased from 10.3 inches at Philadelphia to 17.3 inches at Allentown/Bethlehem, 18.5 inches at Stroudsburg, 20 inches at Montrose, 22 inches at Gouldsboro, and 22.6 inches at Newark, New Jersey. The northern counties tapped moisture from both the western storm and the coastal low, resulting in some extremely heavy falls in the northwestern highlands at Galeton (28 inches) and Kane (24.5 inches).

At the conclusion of the snowstorm on February 4, a record snow depth of 34 inches was measured at Stroudsburg. The greatest snow cover in Pennsylvania on February 4 was 49 inches at Lakeville in Wayne County. In northwestern New Jersey, historic snow depths were observed at Layton (50 inches) and Canistear Reservoir (52 inches).

The two-week cold wave finally broke at the conclusion of the storm on the afternoon of February 4. Many locations enjoyed above-freezing temperatures for the first time in seventeen days, signaling a reprieve from the arctic assault. A mild pattern in late February and March 1961 replaced the harsh conditions that had prevailed since early December.

However, true to form during most severe winters, Mother Nature threw in a few heavy wet snowfalls in early April over northern Pennsylvania. Heavy snow fell over the northern counties as late as April 9–10 and 12–13. A cold snap was accompanied by snow showers in the north on May 27, 1961, with record late traces of snow reported as far east as Stroudsburg and at New York City/La Guardia.

The 1960–61 seasonal snowfall at Harrisburg (81.3 inches) and State College (91.8 inches) set new records. (The State College mark would ultimately be erased in 1993–94.) Stroudsburg (98.6 inches) had its fourth snowiest winter (tied with 1995–96). On the Pocono Plateau, Long Pond (124.4 inches) had the heaviest total in the region.

In the Laurel Highlands of southwestern Pennsylvania, Somerset recorded

178.8 inches of snow in the winter of 1960–61, with the largest totals in December (41.3 inches), January (47 inches), and February (46.5 inches). In the central mountains, 136 inches were measured at Lewis Run and 131 inches fell at Bloserville.

Philadelphia recorded its fourth snowiest winter (46.2 inches) in 1960–61, which ranks behind only 1995–96, 1898–99, and 1977–78. Newark, New Jersey (73.5 inches), had its snowiest winter in modern times, at least until 1995–96 came along.

January 12–13, 1964: Eastern Blizzard

A major eastern blizzard in January 1964 made headlines for a combination of deep snowfalls and relentless northeasterly gales that drove the powdery snow into mountainous drifts across the Keystone State.

The weather map on the evening of January 11 indicated two areas of low pressure. The primary system was located over southwestern Missouri, while a secondary low was forming along the western Gulf coast.

At daybreak on January 12, a new storm center was taking shape along the coast of South Carolina while the western system drifted into western Tennessee. The events over the next twenty-four hours suggested an atmospheric traffic jam. The coastal storm intensified rapidly off the Carolina/Virginia coast, slowed by a blocking ridge of high pressure over eastern Canada. Farther west, low pressure drifted northeast into Kentucky, creating a broad conveyor belt of moisture from the Atlantic coast to the Ohio Valley.

Snow began falling over Pennsylvania during the afternoon hours on January 12 and would gain intensity fairly rapidly. Strong winds gusting up to 45 miles per hour soon created blizzard conditions as the nor'easter deepened east of New Jersey early on the thirteenth. More than 20 inches of snow covered the northern and central mountains.

Some of the larger falls were reported at State College (27.5 inches), Williamsport (24.1 inches—twenty-four-hour record), and Gouldsboro and Pleasant Mount (24 inches). Scranton/Wilkes-Barre (21.1 inches), Stroudsburg (20.6 inches), and Harrisburg (18.1 inches) had substantial falls. Most of the Keystone State received more than 10 inches of snow, except for the extreme southeastern and northwestern counties, where totals averaged near 6 inches. A pocket of twenty-inch-plus snowfalls occurred in the western mountains northwest of Altoona. Major cities in the southern part of the state from Harrisburg (18.1 inches) to Pittsburgh (15.6 inches) were virtually shut down by the blinding snowfall.

Another heavy snowfall in the late winter of 1963–64 dropped more than a foot of snow on eastern sections of the state on February 18–20, with accumulations of 20.3 inches at Harrisburg and 18.1 inches at Stroudsburg.

January 29–30, 1966: Blizzard of '66

A powerful midwinter storm paralyzed the Middle Atlantic region on the closing days of January 1966. The third in a series of winter snowstorms to buffet the Northeast in ten days was the strongest of the group, accompanied by sustained winds of 40 miles per hour and gusts as high as 50 to 60 miles per hour.

The morning weather map on January 28 showed a wave over the Big Bend region of west Texas. In twenty-four hours, the storm had deepened and was positioned near Montgomery, Alabama. A new center would soon take over along the southeast coast and track northward to just east of Atlantic City, New Jersey, by early evening on the twenty-ninth.

Storm totals of 8 to 15 inches were common from Washington, D.C., northward through eastern Pennsylvania and western New Jersey. Some of the heavier snowfalls included 14.1 inches at Bridgeville, Delaware, 13.8 inches at Washington, and 12.2 inches at Harrisburg. Amounts tapered off a little along the coastal plain, averaging 6 to 8 inches from Philadelphia to Boston.

Eastern Pennsylvania was hardest hit with 10 to 20 inches of snow falling, whipped into deep drifts by northeasterly gales. The western counties received 3 to 9 inches, except where lake-enhanced snows pushed storm totals over one foot in Erie County. In New York State, 20.1 inches of snow fell at Binghamton, 26.7 inches at Rochester, and a whopping 39 inches at Syracuse.

The "Storm Summary" in *Climatological Data* estimated that the cost of snow removal in Pennsylvania following Blizzard of '66 exceeded $10 million. The storm commenced on a weekend, but many schools would remain closed for the entire week in eastern Pennsylvania, where drifts were measured as high as 15 feet.

December 24, 1966: Christmas Eve Blizzard

December 1966 brought heavy snowfalls to eastern Pennsylvania on December 13, 20, and 24, leaving record December accumulations of 36 inches at Stroudsburg and 28.4 inches at Allentown/Bethlehem. In all, it was the whitest of all possible Christmases in the Keystone State.

A coastal disturbance of Gulf origin spread a canopy of snow rapidly up the East Coast on the morning of December 24, with temperatures hovering around the freezing mark. During the height of the storm in the afternoon and early evening, snow fell at the rate of 2 to 3 inches an hour in eastern Pennsylvania, accompanied by peals of thunder in southeastern Pennsylvania over a period of six hours.

Snowfall totals ranged from 12.7 inches at Philadelphia to 21.2 inches at Coatesville and 22 inches at West Chester. In the Poconos an observer at Neola, near Tannersville, measured 23 inches. Stroudsburg residents dug out from under a record December snowfall of 18.8 inches and a record depth of 23 inches.

After a balmy, nearly snowless January 1967, February and March brought frequent heavy snows to the Northeast on February 6–7 and 9–10 (coastal sections), March 5, 7, 15–17, and 21–22. Atlantic City, New Jersey, recorded its snowiest month in February 1967 (35.2 inches).

Northeastern Pennsylvania had an exceptionally snowy February and March in 1967. Stroudsburg received 24.5 inches in February and 33.5 inches in March. Two late-April snowfalls on the twenty-fourth and twenty-seventh pushed the seasonal snowfall total to 100.6 inches at Stroudsburg/East Stroudsburg. The northern mountains were whitened again on May 6–7 in the backward spring of 1967.

December 1969: Another Snowy December

The winter of 1969–70 began with a moderate snowfall on December 14, 1969, followed by a bigger storm on December 21–22, leaving a December record snowfall at Scranton/Wilkes-Barre (12.2 inches) and Harrisburg (12.1 inches) that turned to freezing rain in the east for a number of hours. In the northeastern mountains, up to 15 inches of snow fell at Hazleton and Gouldsboro.

A short burst of snow on Christmas Eve 1969 attended the passage of a reinforcing shot of arctic air that left a dusting of snow across the state and another 3 inches at Hazleton. Christmas Day dawned bitterly cold, with temperatures ranging as low as 0 to −10 degrees in the northern highlands. As Pennsylvania residents settled in to enjoy a sunny, frigid holiday, a new storm was brewing in the Gulf of Mexico.

As the system raced northeast to the southeastern Atlantic coast by early afternoon on Christmas Day, an enlarging band of snow overspread the interior Middle Atlantic states northward to Philadelphia by dinnertime. Christmas night 1969 was as snowy as can be, in the tradition of the great post-Christmas blizzards on the same dates in 1872, 1909, and 1947.

Accumulations by mid-morning of the December 26 generally fell in the 10- to 15-inch range in the eastern and central counties, tapering off to less than 6 inches in the west. In the northeast, a fresh 18-inch snowfall was reported by the *Hazleton Standard-Speaker,* for a total of 36 since December 21, 1969. Sleet and freezing rain eventually mixed in near the end of the storm in the Delaware Valley.

As the massive winter storm slowed over southeastern New England, historic snowfalls were measured at Burlington (29.8 inches) and Montpelier (39 inches) in Vermont, northward to Montreal (28 inches). December 1969 was a record snowy month for many locations in northeastern and parts of south-central Pennsylvania, including Gouldsboro (46.1 inches), Tobyhanna (43.1 inches), Hawley (42 inches), Neola (36.8 inches), and Harrisburg (28.3 inches). A maximum snow depth of 35 inches was measured at Gouldsboro (December record).

February 5–7, 1978: Blizzard of '78

The winter of 1977–78 had already established a pattern of heavy snowfalls, with three major snows occurring between January 13 and 20. A blizzard of historic proportions swept the eastern Midwest on January 25–26 but brought only rain to Pennsylvania, as the center of the low crossed Ohio early on the twenty-sixth, with the lowest central pressure reported at Cleveland, Ohio (28.28 inches).

The morning weather map on February 5 showed a low-pressure trough pivoting through eastern Ohio ahead of a cold front and low pressure centered over Michigan. The northern low passed over Lake Erie, while a secondary low was developing a few hundred miles east of the Carolina coast. Upper-level energy infused the coastal "bomb" with the necessary dynamics for intensification as it drifted north-northwest under the guiding influence of a broad upper-air trough.

Intermittent light snow became steady and heavy over the mid-Atlantic states during the morning of February 6 and expanded quickly northward to New England by afternoon. Snow fell quite heavily over the eastern half of Pennsylvania until the early morning of February 7. The heaviest falls were over the eastern third of the state, with amounts diminishing considerably west of the crest of the Appalachians.

In the southeast, Philadelphia was blanketed with 14.1 inches, with amounts increasing over the hilly regions of east-central and northeastern Pennsylvania.

In the upper Delaware Valley, East Stroudsburg tallied 23.7 inches (30-inch depth). Only twenty miles to the northwest on the high plateau, Tobyhanna received 32.5 inches (45-inch depth), and five miles farther northwest, Gouldsboro had 38 inches (52-inch depth). In northern Wayne County, Pleasant Mount reported a snowfall of 22.5 inches (49-inch depth).

The eastern metropolitan areas also received substantial falls north of Washington, D.C. Amounts ranged from 9.1 inches at Baltimore to 14.5 inches at Wilmington, Delaware, and 17.7 inches at New York City (Central Park). Over Long Island, 25 inches fell at Riverhead. Deep falls extended west to Rochester, New York (25.8 inches).

The storm stalled over the eastern tip of Long Island early on February 7, 1978, prolonging the heavy snow over eastern New England. Boston recorded an all-time record snowfall of 27.1 inches and a peak wind gust of 61 miles per hour. In Rhode Island, all-time record accumulations were measured at Providence (28.6 inches) and Woonsocket (38 inches—state record).

The ground at Pittsburgh would remain snow-covered for a record sixty-four consecutive days through the March 12, breaking the mark of sixty-two days set just the previous winter (1976–77). In the northeast, East Stroudsburg had an inch or more of snow on the ground on 101 days in the winter of 1977–78, with a season snowfall of 76.2 inches. Gouldsboro measured 131.2 inches in 1977–78, which was the third highest total behind 1995–96 and 1957–58.

At the end of the winter of 1977–78, Erie had amassed a record accumulation of 142.8 inches of snow, which was not surpassed until 2000–2001 (149.1 inches). In the northeast, Gouldsboro tallied 131.2 inches. Philadelphia received 54.9 inches in 1977–78, 0.5 inch shy of the 1898–99 seasonal record at that time. New York City also topped the 50-inch mark in 1977–78 (50.7 inches).

February 11–12, 1983: Blizzard of '83

The setting for the great snowfall of February 11–12, 1983, featured a dome of frigid air over eastern Canada anchored by high pressure, a fast-moving jet stream disturbance streaking toward the Middle Atlantic coast, and a developing surface wave off the South Carolina coast. The merger of upper-level energy and a low-pressure wave developing along a sharp thermal boundary near the coast provided the necessary ingredients for a snowstorm of historic proportions along the eastern seaboard.

As the storm marched up the coast, moisture-rich Atlantic air rode inland over the top of cold air hugging the surface, causing the snow to come down at record rates in eastern Pennsylvania. Snow reached Washington around midnight, February 11, then spread quickly north, reaching Harrisburg by dawn and southern New England by late afternoon.

During the evening hours of February 11, the snowfall achieved its maximum intensity, with 5 inches falling in one hour at Allentown/Bethlehem and 4 inches in an hour at East Stroudsburg. High winds whipped the snow into deep drifts as blizzard conditions enveloped the eastern counties. Storm totals were record-worthy at Philadelphia (21.3 inches), Harrisburg (25 inches), and Allentown/Bethlehem (25.2 inches), all within twenty-four hours. Farther north, East Stroudsburg received 23.5 inches; Bartonsville, 24.5 inches; Kresgeville, 25 inches; and Tannersville, 27 inches.

The belt of heavy snow covered virtually all of Virginia except the southeast corner. Richmond, Virginia, received 17.7 inches, and Roanoke had an impressive fall of 18.6 inches. Washington's National Airport was buried under 16.9 inches, but 22.8 inches was the measurement at Dulles Airport farther northwest. The snowfall at New York City/Central Park was 17.7 inches, but Kennedy International Airport in Queens had 22 inches. The heavy snow belt extended to Hartford, Connecticut (record 21-inch fall), and Boston (13.5 inches).

December 10–12, 1992: Early Nor'easter

A powerful, slow-moving nor'easter brought hurricane-force winds and record snows on December 10–12, 1992. Wind gusts were clocked at 77 miles per hour at Nottingham and 60 miles per hour at Avoca (Scranton/Wilkes-Barre). Rain alternated with snow in the southeastern part of the state, while huge accumulations buried the west and north.

The greatest accumulations in Pennsylvania were 36 inches at Ogletown and 33 inches at DuBois. The snowfalls at State College (18.1 inches) and Tobyhanna/Mount Pocono (19.5 inches) established December records. Spectacular December falls were observed at high spots in Maryland (35 inches), New Jersey (25 inches), and Massachusetts (48 inches).

March 13–14, 1993: Blizzard of '93 — Storm of the Century

Dubbed the "Storm of the Century" by the media, the Blizzard of '93 was the most accurately forecast major blizzard to hit the eastern United States. Days in advance, meteorologists were warning the eastern seaboard to prepare for the worst.

By March 12, a Pacific disturbance had migrated to the western Gulf of Mexico, where the burgeoning winter storm would encounter favorable conditions for intensification. A series of upper-airstream disturbances traveling along the polar and subtropical jet streams would meet up, causing explosive deepening over the warm Gulf waters.

Meanwhile, arctic air was poised to interact with the storm from the northwest. The arrival of a polar airstream touched off severe weather in the South, spawning eleven tornadoes across Florida on the evening of March 12. A wind gust of 110 miles per hour was registered in Franklin County, Florida. As the storm churned up the East Coast, a canopy of heavy snow overspread the Middle Atlantic region early on Saturday, March 13.

Winds gusted to 101 miles per hour on Flattop Mountain, North Carolina, attesting to the ferocity of the dangerous storm. Mountainous snows piled up across the southern Appalachians, reaching 60 inches at Mount LeConte, Tennessee, and 50 inches atop Mount Mitchell, North Carolina. The storm system passed over southern Georgia on the morning of March 13, picking up additional Atlantic moisture.

Snow broke out over southeastern Pennsylvania around midnight on Saturday, March 13, and quickly spread northward into the northern counties during the wee hours of the morning. Winds increased to 30 to 40 miles per hour, reducing the visibility to near zero in many areas, slowing transportation to a crawl.

Businesses closed in the face of the worst winter storm in memory. Claps of thunder heard during the height of the blizzard signaled a highly unstable atmosphere as warm, moist Atlantic air was drawn into the circulation, colliding with frigid air being pulled down from Canada. Snow fell at the rate of 2 to 4 inches per hour over parts of Pennsylvania during the daylight hours of the thirteenth.

Record low barometric pressure readings were an indication of the severity of the storm and accounted for the extreme winds. A peak wind gust of 75 miles per hour was recorded at the Philadelphia International Airport. The barometer plunged to an all-time low reading of 28.43 inches, breaking the previous record of 28.54 inches observed in a coastal storm on March 7, 1932. The snow tapered off over Pennsylvania after twenty-four hours of fierce winds and blinding snows during the early morning of March 14.

The greatest snowfall in the state (47 inches) was measured at Seven Springs (el. 2,800 feet), a ski resort high in the Alleghenies in Somerset County. A twenty-four-hour snowfall measurement of 40 inches on March 13–14 exceeded the state record daily fall of 38 inches at Morgantown in March 1958.

In the northeast, a new record snowfall of 21.4 inches was measured at Scranton/Wilkes-Barre (20.6 inches in twenty-four hours), edging out the November 24–25, 1971, record of 20.5 inches. It should be noted that these marks would be tied or exceeded less than three years later in January 1996. A top wind speed of 56 miles per hour was clocked at the airport in Avoca during the early morning of March 14, 1993, as swirling winds drove the snow into drifts 8 feet high. A record low atmospheric pressure reading of 28.58 inches was logged at Scranton/Wilkes-Barre during the storm.

In the upper Susquehanna Valley, 20.8 inches fell at Towanda, which was the greatest fall since February 19–20, 1972 (30.4 inches). In the eastern Poconos, snow totals ranged from 20.1 inches at East Stroudsburg to 22 inches at Tobyhanna. The heaviest falls in northern Pennsylvania were 42 inches four miles northeast of Gouldsboro (el. 2,140 feet), 37 inches at Wellsboro, 34 inches at Hollisterville, and 33.1 inches at Long Pond.

In the Lehigh Valley, 17.6 inches fell at Allentown/Bethlehem, but much larger falls were reported to the west. A whopping total of 32 inches was measured about twenty miles to the northeast at Lehighton. In the central part of the state, 27.5 inches fell at State College and 25.7 inches were measured at Shippensburg, exceeding the great snowstorm of March 6–7, 1962 (22 inches). In the lower Susquehanna Valley, 20.4 inches were reported at Harrisburg/Middletown. Pittsburgh was buried under a record January snowfall of 23.6 inches on March 13–14, 1993.

Along the coastal plain, generally 6 to 12 inches of snow fell along a line from Washington, D.C., to Philadelphia and New York City. Wind gusts were clocked at 81 miles per hour at Boston as the storm buffeted eastern New England on March 14. A low pressure reading of 28.38 inches at White Plains, New York, would be comparable to a Category 3 hurricane.

Dramatic snow totals up and down the eastern seaboard reveal the breadth of a storm that deposited an estimated 50 billion tons of snow. Other noteworthy snow totals included 42.9 inches at Syracuse, New York, 35 inches at Lincoln, New Hampshire, 29.3 inches at Beckley, West Virginia, 24 inches at Mountain City, Georgia, and 13 inches at Birmingham, Alabama (17 inches south of the city).

Bitter cold invaded the South and East in the wake of the storm. In northern Pennsylvania, historic late-season cold records were established at Kane (−22 degrees) and Pleasant Mount (−20 degrees). Temperatures slumped to the single digits as far south as Birmingham, Alabama (2 degrees), and chilled to 33 degrees at Orlando, Florida.

The death toll from the Storm of the Century was put at 243 persons from Cuba to Maine. At one point during the storm, 3 million homes in the eastern United States were without power.

By comparison, the Great Atlantic Coastal Storm of March 1962 caused more than $200 million damage from New England to Florida. The nor'easter of March 6–7, 1962, was accompanied by forty-foot high waves that slammed into the Long Island shoreline, driven by 70-mile-per-hour winds. A narrow band of 1 to 2 feet of snow fell in south-central Pennsylvania.

Winter of 1993–94: Three Major Snowstorms

A brief thaw greeted Pennsylvanians on New Year's Day 1994, but a blast of winter was waiting just around the corner. A storm over the central Plains on January 2 yielded to a storm developing near the Gulf coast. On January 3, a secondary low-pressure system formed along the Middle Atlantic coast, causing a wide band of snow to extend westward across the crest of the Appalachians.

Snowfall rates of to 5 and 6 inches per hour were recorded at Pittsburgh and Williamsport on the morning of January 3, 1994. The greatest snowfall in Pennsylvania was 33 inches at Waynesburg, Greene County, southwest of Pittsburgh. The storm total at the Pittsburgh airport was 13.9 inches, but 20 inches were measured in downtown Pittsburgh. In nearby southeastern Ohio, 21 inches of snow fell at Newport.

In northern Pennsylvania the average snowfall was 6 to 12 inches, while the southeastern counties were dealt a nasty blow in the form of an ice storm. Hundreds of thousands of residents in southeastern Pennsylvania and New Jersey lost power from the storm.

The snow fell so quickly that traffic came to a stop along the Pennsylvania Turnpike and Interstates 70 and 79. On January 6, Governor Robert Casey declared a state of emergency for Fayette, Greene, Washington, and Westmoreland Counties in southwestern Pennsylvania, and the Pennsylvania National Guard was called on to assist in the arduous task of snow removal.

The sheer weight of the snow caused roofs of barns and outbuildings to collapse. An NOAA storm summary, citing a Pittsburgh newspaper, reported 10 fatalities due to heart attacks in the region and 185 injuries in southwestern Pennsylvania, mostly from falls.

Moderate snowfalls on January 7–8 and 12, 1994, were followed by a major storm that commenced in western Pennsylvania before daybreak on January 17. Snow came down at the rate of 4 inches an hour at Chambersburg in the south-central part of the state, bringing a total accumulation of 20 inches. A weather observer at Greencastle reported 17 inches. Generally, 6 to 12 inches of snow blanketed the state on January 17. Several barns and a number of small buildings in Franklin and Mifflin Counties collapsed under the weight of the snow.

In the northeast, snow depths on January 18, 1994, averaged around 2 feet, ranging from 22 inches at East Stroudsburg to a record 27 inches at Scranton/Wilkes-Barre (surpassing the 26-inch depth of February 4, 1961). South of Scranton/Wilkes-Barre, the snow depth on January 18 reached 30 inches at Lehighton in eastern Carbon County and 40 inches at Long Pond on the high ground in western Monroe County.

More snow fell on January 26–27, and by the end of the month new snowfall records for January were noted at East Stroudsburg (37.2 inches) and Scranton/Wilkes-Barre (42.3 inches—a new record for any month). Monthly falls soared past 40 inches in the Poconos, including 42.8 inches at Mount Pocono, 47 inches at Honesdale and Long Pond, and 59.1 inches at Hollisterville.

In the Lehigh Valley, 33.9 inches of snow fell at Allentown/Bethlehem in January 1994, which was the greatest monthly total since January 1925 (43.2 inches). In the lower Susquehanna Valley, a new record snowfall at Harrisburg/Middletown of 34.2 inches edged out that of January 1961 by only 0.4 inch. Williamsport reported 34.5 inches in January 1994, illustrating a remarkable uniformity in the snowfall pattern.

Another major snowstorm hit the East Coast on February 8–9, 1994, dropping 10.5 inches at New York City's La Guardia Airport in Queens and 18.5 inches at Boston. Washington, D.C., was paralyzed by several inches of sleet, and Delaware suffered its worst ice storm in modern memory. A day later, on February 10, the Deep South was hit with a glaze storm as a second disturbance rounded the bend and headed northward. New York City took a second hit on February 11 (12.8 inches), while Newark, New Jersey, bore the brunt of the storm (18 inches).

Back-to-back nor'easters on February 8–9 and 11 dropped 9.2 and 9.8 inches, respectively, at Allentown/Bethlehem. A third storm on February 23–24 deposited several inches of snow before changing over to rain. When the month ended, Chicago (26.2 inches), Milwaukee (38.7 inches), and Newark (33.4 inches) had their snowiest February. New York City (26.4 inches) and Boston (36.2 inches) both recorded their second snowiest February on record.

March 1994 came in like a lion. A blizzard hit Pennsylvania on March 2–4, dropping more than a foot of snow over much of the state, except in the far western and southeastern counties, where accumulations averaged 3 to 6 inches. In the northeast, accumulations ranged from 12.1 inches at East Stroudsburg to 21 inches at Long Pond on the Pocono Plateau. Over the north-central highlands, 20 inches fell at Wellsboro.

The heaviest accumulations occurred over the central mountains, where 27.7 inches fell at State College, equaling the March 1993 blizzard accumulation. The March 1994 storm did, however, set a twenty-four-hour intensity mark of 26.6 inches. Other large falls in the region included 27 inches at Rector, 24 inches at Lock Haven, 18 inches at Johnstown, 17.2 inches at Altoona, 14 inches at Punxsutawney, and 7.8 inches at Pittsburgh.

Blowing snow and rare avalanches stranded twenty-five motorists along State Route 120 between Renovo and Lock Haven, where some drifts reached were deeper than 10 feet. Five cars were buried under upwards of 20 feet of snow, which had begun falling around 11:30 P.M. on March 2 and continued for twenty-eight hours. A number of roofs and outbuildings collapsed under the combined weight of this snowfall and the snow and ice built up from previous storms. Property damage was assessed at $5 million in central Pennsylvania.

Snow blanketed the higher elevations on March 18 and 29 to wrap up an exceptional snow season. There was a great deal of variation in snowfall totals across the state in the winter of 1993–94. Accumulations ranged from just 23.4 inches at Philadelphia to 154.9 inches at Bradford in the northwestern mountains.

In the east, the winter totals established new records at Allentown/Bethlehem (75.2 inches) and Scranton/Wilkes-Barre (90.4 inches, edging out 1904–5 by 1.8 inches). East Stroudsburg counted 80.4 inches in the lower Pocono region. In the higher elevations, a weather observer at Mountaintop (el. 1,360 feet) reported 106.7 inches. The largest season totals in the northeast were turned in at Montrose (136.5 inches) and Hollisterville (132.1 inches). In the eastern Poconos, 115.8 inches accumulated at Long Pond, and a Mount Pocono observer measured 105.4 inches.

In northern Wayne County, an inch or more of snow remained on the ground at Pleasant Mount in Wayne County for 110 consecutive days from December 19, 1993, until April 10, 1994. Scranton/Wilkes-Barre recorded ninety-three days of continuous snow cover in 1993–94, and Harrisburg/Middletown had seventy-six consecutive days with snow on the ground until March 21, 1994, setting new station records. In the upper Delaware Valley, snow cover remained at East Stroudsburg until March 25. The Harrisburg/Middletown seasonal snowfall in 1993–94 (75.9 inches) was second only to that of the winter of 1961–61 (81.3 inches).

In the west, State College established a new seasonal snowfall mark of 109.3 inches in 1993–94, and Altoona reported 99.9 inches. The accumulation at Pittsburgh of 76.8 inches was a little shy of the 1950–51 total (82 inches). Erie tallied 131.3 inches, which was at the time the city's second snowiest winter after 1977–78 (142.8 inches).

January 1996: Blizzard of '96

The winter of 1995–96 commenced in early November in Pennsylvania with a blast of polar air on November 11–12, 1995, which brought a coating of snow to the northern counties. A new disturbance formed on the southern boundary of the arctic air along the North Carolina coast on November 13, causing heavy snow to break out over interior sections of Pennsylvania.

By the time the storm eased early on the fifteenth, record early-season accumulations blanketed the southwestern mountains. An observer at Somerset in the Laurel Highlands reported 32.2 inches, and in the northwest 24 inches fell at Kane. Pittsburgh received 10.6 inches on November 13–15, but with a drop in elevation of only 500 feet to the Ohio River near the Ohio border the snowfall was reduced to only trace amounts.

Central Pennsylvania also received a substantial snowfall on November 13–15, with accumulations of 7.6 inches at Williamsport, 16 inches at Mansfield and Troy, and 24 inches in Clearfield County. Five hundred trees on the Pennsylvania State University campus at State College were damaged by the weight of a

17.7-inch snowfall—the second greatest November storm on record (November 12, 1968, brought 22.5 inches). Student volunteers joined maintenance workers clearing snow from Beaver Stadium in time for the Saturday football game.

In the northeast, Scranton/Wilkes-Barre picked up 8.9 inches, with amounts rising to 14.3 inches at Mount Pocono and 17 inches at Tobyhanna. In the eastern and south-central valleys, mixed precipitation held accumulations generally to 2 to 4 inches.

A general snowstorm on November 29, brought another 4 to 7 inches to eastern and central Pennsylvania, including Philadelphia. Monthly snowfall totals reached 9.2 inches at East Stroudsburg, 13.8 inches at Williamsport (a November record), and 22.1 inches at Mount Pocono.

A cold December brought moderate snows on December 9 and 14 and a heavy fall of 6 to 12 inches on December 18–20, with a top accumulation of 16 inches at Lehighton in the east. However, the biggest blow of the winter of 1995–96 was yet to come.

A vigorous jet stream disturbance diving south across the Rocky Mountains on January 5, 1996, was the catalyst for a developing winter storm in the western Gulf of Mexico. The weather map on Saturday morning, January 6, featured a low-pressure center over Louisiana, which drifted to a position along the South Carolina coast the following morning. As the storm gained a head of steam, snowfall totals piled up in Old Dominion.

Storm totals on January 7–8 reached 24.9 inches at Roanoke, Virginia, 24.5 inches at Washington, D.C./Dulles, 22.5 inches at Baltimore, 19 inches at Charleston, West Virginia, 17.1 inches at Washington, D.C./National. A record fall of

Fig. 4.3. January 8, 1996. Fayette County Head Start Program bus is snowbound after the Blizzard of January 6–7, 1996, dumped 2 feet of snow on southwestern Pennsylvania. (Photo by Robin Rombach; *Pittsburgh Post-Gazette* Photo Archives, copyright 1996, all rights reserved)

Table 4.4. Record January 1996 Snow Totals and Depths

Record Monthly Snowfalls (inches)		Record Snow Depths (inches)		Date
Beavertown	59.0	Beavertown	55	12
Hollisterville	55.5	Pleasant Mount	51	16
Reading	46.5	Hollisterville	50	13
State College	41.0	Honesdale	47	13
Harrisburg/Middletown	38.9	Safe Harbor	45	13

48 inches was measured at Big Meadows, Virginia. Farther west, Cincinnati scored 14.4 inches for a then-record snowfall.

The snowy assault in southern and eastern Pennsylvania was under way as the storm passed just east of the Virginia Capes early on January 7, 1996. A spectacular all-time record snowfall of 30.7 inches was measured by estimation at Philadelphia International Airport (27.6 inches in twenty-four hours). Weather service spotters in Perkasie and Spring Grove reported incredible falls of 36 inches! Snowfall totals in excess of 30 inches were recorded at Reading (34 inches), York (31.8 inches), Marcus Hook (30.7 inches), and Grateford (30 inches).

In the Lehigh Valley, an all-time record snowfall was measured at the airport in Allentown/Bethlehem (25.6 inches), surpassing the February 1983 storm blizzard by a mere 0.4 inch. The storm set a January storm record at Harrisburg/Middletown (22.2 inches) and a twenty-four-hour snowfall mark at Scranton/Wilkes-Barre (21 inches), while tying the record storm total set in March 1993 (21.4 inches).

Substantial accumulations were reported in the Pocono region: East Stroudsburg at 21.4 inches, Mount Pocono at 22 inches, and Hawley at 22 inches. On the high plateau, measurements at Long Pond (36 inches) and a site near Gouldsboro (36.5 inches) dwarfed the valley totals. On the fringe of the storm, unexpectedly high totals of 9.8 inches at Pittsburgh (January 6–8) and 17.5 inches at State College snarled traffic for days. Another heavy snowfall on January 12–13 raised snow depths to historic levels in eastern Pennsylvania (Table 4.4).

In New Jersey, 30 inches fell at Hazlet and Moorestown, and a record accumulation of 27.8 inches was measured at Newark (record snow depth of 31 inches). The Blizzard of '96 brought the third heaviest snowfall at Central Park in New York (20.6 inches) and left even more snow at La Guardia Airport (23.7 inches). The unofficial snow depth in Manhattan of 27 inches was comparable to the record depth of 26.4 inches (December 1947). Farther north, 22.8 inches fell at Providence and 18.2 inches, at Boston, where an all-time record snow depth of 32 inches was measured at the conclusion of the blizzard.

The winter of 1995–96 will be long remembered for historic snowfall totals and snow depths unmatched in the twentieth century. In the Laurel Highlands, two Somerset County weather stations reported 162 and 167 inches. The greatest unofficial seasonal snowfall in Pennsylvania in the winter of 1995–96 was 184.7 inches at Montrose, as reported by WNEP-TV (Scranton/Wilkes-Barre). In southern Wayne County, Lehigh Township observer Dennis Rinaldi recorded 176.4 inches of snow four miles northeast of Gouldsboro (el. 2,140 feet) that winter.

The winter of 1995–96 was the snowiest on record at Scranton/Wilkes-Barre (98.3 inches), Williamsport (87.7 inches), New York City (75.6 inches), Philadelphia (65.5 inches), and Baltimore (62.5 inches). Allentown/Bethlehem (71.8 inches) had its second snowiest winter of the twentieth century, East Stroudsburg (98.6 inches) logged its third snowiest winter (tying 1960–61), and Erie (129.2 inches) had its third snowiest winter up to that time. Binghamton, New York (133.5 inches), eclipsed a 1993–94 snowfall mark (130.3 inches).

Out-of-Season Snows

Snow has been observed in every month of the year in Pennsylvania. In the northern mountains, temperatures have occasionally dipped into the twenties in July and August, with scattered frost in the cold pockets on the high Allegheny plateaus. The infamous cold summer of 1816 ("Year without a Summer"; see Chapter 10) featured killing freezes in every month of the growing season, as well as measurable snow in the northern mountains in early June.

Some of the greatest snowfalls in Pennsylvania have occurred in the springtime, which has a great deal to do with the high water content of the snow at near-freezing temperatures late in the season. Deep snowfalls in excess of 2 feet blanketed parts of state on April 14–17, 1854, April 19–21, 1857, April 17–18, 1879, April 10–11, 1894, April 19–20, 1901, and April 27–28, 1928. The greatest April falls at official weather sites were recorded at Salem Corners (31.2 inches) and Coatesville (29.2 inches) in 1894, and at Somerset in 1928 (31 inches).

In the southwest, the Pittsburgh area received a little over a foot of snow on April 2–3, 1901, and again the following spring, on April 8, 1902. In the Delaware Valley, Philadelphia was buried under 19.2 inches of snow on April 3–4, 1915, exceeding a 14-inch fall on April 8–10, 1862 (*Public Ledger*). More recently, a true April blizzard halted transportation across much of Pennsylvania on April 6, 1982, while ice coated the streets of Philadelphia. Large snows (1 to 2 feet) also blanketed the northeastern hills on April 7–8, 1956, April 19–20, 1983, April 22–23, 1986, and March 31–April 1, 1997.

Late Snows

The cool summer of 1859 brought a killing freeze on June 5, 1859, that wiped out entire fields of corn in many parts of Pennsylvania and Ohio, long remembered as the "Great June Frost" (*Monthly Weather Review,* May 1907, 223–225) in the Midwest and Northeast. Even more remarkable, snow flurries flitted through a chilly wind on the Fourth of July 1859 in the mountains of Bradford County near the New York border. Clement Heverling (1926, 573, 591), in his Bradford County history, recalled "a flurry of snow on the 4th of July and so cold that persons wore overcoats at the celebrations." A few snowflakes were also observed in Bradford County on July 2, 1918.

The latest snow or sleet has been officially recorded in Pennsylvania is June 23, 1902 (State College and Washington County), and June 23, 1918 (Mount Pocono).

However, in the *Ohio State Journal* (August 1, 1843), there was a mention of snow mingled with rain on July 11, 1843, on "Allegheny Mountain."

The latest measurable snowfall in the Keystone State occurred on June 11, 1842. The *Pottsville Miners' Journal* reported that it "covered the foliage with its virgin drapery, and giving to the summer livery rather a strange appearance." Snowflakes were seen as far south as Harrisburg. The spring of 1843 also brought snow in June. Historian Luther S. Hoffman was quoted in the East Stroudsburg *Morning Sun* (April 30, 1928) on the unique event: "Snow fell two inches deep and the blossoming grain and rye were covered." A light snow shower was noticed at Philadelphia, according to the weather records of Charles Peirce. Snow also visited Pottsville on June 1, 1843, and the mercury plunged to 24 degrees the following morning, doing great harm to vegetables and fruits (*Miners' Journal*).

The heaviest May snowfall in Pennsylvania records blanketed the northeastern mountains on May 4–5, 1851, with a report of 18 inches at Hazleton, according to the Stroudsburg *Jeffersonian*. In the twentieth century, the biggest May snowfall occurred on May 1, 1945, at Monroeton (9.5 inches) in Bradford County. Measurable snow fell again in the northern mountains on May 3 and 10, 1945, setting a state monthly record (16 inches) at Monroeton. A coastal storm brought a rain-to-snow changeover on the night of May 8–9, 1977, leaving 8.2 inches at Tobyhanna, in the Poconos, and 10 inches on nearby Pimple Hill (el. 2,212 feet).

Measurable snow has not been observed southeast of the mountains since May 3–4, 1861 (2 inches in Lancaster County). In the olden times, near the end of the Little Ice Age, it was different. A 7-inch snowfall covered Lancaster on May 3, 1774 (*Bethlehem Daily Times*, March 14, 1888).

An article in the Stroudsburg *Jeffersonian* (April 20, 1854) recalled a great May snowstorm in 1803: "There was a fall of snow to the depth of six inches." Accompanied by thunder and lightning, rain changed to snow in Philadelphia in the early morning hours of May 8, 1803, bringing measurable snow to the coast for the first time in May since 1774. The glorious shade trees "which lined many of the main streets of Philadelphia" were ruined by the weight of the snow (Ludlum 1966, 167). The *United States Gazette* (May 1, 1841) recalled a fall of "several inches" in Philadelphia on May 8, adding that "sleighs ran as in mid winter."

There was "considerable fall of snow" in the northeastern highlands on May 14–15, 1834 (*Hazard's Register of Pennsylvania*). The following spring, a heavy wet snow on May 20–21, 1835, dropped 15 to 24 inches in Bradford County (Heverling 1926, 569). Another late snowfall blanketed the northern highlands of Pennsylvania on May 24–25, 1838. The *Genessee Farmer* (Rochester, N.Y.) carried a notice of a 10-inch snowfall at Bradford in the northwest, and Heverling (1926, 570) stated that snow fell all night "over a foot deep" in Bradford County to the east (incorrectly listed as 1839). In east-central Pennsylvania, the *Miners' Journal* reported, "A considerable quantity of snow fell on Broad Mountain" north of Pottsville.

The latest measurable snow at Pittsburgh in the twentieth century (0.5 inch) came on May 24–25, 1925, with 3 to 6 inches whitening the mountains in Tioga County. Two inches fell in the north-central mountains again on May 23–24, 1931. The greatest May snowfall in the southwestern counties accumulated 3.1 inches at Pittsburgh on May 9–10, 1966. The Poconos were dusted (1 to 2 inches) on May 17–18, 1973, and May 18–19, 1976. Bradford residents shoveled 8.5 inches of snow on May 7–8, 1989.

Autumn Snows

The earliest visitation of snowflakes in Pennsylvania during the waning days of summer came on August 26, 1885, at Harvey's Lake, near Wilkes-Barre. The snowfall was corroborated by numerous sightings of snow showers in the hills of eastern Pennsylvania on the wings of an unprecedented early chill in the local press. The earliest widespread freeze occurred on September 10–11, 1917.

The greatest September snowstorm in state history blanketed the northern mountains on September 28–29, 1844, remembered as a "remarkable snow-fall, in some parts of the county [Bradford] being 28 inches deep" (Heverling 1926, 571). The *United States Gazette* recalled "several inches in the interior of Pennsylvania."

On September 20, 1956, an unseasonably cold Canadian air mass deposited up to an inch of snow on parts of Erie (only a trace at the official weather site). The growing season ended the next morning over much of northern Pennsylvania, as temperatures dipped into the twenties. A dusting of snow fell at Freeland and atop Pimple Hill, in the Poconos, on September 28, 1984, and sleet was reported in Lancaster County.

The most impressive early-autumn snowfalls in Pennsylvania occurred in the memorable cold fall of 1836. A dusting of snow in the northern Appalachians on September 28–29, 1836, turned out to be only a prelude to twin wintry blasts in early October. The first of two heavy snowfalls buried the highlands of Pennsylvania and New York on October 4–5, 1836.

John Linn (1877, 527), in his *Annals of Buffalo Valley, Pennsylvania (1755–1855),* noted: "A heavy snow-storm; snow one and a half feet deep in Penn's valley and on Buffalo and White Deer mountains" in central Pennsylvania, a little west of the Susquehanna River in Union County. Fifteen inches fell on Broad Mountain, according to the *Miners' Journal,* requiring many men to clear the railroad tracks, and 11 inches fell at Wilkes-Barre (Ludlum 1982, 231). In Bradford County, "snow fell to the depth of nearly two feet" (Heverling 1926, 571).

A second great early-autumn snowstorm on October 11–12, 1836, brought a few inches of wet snow to interior sections of eastern Pennsylvania. A notice in the *Easton Argus* (October 20, 1836), citing a Pottsville dispatch, stated: "On Tuesday night [October 11] it commenced snowing, and continued until Wednesday morning, when it turned to rain at this place. On the Broad Mountain, the snow fell to the depth of 18 inches. . . . At some places on the mountain we learn the snow is two feet deep."

Substantial early snowfalls whitened the higher elevations of Pennsylvania on October 11, 1838, October 13–14, 1855, October 14–15, 1860, October 8–9, 1864, October 6–7, 1873, October 11–12, 1875, October 15, 1876, October 12, 1917, October 9–10, 1925, October 2–3, 1974, and most recently on October 3–4, 1987. A remarkable early nor'easter brushed southeastern Pennsylvania on October 10, 1979, depositing 1 to 3 inches at the earliest date on record in the Delaware Valley. On October 24–27, 1962, a record October fall of 19 inches at Corry fell over four days, and 3 to 6 inches covered the Poconos on October 25–

26, including record October falls of 4.4 inches at Scranton/Wilkes-Barre and 3.5 inches at Stroudsburg.

Moderate snowfalls (1 to 4 inches) have blanketed a large portion of the state, including the southeast, on October 24, 1853, October 26–27, 1859, October 30, 1925, October 19, 1940, October 20, 1952, and October 18–19, 1972. In the west, the greatest October snowfall occurred on Halloween 1993, when 8.5 inches fell at Pittsburgh on October 30–31 (plus 1.7 inches on November 1), and up to 14 inches were measured at Bradford. Heavy autumn snowfalls blanketed the southwestern mountains on October 24, 1917 (13.5 inches at Somerset) and the northeastern highlands on October 16–17, 1977 (17 inches at Freeland).

In the nineteenth century, an early nor'easter struck Pennsylvania on November 7–8, 1862, leaving as much as 14 to 18 inches in the Lehigh and Delaware Valleys. A major early-season snowstorm on November 3–4, 1910, left a blanket of snow 4 to 12 inches deep, while more than 20 inches piled up in the northeastern hills. In the west, the "Great Lakes Hurricane" of November 9–11, 1913, accompanied by fierce winds, paralyzed Pittsburgh and western Pennsylvania under 12 to 18 inches of snow, snarling travel and causing electrical lines to snap.

Later in the century, a remarkable nor'easter on November 6–7, 1953, deposited a whopping 29.8 inches at Lock Haven, 17.5 inches at York, and 8.8 inches at Philadelphia. Another early nor'easter blasted the state on November 12, 1968, starting before dawn, dropping an average of 4 to 12 inches of snow, and setting a November record of 22.5 inches at State College at Pennsylvania State University. The Veterans Day snowstorm on November 10–11, 1987, dropped up to a foot of snow on the state and coated Philadelphia roads with ice. Thanksgiving Day snowstorms have whitened the state in 1886, 1898, 1938, 1958, 1971, and 1989.

5 Cold Waves

'Tis rare to want the wholesome north-wester seven days together.

—William Penn, 1683, in a letter to the Free Society of Traders

A blast of polar air borne on the wings of strong northwesterly winds will send temperatures tumbling as much as 20 to 30 degrees in several hours. As the core of the cold air settles over Pennsylvania beneath an expansive dome of high pressure, the strong winds slowly subside. The lowest temperatures are usually observed under clear skies, calm conditions, and over snow-covered terrain.

The source regions for North American frigid air masses are Siberia and the Canadian Arctic. During the long polar nights, gelid air builds until a mound of dense wintry air breaks off and heads south by way of the North Pole or Hudson Bay, awaiting a shift in the steering winds that guide air masses into the United States.

January 1780: Hard Winter of 1779–80

The Hard Winter of 1779–80 was characterized by an onslaught of deep snowfalls in December and early January, followed by a series of severe cold waves. The Delaware River at Philadelphia was closed to navigation from December 21 until March 4 (Hazard 1828, 379).

The weather was intensely cold across Pennsylvania on January 6–7, 13–16, and 19–29, 1780. Ludlum (1966, 117) compared January 1780 with the coldest month in the Northeast in the nineteenth century: "Due to the imprecise nature of the readings and varying methods of compiling means, it would be reasonable to place January 1780 and January 1857 in a class by themselves, as co-holders of the title of the coldest month in history. January 1857 probably produced greater extremes, but January 1780 stands preeminent for duration of cold without a break."

February 2, 1789: Coldest Morning

An exceptionally cold morning was well documented in eastern Pennsylvania on February 2, 1789. A thermometer belonging to David Rittenhouse in downtown Philadelphia read −5 degrees, nearly matching the low of −6 degrees reached the previous winter on February 5, 1788 (Hazard 1828, 2:380).

Thirteen miles northwest of Philadelphia, Peter Legaux in Spring Mill observed −17 degrees on February 2, 1789, which was the lowest reading in his span of records (1786–1828). The historical notes of Elizabeth Kieffer deposited in the Lancaster Historical Society mentioned a reading of −21 degrees at 7:00 A.M. —"Colder than anyone living can recall" (Ludlum 1966, 79).

January 1792: Cold January

A measure of the severity of a cold regime is the duration of subfreezing conditions and the closure of rivers to navigation due to ice. In late December 1791 the Delaware River at Philadelphia already was filled with ice, but a brief thaw in early January 1792 opened the river for transportation for a short while.

Colder weather arrived in early January, and the river froze again at Philadelphia on January 7 and remained closed through March 6 (Hazard 1828, 2:380). The thermometer of longtime New York City weather-watcher Henry Laight never rose above 30 degrees from January 7 through January 30, 1792, a period of twenty-four days.

A heavy snowstorm hit the Northeast on January 18–19, 1792, creating favorable conditions for the refrigeration of arctic air (Ludlum 1966, 73–74). The records of David Rittenhouse in Philadelphia list a 7:00 A.M. reading of −5 degrees on January 23.

December 1796: Coldest Christmas Eve

A bitter Christmas Eve in 1796 in eastern Pennsylvania brought a reading of −13 degrees at Northumberland, according to the records of Joseph Priestly. A Philadelphia thermometer also descended to −13 degrees on January 9, 1797, and −10 the next day, which ranks with the coldest mornings ever known in the Quaker City (Ludlum 1966, 80).

February 9–11, 1818

An intense winter storm taking a track "probably across Tennessee and North Carolina" turned northeastward or redeveloped along the Virginia coast at the beginning of February 1818 (Ludlum 1966, 237). Dr. Samuel Hildreth at Marietta, Ohio, reported that "26 inches fell on the level" in twelve hours.

A week later, on February 9–11, exceptionally cold weather settled in over Pennsylvania when western Pennsylvania thermometers dipped to −24 degrees at Meadville and −26 in Fayette County, as reported by the *Huntingdon Gazette* (March 5, 1818).

January 1835: Cold Week

Heavy snow blanketed Pennsylvania on December 29–30, 1834, setting the stage for the advent of Cold Week in early January 1835. Accumulations ranged as high as 15 inches at Easton and 22 inches at Pottsville, ranking this storm among the heaviest December storms ever known in the region.

Samuel Hazard, the venerable editor of *Hazard's Register of Pennsylvania,* collected weather dispatches from around the state. The lowest reading reported to his journal was −32 degrees at Pine Grove in rural Schuylkill County in the hills of east-central Pennsylvania. Farther west, along the Susquehanna River, a reading of −31 was observed at Milton.

Table 5.1. Low Temperatures, January 4–5, 1835 (in degrees Farenheit)

Poughkeepsie, N.Y.	−35	Pottsville, Pa.	−24
Albany, N.Y.	−32	Lancaster, Pa.	−16
Hartford, Conn.	−27	Washington, D.C.	−16
Providence, R.I.	−26	Baltimore, Md.	−10

Source: *Hazard's Register of Pennsylvania*, April 11, 1835

The *Miners' Journal* in Pottsville reported readings of −20 degrees on January 4 and −24 degrees on the fifth. The *Easton Centinel and Argus* listed maximum/minimum readings of 8/−12 degrees on the fourth and 10/−16 degrees on the fifth.

Edward Garriott (1906, 11–12), citing an April 11, 1835, article in *Hazard's Register of Pennsylvania,* compiled a table of the minimum temperatures in the Northeast on January 4–5, 1835 (see Table 5.1).

The lowest temperature at Philadelphia during the Cold Week was −6 degrees on January 5, 1835. At Newark, New Jersey, a reading of −13 degrees (Ludlum 1983, 147) is comparable to the modern record of −14 degrees (February 9, 1934). The Boston reading of −15 degrees on January 5 was not surpassed until February 1934 (−18 degrees). In northern New York and New England, readings of −40 degrees or lower were reported at Bangor, Maine; Montpelier, Vermont; Franconia, New Hampshire; and New Lebanon, New York.

After a period of moderate temperatures, harsh winter weather returned to the Midwest and Northeast in late January and early February 1835. A severe cold wave plunged southward across the Midwest on February 5, spreading east over the next few days. Temperatures remained below zero day and night at Fort Dearborn (Chicago) on February 6–8, reaching a 7:00 A.M. nadir of −22 degrees on the eighth.

The core of the cold air engulfed western Pennsylvania February 8, when the temperature dipped to −21 degrees near Pittsburgh (Sewickley Bottom), according to the *Pittsburg Gazette.*

The most dramatic element of the February 1835 cold wave was the degree of the chill south reaching down to the Carolinas, Georgia, and Florida. The temperature plummeted to zero at Savannah, Georgia, at 5:00 A.M., according to the *Savannah Republican* (December 18, 1851), which is lower than the modern record (3 degrees in January 1985).

The lowest reading at Charleston, South Carolina (Castle Pinckney), was 1 degree, significantly below the modern mark (5 degrees in January 1985). Other low readings on February 8, 1835, were quite spectacular: Saint Louis, −25 degrees; Lexington, Kentucky, −20 degrees; Clarksville, Georgia, −15 degrees; and Jacksonville, Florida, 8 degrees.

1835–36: Cold, Snowy Winter

The winter of 1835–36 was outstanding for snow and persistent cold weather in Pennsylvania. Early temperature records maintained at Pennsylvania Hospital in downtown Philadelphia suggest the winter of 1835–36 (27.7 degrees) was comparable to the frigid winter of 1976–77 (28 degrees) in the Delaware Valley. The contemporary mean temperature in Philadelphia for the combined months of December, January, and February is 33.1 degrees.

Samuel Hazard's *Register of Pennsylvania* took notice of a late-November cold snap following a winter storm on the twenty-third. On November 29, 1835, temperatures ranged from 20 to 25 degrees at Philadelphia, ranking among the coldest of November days. Hazard noted on December 12, "The weather for the last week or ten days has been severely cold." A low reading of 12 degrees at Philadelphia was observed on December 3.

An arctic outbreak of historic proportions descended on the Northeast during the daylight hours of December 16, 1835. The network of New York Academy thermometers recorded readings at least as low as −40 degrees in northwestern New York, at which point the mercury congealed (Ludlum 1968, 22). A mid-afternoon reading of −14 degrees at Norfolk, Connecticut, eighty miles north-northeast of New York City, attested to the severe chill.

A terrible fire that broke out in New York City overnight on December 16–17, 1835, consuming hundreds of city blocks over the next several days, was made much worse by fire hydrants' freezing in the near-zero chill (Ludlum 1961, 66). New York City readings dipped to 3 degrees in Jamaica (Queens) and −2 at East Hampton early on December 17. In eastern Pennsylvania temperatures tumbled into the single digits in the afternoon on December 16, and the Schuylkill River was covered with ice. The temperature skidded to 8 degrees at Philadelphia, and −7 degrees at Pottsville early on the seventeenth.

The weather moderated in Pennsylvania toward the end of December 1835, but a series of major winter storms in January 1836 were followed by bouts of frigid weather. The Pottsville *Miners' Journal* listed readings of −16, −22, and −20 degrees on successive nights from January 27–29, 1836. A few days later, the mercury dipped to −4 degrees at Philadelphia on February 2 and reached a maximum of only 10 degrees. Another frigid morning followed on the third (−4 degrees).

The average temperature at Philadelphia in February 1836 was 24 degrees, which ranks fourth among cold Februarys after 1934 (22.4 degrees), 1979 (23 degrees), and 1838 (23.6 degrees). The mean temperature in February 1836 at New York City (Governors Island) was 21.5 degrees (Clayton 1944, 891), which is still the second coldest February in New York City after 1934 (19.9 degrees).

February 5–7, 1855: February Cold Wave

A true measure of the intensity of an arctic air mass is the depression of temperature in the middle of the afternoon. On the afternoon of February 5, 1855, the mercury at Gouvenour, New York, an Academy station, stood at −20 degrees at 2:00 P.M. Afternoon readings on February 6–7 were not much better (−15 and −10 degrees). On successive mornings the thermometer at Gouvenour slumped to −40 degrees, at which point the mercury congealed "in the absence of a spirit thermometer" (Ludlum 1968, 49).

The gelid air sank south into Pennsylvania on the night of February 5–6, 1855. The Smithsonian observer at Pottsville noticed a sunrise reading on February 6 of −3 degrees. A recheck of the thermometer at 2:00 P.M. (−3 degrees) and 9:00 P.M.

(−6 degrees) offered little hope of improvement. Subzero readings were noted at 7:00 A.M. (−6 degrees) and 2:00 P.M. (−2 degrees) on the seventh, before the thermometer rose to 6 degrees as snow commenced to fall in the evening. Adding insult to injury, 14 inches of snow buried Pottsville on February 8–9.

Down at Norristown, the thermometer slipped from 17 degrees at 9:00 P.M. on February 5, 1855, to 4.3 degrees at sunrise the next day. Readings continued to sag on the sixth, drifting down to 2.8 degrees at 2:00 P.M. and later to −2 at sunrise on the seventh. The temperature rose to 2.5 degrees at 2:00 P.M., with snow falling.

Along the coast temperatures plunged to −8 degrees at both Newark and New York City on the morning of February 6, 1855. The Boston *Evening Traveller* reported −44 degrees at West Randolph, Vermont, on the seventh. The *Traveller* thermometer hovered around −10 degrees at Boston, which is the bitterest daylight ever known in the Boston area.

January 1856: Siberian Winter

A moderate snowstorm in Pennsylvania on December 28–29, 1855, opened the floodgates from Canada. Temperatures at Mount Joy in Lancaster County were below freezing through 2:00 P.M. from December 31, 1855, through January 26, 1856. A mean temperature of 17.3 degrees in January 1856 is lower than any month ever known in the region. The average temperature at Philadelphia in January 1856 was 24.2 degrees.

A heavy snowstorm on January 5–6 ushered in one of the bitterest arctic air masses ever known. A weather station at Randolph in Crawford County (el. 1,700 feet) reported −6 degrees at 7:00 A.M. on January 8 and posted the same icy reading at 2:00 P.M. The 9:00 P.M. temperature (−14 degrees) at Randolph preceded a daybreak reading of −22 degrees (January 9, 1856).

The Smithsonian thermometer at Norristown slumped to −9 degrees at 7:00 A.M. on January 9 and recovered to only 1 degree at 2:00 P.M., ranking that duration among the coldest daylight periods (January 18, 1857, and January 17, 1982). The minimum temperature at Philadelphia on January 9, 1856, of −7 degrees was not equaled until January 22, 1984. A low reading of −18 degrees at Pittsburgh stood the test of time until January 19, 1994 (−22 degrees).

A weather station at Nazareth, about ten miles northeast of Allentown/Bethlehem, had a 7:00 A.M. reading of −16 degrees on January 9, 1856, warming to just 1.75 degrees at 2:00 P.M. The weather was still bitter on the tenth (7/−7 degrees). The Pottsville *Miners' Journal* reported extremes of −2/−11 degrees, for a rare zero day on January 9, 1856.

January 1857: Coldest January of the Nineteenth Century

After the severe chill of January 1856, bitter cold returned to the Northeast in January of the next year. The mean temperature at Philadelphia in January 1857 was 22.4 degrees, 2 degrees below that of January 1856. Only January 1977 (20 degrees) has been colder in the city.

At Easton the average temperature in January 1857 was 16.2 degrees, making it slightly colder than February 1934 (16.4 degrees) at nearby Allentown. The mean temperature at New York City in January 1857 was 19.6 degrees, and lower at Flatbush, Queens (19.3 degrees), which is comparable to the modern record (19.9 degrees in February 1934).

At North Whitehall, near Allentown, the temperature did not pass the freezing point (2:00 P.M. observation time) from January 6 through 26, 1857 (twenty-one days), compared to the record of twenty days in January 1893 at Easton.

The first of two exceptionally cold polar blasts arrived on January 17, 1857, when the mercury at Mount Joy in Lancaster County showed a steady fall from 18 degrees at daybreak to 11 degrees at 2:00 P.M., to −6 degrees at 9:00 P.M. The morning of January 18 brought a reading of −12 degrees at Mount Joy, and the temperature only edged up to 3 degrees later on.

In Bucks County along the Delaware River, the Morrisville observer noted 0 degrees at 2:00 P.M. and 9:00 P.M. An Academy thermometer at Copenhagen, New York, registered −42 degrees on January 18. The 2:00 P.M. observation at Cortland, New York, of −10 degrees attested to the extreme severity of the cold wave.

While a cold dome of high pressure hovered over the Northeast, keeping conditions cold and dry, a great mid-Atlantic blizzard developed on the southern margin of the polar front on January 18–19, 1857. The deep snowpack extending from Virginia to Pennsylvania created optimal conditions for cooling. A brief moderating trend on January 21, 1857, accompanied a second coastal disturbance approached the region. However, in the wake of the storm, temperatures plunged to −34 degrees at Craftsbury, Vermont (7:00 A.M.), on January 23 and rose to only −23 degrees at 2:00 P.M. Another Smithsonian thermometer at Norwich, Vermont, recorded −44 degrees.

The second surge of brutally cold polar air arrived in Pennsylvania on January 22, 1857, sending the temperature at North Whitehall tumbling to 11 degrees at 2:00 P.M. and −7 at sunrise on the twenty-third. The afternoon reading recovered slightly to 8 degrees. Temperatures plummeted again overnight, dropping to −22 degrees at 7:00 A.M. on January 24, the lowest ever recorded in the region. The afternoon reading on the twenty-fourth struggled to make it back to 10 degrees.

At Lafayette College in Easton, the morning reading on January 24, 1857, was reported as low as −16 degrees. That same sunrise reading was observed at Norristown, fifteen miles northwest of Philadelphia. Near the coast, a low of −9 degrees was obtained at Jamaica Academy in Queens, and William Whitehead's Newark reading was −12 degrees.

The Morrisville observer along the Delaware River north of Philadelphia recorded frosty lows of −17 degrees on January 24 and −10 degrees on January 26, 1857. In the upper Delaware Valley, readings at Stroudsburg were as low as −29 degrees on January 24 and −26 degrees on the twenty-sixth, according to the *Jeffersonian* (January 19, 1893). In the Susquehanna River valley, the Berwick observer recorded −24 degrees.

A comparison between January 1856 and 1857 observations at Nazareth suggests that January 1857 was slightly colder overall (see Table 5.2). An inspection of long-term records at Washington printed in the *Monthly Weather Review* (March 1891) gives the nod to January 1856 (21.3 degrees) over January 1857 (21.5 degrees) by a frozen whisker. The mean temperature in February 1856 (26.8

Table 5.2. Comparison of Mean Temperatures in Nazareth, January 1856 and 1857 (in degrees Farenheit)

	7:00 A.M.	2:00 P.M.	9:00 P.M.	Mean
January 1856	12	25	15	17.3
January 1857	12.4	22.2	14.4	16.4

degrees) at Washington ensured that January and February 1856 would be the coldest two months in succession in Washington (24.1 degrees).

January 10, 1859: Coldest Daylight

The bitterest daylight of the past two centuries in eastern Pennsylvania occurred on January 10, 1859. A cold wave arrived on January 8 and reached its nadir on the tenth. William Whitehead's thermometer at Newark, New Jersey, plunged to −12.5 degrees early on the tenth, rising to a maximum of −0.5 degree late in the day, marking the coldest daylight in his records back to 1843.

The *Sussex Register* at Newton called the weather on January 10 "the severest cold ever remembered," with temperatures ranging down to −12 degrees in the morning, and inching up to −5 degrees later in the day. A check of observations taken at Easton (Lafayette College) for January 10 show uniformly low readings: 7:00 A.M., −9 degrees; 2:00 P.M., −1.5 degrees; and 9:00 P.M., −7 degrees. Similar numbers were obtained at nearby North Whitehall: 7:00 A.M., −10 degrees; 2:00 P.M., −2 degrees; and 9:00 P.M., −2 degrees. This is the only instance of a true zero day, when the mercury hovered below zero for at least twenty-four hours, in the Lehigh Valley.

Family records maintained by Charles and Alvin Hoffman in East Stroudsburg and later compiled by Luther S. Hoffman listed a morning reading of −14 degrees on January 10, 1859, but there was no mention of a maximum reading. The highest reading at Central High School in Philadelphia on January 10 was 4 degrees. Afternoon values at Norristown ranged from 1 degree at 2:00 P.M. to 3 degrees at 9:00 P.M. on the tenth.

January 8, 1866: Cold Term of '66

A cold wave in January 1866 sent thermometers plunging to the lowest levels ever recorded in January at Philadelphia and New York City. On the evening of January 7, 1866, a 7:00 P.M. reading of −3 degrees was noted at a police station in upper Manhattan. At 6:00 A.M. on the eighth, the temperature had already plunged to −12 to −14 degrees. The *New York Times* stated, "During the afternoon it rose to zero, where it remained up to a late hour."

William Whitehead's thermometer at Newark registered −12.75 degrees, comparable to readings taken on January 10, 1859 (−12.5 degrees), and January 24, 1857 (−12 degrees), and an extreme low from another source on January 5, 1835 (−13 degrees). The modern record low of −14 degrees was observed on February 9, 1934 (Ludlum 1983, 41, 147–148).

It was the same story at Philadelphia, where the official minimum reading downtown on the morning of January 8, 1866, was −9.5 degrees, though the press reported temperatures in the western suburbs of −14 to −18 degrees, "which is said to be the coldest weather ever known there." To the northeast, temperatures ranged from −15 to −20 degrees at Stroudsburg on the morning of January 8.

A weather station at Dyberry registered −19 degrees at 9:00 P.M. on January 7, 1866, lowering to −22 degrees around sunrise on the eighth. The afternoon reading at Dyberry on January 8, 1866, recovered to just −4 degrees and by 11:00 P.M. had slipped back to −11 degrees.

The North Whitehall observer had a reading of −13 degrees at 7:00 A.M. on January 8, 1866, which rose to 4 degrees at 2:00 P.M. The Norristown observer, northwest of Philadelphia, noticed −13 degrees around sunrise and an afternoon temperature of 6 degrees. Temperatures at North Whitehall at the 2:00 P.M. observation reached only the teens during the Cold Term from January 4 to 10, 1866.

1872–73: Two Bitter Outbreaks

A massive dome of arctic air settled over the Midwest in December 1872 during the week before Christmas. On the afternoon of December 22, the temperature at Dyberry stood at 2 degrees, and down in Chester County it was 7 degrees. The intense cold moderated briefly on the twenty-third, but was soon reinforced on Christmas Eve.

Afternoon temperatures at Dyberry during the holiday period from December 24– to 27, 1872, ranged from 8 to 10 degrees and 12 to 13 degrees at Pocopson. The *Easton Express* reported maximum readings during the same period of 11 to 19 degrees. Morning readings on December 24–25, 1872, were zero or lower over much of Pennsylvania. A sunrise report of −10 degrees on Christmas morning at Blooming Grove was one of the lowest readings in the state. A Union County correspondent reported −22 degrees near Lewisburg. In the southeast, the Chester County observer had recorded an even zero degrees.

A massive snowstorm pounded the Northeast on December 25–27, 1872, leaving about 1 to 2 feet of snow on eastern Pennsylvania. Another surge of arctic air swept into Pennsylvania on December 29, sending the mercury in a downward spiral. The records of John N. Stokes in Stroudsburg listed −18 degrees, which is well below the modern December record of −14 degrees in 1963. A weather station near Allentown reached −10 degrees at 7:00 A.M. on December 30. Farther south the mercury dipped to −5 degrees at Pocopson, west of Philadelphia.

On January 18, 1873, a low temperature of −43 degrees was registered at La Crosse, Wisconsin, indicating a mound of cold air was in place, waiting for a shift in the winds to reach Pennsylvania. A heavy snowfall on January 27–28 would be the system to draw the bitter air into Pennsylvania.

On January 29, the temperature at Dyberry fell from 4 degrees at 2:00 P.M. to −19 at 9:00 P.M., eventually bottoming out at −31 at 7:00 A.M. on the thirtieth. The Stroudsburg *Jeffersonian* mentioned a minimum of −32 degrees. The observer at Egypt, near Allentown, recorded −20 degrees at 7:00 A.M., and in Chester County the temperature dipped to −18 degrees. The lowest official state reading (−28 degrees) was logged at Carlisle Barracks, and there was a report of −33 degrees at Lewisburg.

January 3, 1879: Zero Day in West

Bitterly cold air reached Pennsylvania on January 2, 1879, sending temperatures plunging at New Castle from 20 degrees at sunrise down to 7 at 2:00 P.M. and −6 at 9:00 P.M. The next morning found the mercury hovering around −16 degrees. The temperature at New Castle rose to −5 degrees at 2:00 P.M. and −4 at 9:00 P.M. on January 3.

In the east the corresponding 2:00 P.M./7:00 A.M. readings at Egypt on January 3 were 7/−7 degrees, and the Stroudsburg *Jeffersonian* reported a range of 6/−8 degrees. The afternoon observations at New Castle on January 4–5 were below 10 degrees, and the mornings brought subzero sunrise readings. An 8-inch snowfall capped off the cold week at New Castle on January 8–9, 1879.

Another frigid blast arrived on January 18, sending Pennsylvania temperatures to near or below zero over the next few days. A Stroudsburg thermometer dipped to −10 degrees on the nineteenth and −17 on the twenty-first.

December 30–31, 1880: Coldest December Day

An extraordinary cold wave gripped the Northeast on December 30, 1880, bringing the coldest day ever recorded in the Lehigh Valley. The weather observer at Egypt, near Allentown, reported −15 degrees at 7:00 A.M., which rose to just zero at 2:00 P.M. In the northern Poconos, temperatures at Dyberry ranged from −18 degrees (7:00 A.M.) to 1 degree (2:00 P.M.) on the thirtieth. The Stroudsburg *Jeffersonian* reported a low of −10 degrees the morning after a 6-inch snowfall on December 28–29. The 3:00 P.M. temperature on the south side of Main Street struggled to 3 degrees before plunging to −10 degrees on December 31, 1880, and −17 on January 1, 1881.

Farther north, reports came in from Milford (−15 degrees) and Dingmans Ferry (−18 degrees) of extraordinarily low readings. Mount Ararat, sixteen miles west of Carbondale, had a frosty reading of −26 degrees on December 31 and a New Year's morning temperature of −22 degrees.

Philadelphia experienced the coldest December day in weather bureau history (5/−5 degrees) on the thirtieth (see Table 5.3). The New York City extremes (4/−6 degrees) were the lowest in December until 1917. Along the New Jersey coast, Freehold had extraordinary chill (−0.5/−11 degrees). In the northwest, a thermometer at Dodge Mines (el. 1,100 feet) in Morris County read −7 degrees at 2:00 P.M. and −5 degrees at 9:00 P.M.

The cold weather on December 31, 1880, extended south to Richmond, Virginia (−8 degrees), bringing the lowest readings since January 1857. A bitter low

Table 5.3. Maximum/Minimum Temperatures, December 29–31, 1880 (in degrees Farenheit)

	December		
	29	30	31
Dyberry	10/5	−1/−18	−6/−19
Philadelphia	14/4	5/−5	14/0

of −13 degrees was reported at Washington, D.C., on the thirty-first, and New Year's Day 1881 was even colder there (−14 degrees). These are the lowest December/January readings in city history.

January 1893: Record Streak of Subfreezing Temperatures

Arctic air was a frequent visitor to Pennsylvania in early January 1893. Philadelphia endured two consecutive weeks of subfreezing weather, and January 1893 (24 degrees) ranks behind 1977 (20 degrees) and 1857 (22.4 degrees) among the coldest Januarys in the city's weather history.

In northern Pennsylvania, a record-breaking string of twenty-two subfreezing days began on January 3 and lasted through the January 24. The thermometer at Easton could not even manage a high of 20 degrees from January 10 to 18, 1893, making that month's mean temperature (16.5 degrees) only a fraction higher than that of January 1857 (16.2 degrees).

The Stroudsburg press reported readings as low as −18 to −25 degrees on January 16, −22 to −27 degrees on the seventeenth, and −18 to −22 degrees on the eighteenth. Binghamton, New York, had an all-time record low of −28 degrees. The *Philadelphia Inquirer* carried a summary of chilly readings ranging down to −24 degrees at Bear Gap, near Shamokin, and Spring Grove. (Official minimum readings in the January 1893 cold wave appear in Table 5.4.)

February 9–15, 1899: Great Cold Wave

Two heavy snowfalls on February 5–6 and 7–8, 1899, created the requisite conditions for preserving the extraordinary chill of the greatest arctic outbreak in recorded meteorological history in the eastern half of the United States.

In northern Minnesota, Leech Dam registered −59 degrees on February 9, 1899, signaling the intensity of the arctic surge. The core of the cold would soon arrive in Pennsylvania and hold the state in an icy stranglehold for a solid week. The *Stroudsburg Daily Times* reported low temperatures in that city of −10, −16, and −14 degrees (February 9–11, 1899), and −17, −25, and −26 degrees at Tobyhanna on the high plateau.

The lowest readings in Pennsylvania were reported on February 10, which was a zero-day at Dyberry, Harrisburg, and South Bethlehem. Maximum/minimum readings at Philadelphia (5/−6 degrees) on February 10 represent the coldest daily mean temperature in city history. At Washington, D.C., high/low readings (5/−15 degrees) marked the coldest day ever in the nation's capital. Baltimore also endured its coldest day on record (3/−7 degrees) on February 10, 1899.

In western Pennsylvania, Pittsburgh shivered through a record seven consecutive days with subzero lows from February 8– to 14, 1899. Temperatures remained below zero day and night on February 9 and 10, with maximums of −3 (ninth) and

Table 5.4. Minimum Temperatures, January 17–18, 1893 (in degrees Fahrenheit)

Dyberry	−22	Easton	−14
Somerville, N.J.	−20	York	−14
Millsboro, Del.	−17	Quakertown	−14

−2 degrees (tenth). Pittsburgh reached an all-time February minimum of −20 on February 10.

In the central part of the state, State College had its bitterest day ever on February 10 (−5/−20 degrees). The lowest official reading in the state was −39 degrees at Lawrenceville, Tioga County, in the north-central hills.

A great blizzard swept up the East Coast on February 11–14, 1899, dumping up to 3 feet of snow as it went. Another frigid morning on February 15 brought readings of −10 degrees or lower in northern and western sections of Pennsylvania. There was a reversal of fortune, however, on February 20–22, when temperatures soared into the fifties.

January 5, 1904: Coldest Morning in Pennsylvania

A heavy snowstorm on January 2–3, 1904, paved the way for a frigid arctic outbreak that would bring the lowest temperature ever recorded at an official government weather station in Pennsylvania. In the southeast, the temperature rose to only 13 degrees at Philadelphia on January 4, the day after the storm, and readings were barely above zero in the northern mountains.

On January 5, the bottom fell out of the temperature across Pennsylvania under clear skies with light winds, which is summarized in Table 5.5. North and west of Philadelphia, readings plunged to between −10 and −30 degrees. A state record low temperature of −42 degrees was recorded at Smethport in McKean County, exceeding the extreme lows reached in February 1899. The next lowest reading (−38 degrees) was reported at Lawrenceville in Tioga County.

The *Stroudsburg Times* reported readings in the community as low as −26 to −31 degrees. A follow-up story in the *Stroudsburg Daily Times* on January 13, 1904, mentioned even lower readings: −34 degrees on Samuel Eschenbach's farm near Pocono Summit; −32 at Blakeslee; and −28 two miles from Stroudsburg at the home of local "weather prophet" Reverend Ira H. Hicks (see Table 5.6).

Another cold wave arrived on January 18–19, 1904, driving nighttime readings far below zero again in the northern highlands and valleys. On January 21, the *Stroudsburg Times* described the difficulty local residents were having trying to stay warm during the frigid January nights: "Furnaces heaped with coal failed to

Table 5.5. Minimum Temperatures, January 5, 1904 (in degrees Farenheit)

East		Central		West	
Towanda	−31	Lewisburg	−29	Coudersport	−33
Pocono Lake	−27	Wellsboro	−25	Grampian	−32
Milford	−24	Selinsgrove	−24	Franklin	−30
Wilkes-Barre	−18	Montrose	−21	Emporium	−29

Table 5.6. Minimum Temperatures, January 5, 1904 (in degrees Farenheit)

Greentown	−34	Tannersville	−28
Bushkill	−33	Marshalls Creek	−28
Pocono Summit	−30	Brodheadsville	−20

Source: The *Stroudsburg Daily Times*

Table 5.7. Minimum Temperatures, January 14, 1912 (in degrees Farenheit)

Stroudsburg	−35	Lancaster	−27
Pocono Lake	−35	Lebanon	−17
Mifflintown	−31	State College	−16
Emporium	−31	Bethlehem	−16

keep a house warm and water pipes in many places were frozen shut." The paper reported extreme readings of −36 degrees at the Transue Farm in Echo Valley (between Shawnee and Frutchey), −30 at Analomink, and −28 at Bushkill. In the Stroudsburgs temperatures dipped to −16 to −22 degrees, with a "bitter, cutting wind."

January 14, 1912: Bitter Cold

Snow cover and clear skies were responsible for another extremely cold January morning eight years after the historic low temperatures recorded in January 1904. The core of bitterly cold air was centered west of Pennsylvania on January 12, 1912. A low temperature of −47 degrees was observed at Washta, Iowa. The capital city of Des Moines endured its coldest day of the century (−14/−29 degrees) on the twelfth.

The cold air spilled east into Pennsylvania on January 13. Pocono Lake (el. 1,660 feet) had a maximum temperature of 3 degrees, before the mercury plunged to −16 degrees by 9:00 P.M. Readings as low as −35 degrees were recorded at official weather stations in Stroudsburg and Pocono Lake on the morning of January 14.

An all-time minimum reading of −27 degrees was recorded on January 14, 1912, at Lancaster. A minimum of −16 degrees at Bethlehem is comparable to the modern record of −15 degrees on January 21, 1994, at the Lehigh Valley International Airport. In central Pennsylvania a temperature of −17 degrees at the Pennsylvania State University in State College was the lowest since February 1899 (−20 degrees). The frigidity of January 14, 1912, is shown in Table 5.7.

The "urban heat island" afforded some protection for Philadelphia, where the lowest reading was zero. However, at Washington, D.C., city warmth didn't prevent the temperature from plunging to −13 degrees on January 14, 1912, which was the lowest reading in the nation's capital since January 1, 1881 (−14 degrees).

1917–18: Coldest Winter

The winter of 1917–18 was the coldest in Pennsylvania weather history since records began in 1888, averaging 20.7 degrees. December 1917 was the coldest December in state records until 1989, and January 1918 was chilliest January until 1977.

Several waves of frigid air descended on Pennsylvania in December 1917 following heavy snowfalls on the eighth and fifteenth. The bitterest air mass arrived during the daylight hours of December 28, sending temperatures plummeting into the single digits, and below zero in the northern mountains.

Scranton recorded its lowest December maximum of the century (2 degrees) on

Table 5.8. Maximum/Minimum Temperatures December 29, 1917–January 4, 1918 (in degrees Farenheit)

	Stroudsburg	Scranton	Mt. Pocono	Harrisburg
December 29	10/−5	2/−10	5/−8	5/−2
December 30	5/−12	3/−13	−7/−22	7/−3
December 31	9/−13	5/−7	−2/−16	8/0
January 1	14/−10	12/−3	0/−15	14/4
January 2	9/−10	10/0	−2/−12	10/5
January 3	12/−8	6/−5	8/−5	12/4
January 4	18/−6	16/−5	6/−18	19/3

December 29, and some mountain locations experienced a zero day. Temperatures slipped below zero in northern Pennsylvania before midnight on December 28 and would not rise above zero at Mount Pocono (el. 1,720 feet) again until the afternoon of January 3, 1918.

The core of the cold air was over eastern Pennsylvania on December 30, when Mount Pocono endured its coldest December day (−7/−22 degrees). On the thirtieth, Scranton (3/−13 degrees) also recorded the lowest daily mean for any December day. An extreme low of −28 degrees at Ebensburg in Cambria County equaled the state record for December (1894, 1914). Along the coast, New York City (Central Park) experienced its coldest day of the century on December 30, 1917 (4/−13 degrees), which felt closer to −50 or −60 degrees with 20-mile-per-hour winds whipping through town.

Maximum readings in Pennsylvania remained below 20 degrees for eight straight days (December 28, 1917, through January 4, 1918), except in the extreme southeast (Table 5.8). The lowest mean temperature in January 1918 was 9.6 degrees at Drifton in Luzerne County (el. 1,633 feet).

1934: Coldest February

Bitterly cold arctic air plunged into Pennsylvania on February 8, 1934, holding maximum readings to the single digits following subzero chill in the north. Late-afternoon readings dipped below zero in the northeastern mountain section before sunset, reaching −15 at Gouldsboro at 5:00 P.M. and −22 at Skytop by midnight.

Historic chill greeted residents of Pennsylvania on the morning of February 9, 1934. In the central part of the state, Bellefonte reported a low of −31 degrees, and in the north-central mountains Wellsboro checked in with −30 degrees. Scranton had its coldest day (0/−19 degrees) on February 9, and Stroudsburg reported 5/−16 degrees.

At Mount Pocono, the morning minimum of −25 degrees established a February record, and daytime readings struggled to rise above −10 degrees. The Stroudsburg press reported lows of −18 to −24 degrees in the colder spots and −30 degrees in the West End.

Record-breaking cold extended to the coastal plain and major urban centers of the Northeast. Philadelphia (−11 degrees), Newark (−14 degrees), New York City (−15 degrees) and Boston (−18 degrees) established all-time record lows.

Temperatures around the state were generally below freezing from January 29 to February 10, 1934, and again from February 23 to 28. The last cold spell clinched a record low monthly mean temperature for the state of 16.5 degrees (10.4 degrees below normal). The coldest reading was −34 degrees at Lawrenceville, Tioga County, on February 28.

Many Pennsylvania cities observed a record cold month in February 1934. The lowest average temperature was 7.4 degrees at Mount Pocono (state record for February). The average temperature at Erie (14 degrees) set a February record, as did the value at Philadelphia (22.4 degrees), tying January 1857 for the coldest month up to that time.

1935–36: Frigid January/February

The winter of 1935–36 brought a series of cold waves across the eastern two-thirds of the United States. A cold December 1935 gave way to moderate conditions in early January 1936, but frigid air continued to build in western Canada, destined to reach Pennsylvania in stages later in the month.

A heavy snowstorm on January 18–20 buried the eastern half of the state with as much as 27 inches at Gouldsboro, 20 inches at Scranton, and 15.9 inches at Stroudsburg. After a few wintry days with subzero mornings, a brief thaw on January 22 saw temperatures rebound to near 40 degrees over southeastern Pennsylvania. Meanwhile, several hundred miles to the west, at Columbus, Ohio, the mercury plunged from 33 degrees at 8:00 A.M. to −5 degrees by 5:00 P.M., heralding the arrival of a new surge of arctic air. At 10:00 P.M. on January 22, the temperature at Columbus had fallen to a frigid −16 degrees, with an estimated wind chill around −70 degrees.

We can pick up the progress of the Polar Express in western Pennsylvania shortly before midnight on the twenty-second, when the temperature at Pittsburgh had dipped to −14 degrees. Farther east, readings had fallen into the single digits as arctic air pushed across the mountains.

The core of the cold air settled over western Pennsylvania early on January 23, 1936. The maximum temperature at Pittsburgh was −2 degrees, for a true zero day, after a morning low of −16 degrees. The lowest reading in the west was reported at Ebensburg (−30 degrees) in Cambria County. In the northeast, Gouldsboro had maximum/minimum readings of −3/−18 degrees on January 23.

In the southeast, Harrisburg had extremes of 9/−6 degrees on January 23, 1936, and Allentown was equally frigid at 10/−5 degrees. Morning lows on January 24 in the east ranged from 5 degrees at Philadelphia to −5 at Allentown to −10 degrees at Mount Pocono. In the west, the mercury dipped to −11 at Pittsburgh, where the maximum only climbed to 7 degrees on the twenty-fourth.

The twelve-day period from January 23 through February 3, 1936, was one of the coldest in Pennsylvania weather history, rivaling periods of prolonged chill observed in January 1856, 1857, 1893, and 1918. The thermometer failed to rise above 20 degrees at Pittsburgh and Scranton for nearly a week (January 23–29, 1936). Pittsburgh shivered through six consecutive subzero mornings, which is the second longest streak in city weather records.

A reinforcing blast of arctic air arrived in Pennsylvania on January 27, when Gouldsboro registered a daylight maximum of −1 degree, while most locations in northern Pennsylvania never rose above the single digits. Maximum temperatures were held to the teens and low twenties in Pennsylvania from January 31 through February 3, 1936. Subzero readings were recorded on the mornings of February 1 and 3, 1936, with the lowest reading reported at Gouldsboro (−22 degrees) on the third. Gouldsboro recorded thirty-two consecutive subfreezing days (January 16– February 16, 1936).

High temperatures at Allentown ranged from 10 to 26 degrees during the period from January 23 through February 3, 1936, before finally edging up to 34 degrees on the fourth. The cold moderated briefly in the middle of February, though several snowfalls beefed up the already deep snowpack. Another arctic high-pressure area over the upper Midwest drove the temperature down to a record minimum of −60 degrees at Parshall, North Dakota, on February 15.

Within a few days, temperatures plunged below zero again across northern Pennsylvania. A cold daylight on February 19, 1936, brought maximums in the single digits in the northwest and near 20 degrees in the southeast. The lowest temperature was −27 at Brookville (Jefferson County). Minimum readings at Gouldsboro on successive mornings from February 18 to 22 were −14, −18, −13, −7, and −13 degrees.

1942–43: Two Frigid Outbreaks

The winter of 1942–43 was not unusually cold, but it did feature two noteworthy cold spells. Arctic air plunged southeast across Pennsylvania on December 19, 1942, following a light snowfall. The morning of December 20 brought subzero readings to all but the southeastern corner of the state.

Daytime readings on the twentieth were hard-pressed to reach zero in the northern mountains and barely edged above 10 degrees in the southeast. Mount Pocono recorded extremes of −2/−12 degrees on December 20, which was the earliest recorded zero day. Another cold morning (−7 degrees) followed on the twenty-first.

In the middle of February 1943, a second polar outbreak of historic proportions interrupted a generally mild midwinter pattern. Scranton recorded a maximum of zero on February 15, 1943, after sinking to −13 degrees early in the day. Mount Pocono had a record low maximum of −7 degrees, following a minimum of −19 degrees, for the coldest daily mean (−13 degrees) on record. Montrose also observed a record cold daily mean (−13 degrees) based on extremes of −6/−20 degrees.

In the eastern valleys, Palmerton registered its coldest day on record (2/−16 degrees) on February 15. Stroudsburg had extremes of 7/−16 degrees on this same day. The press listed lower Pocono readings: Scotrun, −32 degrees; Scioto, −31 degrees; Skytop, −30 degrees; Saylorsburg, −26 degrees; and Swiftwater, −25 degrees. New York City had maximum/minimum readings of 6/−8 degrees on February 15, for the coldest daily mean (−1 degree) so late in the winter.

The morning of February 16, 1942, was frigid again, with a low of −21 degrees at Stroudsburg (February record), though the mercury would recover to the sixties on the twentieth. (An earlier reading of −21 degrees on February 1, 1936, was likely erroneous.)

The February 1943 cold wave was especially severe in New England. All-time records lows were observed at Concord, New Hampshire (−43 degrees), Portland, Maine (−39 degrees), and Falls Village, Connecticut (−32 degrees—state record).

January 1961: Lowest Temperatures since 1934

A major nor'easter brought heavy snow to Pennsylvania on January 19–20, 1961, commencing a long period of subfreezing weather. The maximum temperature at Scranton/Wilkes-Barre failed to reach 20 degrees for nine straight days (January 20 to 28, 1961).

At Philadelphia the thermometer did not exceed freezing for two full weeks (January 19–February 2, 1961), breaking the previous record of thirteen straight days in January 1893. Stroudsburg had a record seventeen consecutive days of subfreezing weather (January 19–February 4, 1961). During this remarkable cold span, a record of fourteen consecutive subzero mornings (January 21–February 3, 1961) was observed at both Stroudsburg and York.

The coldest morning in Pennsylvania occurred on January 22, 1961, when temperatures fell below zero over virtually the entire state, except Erie (2 degrees). In the southeast, minimum readings of −19 degrees were observed at Quakertown and Phoenixville. In the Susquehanna Valley, Berwick turned in a low temperature of −20 degrees, and Philadelphia endured its first subzero morning (−4 degrees) since January 23, 1936.

Farther east, a new January record low of −12 degrees at Allentown/Bethlehem was reached on January 22, 1961, which lasted until 1994 (−15 degrees). A report of −25 degrees at Stroudsburg noted the coldest reading since January 14, 1912. The Hawley observer read −27 degrees, which was the coldest morning on record in the region until January 21, 1994 (−31 degrees). The lowest reading in the state, on January 22, 1961, was turned in at Mercer (−32 degrees).

Exceptionally low readings persisted during the opening days of February 1961. The morning of February 2 brought low readings of −4 at Philadelphia, −14 at Quakertown, and −25 at Hawley. Erie finally recorded a subzero reading (−6 degrees) during this cold spell. In the Allegheny highlands, readings as low as −26 degrees were reported at Clarion and Indiana. The lowest official temperature (−35 degrees) was recorded at a station seven miles east of Dubois, and also at Ridgway. An unofficial thermometer registered −40 at St. Marys in Elk County.

A heavy snowstorm on February 3–4, 1961, was actually the end of the frigid pattern, after which time temperatures moderated into the thirties and forties. During the third week of February 1961, readings climbed into the sixties and lower seventies!

January 24–25, 1963: Polar Express

A blast of frigid air swept across Pennsylvania early on January 24, 1963, bringing frigid maximums at Pittsburgh (−2 degrees) and State College (0 degrees). At Williamsport the high temperature was only 7 degrees. The following morning (January 25) ushered in subzero readings across much of the state, including −16 degrees at State College, which was the lowest reading at the Pennsylvania State University since February 9, 1934 (−17 degrees).

The coldest readings in eastern Pennsylvania actually came a few days later, on January 29, when the minimum temperature at Philadelphia dipped to −5 degrees (the coldest morning since February 1934). Very low readings were also reported at Lancaster (−11 degrees) and Quakertown (−18 degrees). In the northeast low temperatures of −18 degrees at Stroudsburg and −20 at Tobyhanna led the pack.

January 1977: Coldest Month

The winter of 1976–77 is synonymous with extreme chill in the East and the first visitation of snowflakes in modern history in southern Florida. A sinuous jet stream dove exceptionally far south across the eastern half of the country, forcing a succession of arctic air masses into the eastern half of the country.

The monthly mean temperature in Pennsylvania in January 1977 was an icy 13.4 degrees (11.2 degrees below normal), which is the coldest month in state weather history. The coldest periods occurred on January 11–13, 16–18, and 28–31. To the northwest, temperatures remained below freezing at Bradford from December 29, 1976, through February 9, 1977 (a record-breaking period of forty-three days).

The Bradford weather site (el. 2,142 feet), four miles west of town, reported a record low monthly mean temperature for Pennsylvania that January (4.3 degrees), along with the lowest temperature (−36 degrees) of the month on the thirteenth. The average maximum/minimum temperatures at Bradford FAA in January 1977 were 12/−3.5 degrees.

On January 17, 1977, Pittsburgh had a zero day (−2/−17 degrees). The coldest figures again were turned in at Bradford FAA, where the mercury plunged to −21 degrees and rose to only −10 degrees later in the day, establishing another state record for the lowest maximum reading. Williamsport tied its all-time cold mark of −17 degrees (February 1899 and January 1912) on the eighteenth, though this figure would be eclipsed in January 1994 (−20 degrees).

The fiercest wintry blast of the month arrived on the afternoon of January 28, 1977, as an arctic front crossed the state accompanied by blizzard conditions. The weather change across the front was dramatic. Shortly before 7:00 P.M., the temperature rose to 44 degrees at Philadelphia just ahead of the front, while readings had already tumbled to −10 degrees at Pittsburgh. The temperature at Scranton/Wilkes-Barre would plunge from 37 to 4 degrees as the cold air blasted through the mountains. Early on January 29, 1977, the temperature had slumped to −25 degrees at Bradford FAA, where the maximum would reach only −6 degrees.

The mean January temperature at Pittsburgh was an icy 11.4 degrees, six degrees lower than that of the previous coldest January (1940) and a spectacular 14.7 degrees below normal. At the opposite end of the state, the average temperature at Philadelphia in January 1977 (20 degrees) edged out January 1857 (22.4 degrees) and February 1934 (22.4 degrees) for the coldest month on record.

February 1979: Second Coldest February

The winter of 1978–79 was severe in the Midwest but not extreme in the East until February 1979, when arctic air eventually found its way into the Northeast. A temperature of −52 degrees at Old Forge, New York, tied the all-time low temperature record in the East, previously recorded at Stillwater Lake, New York, on February 9, 1934.

As the core of the cold weather settled farther east in late January 1979, some northern mountain locations recorded subfreezing temperatures for twenty consecutive days, from January 31 through February 19. The coldest period of February 1979 would commence on the ninth and continue for ten days, when maximum readings at Scranton/Wilkes-Barre remained below 20 degrees.

At Philadelphia daily maximum readings edged above 20 degrees only twice (February 15–16, 1979) during a ten-day mid-February cold snap, and rare subzero mornings occurred on February 10–11 (−1 and −2 degrees), in addition to a 0-degree minimum on the eighteenth.

The lowest temperature in Pennsylvania observed in February 1979 was −34 degrees at Warren and Clermont 4 NW (last reached on February 18, 1979). The lowest monthly mean temperature was 10 degrees at Bradford FAA. Among stations with longstanding weather records, Pittsburgh had its coldest February (18 degrees), and Philadelphia (23 degrees) had its coldest February since 1934 (22.2 degrees). In Pennsylvania, the average temperature in February 1979 was 17.2 degrees (9.7 degrees below normal), which was fractionally higher than that of February 1934.

December 25, 1980: Frigid Christmas

An icy polar air mass descended on the Northeast on Christmas Eve 1980, bringing the lowest December temperature ever recorded in Pennsylvania at Clermont 4 NW, −29 degrees, on Christmas morning 1980. Gusty northwesterly winds buffeted the state on Christmas Eve as temperatures plunged through the teens into the single digits.

Christmas morning brought subzero readings to most of Pennsylvania, except in the extreme southern counties. In the northern highlands, temperatures of −10 to −20 degrees were not uncommon. Philadelphia recorded a minimum of 1 degree, and Bucksville reported −5 degrees in the normally moderate southeast.

Daylight maximums on Christmas Day 1980 were exceedingly low. Boston (−5 degrees) had its coldest daylight in modern times. Northeastern Pennsylvania had the lowest daylight maximums in the state on December 25, 1980. Montrose reached only 0 degrees, Pleasant Mount and Freeland peaked at 1 degree, and East Stroudsburg managed a high of 5 degrees. Pittsburgh recorded a high of 11 degrees on that Christmas after dipping to 0 earlier in the day. Philadelphia endured its coldest Christmas daylight with a high of 9 degrees and a morning low of 1 degree.

January 1982: Two Cold Sundays

A vast polar high-pressure system over Alberta, Canada, on January 9, 1982, carried a central atmospheric pressure of 31.10 inches, indicative of a huge mound of frigid air ready to be unleashed on the Midwest and Northeast. Sunday morning, January 10, was the coldest on record at Chicago (−26 degrees), though, remarkably, this record would be surpassed in January 1985. A heavy burst of lake-effect snowfall of 28 inches fell at Buffalo, New York (25.3 inches in twenty-four hours).

In the Southeast the temperature plunged to −5 degrees at Atlanta on the

Table 5.9. Daylight Maximum Temperatures, January 17, 1982 (in degrees Farenheit)

Binghamton, N.Y.	−7	Atlantic City	1
Scranton/Wilkes-Barre	−2	Allentown/Bethlehem	3
East Stroudsburg	0	New York City	4

eleventh, and the next morning the citrus crop sustained heavy damage in central Florida. A mixture of snow and ice fell along the Gulf coast on January 12, before turning northward along the eastern seaboard on the thirteenth and spreading snow up the coast. Meanwhile, a second surge of frigid air was building up to the northwest.

On January 16, 1982, readings bottomed out at −52 degrees in northern Minnesota, −25 at Chicago, and −26 degrees at Milwaukee (record). The bitter air swung southeastward on January 17, 1982, Cold Sunday II, bringing even lower temperatures than did the previous outbreak. Temperatures plummeted across Pennsylvania, reaching the lowest levels since February 1899 at Pittsburgh and February 1934 at Philadelphia.

The maximum reading at Pittsburgh on January 17 was only −3, which equaled the previous lowest maximum from February 9, 1899. The Pittsburgh minimum of −18 degrees set a new all-time cold mark, which was later tied in 1985, and exceeded in 1994. Daylight highs at DuBois (−8) and Altoona (−9) were historic lows.

Philadelphia shivered through its coldest day on record on January 17, 1982. The daylight maximum was 0 degrees at 2:48 P.M., which is the only known instance of a zero daylight in the Delaware Valley (see Table 5.9). The morning minimum of −7 degrees established a new January record at Philadelphia, which was later tied in 1984.

Another cold morning followed on January 18, 1982, when readings nose-dived to −10 degrees at Wilmington, Delaware, and −7 at Baltimore (January record). Other chilly minimums included −8 degrees at Scranton/Wilkes-Barre, −5 at Washington, D.C. (lowest since February 1934), and −4 at Philadelphia. Temperatures generally remained below freezing in northwestern Pennsylvania from January 8 through 28, 1982 (twenty-one days). In the southeast, the monthly mean temperature at Philadelphia in January 1982 (24.7 degrees) ranks it as the seventh coldest January.

1983–84: Frigid Christmas and a January Polar Blast

Polar air began invading the midsection of the United States in early December 1983, even as temperatures remained comfortably above normal in the East. A low-pressure wave developed along the polar boundary lying across Montana and North Dakota on December 14–15, forcing bitterly cold air southward into the middle of the nation, commencing one of the great cold waves in United States history.

Temperatures dipped below zero at Omaha, Nebraska, at 3:00 A.M. on December 17 and would remain below zero for a record 202 consecutive hours, until 1:00 P.M. on the twenty-sixth. The cold seeped into Pennsylvania by the twentieth, though the core of the cold air stayed over the Midwest until a weak low-pressure wave tracked across the Great Lakes on December 21–22, 1983. More than an inch of mixed precipitation fell on Pennsylvania on the opening days of winter, but, more critically, upper-level winds turned northwesterly in the wake of the system, drawing bitterly cold air into the Northeast a few days before Christmas 1983.

The central barometric pressure beneath a dome of frigid air over the Yukon Territories reached 31.45 inches on December 22 as temperatures plummeted to −52 degrees in Montana (Ludlum 1984, 47–48). On Christmas Eve a vast high-pressure region of dense cold air now stretched from the shores of the Arctic to the Gulf of Mexico.

The high-pressure ridge crested near Miles City, Montana, setting a record high barometric pressure reading of 31.42 inches in the Lower Forty-eight. Polar air penetrated all the way to the western Gulf coast, where Houston, Texas, recorded ninety-one hours of continuous subfreezing temperatures. Morning readings on December 24 bottomed out at −25 degrees at Chicago (O'Hare), recovering to only −11 degrees in the early afternoon for a record low maximum reading.

The arctic air, accompanied by bitter winds, spilled east across western Pennsylvania, dropping temperatures below zero before dawn on Christmas Eve. The mercury at Pittsburgh slipped below zero by 6:00 A.M. on December 24 and did not climb above zero for fifty-one hours, until 9:00 A.M. on the twenty-sixth. (The cold intensity record would be surpassed in January 1994.) The high temperature at Pittsburgh on Christmas Day 1983 was 0 degrees after a record daily low of −12 degrees.

In the eastern part of the state, temperatures plunged through the teens and single digits on Christmas Eve, falling below zero by Christmas morning. Christmas Day 1983 was a zero day at Freeland (el. 1,970 feet), with extremes of −5/−15 degrees. Single-digit maximums were the rule over the remainder of eastern Pennsylvania on Christmas Day, rivaling the frigid readings on Christmas Day 1980: Scranton/Wilkes-Barre, 4 degrees; East Stroudsburg, 6 degrees; Allentown/Bethlehem, 8 degrees; and Philadelphia, 10 degrees.

The Southeast was subjected to snow and freezing rain followed by a damaging freeze on December 24–26 Christmas Day 1983 brought record chills to Atlanta (1 degree), Jacksonville (10 degrees), and Orlando (19 degrees). Another freeze on the twenty-sixth sent readings down to 33 degrees at Miami. A total of 125 weather stations in twenty-four states broke record minimum temperatures on December 25, 1983, and the nation's capital had its coldest Christmas Day (14/3 degrees).

Temperatures moderated after Christmas, but another brutal surge of arctic air infiltrated the country in mid-January 1984. A huge vortex of frigid air over Hudson Bay in eastern Canada funneled arctic air south into the eastern states on January 19–21, bringing all-time record lows at Toledo, Ohio (−20 degrees), and Elkins, West Virginia (−24 degrees) on January 21, 1984.

The morning of January 22 was exceptionally bitter across Pennsylvania. Monthly record low temperatures were broken or tied at Philadelphia (−7 degrees) and Baltimore (−7 degrees). In the northeast temperatures were as low as −18 degrees at East Stroudsburg and −23 at Tobyhanna. An all-time record low temperature of −18 degrees was observed at Dulles Airport, twenty miles west of Washington, D.C, compared with a balmy minimum of 3 degrees across the river from the capital.

A thaw followed the cold wave in January 1984, sending temperatures into the forties and fifties on the twenty-fifth through the twenty-seventh. In contrast to the frigid early winter pattern, February 1984 was one of the mildest on record, ending with a "heat wave" on February 23–24, when readings soared to near 70 degrees.

However, like a recurring literary theme, winter was still not through with Pennsylvania in March 1984. A snowstorm on March 8–9 brought another blast of frigid weather, sending thermometers below zero in many sections of the state on the tenth. March 1984 was the coldest March in Pennsylvania since 1960.

January 20–21, 1985: Great Arctic Outbreak

A warm December 1984 may have given the impression that the winter of 1984–85 would be much milder than the previous one. The warmth was misleading, of course. A large Canadian high-pressure area migrated southward into the north-central United States on January 19, 1985.

The morning of January 20 brought an all-time record low at Chicago of −27 degrees. The coldest weather since February 1899 wiped out two-thirds of the vegetable crops in the Southeast, where temperatures plunged to 5 degrees at Pensacola, 16 at Daytona Beach, 21 at Tampa, and 31 at Miami.

The Arctic Express rolled into Pennsylvania on January 20–21, 1985, with temperatures falling to −10 to −20 degrees and wind chills exceeding −50 degrees. Pittsburgh tied the city's all-time minimum on January 20–21 (−18 degrees) and reported a maximum of 1 degree on the twentieth. Bradford (−2/−17 degrees), to the northwest, experienced a zero day on the twentieth.

Temperatures across northern Pennsylvania generally bottomed out between −10 and −20 degrees on the morning of January 21, 1985. The lowest reading in the state was −29 degrees at Derry on January 21. Farther east, Williamsport dipped to −14 degrees and Tobyhanna reported −20 degrees. Along the coastal plain, Philadelphia and Baltimore both reported −6 degrees, one degree shy of the January 1984 records. Even more impressive, Wilmington, Delaware, established a new monthly mark (−14 degrees) and tied the all-time record low (February 9, 1934).

Maximum/minimum readings were uniformly frigid on January 21, 1985, at State College (3/−17), Scranton/Wilkes-Barre (3/−14), Lebanon (9/−21), and Philadelphia (8/−6 degrees). On that day, a noon reading of 7 degrees at Washington, D.C., forced the presidential inauguration indoors for the first time ever.

In the Southeast, the morning of January 21 brought historic chill. All-time low temperature records were shattered at Knoxville (−24 degrees), Nashville (−17 degrees), and Birmingham (−10 degrees). Near the coast, record lows were reported at Savannah (3 degrees) and Charleston (6 degrees). A record state minimum of −22 degrees was noted at Hogshead Mountain, South Carolina. South Florida suffered through another freeze, posting lows of 16 degrees at Daytona Beach and 31 at Miami.

At Buffalo, the lake-effect snow machine was in full gear in late January 1985, depositing 30 to 42 inches of snow. Up to 5 feet of snow piled up downwind of Lake Ontario as wind chills reached −60 degrees, shutting down the New York State Thruway from Rochester, New York, to the Pennsylvania line.

December 1989: Coldest December

When winter arrived in late November 1989 with a Thanksgiving Day snow-storm along the eastern seaboard, it decided to stay through the Christmas holiday season.

Frequent snow showers and squalls visited the northwestern part of the state in December 1989. Measurable snow fell at Erie every day from December 11 to 23, 1989, with the greatest contribution coming during the four-day period of December 19–22 (26.6 inches), leading to a record snow depth of 39 inches on the twenty-first. A record monthly snow accumulation at Erie of 66.9 inches in December exceeded all previous months. The heaviest monthly tally was 71.3 inches at the Union City Filtration Plant.

Maximum readings at Bradford, to the northwest, never rose past the teens from December 15 to 27, 1989, during the heart of the cold term. Pittsburgh registered subfreezing conditions from December 7 to 28 (twenty-two days). In northeastern Pennsylvania, East Stroudsburg counted a record nineteen consecutive subfreezing days from December 12 to 30. During an eight-day stretch (December 18–25), minimums at East Stroudsburg were zero or lower, while highs from the nineteenth through the twenty-fifth ranged from 15 to 24 degrees.

The core of the cold air gradually spilled eastward. Pittsburgh had its coldest day on December 22, 1989 (7/−12 degrees). On the twenty-third, the mercury dipped to −17 at Bradford 5 SW. The core of the cold air reached eastern Pennsylvania on Christmas Eve, setting numerous daily records as the mercury plunged to −5 at Scranton/Wilkes-Barre, −12 at East Stroudsburg, −20 at Tobyhanna, and −22 at Francis E. Walter Dam in Luzerne County.

December 1989 was the coldest in state history (17.8 degrees) since at least 1888, averaging 12.1 degrees below normal. The persistent chill that month was reflected in record low December mean temperatures at Bradford (12 degrees), East Stroudsburg (17.9 degrees), Scranton/Wilkes-Barre (18.6 degrees), and Erie (21.7 degrees).

January 19–21, 1994: Historic Cold Wave

A heavy snowfall over the Ohio Valley and Middle Atlantic region on January 16–17, 1994, laid the groundwork for the arrival of a gelid air mass that would undergo little modification. On January 18, 1994, St. Cloud, Minnesota, had an icy maximum reading of −17 degrees and a minimum of −34 degrees before bottoming out at −40 degrees early on the nineteenth.

Daytime maximums across Ohio on January 18 were exceptionally cold at Dayton and Findlay (−11 degrees). The frigid air spilled into Pennsylvania on the morning of January 18, when the mercury dipped below zero at about 6:00 A.M. at Pittsburgh. The temperature remained at or below zero at Pittsburgh for a record fifty-two consecutive hours until 10:00 A.M. on the twentieth, exceeding the previous record in December 1983 by one hour. The calendar day of January 19, 1994, was the coldest ever known at Pittsburgh ($-3/-22$ degrees). An all-time record minimum of -18 degrees was observed at Erie.

In the central mountains a low of -18 degrees was reported at State College on January 19, 1994. Farther east, minimums reached -21 at Tobyhanna and an unofficial -25 at Gouldsboro. Scranton/Wilkes-Barre residents venturing outdoors braved the city's coldest daylight (-2 degrees). A private weather station at Canadensis (el. 1,900 feet) recorded a high temperature of -5 degrees.

Weather history was also made in southeastern Pennsylvania on January 19. Harrisburg/Middletown and Coatesville experienced their only zero day (-1 degree) in the twentieth century. Allentown/Bethlehem had its lowest maximum (2 degrees), and record low January maximums were recorded at East Stroudsburg (3 degrees), Philadelphia (6 degrees), and Washington, D.C. (7 degrees).

Historic low temperatures were recorded over the eastern half of Pennsylvania on the morning of January 21, 1994, under clear skies and light winds: Harrisburg/Middletown, -22 degrees; Scranton/Wilkes-Barre, -21 degrees; Williamsport, -20 degrees; and Allentown/Bethlehem, -15 degrees. In northeastern Pennsylvania, readings plunged to -25 degrees at East Stroudsburg (lowest since January 22, 1961), -31 at Tobyhanna (lowest since January 14, 1912, at nearby Pocono Lake), and -31 at Hawley (all-time record).

The wintry pattern in Pennsylvania in January 1994 averaged a frosty 18.3 degrees (6.3 degrees below normal), moving it into fifth place among the coldest Januarys in the state since records became available in 1888.

6 Heat Waves

The weather has been so hot for a week past, as has not been known in the memory of man in this country, excepting the "hot summer" about seven years since.

—*Pennsylvania Gazette,* July 1734, in *Annals of Philadelphia and Pennsylvania, in the Olden Time*

Heat waves in Pennsylvania are common on the average of once or twice each summer. During a typical hot weather spell, the mercury soars past 90 degrees for several days in a row, which may be accompanied by uncomfortable humidity levels. The combination of heat and humidity places considerable stress on the human body. Vigorous activity on a hot, muggy day increases the risk of dehydration, heat exhaustion, and heat stroke.

National Weather Service statistics reveal that in an average year, 175 persons die from heat-related illnesses in the United States. Data provided by the United States Centers for Disease Control and Prevention in Atlanta suggest the national heat mortality toll (an average of 361 deaths per summer) is considerably higher during hot summers.

A series of hot summers in the 1930s brought a record number of 100-degree days in Pennsylvania. The interior United States was scorched by intense heat with scant summer rains through much of the decade. Crops withered in fields that turned to dust, forcing thousands to board up their homes and head west in search of a new livelihood.

The summer of 1936 brought the highest temperatures ever recorded in Pennsylvania (111 degrees), West Virginia (112 degrees), New Jersey (110 degrees), and Maryland (109 degrees). The death toll from heat-related illnesses in the United States that year was estimated at 4,678 and was probably much higher.

The sizzling summer of 1980 was memorable in Dallas, Texas, for a record forty-two consecutive 100-degree days and a mean temperature of 92 degrees. Rain fell on just one day in the area, and at least 1,700 persons succumbed to the heat. The combination of heat and drought in the United States brought economic losses of $20 billion.

The notoriously hot summer in the Midwest in 1995 was blamed for more than seven hundred fatalities in the United States, mostly in the Chicago area. Relentless heat and worsening drought in July 1999 claimed hundreds of lives from Missouri to Pennsylvania, and torrid conditions coupled with intense drought afflicted the southern states in the summer of 2000.

Historic Pennsylvania Heat Waves

A summary of the weather and climate in the *Annals of Philadelphia and Pennsylvania, in the Olden Time* (Watson 1868, 353) recalled the hot summers of 1727 and 1734, which caused instances of heat prostration and even a few deaths from exertion in the fields. A spell of hot weather in July 1789 in Philadelphia caused problems with food preservation: "By 10 o'clock, A.M., the meats in the market putrefy, and the city mayor orders them cast into the river—merchants shut up their stores—thermometer at 96° for several days" (Watson 1868, 361).

Early Philadelphia weather records taken at the Pennsylvania Hospital did not indicate a temperature above 100 degrees in the city between 1825 and 1875, though the *United States Gazette* mentioned that on a sweltering day on July 14, 1841, "The thermometer at noon in the shade stood at 100 degrees." The thermometer at the Philadelphia Naval Yard showed that a 100-degree day occurred on July 1, 1843.

Urban development in the Delaware Valley has contributed to generally warmer summers with more frequent occurrences of 100-degree readings at Philadelphia in recent years. A typical Delaware Valley summer brings more than twenty days of 90-degree heat, compared to summers in the northern and western mountains of Pennsylvania, which often go by without a single 90-degree reading.

1866: Mid-July Heat Wave

A hot July brought a week of 90-degree heat (July 12–18, 1866) in the eastern counties. The weather station at Nazareth reached 97 and 98 degrees on July 15–16 at 2:00 P.M. In the northeast, Blooming Grove and Dyberry both reached 96 degrees at 2:00 P.M. on the sixteenth.

1868: Hottest July in the Nineteenth Century

The mean temperature at Philadelphia in July 1868 (81.4 degrees) was higher than in any month in city weather records until July 1955 and 1993 and was eventually dispatched in July 1994 (82.1 degrees). Nonetheless, the 1868 heat record at Philadelphia is outstanding in light of modern urbanization that has contributed to generally hotter summers in the Delaware Valley in more recent times.

The weather site at Dyberry in the northeastern hills registered a maximum reading of 98 degrees at 2:00 P.M. on July 14, 1868, for the warmest day in station records (1865–1903). In the western part of the state, the observer at New Castle recorded 90 degrees or higher at 2:00 P.M. during hot spells lasting July 1–5 and July 11–21, with extremes of 97 and 98 degrees on the fourteenth and fifteenth. The mean monthly temperature (80.3 degrees) is comparable to Pittsburgh's hottest month (1887).

1876: Hot July

The centennial summer of 1876 was an especially hot one in Pennsylvania. The mercury at Philadelphia soared to 90 degrees or higher on thirteen of the first twenty days of the month.

The first heat spell arrived in Philadelphia on July 2–5, and the highest readings were reported there on July 8–10 (98, 100, and 95 degrees). Pittsburgh observed six straight days in the nineties from July 7 to 13, 1876.

The observer at Egypt, a little northwest of Allentown, recorded 102 degrees at 2:00 P.M. on July 10, during a record fourteen-day heat spell that sent the mercury into the nineties by 2:00 P.M. (July 7 to 20, 1876). Farther north the Stroudsburg *Jeffersonian* noted a reading of 98 degrees on the tenth. In the cooler hills of western Pike County, the weather station at Blooming Grove recorded ten 90-degree days in July 1876.

1881: Great September Heat Wave

A period of intense heat developed toward the end of a very dry summer in Pennsylvania in 1881. Newspaper reports described wells going dry, brown pastures, and endless fields of stunted corn and wheat. Wagons traveling through the rural country stirred up great clouds of dust in a scene that must have resembled something out of the Old West. On July 10, the thermometer in downtown Pittsburgh registered a record maximum reading of 103 degrees.

A protracted heat wave developed on August 26, 1881, when many Pennsylvania cities reached the nineties. In the northeast, the Blooming Grove observer reported 2:00 P.M. readings of 100 and 98 degrees on August 30–31. The hot weather persisted through the first week of September, when Blooming Grove reached 100 and 99 degrees on September 6–7.

The hot, dry weather brought extreme highs of 101, 102, and 100 degrees at Pittsburgh during September 5–7, 1881. In the east, the *Jeffersonian* described the desertlike conditions on the seventh: "From one o'clock to four o'clock, was about as hot a day as Stroudsburg has any record of. The mercury ranged from 100 to 105 degrees. The air rolled along and felt as if it was heated by a furnace."

All-time September record maximum temperatures were observed on September 7, 1881, at Washington, D.C. (104 degrees), and Philadelphia and Boston (102 degrees). Temperatures soared into the nineties again on September 8 in eastern Pennsylvania, ahead of a strong cold front that was accompanied by heavy thunderstorms and welcome rains on the ninth.

The autumn of 1881 (September, October, November) was the warmest on record at Philadelphia, averaging 4.2 degrees above the modern normal and being slightly warmer than the balmy autumns of 1901 (+4.1 degrees) and 1971 (+3.4 degrees).

Three years later, another outstanding September heat wave brought 90-degree weather to parts of southeastern and southwestern Pennsylvania from September 4 to 11, 1884. The 100-degree reading that came the latest in the year in Pittsburgh was recorded on September 10, 1884.

1887: Hottest July at Pittsburgh

A hot, steamy pattern wilted the East and Midwest through much of July 1887. Pittsburgh endured its hottest month on record (80.3 degrees) that month, which edged out July 1878 (79.5 degrees). Philadelphia recorded twenty days of 90-degree heat in July 1887.

The heat peaked during the middle part of the month, when Philadelphia recorded daily extremes of 100/73, 96/77, and 94/78 degrees on July 16–18. In the western part of the state, Pittsburgh reached a maximum of 101 degrees on the seventeenth. The Midwest also broiled on July 17, when temperatures soared to 107 degrees at St. Louis 104 at Rockford, Illinois. Severe thunderstorms rumbled across the Northeast in the evening, causing pockets of wind damage in Pennsylvania, temporarily breaking the heat wave.

Another sizzler on July 18, 1887, brought readings of 106 degrees at Lynchburg, Virginia, 104 at Raleigh, North Carolina, and 103 at Washington, D.C. Severe thunderstorms lashed the Northeast and Middle Atlantic states on a number of days from July 17 to 26, with reports of localized flooding and wind damage almost daily. Temperatures rose to 90 degrees or higher each day from July 25 to 31 at Philadelphia, pushing up the mean monthly temperature to 80.7 degrees.

June/July 1894: Drought Summer

Dry conditions that prevailed across the middle of the country and parts of the East during the middle 1890s were associated with a series of hot summers. Solar energy was not spent evaporating ground moisture, so the air above picked up the extra warmth.

The thermometer at Philadelphia topped 90 degrees from June 22 to 25, 1894, with a high of 97 degrees on the twenty-fourth. Temperatures reached the century mark at Hamburg (102 degrees), Aqueduct (101 degrees), and Lock Haven (101 degrees) in June.

Periods of searing heat returned as the drought summer of 1894 wore on, with very high temperatures across Pennsylvania on July 13 and 19–20. An eight-day heat wave at the close of the month from July 25 to August 1 sent readings back into the nineties in southeastern Pennsylvania. The state temperature extremes in July 1894 were both observed at Lock Haven (102/31 degrees), which is a unique Pennsylvania weather event.

1895: Record May Heat

An outstanding heat wave on May 30–31, 1895, brought a state record May maximum of 102 degrees at Lock Haven (equaled on May 27, 1941, at Marcus Hook). The thermometer soared to 100 degrees at Holidaysburg and Carlisle. May heat records were also established at Williamsport (96 degrees) and Wilkes-Barre (97 degrees) in 1895.

1896: August Heat Wave

A protracted heat wave in early August 1896 brought nearly two weeks of ninety-degree heat to most of Pennsylvania. At Philadelphia the mercury ascended to 90 degrees or higher on ten consecutive days from August 4 to 13, with a maximum of 97 degrees on the eleventh. The highest readings in the state were 101 degrees at both Aqueduct on the ninth and Honesdale on the eleventh.

Scranton observed eight days of 90-degree heat from August 5 to 12, with a peak reading of 95 degrees. The *Stroudsburg Times* reported the summer of 1896 was "the most disagreeable summer since 1876," even when compared to the hot, droughty summers of 1893 and 1894. The *Times* stated, "The daily list of deaths and prostrations is appalling in large cities, and business was almost at a standstill, while humanity gasped and prayed for relief."

July 1898: Hot Holiday

A four-day heat wave that commenced on July 1, 1898, in Pennsylvania culminated in extreme readings across the interior southeastern counties on the third, ranging as high as 107 degrees at Hamburg and 106 at Aqueduct. The nation's capital roasted at 104 degrees on July 3, one of the hottest readings ever known in the city. Wilkes-Barre endured a rare 100-degree reading in the northeast.

1900: Hottest Summer

The summer of 1900 was the hottest on record in Pennsylvania. The mean temperature for the months of June, July, and August 1900 was 72 degrees (3.7 degrees above normal). A string of 90-degree days from July 4 to 7 at Easton kicked off a blistering summer, and another streak of 90-degree heat from July 15 to 22 brought the maximum reading of 97 degrees on the seventeenth.

The highest readings in the state in July 1900 were 104 degrees at Quakertown, 103 at Chambersburg, East Mauch Chunk, Ephrata, and York, and 102 at Carlisle, Huntingdon, Lewisburg, and Lock Haven. Temperatures reached 100 degrees as far north as Wilkes-Barre in July 1900, which stands out as the second hottest July in the state after 1955.

August 1900 was hot, too, featuring an average temperature of 73.9 degrees (4 degrees above normal)—the warmest August since statewide records began in 1888. The highest readings were 103 degrees at Lebanon, 102 at Huntingdon, Lock Haven and York, and 101 at Coatesville and Philadelphia. The warmest period lasted from August 6 to 12, when readings soared to 90 degrees or higher in southeastern Pennsylvania.

1901: Second Consecutive Simmering Summer

The summer of 1901 was the third warmest in Pennsylvania weather records since 1888, following the hot summers of 1900 and 1949.

The second consecutive hot summer at the turn of the century in Pennsylvania commenced with an exceptional heat wave on June 25, 1901, lasting through July 6. Philadelphia recorded twelve consecutive days with temperatures exceeding 90 degrees, eclipsing the previous mark of eleven days (August 16 to 26, 1885). This figure would not be surpassed until August/September 1953.

The thermometer at Philadelphia climbed to 98 degrees on June 30, 1901, and then reached extreme levels of 102, 103, and 98 degrees on July 1–3. To the west, Pittsburgh had its highest minimum reading for any day (82 degrees) on July 1, and afternoon temperatures would approach 100 degrees.

The highest temperatures in Pennsylvania were reported on July 2, 1901. The maximum reading was 107 degrees at York, twenty-five miles southeast of Harrisburg, establishing an all-time record for the city. Other notable high temperatures on that day were 103 degrees at Coatesville and 102 at East Mauch Chunk, Ephrata, Huntingdon, and Lock Haven. Northern and western mountain sections generally reported maximum readings between 93 and 98 degrees on the second.

In the northeast the *Stroudsburg Daily Times* reported a temperature of 99 degrees on June 30, which was topped on July 2 by a reading of 103 degrees. Pocono thermometers in the upper elevations registered 98 degrees at Mount Pocono and

94 at Tobyhanna, comparable or perhaps exceeding the modern records of 95 degrees at Mount Pocono (September 2, 1953, and July 31, 1954) and 94 degrees at Tobyhanna (July 6–7, 1988).

At Easton the record high average temperature in July 1901 (78.4 degrees) was not surpassed until July 1955 (79 degrees) in the area. Bouts of searing heat and humidity in August 1901 at Pittsburgh (78.7 degrees) brought the hottest August ever, locally.

1911: Hot as a Firecracker

The Fourth of July 1911 brought the highest temperatures ever recorded in northern New England. All-time state records were noted at Nashua, New Hampshire (106 degrees), North Bridgton, Maine (105 degrees), and Westboro, Massachusetts (105 degrees).

The top temperature in Pennsylvania was 105 degrees, which occurred at Marion on July 3, 1911, and at Brookville and Selinsgrove on the Fourth of July. The reading at Brookville in the northwest was especially notable, considering the mean elevation (1,400 feet) of the weather station. Readings of 103 degrees were reported at George School, Gettysburg, and Huntingdon in July 1911, but a reading of 103 at Pocono Lake (el. 1,660 feet) should be disregarded, due to questionable maximums in the summer of 1911.

1918: Hottest August Day

An early August heat wave in 1918 brought the highest temperatures ever recorded in August in Pennsylvania up to that time. The heat peaked in western Pennsylvania on August 6, when the mercury soared to all-time record highs of 108 degrees at Claysville in Washington County (August state record) and 107 degrees at Coatesville, Lancaster, and Sadysburyville (Chester County). An exceptional reading of 106 degrees occurred at Clearfield (el. 1,120 feet) in the northwest and at Beaver Dam in the southwest on August 6.

On August 7, the heat peaked in the eastern part of the state, when the temperature at Philadelphia reached an all-time high of 106 degrees, which, added to a minimum of 82 degrees, yielded a record daily mean temperature of 94 degrees! New York City also recorded a record August maximum temperature (104 degrees) on the seventh. Ten Pennsylvania weather stations reached 105 degrees or higher on August 6–7, 1918. Bethlehem (Lehigh University) reached a high of 105 degrees on the seventh, setting a mark that would not be tied until July 3, 1966, at the airport. The coolest maximum reading was 90 degrees at Mount Pocono (el. 1,720) in the northeast.

At Pittsburgh the heat wave lasted from August 4 to 8, 1918, with extremes of 94, 101, 103, 101, and 93 degrees. The maximum of 103 degrees on the sixth established an August heat record and equaled the all-time mark reached on July 10, 1881, and later attained on July 16, 1988. A minimum of 81 degrees on August 6, 1918, is the highest minimum at Pittsburgh in any August, making that day (average of 92 degrees) the city's hottest.

1919: Early Hot Spell

An intense three-day heat wave in early June 1919 brought record-breaking monthly temperatures. In northeastern Pennsylvania, Stroudsburg reached 95, 99, and 97 degrees on June 2–4, 1919. Scranton also hit 99 degrees on June 3, setting an all-time June heat record.

1923: Another June Heat Wave

The heat arrived early in June 1923, sending temperatures into the lower nineties at Allentown from June 2 to 6. A more remarkable extended heat wave developed on June 17, when temperatures rose to near 90 degrees over southeastern Pennsylvania. Allentown registered nine consecutive days of 90-degree heat from June 18 to 26. Peak warmth occurred on June 20–21 (100 and 98 degrees) and 24–25 (98 degrees). Temperatures reached the century mark on June 20, with top readings of 103 degrees at Lancaster, 102 at Mifflintown, and 101 at Catawissa, Reading, and Williamsport. June 1923 ended with a cool spell and frost in the northern mountains on the thirtieth, and a low reading of 32 degrees at West Bingham.

1925: June Swoon

The third memorable early heat wave in seven years gripped Pennsylvania during the first week of June 1925, sending temperatures to the highest levels known for that early in the season at some eastern locations. Most eastern Pennsylvania valley cities recorded seven consecutive days of 90-degree heat from June 1 to 7, 1925 (Table 6.1). All-time June heat records were established at Williamsport (104 degrees) on the fifth and Allentown (100 degrees) on the sixth (equaled in June 1966).

1930: Blistering Summer

The summer of 1930 commenced the first in a series of torrid summers during the great Dust Bowl years that enveloped the American Plains and Midwest. An expansive ridge of high pressure in the upper atmosphere became the persistent theme during the hot, dry summers of the 1930s. Desertlike heat periodically wafted eastward around the northern edge of the Bermuda high, helping to establish many all-time heat records.

The calendar year 1930 was the driest on record in the state of Pennsylvania,

Table 6.1. Maximum Temperatures, June 1–7, 1925 (in degrees Farenheit)

	June						
	1	2	3	4	5	6	7
Williamsport	96	93	94	100	104	100	96
Harrisburg	92	94	95	98	99	99	96
Allentown	91	96	98	98	98	100	98
Philadelphia	92	98	96	98	100	100	98

which undoubtedly contributed to the intense heat because of the lack of sufficient moisture to provide even modest evaporative cooling or heat-breaking thunderstorms.

A pattern of recurring heat developed by the middle of July 1930 and intensified through the latter half of the month, continuing into early August. A hot period in the Keystone State on July 21 brought many 100-degree readings in southeastern Pennsylvania, as well as an all-time maximum of 106 degrees at Washington, D.C. During the hot spell lasting from July 19 to 23, Chambersburg and Lancaster recorded four consecutive 100-degree days with identical readings of 102, 102, 104, and 100 degrees.

York endured two straight weeks of 90-degree weather from July 17 to 30, 1930, before temperatures briefly dipped into the high eighties. The thermometer on Academy Hill in East Stroudsburg soared to 102 degrees on July 21, setting a July heat mark that lasted until 1953. Huntingdon reached 101 degrees on July 26, and 100 degrees on July 28.

A second blast of hot, dry air in early August 1930 enveloped southeastern Pennsylvania. A torrid week at York that lasted from August 2 to 10 brought two hot periods: August 3–5 (102, 104, 103 degrees) and 8–9 (102, 100 degrees).

Generally, the warmest readings in Pennsylvania occurred on August 4, 1930, ranging as high as 106 degrees at Lykens and Mifflintown in the Susquehanna Valley. Farther south the thermometer climbed to 105 degrees at Catawissa and Chambersburg that day, and Altoona established an all-time maximum of 102 degrees (el. 1,615 feet). There was an extreme reading of 108 degrees at Carlisle, but maximum temperatures in July and August 1930 appear to be questionably high upon further inspection. Three consecutive days of 100-degree heat were recorded at Huntingdon (102, 105, and 100 degrees), Selinsgrove (102, 105, 101), and Mauch Chunk (102, 103, 101) on August 3–5.

1931: July Heat Wave

An early heat wave on June 30 and July 1, 1931, sent the mercury soaring to 100 and 102 degrees at Williamsport. The first day of July 1931 brought searing heat to the central counties, with maximums of 105 degrees at Lock Haven and Hyndman and 103 at Clearfield in the northwest.

June 8–9, 1933: Another June Sizzler

Scorching heat brought a state record maximum for June 1933, when the maximum reading at Sharon, in the northwestern corner of the state, topped out at 107 degrees on June 8. The heat peaked in the eastern part of the state on June 9, with maximum readings approaching 100 degrees, setting numerous daily records. The mercury at Scranton and Lancaster rose to 98 degrees, among the warmest readings. An all-time June maximum of 92 degrees was observed at Mount Pocono (el. 1,720 feet) in the northeast (tied in 1952).

Unusually high temperatures persisted through July 1933 in areas where soils were dry. Even the northwest was toasty. Brookville notched a high of 101 degrees on July 24, 1933.

1934: Hot, Dry Summer

The exceptionally dry weather that enveloped the midsection of the nation in the summer of 1934 brought periods of intense heat to Pennsylvania. Temperatures soared past 90 degrees on the first six days of June in the western part of the state at Corry (Erie County) and Franklin (Allegheny County). A record early-season 100-degree reading was observed at Franklin on June 3.

A long heat wave commenced on June 21 in Pennsylvania, when temperatures frequently mounted past 90 degrees over most of the state, except the northern and western mountains. The heat wave peaked in the east on June 29–30, with a maximum reading of 104 degrees at Marcus Hook (June 30), and 103 degrees at Lancaster (June 29) and Mifflin (June 29–30), all establishing June heat records.

Record June heat was noted on June 29, 1934, at Catawissa, Chambersburg, Williamsport, York, and Philadelphia (102 degrees). Harrisburg also joined the century club (100 degrees). In the west, temperatures on June 29 peaked at 96 degrees at Pittsburgh and 100 at Vandergrift. The only Pennsylvania weather site that did not reach 90 degrees in June 1934 was Montrose (el. 1,656 feet) in Susquehanna County.

Simmering conditions prevailed in July 1934 over very dry sections of southern Pennsylvania. Pittsburgh suffered through its sixth hottest July (77.6 degrees) since records began in 1878. In the lower Susquehanna Valley, temperatures consistently hit the nineties at York on the first seven days of the month, and a few locations reached the century mark.

High heat returned on July 14, when maximum temperatures climbed to 90 degrees or higher at York on all but two days from July 14 and 31, 1934. In the south-central part of the state, Huntingdon reached 100 degrees on the twenty-first and highs of 103 and 101 degrees on July 25–26. In the central mountains, State College (el. 1,217 feet) had a rare instance of consecutive 100-degree days on July 25–26, 1934 (100 and 101 degrees). Higher readings at Mifflin appear to be too high relative to surrounding locations to be considered valid.

Fewer bouts of heat occurred in August 1934, though parts of the Midwest continued to sizzle in the midst of a severe drought. The thermometer at Springfield, Illinois, topped out at 108 degrees on August 8–9, 1934 (August record).

1936: Hottest Ever in Pennsylvania

Unrelenting heat gripped the Midwest during the torrid summer of 1936 in the heart of the Dust Bowl era. Fifteen state maximum temperature records from the Midwest to the Middle Atlantic states established in the summer of 1936 still stand to this day.

During the second week of July 1936, sizzling conditions brought all-time July heat records to many parts of Pennsylvania. On July 9–10, a state mark was established at Phoenixville in Chester County, where the mercury topped out at 111 degrees on consecutive days. South of Philadelphia, a high reading of 108 degrees was obtained at Marcus Hook.

A searing heat wave that originated over the High Plains arrived in Pennsylvania on July 7, and over the period of July 8–15, temperatures reached unequaled

Table 6.2. Maximum Temperatures, July 9–11, 1936 (in degrees Farenheit)

| | July | | |
	9	10	11
Williamsport	106	104	101
Bethlehem	104	103	103
York	104	105	101
Harrisburg	103	103	100
Scranton	103	101	99
Philadelphia	103	104	98
Pittsburgh	101	101	94

levels in many Pennsylvania towns and cities. Pittsburgh endured eight consecutive days of 90-degree heat, with temperatures ranging from 91 to an extreme of 102 degrees on the fourteenth.

The desiccating heat peaked in Pennsylvania on July 9–11, 1936, with three days of triple-digit readings in many locations below 1,200 feet (Table 6.2). Many northern Pennsylvania communities established all-time heat marks on July 9, including Lawrenceville (107 degrees), Williamsport (106 degrees), Towanda (104 degrees), and Scranton (103 degrees). Towanda and Lawrenceville weathered a record four straight days of 100-degree heat (July 8–11). The central mountains also experienced extreme heat on July 9, which set all-time records at State College (102 degrees) and Clearfield (103 degrees—tying July 1931).

The heat eased a little in eastern Pennsylvania after the eleventh, but temperatures soared again west of the crest of the Appalachians. Franklin recorded seven consecutive 100-degree days (July 8–14), with maximum readings of 106 degrees on the ninth and fourteenth. A blast of hot, dry air brought all-time maximum readings to Corry (110 degrees) in Erie County and Vandergrift (106 degrees) in Westmoreland County on July 14. The highest official readings on that day at Pittsburgh were 103 degrees at the Federal Building downtown and 102 degrees at the county airport.

Southwesterly winds overcame the usual cooling effect of Lake Erie, and the city of Erie sizzled at 98 degrees on the afternoon of July 14, 1936, setting a long-time record heat mark that lasted until July 1988 (100 degrees).

Along the coast, New York City endured its hottest day in over a century of weather records maintained at Central Park, when the mercury reached 106 degrees in July 1936. In New Jersey, an all-time state heat record was observed at Runyon during the three-day heat wave of July 9–11 (109, 110, and 105 degrees). State heat records were observed at Martinsburg, West Virginia (112 degrees), and Cumberland and Frederick, Maryland (109 degrees), on July 10.

The scorching heat in July and August 1936 was even more extreme in the parched Midwest. Maximum/minimum readings at Springfield, Illinois, on July 14 (108/84 degrees) were among the hottest readings observed during an unprecedented twelve-day stretch of 100-degree heat from July 4 to 15. The hot week accounted for a spectacular mean temperature at Springfield of 86.2 degrees in July 1936 (9 degrees above normal).

Extreme readings in July 1936 of 121 degrees in North Dakota, 112 in Manitoba, and 108 in Ontario, Canada, reflect the northern extent of the hot air bubble. Desertlike heat persisted in the Plains through much of August 1936 and wafted into western Pennsylvania several times: August 1–5, 12–15, and 20–25. Pittsburgh recorded five days in a row in the nineties (August 21–25).

From August 7 to 26, 1936, Wichita, Kansas, suffered through twenty straight days with cloudless skies offering no relief. The weather bureau at Kansas City, Missouri, collected a scant 1.12 inches of rain during the months of June, July, and August that year, while temperatures soared past 100 degrees on a record fifty-three days.

1948: Late-August Heat Wave

Temperatures soared to the highest levels of the summer in 1948 in Pennsylvania during the last week of August. Ninety-degree readings were common across Pennsylvania over a seven-day period from August 24 to 30, 1948.

The highest readings were recorded in the southeastern tip of the state at Marcus Hook on August 26–29 (106, 105, 104, and 101 degrees). York also recorded four consecutive 100-degree days on those dates, though the maximum was only 101 degrees. The northwestern highlands of Pennsylvania escaped the extreme heat, with readings hovering around 90 degrees during the late August heat wave.

In the northeastern highlands, temperatures at the Mount Pocono Airport (el. 1,915 feet) reached an August record high of 93 degrees on the twenty-sixth, while valley readings fifteen miles to the southeast at Stroudsburg topped out at 102 degrees.

July 1949: Hot and Humid

Very dry weather in June 1949 brought the lowest monthly average precipitation (1.92 inches). The dry soils provided little moisture for incoming weather systems to work with, contributing to a persistently hot, dry pattern through the summer of 1949. Selinsgrove received a scant 0.31 inch of rain in June 1949.

July 1949 was relentlessly hot in the Northeast. Temperatures exceeded 90 degrees across much of Pennsylvania on July 2–6, 1949, with the hottest weather generally observed on the Fourth of July. Maximum readings in the southeast on July 4 reached 103 degrees at Columbia and 102 at Wellsville.

Temperatures hit 90 degrees or higher at Philadelphia from July 18 to 22, followed by another round of intense heat statewide that lasted from July 25 to 30. In July 1949, average minimum temperatures were among the highest ever recorded for any month in Pennsylvania, reflecting increasingly humid conditions that contributed to higher nighttime readings.

Hot and muggy weather returned in early August 1949, culminating in another heat wave from August 9 to 11. The summer of 1949 was the hottest on record in Pennsylvania since 1888, though the summer of 1955 would subsequently turn out to be even warmer and more miserable in the Northeast.

1952: Hot, Dry June and July

June 1952 was the second driest June in Pennsylvania weather history (2.23 inches) after 1949, again resulting again in diminished crop yields. Several days of

90-degree weather were observed in the valleys in the middle of June 1949, but that was only a prelude to record-breaking warmth during a three-day heat wave on June 25–27, 1952.

A maximum reading of 104 degrees was reported at Newport on June 26 and 29, 1952. The hottest day around the state was June 26. Carlisle reported a high of 103 degrees, and maximums of 102 were recorded at Lewisburg, Lock Haven, Reading, and Williamsport, establishing June heat records. Williamsport had consecutive 100-degree days (100 and 102 degrees) on June 25–26. In the eastern counties, high readings reached 99 degrees at Allentown/Bethlehem and 98 at Scranton/Wilkes-Barre and Stroudsburg on the twenty-sixth. The downtown Pittsburgh maximum reading of 99 degrees also set a June record.

July 1952 was also a hot month in Pennsylvania. In the northeast, Stroudsburg recorded seventeen days of 90-degree weather, with maximum readings in the upper nineties observed on July 13–15 and 22–23.

1953: Longest Heat Wave

The summer of 1953 featured recurring heat beginning at the summer solstice. Extreme heat was reported in the east on June 20–21. Stroudsburg hit a June record high temperature of 100 degrees on the twenty-first, one of several Pennsylvania cities to reach the century mark.

July 1953 continued the pattern of sweltering weather, with temperatures in the nineties right off the bat. The hottest weather in the summer of 1953 arrived mid-month. During the period of July 15 to 21, temperatures in the east frequently topped 90 degrees. Stroudsburg had highs of 100 degrees on the seventeenth and 103.5 degrees on the eighteenth (July record).

August 1953 was not unusually hot in Pennsylvania until late in the month. A prolonged heat wave began on August 24, which would be the first of a record twelve consecutive 90-degree-plus days at Stroudsburg and New York City (Table 6.3). At Philadelphia the mercury soared to 90 degrees or higher for thirteen consecutive days through September 5, edging out the June/July 1901 mark by one day. (This record would later be broken in July/August 1995.)

Extreme heat was observed across Pennsylvania and New Jersey on September 2, 1953, with highs of 102 degrees at Williamsport (102 degrees), 101 at Scranton/Wilkes-Barre, and 100 at Palmerton (all-time September records). The temperature at Mount Pocono Airport on the high plateau shot up to 95 degrees, equaling the all-time record maximum for the site (July 31, 1954).

A state record for heat in September was achieved at Stroudsburg on September 2, 1953, when the thermometer topped out at 105.5 degrees (all-time station record). The accuracy of the data was corroborated by record highs in northern

Table 6.3. Maximum Temperatures, August 25–September 4, 1953 (in degrees Farenheit)

	August							September			
	25	26	27	28	29	30	31	1	2	3	4
Stroudsburg	94	91	96	99.5	100	100	100.5	99	105.5	104	93
Philadelphia	90	92	93	96	98	98	100	101	101	97	92

New Jersey on the same day, which ranged as high as 106 degrees at Paterson, 105 at Newark (tied in July 1995), and 104 at Belvidere and Layton. The weather station at Layton in northwestern New Jersey recorded three consecutive 100-degree readings on September 1–3 (102, 104, and 103 degrees). The maximum temperature of 102 degrees at New York City on September 2 surpassed the September mark of 101 degrees (September 7, 1881).

1954: Searing July Heat

Extreme drought conditions prevailed across a large portion of the eastern and central United States in the summer of 1954, contributing to extreme heat. Many town and cities in Pennsylvania received less than half of the normal July rainfall. On the whole, July 1954 was the driest seventh month in the Keystone State since July 1909 and 1910.

The first hot blast in the summer of 1954 in Pennsylvania arrived at the beginning of astronomical summer (June 21–22). A brief hot surge on July 13–14 sent readings soaring to 100 degrees in eastern and extreme western Pennsylvania. The highest reading on the fourteenth was 104 degrees at Sharon in the northwest. In the east maximum temperatures included 102 degrees at Stroudsburg and Lebanon and 101 at Harrisburg.

A longer spell of high temperatures developed on July 26 and lasted through August 2. The highest readings were observed on July 31 in the east, with top figures of 104 degrees at Phoenixville and Wellsville. Stroudsburg recorded maximums of above 90 degrees on the final six days of July 1954 (90, 96, 96, 97, 99, and 102 degrees). In the higher elevations, Mount Pocono (el. 1,915 feet) set a July maximum record (95 degrees) on the thirty-first, tying the September 1953 record.

Over in northern New Jersey, Newark and Plainfield sizzled at 104 degrees on July 31, 1954, but even those readings paled in comparison to a high temperature of 115 degrees at St. Louis, Missouri, on the same afternoon.

1955: Hottest July/August

The months of unrelenting heat and humidity that plagued the Northeast in the summer of 1955 rate as the warmest and most uncomfortable two months of the twentieth century. In the stifling summer of 1955, heat records were established at Allentown/Bethlehem in both July (79 degrees) and August (75.8 degrees), though the August mark would fall in 1980.

Stroudsburg recorded 90-degree-plus temperatures on a record twenty-five days in July 1955, adding up to a mean monthly maximum of 92.7 degrees, with a maximum of 102 degrees on the twenty-second. Hot spells occurred on July 3–5 and, most notably, beginning on July 15 and lasting through July 23. The average temperature at Philadelphia in July 1955 was a simmering 81.4 degrees (4.9 degrees above normal), which at the time equaled the warmest month ever in the city (July 1868).

August 1955 opened up with sizzling heat and high humidity. The first day of the month brought a record high of 103 degrees at Stroudsburg during a seven-day stretch of 90-degree-plus heat. The thermometer reached the century mark again on August 5–6 (100, 101 degrees). The hot pattern might have continued, except for the arrival of ex-Hurricanes Connie, on August 12–13, and Diane, on August 18–19, which brought flooding rains and cooler temperatures. Despite a record wet month (23.55 inches), Mount Pocono (el. 1,915 feet) had a record high August mean temperature of 70.7 degrees.

1966: Searing Fourth of July

The summer of 1966 occurred in the midst of a drought that had prevailed in the Northeast since 1962. Hot weather arrived in late June 1966, setting the tempo for a searing summer. The Bermuda high brought southwesterly winds and extreme heat on June 27. The thermometer mounted to 98 degrees at Stroudsburg, and Allentown/Bethlehem and Harrisburg reached 100 degrees to tie local June heat records. New York City hit a record June high of 101 degrees.

The high point of the summer came on the Fourth of July holiday weekend, sending Pennsylvanians flocking to neighborhood pools and mountain resorts. On July 3, 1966, the mercury reached dizzying heights in southeastern Pennsylvania. All-time hot weather marks were established at Harrisburg (107 degrees) and Allentown/Bethlehem and West Chester (105 degrees). Philadelphia notched a July record maximum of 104 degrees, which was two degrees shy of the all-time mark in August 1918.

The highest reading in the state on July 3 was 108 degrees at Bedford in the south-central hills. In the normally cooler northeastern highlands, Scranton/ Wilkes-Barre and Stroudsburg both hit 101 degrees. The weather station at Tobyhanna on the Pocono Plateau hit 94 degrees, coming within a degree of the 1954 Mount Pocono record.

1980: Sweltering Summer

The 1980s marked a return of the hot summer patterns that were recurrent in the 1920s through the 1950s but generally absent in the cooler 1960s (except 1966) and the wet 1970s. Two especially hot days on July 20–21, 1980, pushed the thermometer to the century mark in parts of southeastern Pennsylvania.

The hot, dry pattern continued in August 1980, which would go down as the hottest August at Philadelphia (mean 80 degrees), Allentown/Bethlehem (78.2 degrees), and Scranton/Wilkes-Barre (75.2 degrees). The mean temperature at East Stroudsburg (74.1 degrees) was the warmest August since 1938 (75.2 degrees), and a late-season heat wave there brought a week of 90-degree weather from August 25 to September 2, 1980, culminating with a high of 97 degrees.

The heat in the summer of 1980 was especially extreme in the southern Plains. Wichita Falls, Texas, had a maximum of 117 degrees in July 1980. Brutally hot conditions in the South on July 13, 1980, saw the mercury skyrocket to 108 degrees at Memphis and Macon, Georgia (all-time records). The average temperature at Washington, D.C., was hot enough to establish an August record (82.8 degrees).

1988: Drought Summer

Very dry conditions developed across the East and Midwest during the late spring of 1988. June 1988 brought less than an inch of rain to many places in Pennsylvania. The driest spots in the state were Honesdale (0.29 inch) and Hanover (0.34 inch).

Dry conditions contributed to some unusual temperature extremes in June 1988. On June 11, temperatures dipped as low as 28 degrees at Bradford in the northwest and 29 degrees at the Rodale Research Center in the east-central hills. A few days later, temperatures soared, ranging from 92 to 97 degrees at Philadelphia on June 13–16.

Western Pennsylvania caught the warm southwesterly flow on June 20–22, when temperatures soared to June record highs of 98 degrees at Pittsburgh (tying June 4, 1895) and 101 at Mercersburg on the twenty-second. Philadelphia baked in 90-degree-plus heat from June 19 to 23, 1988 (90, 94, 97, 100, and 95 degrees).

A few days later, history was made in western Pennsylvania when Erie recorded its first and only 100-degree reading on June 25. Pittsburgh reached 98 degrees on the twenty-fifth, tying the June mark set three days earlier.

A cool spell brought temporary relief to Pennsylvania on July 1, with frost in the northwest at Clermont 4 NW (31 degrees) and Kane (32 degrees). In the northeast, Pleasant Mount recorded maximum/minimum readings of 55/42 degrees on July 1, and Scranton/Wilkes-Barre had an unusually chilly summer day (63/42 degrees).

The break was short-lived, because the hottest portion of the summer of 1988 would commence on the Fourth of July and continue unabated through the eighteenth, comparable to the lengthiest heat waves ever known in Pennsylvania.

Harrisburg and Philadelphia reached 90 degrees on fourteen of fifteen days between July 4 and 18, 1988. Harrisburg attained 101 degrees on July 7–8 and 11, peaking at 104 degrees on the sixteenth. Philadelphia sweltered on July 7–8 with readings of 100 degrees, which would later reach 102 degrees on July 16–17.

On July 16, Pittsburgh and Williamsport hit extremes of 103 degrees, marking the thirteenth consecutive day of 90-degree-plus heat at both cities, dating back to the Fourth of the July. (The previous record of eleven straight 90-degree days was set on June 30 to July 10, 1878.) Pittsburgh's extreme reading of 103 degrees on the sixteenth tied the all-time mark observed in July 1881 and August 1918.

Scranton/Wilkes-Barre had a rare 100-degree day (101 degrees) on the sixteenth, and the same hot afternoon Binghamton (98 degrees) set a Broome County Airport (el. 1,590 feet) record, surpassing the previous high of 96 degrees (September 1953). In the normally cooler Poconos, Tobyhanna hit 94 degrees on July 6–7, 1988, and 93 degrees on July 10 and 16, tying the July 1966 record. East Stroudsburg had maximums of 99, 99, and 97 degrees on July 6–8, followed by 100 and 99 degrees on July 10–11 and 99 degrees on the sixteenth.

Excessive heat in the Middle Atlantic region on July 16, 1988, brought record high temperatures of 107 degrees at Martinsburg, West Virginia, and 104 degrees at Charleston, West Virginia, Baltimore, and Washington, D.C.

Heavy thunderstorms during the last two weeks of July 1988 in Pennsylvania cooled the air and brought drought relief, but a hot, dry southwesterly circulation returned in August 1988. During a ten-day stretch from August 8 to 17, Pittsburgh sizzled through nine days with maximums of 90 degrees or higher, capped off by an extreme of 100 degrees on the seventeenth.

Philadelphia recorded forty-nine 90-degree days in 1988, a record that lasted all of three years. Williamsport counted a record forty-two days of 90-degree heat in 1988. In the Midwest, Chicago broiled on a record forty-seven days of 90-degree-plus heat, including seven days with temperatures hitting the century mark.

1991: Hot and Dry

The hot, dry summer of 1991 began in the middle of May and continued with little break for the next three months. As in 1988, a dry spring promoted high evaporation rates that contributed to the very warm conditions in Pennsylvania in May 1991.

Philadelphia recorded its warmest May (70.8 degrees), a substantial 8 degrees above normal, easily besting the previous warmest May in 1880 (69 degrees). The thermometer climbed to 90 degrees or higher on a record twelve days in May 1991, with maximum readings of 97 degrees on May 30–31, establishing a May high mark. At the end of June, the mercury would reach 100 degrees at Philadelphia for the first time.

The primary heat wave in 1991 arrived on July 16 and continued through the twenty-third. Scranton/Wilkes-Barre had eight consecutive 90-degree days, the longest such spell since 1953. East Stroudsburg hit 99 degrees on July 20–21 and 97 on the twenty-third. Williamsport had its two hottest days on July 19–20 with highs of 100 and 101 degrees.

The three summer months of 1991 at Philadelphia averaged 77.9 degrees, eclipsing the hot summers of 1901 and 1988 (77.1 degrees) and 1949 (76.9 degrees). However, the new record would not survive the heat of the summers of 1993, 1994, and 1995.

August 1991 marked the eleventh consecutive month of above-normal temperatures at Scranton/Wilkes-Barre, and more hot weather followed in September 1991. On September 16, maximum values soared to 95 degrees at Philadelphia and 98 degrees at Baltimore. Another scorcher on the seventeenth marked a record fifty-three 90-degree days at Philadelphia.

Williamsport observed forty 90-degree days in 1991, just two days fewer than the 1988 stretch. New York City recorded thirty-nine 90-degree days in the summer of 1991, two more than the previous record in 1944.

1993: Hot and Muggy

After a cool summer in 1992 that was mainly attributed to the eruption of Mount Pinatubo in the Philippines in June 1991, the heat and humidity returned in earnest in the East in the summer of 1993. The summer of 1993 featured a heat wave that lingered from July 4 to 14, accompanied by eleven consecutive 90-degree days at Philadelphia, including three days of simmering 100-degree temperatures on July 8–10. The maximum reading at Philadelphia was 101 degrees on the tenth.

The mean summer temperature (June, July, August) in 1993 at Philadelphia was a sweltering 78.2 degrees, 3.5 degrees above the thirty-year normal and slightly warmer (0.3 degree) than the previous hottest summer (1991). July 1993 (81.4 degrees) tied 1868 and 1955 for the warmest July, though this record would be broken in 1994.

Newark, New Jersey, had its hottest month ever in July 1993 (82.6 degrees), plus the earliest 100-degree day ever recorded at that city on June 19 (102 degrees). This record was beaten by four days in June 1994! Newark ended up with a record forty-nine 90-degree-plus days in 1993, highlighted by a record eight 100-degree days.

1994: Record Heat Again

The pattern of hot summers in the early 1990s continued in 1994, when Pittsburgh endured its longest June heat wave from June 13 to 20. Temperatures soared to 90 degrees or higher, with top readings of 97 degrees on June 16 and 18–19. Columbus, Ohio, set a record with eleven consecutive 90-degree days from June 13 to 22, 1994.

The mercury at Newark soared to 101 degrees on June 15, which was the hottest reading at that city so early in the season. June 1994 was the warmest sixth month ever at Newark (77.8 degrees), beating out June 1993 by a full two degrees. June 1994 was also the hottest on record at Philadelphia (78.1 degrees), Baltimore (77.2 degrees), and Washington, D.C. (79.4 degrees). Washington simmered during seventeen days of 90-degree heat in June 1994, including a record fourteen consecutive days in the nineties.

July 1994 kept up the torrid pace, becoming the warmest month ever at Philadelphia (82.1 degrees) and the second warmest at Newark (81.9 degrees) after 1993. The months of June, July, and August 1994 averaged 78.4 degrees at Philadelphia, breaking the 1993 mark by merely 0.2 degree. The summer of 1994 was the fifth summer of the preceding ten years to rank among the ten warmest in Philadelphia since 1825.

High humidity levels in July 1994 made the summer extraordinarily uncomfortable in Pennsylvania. The mean minimum temperature at East Stroudsburg of 63.4 degrees was the highest since July 1949 (63.9 degrees), attesting to the muggy nature of the month, because humid nights inhibit radiative cooling.

1995: Hot and Dry

The summer of 1995 was notoriously hot and humid in the East, following its predecessors in 1993 and 1994. In the Northeast the summer of 1995 was the most uncomfortable since 1955 in terms of heat and humidity, and it was also the driest summer since 1913, generating only 64 percent of the normal rainfall.

The heat first appeared in the upper Midwest, when International Falls, Minnesota (not generally regarded as a hot spot), hit 99 degrees on June 17–18, 1995, on the road to seven straight record high temperatures. On June 19, the temperature soared to 103 degrees as far north as Alpena, Michigan.

By the middle of July 1995, the Midwest was in the grip of a killer heat wave that caused more than 500 deaths in the Chicago area alone as the heat index (temperature plus humidity) reached a sweltering 125 degrees. The high temperature at Midway Airport of 106 degrees on July 13, set an all-time record the day after Omaha, Nebraska, had reached 109 degrees. Milwaukee, Wisconsin, topped out at 103 degrees, without the benefit of a cooling lake breeze that normally mitigates the afternoon heat.

The origin of the July 1995 heat wave could be found in Kansas as early as July 11 (112 degrees), and it reached Toledo, Ohio (104 degrees), on the fourteenth.

On July 15, the heat index at Philadelphia soared to an unfathomable 129 degrees! Dew points topped 80 degrees in the Ohio Valley eastward to southern Pennsylvania, creating the equivalent of a day in the Amazon jungle.

The highest readings in the Northeast came on July 15, 1995. Williamsport and Philadelphia sizzled at 103 degrees, New York City (Central Park) hit 102 degrees, and Boston, Pittsburgh, and Scranton/Wilkes-Barre all reached 100 degrees. Poughkeepsie, New York, and Danbury, Connecticut, set all-time highs of 106 degrees on that day. Burlington, Vermont, recorded two 100-degree days in 1995 (June 19 and July 14), doubling the previous record. July 1995 averaged 74.6 degrees at Burlington, tying July 1975 for the second warmest seventh month.

A lengthy spell of 90-degree heat in eastern Pennsylvania lasted from July 25 to August 4, 1995. The mercury climbed to 90 degrees or higher at East Stroudsburg thirteen times in August 1995 (August record). Philadelphia endured a record seventeen consecutive days with 90-degree-plus temperatures from July 20 to August 5, 1995. The total of twenty-one 90-degree days in July 1995 set a local mark.

The mean monthly temperature at Philadelphia in July 1995 (81.5 degrees) averaged 4.8 degrees above normal, qualifying it as the second warmest July there after 1994. August 1995 was the second warmest in Philadelphia (79.9 degrees), with a departure of +4.4 degrees (0.1 degree below the August 1980 record).

The months of July/August 1995 were the warmest consecutive months (mean 80.7 degrees) ever measured at Philadelphia, breaking a summer (June, July, and August) heat record for the third straight year with an average temperature of 78.6 degrees. In all, the temperature climbed to 90 degrees or higher on forty-five days at Philadelphia in 1995.

Pittsburgh suffered through seven straight days of 90-degree heat from July 28 to August 3, and another eight in a row from August 13 to 20, culminating in the hottest August (77.7 degrees) in Pittsburgh records. August 1995 was also the hottest on record at Binghamton (70.9 degrees). Baltimore had its hottest July (81.5 degrees) and August (80.1 degrees), bolstered by a record twenty-five straight days of 90-degree heat (July 12–August 5), which added up to the city's warmest summer (78.8 degrees), including June 1995.

The dryness of August 1995, the driest August on record in the city, was reflected that month's rainfall at New York City of 0.18 inch. Washington, D.C., went without measurable rain for thirty-three days beginning on August 7, eclipsing the record of thirty-two consecutive days (September 30–October 31, 1963). In the Midwest, the summer of 1995 was the second hottest at Chicago (76.3 degrees), a mere 0.1 degree cooler than the record warm summer of 1955, when readings were taken at Midway Airport, generally a warmer location than the present site at O'Hare Airport.

July 1999: Searing Heat and Drought

The drought of 1998–99 certainly contributed to the brutal heat that developed in early July 1999 and continued into early August. High evaporation rates and parched soils allowed the lower atmosphere to heat up day after day in July and August 1999, particularly in eastern Pennsylvania.

The differences in average temperatures in July 1999 between western and eastern Pennsylvania were dramatic, reflecting local drought conditions. In the southeast, the weather station at Philadelphia's Franklin Institute recorded the highest mean temperature (84.1 degree) on record in the state, exceeding the July 1955 record (82.6 degrees) set at Philadelphia's Drexel Institute and Point Breeze sites.

In Harrisburg/Middletown July 1999 (81.9 degrees) went down as the hottest month ever recorded in the capital city. In the northeast at East Stroudsburg, that month (76.5 degrees) ranks second only to July 1955 (77.9 degrees). At Allentown/Bethlehem, the misery of July 1999 included the driest (0.33 inch of rain) and third warmest (78 degrees) July on record. The only warmer months in the Lehigh Valley were July 1955 (79 degrees), July 1901 (78.4 degrees/Easton), and July 1949 and August 1980 (78.2 degrees). In contrast, the mean temperature at Pittsburgh in July 1999 was 76 degrees, merely tied for the twentieth warmest July!

Extreme heat developed across much of Pennsylvania in time for the Fourth of July. The first major heat wave lasted from July 3 to 7, 1999. The maximum reading of 104 degrees at the Franklin Institute in downtown Philadelphia occurred on the fifth. The weather station at Harrisburg/Middletown recorded three consecutive 100-degree days on July 4–6 (101, 102, and 102 degrees). On July 5, the mercury at East Stroudsburg reached 100 degrees for the first time since July 10, 1988. Allentown/Bethlehem also reached the century mark (July 6, 1999).

The next heat wave arrived on July 15–20, sending the thermometer soaring to 100 degrees or higher at Harrisburg/Middletown on the sixteenth through the eighteenth (100, 101, and 100 degrees). The hottest temperature of the month was measured at Grateford (106 degrees) in the southeast on July 18. During the last week of July 1999, Governor Thomas Ridge had declared a drought emergency in all but twelve northwestern Pennsylvania counties.

The mercury at East Stroudsburg reached 90 degrees or higher on twenty-two days in July 1999, a hot streak that is surpassed only by that of July 1955 (twenty-five days). With a mean temperature of 76.5 degrees, July 1999 edged out July 1949 (76.4 degrees) to move into second place after July 1955 (77.9 degrees) for hottest month. A protracted heat wave in tinder-dry eastern Pennsylvania commenced on July 23 and lasted into August. The thermometer at East Stroudsburg reached 90 degrees or higher on eleven consecutive days through August 2, a stretch nearly eclipsing the record of twelve days set in August/September 1953.

Philadelphia endured twelve consecutive 90-degree days from July 23 to August 3, 1999. By contrast, on the "air-conditioned" high Allegheny Plateau in northwestern Pennsylvania, Bradford (el. 2,117 feet) did not touch 90 degrees in July 1999 until the last day of the month.

Early Warm Spells

The earliest 90-degree weather in Pennsylvania was observed at Hanover (90 degrees) and Everett (93 degrees) on March 23, 1907. The warmest March in Pennsylvania, 1945, included remarkably warm weather on March 25–26 in the west, and then in the east on March 28–29, with a top reading of 91 degrees at Marcus Hook. A five-day warm spell on March 27–31, 1998, brought a state record–tying high of 91 degrees on March 30 at Octoraro Lake in the southeast.

Record April warmth in 1915 included summerlike heat on April 19–20 and April 24–27. A top temperature of 98 degrees was observed at Bloserville, Cumberland County, on the twenty-fifth, and at Punxsutawney, Jefferson County, on the twenty-sixth.

A hot Easter weekend in 1976 tied the April 1915 state heat records, with a maximum reading of 98 degrees on Easter Sunday, April 18, at Norristown and Port Clinton. Temperatures reached the nineties in the Pennsylvania valleys on April 17–19, setting records at East Stroudsburg (94 degrees) and State College (94 degrees) on April 18. Another famous hot Easter weekend, April 17–18, 1896, brought highs of 91 degrees at Stroudsburg and Philadelphia and 90 at Pittsburgh. The *Stroudsburg Times* stated that April 18, 1896, was "the hottest [April] day in seventy-two years [since 1824]."

Late Warm Spells

An early autumn blast of hot, dry air in September 1895 sent temperatures into the lower nineties for five straight days at Pittsburgh (September 18–22). Another five-day heat wave in a dry autumn lasted from September 10–14, 1931, with extreme warmth at Stroudsburg (97 degrees) and Williamsport (100 degrees) on the eleventh, the warmest readings ever recorded so late in the season at both locations. Philadelphia experienced five days of 90-degree heat September 22–26, 1970, with a maximum of 95 degrees.

An early October heat spell in 1941 pushed temperatures to 100 degrees at Phoenixville on the fifth, setting an all-time state record for the month. Other hot spots in southeastern Pennsylvania on October 5, 1941, included Ardmore (98 degrees), Harrisburg (97 degrees), and Lancaster (95 degrees). York had three consecutive 90-degree days on October 5–7 (97, 94, and 96 degrees), while the western half of the state had cooled down by the seventh. The spring and summer of 1941 also had been unusually warm, featuring record heat waves in mid-April, late May, and from July 23 to August 2, when a peak reading of 104 degrees was observed at Marcus Hook (July 28, 1941).

November 1950 opened with two days of 80-degree weather in most of Pennsylvania, establishing all-time marks in practically every Pennsylvania community. The highest reading was 87 degrees at Marcus Hook. Even the northwestern highlands did not escape the unusual autumn warmth. Highs of 85 at Warren and 82 at Erie set November marks. In the northeast, Mount Pocono enjoyed a balmy 77-degree day.

Winter Warm Spells

A Lebanon correspondent in *Hazard's Register of Pennsylvania* (January 16, 1830) recalled two pleasant Christmases in 1824 and 1829 (66 degrees). Christmas 1964 was the warmest holiday in modern times, featuring a high of 68 degrees at Philadelphia, eclipsing the previous warmest December 25 in 1889 (66 degrees). The warmest location in the state on Christmas Day 1964 was Newell (70 degrees). The mercury hit 70 degrees again on Christmas Day in 1982 at Uniontown and Waynesburg in the southwest.

The warmest December day in Pennsylvania weather history occurred on December 3, 1982, which brought a summerlike reading of 82 degrees at Washington in the southwest. Other warm spots on December 3, 1982, were Uniontown (79 degrees), Erie (75 degrees), and Pittsburgh (74 degrees). A spectacular year-end warm spell brought the latest 70-degree day at Pittsburgh (71 degrees) on December 28, 1984. The next day, temperatures soared in the east to 75 at Harrisburg and 72 at Philadelphia and Allentown/Bethlehem.

The greatest December heat wave in Pennsylvania occurred in 1998, with a maximum of 78 degrees in Adams County. Temperatures first hit record-breaking levels on December 4 at Philadelphia (73 degrees) and East Stroudsburg (71 degrees) and tied records at Allentown/Bethlehem (72 degrees) and Scranton/Wilkes-Barre (69 degrees). Harrisburg/Middletown had three consecutive 70-degree days starting with December 3 (72, 74, and 73 degrees).

On December 7, 1998, Harrisburg/Middletown (75 degrees), Philadelphia (73 degrees), and Scranton/Wilkes-Barre (69 degrees) tied records set days earlier, and Williamsport (69 degrees) established a new December mark on both the sixth and seventh.

The traditional January thaw is actually statistically reproducible around January 22–26, suggesting a seasonal exhaustion of arctic air masses that is normally temporary. On January 12, 1890, the thermometer hit 77 degrees in Coatesville during a record warm winter in the state. Two very warm days on January 22–23, 1906, featured record January highs of 85 degrees at Freeport, 83 at Derry, 79 at Irwin, 78 at Uniontown, and 75 at Pittsburgh.

Another surprisingly warm day on January 29, 1914, brought readings of 81 degrees at Irwin and 79 at Uniontown. A warm spell in January 1950 tied a record at Pittsburgh (75 degrees) on the twenty-fifth, established a monthly mark at Johnstown (80 degrees), and tied the January record at Uniontown (79 degrees). The heat moved eastward the next afternoon, with highs of 78 at York, 77 at Reading, 72 at Allentown/Bethlehem, and 69 at Mount Pocono on January 26, 1950, during a nearly snowless month in parts of the state.

Two historic warm February days occurred in the early 1930s. On February 25, 1930, temperatures soared to 80 degrees at Quakertown, 79 at Philadelphia, 74 at Stroudsburg, and 70 at Mount Pocono (all-time marks). An even warmer day occurred in the south-central part of the state on February 11, 1932, which brought a state record high for February of 83 degrees at Hyndman in Bedford County.

7 Thunderstorms and Damaging Windstorms

When it thunders, the mountain men are bowling.

—Old weather saying (New York origin)

There is a sense of excitement and urgency when a thunderstorm rumbles off in the distance, offering up the prospect of relief after a hot, muggy summer day. We eagerly anticipate a blast of rain-cooled air, heralding the arrival of the storm. In time, a brief downpour cleanses the air and replenishes soil moisture, rejuvenating wilted flowers and dry crops before moving on.

At any given hour, there are approximately 1,800 thunderstorms in progress, which amounts to around 40,000 storms occurring around the world every day. Lightning strikes the earth an average of 100 times every second. In the equatorial rain forests of South America and Africa, an afternoon thunderstorm is practically a daily occurrence. In the United States, central Florida experiences about a hundred days with thunderstorms in a year.

The typical life cycle of an individual thunderstorm lasts about an hour. Rising currents of warm, moist air cool by expansion, condensing into tiny water droplets that aggregate to form fluffy cumulus clouds. Billowy clouds grow vertically under favorable conditions, and soon water droplets become heavy enough to overcome gravity and fall as rain.

A thunderstorm goes through the phases of growth, maturity, and decay. An individual thunderstorm dissipates when a large mass of rain-cooled air finally collapses toward the ground, effectively choking off the updraft that fueled the cell. Sometimes a cooling downdraft will lift warm, moist air nearby, creating new updrafts and promoting the growth of new storms at the expense of dying cells.

Pennsylvania has an average of thirty to forty thunderstorm days annually. The greatest frequency of thunderstorms is in the western part of the state. The fewest number of storms is reported in the upper Delaware Valley in the northeastern corner of Pennsylvania, where the air is little cooler and more stable in the summertime. The western arm of the Bermuda high in some seasons is strong enough to deflect moisture to the north and west during a droughty summer, limiting the number of thunderstorms in the eastern counties.

Solar heating plays a significant role in the development of thunderstorms on humid summer days. The ground readily absorbs solar heat and then transfers warmth to the air, which becomes buoyant relative to the surroundings. On sunny days, the tops of the ridges absorb more direct solar energy, which can spark isolated storms over the mountaintops when the humidity is high and the atmosphere is somewhat unstable.

Thunderstorm Formation

The key components that favor the formation of thunderstorms are warmth, moisture, and atmospheric instability. Thermals will continue to rise as long as the air inside an invisible air packet is warmer than the environment. Strong heating, a weather boundary, or an upper-level disturbance can propel invisible air parcels to high, chilly altitudes. If the atmosphere is unstable, rising air parcels cool and become saturated at some level, which may result in the formation of millions of microscopic cloud droplets.

Atmospheric *stability* refers to the tendency of an air parcel or perhaps a layer of air to either remain in its present position (stable) or become buoyant (unstable). Rising air packets cool by expansion because there is less pressure on the outside pushing inward. An intrusion of dry, chilly air around 10,000 feet cools the upper portion of an unstable layer at a more rapid rate than it cools the lower layers. Differential cooling through the lower atmosphere favors strong updrafts and downdrafts often associated with severe storms.

Classification of Thunderstorms

Thunderstorms are classified by the nature of the conditions under which they form: *Air-mass* thunderstorms may develop as isolated or multicell storms that frequently organize in bands or clusters after intercepting a plume of Gulf moisture. Multicell storms are usually preceded a *gust front* that may take the form of a broad *shelf cloud* spectacularly set off against a pale yellow or milky summer sky. At times a gust front will rotate horizontally (*roll cloud*) and can be mistakenly identified as an incipient tornado by an untrained spotter.

Frontal thunderstorms are created by the forced lifting of moist air along a boundary separating air masses of different temperatures and moisture properties. A squall line of gusty thunderstorms typically forms in the late spring and summer during the heat of the day, usually when a cold front undercuts a mass of warm, muggy air that has been subjected to hours of insolation.

Elevated thunderstorms typically develop along a warm front that marks the boundary between a surge of warm, moist air and a stubborn layer of cold air. The temperature difference between warm air forced to rise over chilly air hugging the surface and a pocket of very cold air around 15,000 feet overhead may result in the formation of thunderstorms embedded in a broad rain shield along a slow-moving thermal boundary.

Orographic storms are the product of forced ascent of moist air over higher elevations, resulting in further cooling and condensation. In addition, ridge tops receive more direct solar energy on clear days. Uneven heating of mountainous terrain promotes updrafts that quickly encounter a cooler environment in the higher elevations, leading to the growth of isolated thunderstorms. Storms forming over the Pennsylvania ridges far away from organized weather systems tend to remain nearly stationary or simply drift along in the weak upper-air flow, until the loss of daytime heating causes the storm to fall apart and die.

Lightning and Thunder

Lightning strikes the surface in the United States about 25 million times annually. In an average year, lightning strikes kill seventy-three people, more than tornadoes (sixty-eight) or hurricanes (sixteen). States reporting the highest number of lightning deaths over the past thirty years are Florida, Texas, North Carolina, and New York.

Lightning also ignites about 10,000 forest fires around the nation each year, resulting in hundreds of millions of dollars of damage. Dry thunderstorms pose a serious fire danger in the western United States, because rain evaporates in dry air before reaching the ground. Lightning strikes ignite thousands of wildfires during hot, dry summers.

Most lightning casualties occur on golf courses and athletic fields, at outdoor recreational events, and in parks and campgrounds. In Pennsylvania, lightning struck tent poles at the Crawford County Fairgrounds on August 24, 1968, killing two people and injuring seventy-two others. On September 18, 1984, lightning struck a soccer field in Chester County, killing one person and injuring twenty-six others on the playing field.

Thunderstorm Electrification

A single bolt of lightning is only about as wide as a pencil, but the temperature in the core of heated channel of air may reach 54,000 degrees Fahrenheit—about five times higher than the temperature of the sun's surface.

Electrical storms most commonly occur during the late-afternoon hours on hot, steamy summer days, when thunderheads soar into the cold upper regions of the atmosphere, resulting in more contact between ice crystals and water droplets. A growing cumulus cloud becomes electrified in complex interactions involving water droplets, ice crystals, and hailstones.

The electrification of a thunderstorm is not completely understood. According to one theory, the process begins when droplets interact with hailstones; water droplets freeze on contact, which gives off some heat. The warmer hailstones develop a negative charge as they fall toward the base of the cloud. At the mid-cloud level (15,000 feet), where temperatures are slightly above zero, *graupel* (soft hail) acquires a positive charge from coming in contact with smaller ice crystals.

A strong updraft carries positively charged ice crystals to the upper regions of the storm. Meanwhile, negative charges collecting near the base of the cloud induce a positive charge near the ground, which follows the storm like a shadow. Lightning occurs when the difference in electric charges is great enough to break down air resistance, initiating a downward surge of electrons.

Cloud-to-ground lightning begins as a barely visible *stepped leader,* traveling at a speed of 200,000 miles per hour. Electrons flow from the middle of a thunderstorm downward in discrete steps. As the leader nears the ground, the potential gradient increases, causing an upward-moving streamer to move along protruding objects about to be struck by lightning, effectively short-circuiting the storm.

Scientists have recently discovered that electrons sometimes flow upward from the ground to create a pathway for lightning. A stepped leader actually develops along a tall building or tower before branching out in an upside-down manner. Downward-moving electrons eventually meet up with upward-moving positive charges. When the flow of electrons unites in a single channel, a series of discharges, or sparks, constitutes a flash called *forked lightning.*

Electrons flow freely from the cloud to the ground and back, creating a luminous *return stroke* that follows the path of the stepped leader at a speed of about 60,000 miles per second. One or several *dart leaders* may follow along the essentially same channel in a fraction of a second. This process may be repeated, resulting in a series of return strokes propagating upward in less than a second.

A particularly dangerous form of cloud-to-ground lightning is called a *positive flash.* Positive lightning is often referred to as "a bolt from the blue" because an observer may be shocked by an unexpected lightning strike from an approaching storm. A positive stroke usually occurs near the front of a storm, when a bolt of lightning is thrown off the top of a thunderhead that has been tilted by strong upper-level winds. Positive charges at the front of a storm are lowered by the initial strokes, making a connection with the negatively charged ground up to ten miles ahead of the storm possible.

Most lightning (80 percent) occurs within a storm cloud. *Cloud-to-ground lightning* is the most spectacular and also the most dangerous form of lightning. *Sheet lightning* occurs with in-cloud or cloud-to-cloud discharges between neighboring storms, appearing to an observer as if a cloud is being illuminated by a fluorescent light. Colorful lightning has been observed as high as thirty miles above the top of a thunderstorm and goes by various quaint names such as *blue jets, red sprites, elves,* and *trolls.*

A vivid description of *ball lightning,* an uncommon and largely unexplained phenomenon, was included in the April 1947 issue of *Climatological Data:* "Electrical phenomena of a peculiar nature occurred in Buchanon Valley, near Cashtown, in Adams County" on April 2, 1947. Local observers reported that "balls of fire floated inside and outside of houses. A witness by the name of W. E. Cole heard what sounded like a "pistol shot" around 10:15 P.M. Cole then observed "a red ball of fire more than a foot in diameter." Racing to the basement to turn off the electricity, he heard "another shot-like sound, and more glowing balls of fire appeared." Outside, tree trunks appeared to be "dynamited" and the ground was "almost white with fragments."

Severe storms struck Pennsylvania again on April 4–5, 1947, accompanied by heavy downpours that caused damaging flash floods in the northeast at Towanda, Wilkes-Barre, and in the Lackawanna Valley, claiming the life of a fourteen-year-old boy in Meadville and wrecking thirty-four bridges. Storm damage was put at nearly $1 million. Very windy conditions prevailed on Easter Sunday (April 6), with gusts as high as 80 miles per hour at Pittsburgh damaging "utility poles, trees, porches, roofs and windows."

Another dramatic lightning strike occurred in the middle of winter at Eynon, near Scranton, at 2:30 P.M. on January 13, 1993. The *Storm Data* report stated that lightning struck the backyard of a home, "breaking an underground water main then traveling through the cellar and out the front of the house. Chunks of sod were blown all over the place with some on the house roof 80 feet away. The foundation of the house and garage were damaged and a wall was blown off the garage. The electric meter was found 100 feet from the house." A five-year-old boy in a nearby garage suffered minor burns.

Thunder

The discharge of electricity causes the rapid expansion of the air, which promptly explodes as sound waves resonating as thunder. Sound waves travel at a much slower speed (0.2 miles per second) than light waves (186,000 miles per second), which is why we usually don't hear thunder until a few seconds have passed after a close lightning flash. In the mountains, "rolling" thunder reverberates for as long as twenty seconds, echoing between the ridges and valleys.

Severe Thunderstorms

Much has been learned in recent years about the nature of cloud-to-ground lightning from a nationwide network of lightning-detection sensors. A severe thunderstorm will typically deliver several thousand strikes over the course of a few hours.

The frequency of lightning discharges has been linked to the severity of a thunderstorm. A great number of in-cloud and cloud-to-ground strikes is an indication of an intensifying storm. A thunderstorm system over southeastern Ohio and West Virginia averaged about 11,000 cloud-to-ground lightning strikes per hour during the evening of August 9, 2000, which amounted to nearly 200 strikes each minute.

A severe thunderstorm *watch* is issued by the Storm Prediction Center (SPC) in Norman, Oklahoma, when the potential exists for the formation of powerful thunderstorms over a period of about six hours. A watch area generally covers 25,000 to 50,000 square miles. A severe thunderstorm *warning* suggests that a dangerous storm is in progress, packing winds in excess of 58 miles per hour and/or hail three-quarters of an inch in diameter or larger.

Thunderstorm Systems and Straight-Line Winds

Clusters of thunderstorms may organize into a self-sustaining *mesocale convective system* (MCS) propagating along a moisture convergence boundary. A larger *mesocale convective complex* (MCC) usually feeds off a persistent low-level jet stream that transports warm, moist Gulf air northward. The merger of colliding downdrafts, or boundaries of rain-cooled air flowing out from individual cells, helps sustain the growth of more storms.

One of the greatest dangers of a thunderstorm complex or an evolving squall line is the threat of damaging winds. Thunderstorms normally bring a cooling downdraft that may briefly gust past 30 miles per hour. However, a layer of dry air around 10,000 feet and a strong mid-level wind field may combine to mix powerful winds to the surface.

Rain evaporating into dry air causes a surge of cold air to blast out of the front end of a thunderstorm at speeds occasionally in excess of 50 miles per hour. Rain-cooled air slamming into the ground may splatter with a force that sometimes topples trees, peels the roof or pieces of siding off buildings, and even overturns small structures.

Mature thunderstorms have strong updrafts and downdrafts. A *downburst* is an intense downdraft that can cause localized wind damage, typically in a starburst pattern when viewed from a point overhead. If the downburst is less than 2.5 miles wide, it is classified as a *microburst.* Microbursts are usually associated with tall thunderstorms that entrain dry air in middle levels (around 10,000 feet). A *wet microburst* occurs when a big, soggy thunderstorm collapses in a swirl of rain and wind.

Severe thunderstorms without a history of damaging winds may suddenly intensify, or "pulse," when two cells merge into one large storm or when a narrow line of storms intersects another storm boundary. In a few instances, downburst damage may extend a width of several miles over a distance of five to ten miles. Wind shear presents a major hazard to aviation, because shifting winds within a few feet of the ground give an airplane taking off or landing in the vicinity a sudden unexpected lift, causing the pilot to compensate by reducing power. Moments later, sinking air creates a tail wind that causes an aircraft to lose aerodynamic lift, triggering a rate of descent that might not be recoverable.

On June 24, 1975, wind shear was blamed for causing Eastern Airlines Flight 66 from New Orleans to crash as it approached the runway at Kennedy International Airport, killing all 112 people on board. A wind-shear disaster in July 1982 at New Orleans took the lives of all 145 passengers and crew, as well as 8 people in their homes. A U.S. Air flight hit the ground under wind-shear conditions in July 1994 at Charlotte, North Carolina, killing 37 passengers.

When the mid-level winds are quite strong, momentum is transferred downward as rain-chilled air hits the ground with great force. Intense downbursts may attain velocities in excess of 100 miles per hour, which approximates the speed of a weak tornado. During a thunderstorm that passed over the Allentown/Bethlehem/Easton Airport on June 15, 1964, the weather bureau anemometer caught a one-minute average wind speed (fastest mile) of 81 miles per hour and a peak gust of 109 miles per hour—both state records.

A powerful system of storms with a path length of at least 280 miles that lasts more than twelve hours is called a *derecho.* To be classified as a derecho, the damage pattern must show an orderly progression with no more than three hours' time elapsing between pockets of wind damage, and there must be at least three reports of wind gusts of at least 74 miles per hour at a minimum of 45 miles apart.

During the summertime, a derecho often forms over the forests of northern Minnesota, Wisconsin, and Michigan, picking up a considerable moisture from the heavy vegetation evaporated into the air. A derecho can travel at speeds reaching 50 miles per hour across the Great Lakes and Ohio Valley before crossing into Pennsylvania. Pockets of microburst damage with embedded small tornadoes are a common occurrence in the summertime.

Hail

The presence of hail in a thunderstorm indicates considerable vertical development associated with powerful updrafts. Hail reflects more microwave radiation toward the antenna and usually appears as a bright area on a weather radar screen.

Hail damage in the United States averages $1.5 billion annually. Hailstorms occur most frequently in the High Plains of northeastern Colorado and southeastern Wyoming, where the elevated terrain naturally boosts the height of thunderstorms into the cold upper atmosphere. One of the worst hailstorms struck Denver, Colorado, on July 11, 1990, causing forty-seven injuries and $625 million of damage. Over a period of fifteen minutes, hailstones as large as softballs (diameter of 4.5 inches) bombarded the metro area.

A severe hailstorm blasted the Dallas/Fort Worth area on May 5, 1995. Fort Worth was pounded by hail 4 inches in diameter, shattering car windows and causing considerable property damage. In the Dallas area, the same storm brought torrential rains and flash floods that claimed sixteen lives and resulted in $2 billion of damage.

Large hail is associated with severe thunderstorms fed by powerful updrafts that suspend water droplets and ice crystals in the cold upper atmosphere long enough to form larger chunks of ice. Supercooled droplets freeze on contact with ice crystals and other particles to form embryonic hailstones. Eventually, the weight of gravity pulls hailstones toward the ground at speeds that can approach 100 miles per hour.

Hailstones sometimes accumulate on the ground to a depth of several inches, resembling a wintertime snowfall except that temperatures may have been near 90 degrees before the storm arrived. A pool of unseasonably chilly air above 15,000 feet in the spring or fall is often responsible for small hail (less than 0.75 inch in diameter).

Occasionally, large hail causes property damage in Pennsylvania. A violent hailstorm struck Carlisle on August 9, 1915, breaking thousands of panes of glass during a single hour with hailstones measuring as large as 1.5 inches in diameter. On the afternoon of July 21, 1929, a severe thunderstorm at Johnstown unloaded a barrage of hailstones that broke more than two thousand windows and piled up in drifts as deep as two to four feet (*Climatological Data—Pennsylvania Section*).

Historic Severe Thunderstorms

July 5, 1841: York County Hailstorm

The *York Gazette* of July 13, 1841, carried a story of an "extraordinary storm of wind, hail & rain" that swept through York and Cumberland Counties around 3:00 P.M. on July 5. The storm traveled south, hitting Dillsburg (York County) before moving on toward York. The story noted that "nearly all the panes of glass in the village of Dillsburg were broken." There was a considerable hailstreak: "The hail was found in the hollow—to the depth of two feet," still evident the following morning.

The path of wind and hail damage averaged one and a half to five miles wide northeast of York, suggesting a *macroburst,* or wide downburst. The storm "uprooted trees, prostrated fences, and unroofed numerous barns," according to the press account. Dickinson and South Middleton Townships in Cumberland County bore the brunt of the damage, where "the grain on numerous farms was utterly destroyed."

Spring/Summer of 1842: Severe Storms Lash

A severe thunderstorm lashed the country north of Lebanon on May 29, 1842, according to an item in the *United States Gazette:* "A storm of unusual violence passed over a section of country . . . prostrating trees and fences, and doing other damage." The storm dropped large hailstones on Lebanon.

In a *History and Geography of Bradford County, Pennsylvania,* Heverling (1926, 570) described "a tornado three miles wide" on June 26, 1842, that crossed southeastern Bradford County in the northern portion of the state. The wide damage path suggests a broad downburst, though a tornado may have been responsible for some of the damage. The storm "leveled forests, scattering fences, wrecking buildings and destroying crops."

Yet another notable storm blasted the Philadelphia area in early July 1842. A story in the *Philadelphia Gazette* described a severe thunderstorm that socked Philadelphia on the evening of July 1. The storm lasted from 7:00 to 10:00 P.M., dumping 5.13 inches of rain in the Pennsylvania Hospital rain gauge, flooding city streets, and swamping hundreds of cellars in dwellings near the Delaware River.

July 20, 1859: Delaware County Hailstorm

A nasty hailstorm bombarded northern Delaware County north of Philadelphia on the afternoon of July 20, 1859. A correspondent to the *Country Gentleman* wrote: "In some fields one-third of the corn is cut short off at the joints, and cabbage, melons, &c., very much injured, and in some cases entirely destroyed."

October 16, 1875: Severe Gale in the Upper Delaware Valley

A strong cold front crossing northeastern Pennsylvania on October 16, 1875, was accompanied by a "severe gale" that caused property damage at Milford. A dispatch in the Stroudsburg *Jeffersonian* (October 21, 1875) relayed the following: "A terrific tornado accompanied by heavy bursts of rain . . . between six and seven o'clock last evening [October 16]. Trees were uprooted, fences were blown down, outbuildings overturned, and windows broken in."

June/July 1880: Two Bradford County Storms

Two notable storms blasted Bradford County in northern Pennsylvania in the summer of 1880. On June 21, 1880, "a terrific and destructive storm of wind and hail" struck the western part of the county from Wells to LeRoy. Another storm on July 31 brought heavy rain and high winds that "swept everything before it, half a mile wide, across Ridgebury," which may have been the work of an embedded tornado (Heverling 1926, 579).

August 7, 1882: Eastern Squall Line

The press reported the passage of a vicious line of thunderstorms over eastern Pennsylvania on the afternoon of August 7, 1882. Reports from the Scranton area stated that "trees were uprooted and houses unroofed." Lightning strikes ignited many fires, causing considerable damage at localities along the Delaware Valley from Milford to Easton.

June 24, 1884: Violent Storms in West

A violent thunderstorm system crossed eastern Ohio into western Pennsylvania on June 24, 1884, accompanied by frequent cloud-to-ground lightning, flooding rains, and powerful winds. At least four persons were killed by lightning strikes, including two in northeastern Ohio, one in Murraysville, Pennsylvania, and another at Richfield Springs, New York. Many others were injured in various communities by the vicious electrical storms. Strong winds "wrecked trees, blew down fences and did great damage to grain" at Newcomerstown, Ohio.

In southeastern Pennsylvania, torrential downpours and strong winds flattened crops and washed out railroad lines from Gettysburg to Lancaster. Creeks overflowed in Chester County, and one cluster of storms dumped 11.00 inches of rain at York on June 24–25, causing major flooding on Cordorus Creek.

August 1–2, 1886: Wyoming Valley

The Wilkes-Barre area was visited by a severe thunderstorm overnight on August 1–2, 1886, killing a young man along Toby's Creek near Plymouth. High water tore through several mills, pushing Harvey's Creek ten feet higher than had ever been known at any time before. Flash floods swept away "saw and grist mills, and ponte and iron bridges" at Huntsville, Trucksville, Harvey's Lake, and Luzerne (*Jeffersonian* [Stroudsburg], August 5, 1886).

July 5, 1888: Lackawanna Valley

A Scranton dispatch reported a severe storm that passed over the Lackawanna Valley on the afternoon of July 5, 1888, killing two persons and causing extensive wind damage: "The Lackawanna Valley was visited this afternoon by the most furious storm ever known here. Two men and two horses were killed by lightning in Scranton and great damage was done throughout the valley. The rain fell in torrents, while the lightning flashes were incessant. The streets were flooded with water, and in unpaved portions deep gullies were worn, especially on hillsides" (*Jeffersonian* [Stroudsburg], July 12, 1888).

May 1889: Stormy Spring

A stormy pattern in May 1889 was likely due to a robust jet stream circulation directing vigorous weather systems across Pennsylvania throughout the month. A powerful squall line caused widespread wind damage during the middle of the afternoon on May 10, 1889, wreaking havoc in the eastern two-thirds of the state. High winds tore down tents at the Barnum & Bailey's circus show in Williamsport, seriously injuring six performers. A New York man was struck and killed by lightning in Susquehanna, and several persons were injured in stormy weather at Easton and Pottsville.

At Pottsville, where the storm may have briefly assumed the form of a small tornado, roofs were torn off buildings and several homes were "blown down." The *Monthly Weather Review* reported that a tornado touched down in Susquehanna

County, destroying several buildings at Hop Bottom between 2:45 and 3:35 P.M. Throughout eastern Pennsylvania, violent winds knocked down telephone, telegraph, and electric lines, throwing some communities in the dark for hours.

The *Philadelphia Inquirer* described a "furious wind storm" that struck the city from the northwest just after 5:00 P.M. on May 10, 1889, and lasted fifteen to twenty minutes. The report stated that "thousands of tons of dirt were whirling in the air, and made a cloud so thick as to be almost impenetrable and of a peculiar yellow appearance." Storm damage included trees and signs blown over and many homes unroofed in the "lower section of the city."

A crowd of about two thousand at the Philadelphia Base Ball Grounds huddled in protected areas or on the field as the winds blew suddenly and violently through the pavilion, though luckily no one was seriously hurt. Wind damage was widespread northwest of downtown Philadelphia, particularly in Germantown, Chestnut Hill, and Olney. Several skiffs were overturned and lost in the Delaware River, though no loss of life or serious injuries were reported in the Delaware Valley. One report stated that fifty buildings were unroofed in the storm on the west side of Philadelphia. A press notice from Reading reported, "Four of a handsome row of houses covering an entire block on Eleventh, from Center to Douglass streets, had their roofs torn off."

Seventy miles above Washington, D.C., twenty-five men laboring on a railroad trestle over the Potomac River were tossed into the water sixty feet below, killing several workers. In Geneseo, New York, three laborers were blown off a building under construction, and one man died in the fall. In northern New Jersey, a young girl was killed by lightning at Chadwick, and high winds caused "considerable damage" to homes and trees at the Oranges and Newark about 5:00 P.M.

On May 19, severe storms struck again and were described in the *Monthly Weather Review*. Near Norway, in Chester County, lightning ignited an oil tank, which exploded into flames. In Rouseville, Venango County, a church burned to the ground after being struck by lightning.

The weather in Pennsylvania turned violent again on May 20, 1889. An apparent tornado tore through open farm country seven miles north of Scranton between Clarks Summit and Clark's Green, which was reported in a dispatch to the *Pittsburgh Commercial Gazette:* "Several buildings were demolished, and every orchard in the path of the storm was wrecked, trees being torn up by the roots and carried many yards."

Along the same squall line, a "terrific wind and rain storm, which afterwards turned into a hail storm" passed over the Wyoming Valley. A second tornado likely touched down near Wilkes-Barre, where several houses were destroyed. In one instance, two homes were "swept from their foundations and all the inmates injured."

September 17, 1896: Hail and High Winds Batter Eastern Pennsylvania

The *Philadelphia Inquirer* headline on September 18, 1896, blared, "Hail and Wind Wrought Havoc" after severe storms rolled through eastern Pennsylvania on the afternoon of the seventeenth.

At Bloomsburg the storm was accompanied by "the most disastrous hail storm ever known in this vicinity" around 3:00 P.M. on September 17. The storm arrived from the north, suggesting that an upper-level pool of chilly air favoring northerly winds aloft hovered above Pennsylvania. Property damage was estimated above $20,000 from hail, lightning, and strong winds that unroofed buildings.

In the east-central hills, the barrage of hail and winds was no less severe. At Shenendoah, the hailstones were "the size of large plums" and shattered about three thousand windows. Another dispatch reported, "Nearly all the telegraph and telephone poles between Bristol and Croyden are down."

The storm at Sellersville brought large hail and a probable tornado. A stone pillar was torn out of a barn building, and about a hundred tall oak trees were "shattered and twisted." The storm destroyed a stable, carried a large water tank four hundred feet, and tore a railroad platform from its foundation that was "stood on ends." Many businesses and homes suffered broken windows, especially on the north sides, and the skylights of the cigar factories "containing 150 panes of glass" were completely destroyed. The storm that hit Perkasie at 4:30 P.M. was described as the worst since 1871, damaging small buildings and ruining hundreds of thousands of bushels of apples.

July 19, 1898: Terrifying Electrical Storm in Monroe County

The *Stroudsburg Daily Times* reported that a "fierce electrical storm" caused considerable damage throughout Monroe County on the night of July 18–19, 1898. Homes and businesses were struck by lightning, a number of them burning to the ground, and several people were injured. The storm was especially severe northwest of Stroudsburg in Coolbaugh Township and at Mount Bethel, where a barn and many crops were destroyed.

March 28, 1919: High Winds in Wayne County

Winds estimated at around 60 miles per hour tore off forty feet of cornice at the Welwood Silk Company in Honesdale. Window lights were blown out, and roof damage was reported to a number of nearby dwellings, according to the *Wayne Independent* (February 4, 1978).

July 1920: Statewide Storms

A stormy July in 1920 featured the passage of several unseasonably strong cold fronts, indicative of a powerful jet stream overhead, conducive to severe weather in Pennsylvania. The area around Union City experienced "very severe hailstorms" on the eighth. On July 14, 1920, a small storm at Carlisle of "possibly tornadic character, unroofed buildings, broke down numerous trees, a silo, and ruined crops along a narrow path of nearly three miles in length," according to the storm summary in *Climatological Data*.

A pattern of severe electrical storms hit Monroe County from July 18 to 24 on alternating days. On July 18 a storm took out an electrical light plant at Mount Pocono, causing widespread damage and claiming one life. The rainfall on that day totaled 3.50 inches at Mount Pocono and was even heavier at Milford (5.11 inches).

Greensburg was hit by a severe storm on July 23 in the western part of the state. The next day another round of severe storms lashed Monroe County, accompanied by "terrifying thunder and destructive lightning, excessive rainfall, many washouts." Other severe storms in July 1920 struck Selinsgrove on the thirtieth (high winds) and New Kensington on the thirty-first (fallen trees, high winds, hail).

May 23, 1925: Strong Cold Front Brings High Winds in the East

A strong cold front that would bring snow flurries to parts of northern Pennsylvania ignited a fierce line of thunderstorms across the Keystone State during the afternoon of May 23, 1925. Ahead of the front, temperatures soared into the nineties over eastern Pennsylvania under partly sunny skies. The afternoon maximum at Philadelphia reached 96 degrees. At the time that summer was taking hold, a late-winter cold front was barreling southeast across the Great Lakes.

The inevitable clash of air masses caused an intense squall line, accompanied by hail and damaging winds, to form over the eastern half of the state. The Stroudsburg *Morning Press* described the storm in the northeastern corner of the state: "The Pocono Mountain section was swept by a large hailstorm that drove men and animals to shelter, so large were the stones and so heavy was the bombardment." The rushing winds may have spawned a ground tornado in downtown Stroudsburg: "At times a miniature tornado prevailed . . . great trees were twisted and snapped off."

Pittsburgh measured a late-season record snowfall (0.5 inch) on May 24–25, 1925, and 3 to 6 inches blanketed the high ridges in Tioga County.

June/July 1928: Stormy Early Summer

Violent winds were churned up by a severe thunderstorm around Newville and Bloserville on June 14, 1928. The storm "damaged or destroyed many buildings, uprooted many trees, and beat down a considerable amount of grain and corn" (*Climatological Data*). Wind damage was reported in Juniata, Perry, Cumberland, and York Counties. A substantial monthly rainfall of 13.14 inches was reported at West Chester for June 1928.

Severe storms accompanied by damaging winds struck Pennsylvania again in Allegheny County southeast of Pittsburgh on the Fourth of July, 1928: "At Rainbow Gardens and Olympia Park, 400 automobiles were destroyed in landslides, and 2000 persons were marooned by floodwaters" (*Climatological Data*).

Another round of heavy weather brought localized flooding in Westmoreland County on July 11. Either a small tornado or a downburst carved a narrow damage path several miles long near Mifflintown on the twentieth. On July 22, hail, high winds, and lightning strikes were responsible for "upwards of $25,000" of damage at Carlisle.

July 1934: Electrical Storms Hit Scranton Repeatedly

July 1934 was one of the hottest and driest months on record in the Midwest. Pennsylvania was on the fringe of the scorching heat throughout much of the month, though western localities often saw the mercury flirt with the century mark. The boundary between hot, dry air and cooler air to the north was active on several occasions, and the Scranton area was on the receiving end of much of the action.

The *Climatological Data* report mentioned severe storms in northeastern Pennsylvania, causing pockets of wind and lightning damage on July 4, 13, and 26–28, 1934. On July 13, lightning killed two persons in Scranton and seriously injured a third. Flooding rains and damaging winds hit nearby Wayne County on July 27–28. An article in the *Wayne Independent* (February 4, 1978) described a small tornado that crossed East Dyberry, north of Honesdale (dated incorrectly as July 21, 1934). During a ten-minute period, the winds flattened crops and uprooted trees covering a distance of a quarter-mile. One farm reportedly lost about a hundred trees. Churning winds tossed a silo one hundred feet while destroying another and causing pockets of minor property damage.

June 13, 1939: High Winds Rip through Philadelphia

A squall line accompanied by high winds in the late evening hours of June 13, 1939, uprooted hundreds of trees around Philadelphia, while downpours flooded streets and basements. A storm account in the *Philadelphia Inquirer* described the events: "A severe electrical storm, freakishly combined with high, twisting, tornado-like winds, last night ripped the roofs from four houses in two sections of Philadelphia, partially deroofed a dozen other houses, and spread a wide trail of damage through the city and its suburbs."

The storm that struck the Philadelphia area around 9:30 P.M. may have spawned a narrow funnel eighty yards wide in suburban West Oak Lane that traveled about a half-mile (Grazulis 1993, 908). Storm damage was confined mostly to rooftops, and no injuries were reported.

July 9–10, 1945: Carbon, Northampton, Lehigh Counties

Severe electrical storms raked east-central Pennsylvania on the evening of July 9–10, 1945, flooding streets, sparking fires, and causing widespread crop damage. Two persons died in the barrage of storms and resultant flooding in Northampton and Lehigh Counties, and four others perished in Phillipsburg, New Jersey.

An early indication of a building cluster of severe storms over the central mountains of Pennsylvania came from the town of Boalsburg in Centre County, which was hit by a severe hailstorm around 5:00 P.M.: "Stones were reported 2 to 2¼ inches in diameter, and a few compound stones as large as 4 inches." A bombardment of hailstones "as large as hickory nuts" accompanied a group of violent storms that pounded Carbon, Northampton, and Lehigh Counties between 7:00 P.M. and 11:00 P.M. on July 9, 1945.

In eastern Pennsylvania, torrential rains caused creeks to rise out of their banks, though the flooding was localized and did not affect the Delaware or Lehigh Rivers. The Aquashicola Creek reached its highest level in forty-four years of records. The town of Bath was completely flooded as the Monocacy Creek roared out of its banks. Considerable debris was left in the wake of the flooding, leaving a "deposit of silt, stones, and rubble to a depth of 3 feet."

Wild Creek Reservoir in Carbon County received 5.33 inches of rain on July 9–10, 1945, en route to a monthly rainfall of 17.89 inches. This broke the previous all-time state monthly rainfall record of 17.70 inches at York in August 1933. Rainfall totals in eastern Pennsylvania near the Delaware River were reported to have measured as much as 8.00 inches near Bangor, about ten miles south of Stroudsburg. A rain gauge at Easton measured 6.20 inches.

A final comment in the state *Climatological Data* report for July 1945 mentioned some Greene County folklore: "The unique tradition that rain will fall at Waynesburg on July 29th was fulfilled. Only three times by oral or written records has rain failed to fall on the 29th, in that community, in the past 69 years."

June 10–11, 1954: Severe Storms Hit Southwestern Pennsylvania

Powerful thunderstorms raked southwestern Pennsylvania during the night of June 10–11, 1954, accompanied by downburst winds of at least 90 miles per hour northwest of the city of Pittsburgh (*Climatological Data*). A tornado (F2) touched down at 12:04 A.M. in Beaver County on that day, tracking seven miles and injuring three persons and causing $50,000 of damage around New Brighton. About five miles to the north, hail pounded Ellwood City in southern Lawrence County, resulting in widespread property damage. Another storm in Allegheny County with a narrow path (30 yards) contributed to a $500,000 damage toll.

Severe storms continued to develop near an active weather boundary across western Pennsylvania on June 12–13. Shortly before midnight on the twelfth, one of those storms spawned a tornado (F2) in Potter County that was responsible for $50,000 of damage.

July 27–28, 1969: Eastern Storms

The month of July 1969 was especially stormy in Pennsylvania, marked by intense downpours that led to record July rainfall totals in the eastern portion of the state. The heaviest unofficial rainfall in the state in twenty-four hours occurred on July 11 near Smithfield in the southwestern corner of the state, where an estimated 6.00 to 8.00 inches of rain fell in a relatively short period of time.

A weather boundary lying over Pennsylvania during the last week of July 1969 separated unstable tropical air and cooler air to the north. An active jet stream pattern brought a series of disturbances rippling across the state, triggering rounds of heavy thunderstorms that resulted in serious flooding. During the month of July 1969, a total of five Pennsylvanians died and twenty others suffered injuries related to the severe weather.

The Harrisburg area received 5.02 inches of rain on July 22–23 and a total of 8.43 inches during the week of July 21–28. In the northeast, Long Pond had 8.80 inches during the closing days of the month (July 26–30). Flood damage in Monroe County alone totaled $1 million, according to the *Climatological Data* report.

Storms winds toppled a pavilion at Highland Park in Sellersville on the afternoon of the twenty-seventh, injuring a young boy. The same afternoon a tornado touched down five miles west of the Harrisburg-York Airport, resulting in serious damage, costing $300,000, over several city blocks. Thunderstorm winds gusted to 60 miles per hour on the twenty-eighth at Philadelphia.

June 29–30, 1987: Violent Southeastern Storms

Severe thunderstorms raked Pennsylvania on June 29–30, 1987, causing widespread property damage (*Storm Data*). The storms were severe during the evening hours of June 29 in western Pennsylvania and were accompanied by hail, heavy rain, and a few funnel clouds. A tornado touched down at Paris in Washington County, damaging fifty homes (ten heavily). Lightning induced fires around Titusville in Crawford County, and there were many reports of wind damage all over western Pennsylvania.

Severe thunderstorms raked parts of southeastern Pennsylvania during the middle of the afternoon on June 30, 1987. High winds over northern Lancaster County between Mount Joy and Reinholds damaged "at least 100 farm buildings, 30 silos and 100 pieces of farm equipment," along with thirty homes. In Manheim, where the storm struck at 3:42 P.M., barns were destroyed, homes damaged, and a greenhouse was lifted over two others and wrecked in the process. The storm continued east, passing north of Lititz, tearing the roofs off at least four homes, and damaging quite a few barns and other farm buildings.

Hail accompanied the violent storm, which shredded corn in the fields. In Elizabeth Township, the storm took the roof off another twenty-five to thirty homes just before 4:00 P.M. and caused major damage to eighteen barns. The path of damage continued through Reinholds at 4:22 P.M., where tree limbs were shattered and roofs were stripped from houses and a mobile home was overturned. The thunderstorm caused more damage as it crossed Berks County over the next half-hour, passing several miles southeast of Reading.

Down in Adams County, another powerful cell hit around 4:30 P.M., causing property damage and taking one life. An anemometer located at a radio station in Gettysburg was torn from the roof after registering winds of at least 100 miles per hour. One woman was killed when a garage roof was ripped off and landed on top of her.

June 1996: Stormiest Month

June 1996 brought a record number of severe storm reports (269) in Pennsylvania. Waves of heavy thunderstorms lined up along stalled or slow-moving weather fronts for days at a time. Economic losses for the month totaled over $44.2 million.

The most active days in Pennsylvania, based on reports of hail, damaging winds, flooding rains, and tornadoes, were June 4 (24 reports), 11 (36), 18 (28), 22 (26), and 24 (55). Three especially stormy periods occurred during June 7–14, 17–20, and 20–24, when there were only a few days without a severe weather report in the state.

Severe storms raked central and southeastern Pennsylvania on June 7–8 and 11–12, 1996. A destructive flood accompanied training thunderstorms over southeastern Bucks County on the evening of June 12 after 11.55 inches of rain fell at Langhorne in four hours. A rain gauge in Gettysburg measured 10.72 inches. Flooding affected more than 650 homes and businesses, killing two people. Local storm reports (NOAA) noted rescues of two hundred to three hundred people after a canal inundated a portion of town after Brock and Silver Creeks spilled out of their banks. Flooding was also a problem along the Neshaminy Creek. Storm damage was estimated at $14.5 million.

Central and western sections of Pennsylvania were hit hard by high winds and localized flooding on June 17–20. State College received over 5.00 inches of rain in a few hours in the late afternoon on June 17, sending torrents of water coursing down Beaver Avenue, which resulted in property damage in and around the Pennsylvania State University. Nearly one hundred homes were affected by the storm.

On June 19–20, 1996, flash floods caused extensive damage in the western counties, with the worst damage at Freedom ($7.5 million) and McKeesport ($3.1 million). Another severe storm caused $15 million damage at Logantown around 4:00 P.M. on the twentieth.

Fig. 7.1. November 8, 1996. Straight-line winds felled dozens of trees in southern Monroe County after a line of severe thunderstorms moved through the area with winds estimated at more than 50 miles per hour. (Courtesy Michael Pontrelli)

Small tornadoes that formed along a warm front draped across northeastern Pennsylvania struck Wyalusing, Laceyville, and Duryea/West Avoca, causing damage in Bradford and Luzerne Counties between 3:00 and 4:00 P.M. on the afternoon of June 22. Monroe County was bombarded with softball-sized hailstones that left a hailstreak extending from Kresgeville to Saylorsburg. Many areas reported 2.00 to 4.00 inches of rain.

Another wave of severe storms erupted in the early afternoon of June 24, 1996, in the western part of the state. Flash floods caused $150,000 of damage around Pittsburgh, where 3.11 inches of rain fell in a few hours' time. The rainfall total at Langhorne in June 1996 of 18.48 inches was the greatest accumulation in the state since June 1972.

November 8, 1996: Late-Autumn Squall Line

A powerful autumn cold front swept across Pennsylvania on November 8, 1996, accompanied by damaging winds and several small tornadoes. Tornadoes were sighted in Bedford County (F1) and at Centre Hall (F0) near State College in the central part of the state during the mid-afternoon. Around 4:00 P.M., a stronger F2 twister touched down near the Blue Mountain Ski Area in northern Northampton County. A little later, a weaker (F1) tornado with estimated 90- to 120-mile-per-hour winds, associated with the same cell, caused more damage along Kunkletown Road west of Saylorsburg.

As the funnel lifted, a ten-mile pattern of damaging straight-line winds accompanied the supercell traveling northeast at 40 miles per hour. Five homes, an airplane hangar, and a number of planes sustained significant damage in Ross Township, a few miles southwest of Stroudsburg. A roof was carried about a hundred yards. One eyewitness saw a "huge black mass" suggestive of an embedded tornado, likely increasing the force of the wind. Farther north in Monroe County there was plenty of scattered wind damage, and two persons were hurt when a tree fell on the van they were driving on State Route 447.

July 18, 1997: Microburst Damage in the Central Mountains

Weather personnel from the Pennsylvania State University embarked on a detailed investigation on widespread wind damage that occurred in central Pennsylvania during the afternoon of July 18, 1997. The results showed the concurrence of a microburst with embedded small tornadoes. Such was the case in Union County, where two small pockets of circular damage were discerned within a broader microburst damage path. Downburst damage extended across southern Lycoming and northern Clinton Counties.

Another tornado was identified in Clinton County that passed through Crestmont and Woolrich, five miles east of Lock Haven, around 4:40 P.M. The damage path of the tornado, which traveled four miles, extended up to a half-mile wide. However, the tornadic winds were part of a broader downburst damage pattern that extended two miles wide and six miles long. Thousands of trees and several homes were damaged in a rural section of Clinton County. Downburst damage continued east within a cluster of severe storms across the Susquehanna River through the town of McElhatton.

Tornado damage was also discovered in damage patterns observed in Potter County, along with additional pockets of wind damage in Clinton County east of Renovo and in Cameron and McKean Counties.

8 Tornadoes and Whirlwinds

The phenomenal force of the wind can only be imagined from the visible evidence of its destruction, and its power seemed to be almost supernatural.

—*Philadelphia Inquirer,* August 4, 1885

A whirling mass of cloud and debris beneath a roiling sky is a truly awesome and frightening sight. The twisting winds inside a tornado average between 100 and 150 miles per hour, but some storms generate winds in excess of 200 miles per hour.

A portable Doppler radar measured a wind speed of 318 miles per hour in a tornado that struck Oklahoma City on May 3, 1999. The previous top wind gust of 286 miles per hour was measured in a storm near Red Rock, Oklahoma, on April 26, 1991.

In an average year, more than a thousand tornadoes are likely to touch down across the United States. Fortunately, the loss of life attributed to tornadoes and has dipped significantly in recent years, thanks to timely warnings and greater public awareness of tornado safety.

A broad swath from central Texas to eastern Nebraska comprises the heart of "tornado alley," which extends southward through the Gulf states and eastward to the Ohio Valley. No other place in the world experiences more tornadoes than the nation's heartland, although twisters are not confined to the Midwest and southern states.

Pennsylvania Tornadoes

Pennsylvania experiences an average number of eleven tornadoes annually, based on the statistical period of 1950 through 1999. However, during a ten-year period from 1989 to 1998, the average number of Pennsylvania tornadoes doubled to twenty-two. The more recent value was inflated by two super tornado outbreaks that hit the Keystone State over a three-day interval between May 31 and June 2, 1998. Fifty-nine tornadoes, plus several waterspouts over the open waters of Lake Erie, were counted in Pennsylvania in 1998, setting a single-season record for the state.

Most Pennsylvania tornadoes are relatively weaker cousins of the stronger midwestern and southern storms. The most damaging tornado outbreaks in Pennsylvania history (1865, 1896, 1944, 1985, and 1998) struck in the late spring, when the sun is fairly high in the sky and the ground and lower atmosphere are soaking up lots of energy. At the same time, the upper atmosphere is fairly chilly, creating highly unstable conditions ripe for severe storms if there is abundant low-level moisture and a lifting mechanism.

The greatest death toll in Pennsylvania in a single tornado outbreak occurred on May 31, 1985, when sixty-three residents lost their lives in a rampage of violent storms. Another stormy evening on June 23, 1944, brought several large tornadoes that raked southwestern Pennsylvania and northern West Virginia, killing forty-five Pennsylvanians.

Favorable Weather Conditions for Tornadoes

Tornadoes are born in an environment in which winds are increasing with altitude and changing direction, known as *wind shear.* The core of the jet stream is usually located in the vicinity of a sharp vertical temperature contrast, which supplies available energy for burgeoning storms.

Most tornado outbreaks in Pennsylvania develop when a cool, dry northwesterly flow is superimposed over surging tropical air. On the southern edge of the jet stream, diverging air currents force a compensating low-level inflow of warm, moist air from the southwest. A severe weather outbreak is triggered by a pocket of fast-moving winds interacting with moist air in an unstable environment and creating waves in the atmosphere, much like a paddle wheel moving through a river.

Faster westerly winds passing over a layer of weaker southerly currents near the surface may cause a layer, or "tube" of air to begin to roll horizontally. The arrival of a vigorous upper-level disturbance over a relatively clear area that has been subjected to hours of solar heating promotes strong updrafts. Rising air currents eventually punch through a rolling tube, causing it to tip vertically. A tilted updraft prevents a rain-chilled downdraft from choking off the influx of tropical air fueling the storm, which allows a storm to continue to grow.

The greatest risk of tornadoes comes from isolated supercells with rotating updrafts sustained by strong wind shear in advance of a squall line. The formation of a whirling *mesocyclone,* usually in response to shifting winds aloft, or the merger of rain-cooled outflow boundaries sometimes initiates rotation in the middle levels (5,000 to 10,000 feet) of the atmosphere. As the circulation of a rotating thunderstorm slowly contracts to a diameter of about two to six miles, the swirling winds increase, much like a figure skater who spins faster by pulling in his or her arms.

Condensation gives rise to a characteristic dark, amorphous *wall cloud* that often appears below a rain-free cloud base. The ominous, roiling sky conditions are normally observed in the southwest portion of a thunderstorm along the interface of the *rear-flank downdraft* and a region of strong inflow. Suddenly, a writhing pendant emerges from the wall cloud, bobbing up and down before making contact with the surface. Once on the ground, dirt and debris drawn into the funnel darken the storm, providing an outline for a severe-storm spotter.

The average path width of a tornado is only few hundred yards, though a few storms have a damage path more than a half-mile wide. Multiple funnels are often responsible for pockets of damage that apparently skip over one home while leveling another building next door. Some of the most devastating storms have formed through the merger of several smaller funnels, spawning a monster tornado whirling through the countryside like a giant rotary blade.

Tornado Detection

Meteorologists now have the tools to view and track the circulation inside a severe thunderstorm with the aid of Doppler radar analysis, and in the process have learned a great deal about how tornadoes form. The principle behind Doppler weather radar is that the movement of raindrops either toward or away from the antenna alters the frequency of reflected microwaves, much like the pitch of an approaching train whistle changes relative to an observer waiting on a station platform.

The advantage of using today's Doppler radar (88-D, for the 1988 model) over conventional weather radar (WSR-57, for the 1957 design) is the ability to gauge wind speed and the direction of a storm. By analyzing data obtained from ground-based and airborne Doppler radar units, in conjunction with atmospheric soundings (temperature, wind, air pressure, and moisture profiles), meteorologists have improved the average lead time for the issuance of tornado warnings from several minutes twenty years ago to about twelve minutes today.

Tornado Classification

Professor T. Theodore Fujita of the University of Chicago and Allen Pearson, a former director of the National Severe Storms Forecast Center (now the Storm Prediction Center), devised a tornado intensity scale that allows meteorologists to rank tornadoes by wind speed, path length, path width, and typical damage. Table 8.1 shows the features examined to rank a tornado on the Fujita-Pearson scale from F0 to F5.

A little more than 60 percent of the tornadoes that touch down across the country are considered weak, with winds estimated at less than 113 miles per hour. Light damage associated with weaker storms usually consists of broken tree branches and signs blown down. Stronger storms may leave a trail of twisted trees and broken windows.

Stronger tornadoes are capable of uprooting large trees, overturning cars, wrecking outbuildings, and collapsing the walls of a frame home. Violent tornadoes can sweep a home off its foundation, toss vehicles through the air, shear trees off at the stump, and otherwise cause near-total destruction in the storm path.

Table 8.1. Fujita-Pearson Scale for Damaging Wind

Category	Wind speed (mph)	Path length (miles)	Path width (yards)	Expected damage
F0	< 72	< 1	< 17	light
F1	73–112	1.0–3.1	18–55	moderate
F2	113–157	3.2–9.9	56–175	considerable
F3	158–206	10–31	176–556	severe
F4	207–260	32–99	556–1,584	devastating
F5	261–318	100–315	1–3 miles	incredible

More than two-thirds of the fatalities associated with tornadoes in the United States occur with violent tornadoes. Only about 2 percent of violent tornadoes that strike the United States are classified as F4 (207 to 260 miles per hour) or F5 (261 to 318 miles per hour), but these huge storms are responsible for more than three-quarters of the fatalities caused by tornadoes around the country.

Gustnadoes and Landspouts

For a long time it was assumed that most tornadoes spun down from a rotating thunderstorm. Modern research has confirmed that small tornadoes occasionally spin up from the ground.

The leading edge of fast-moving band of storms may spawn one or more short-lived tornadoes in a zone of strong low-level wind shear. When a powerful down-draft slams into the ground, dense rain-chilled air splatters in all directions. One theory is that the air attains some rotation near the surface, perhaps from a collision between two strong thunderstorm downdrafts.

A *gustnado* sometimes develops near the apex of a *bow echo,* or a bulge in a line of fast-moving severe thunderstorms, where strong mid-level winds plunge toward the ground and fan out. A gustnado is not a true tornado, because there is no direct connection to a rotating column of air at the base of a thunderstorm. Wind damage with these storms tends to be confined to rooftops, outbuildings, fences, and lawn furniture.

Clear, breezy, and very warm days occasionally give rise to a *landspout* or *dust devil.* Ground whirls resembling miniature tornadoes tend to form on hot, sunny days where heated air rises and mixes with cooler air above. Air flowing into a warm pocket, such as a sun-baked field or paved parking lot, may begin to rotate clockwise or counterclockwise, perhaps aided by small obstacles or natural barriers.

Most landspouts and dust devils are small and harmless, picking up leaves or dust as they swoop across an open area for a short distance. Occasionally, a strong dust devil can spin at speeds around fifty miles per hour, causing minor damage. On April 26, 1987, a dust devil was observed three miles northwest of Williamsport in the early afternoon, ripping the plastic off a greenhouse and lifting a pickup truck camper off its blocks, moving it a distance of fifteen feet. The dust devil scattered debris over a three-hundred-foot area.

An unusual whirlwind, possibly a dust devil, hit a Reading neighborhood around 5:30 P.M. on April 21, 1963. The path width was only fifteen yards, though the storm was classified as a weak tornado. Richard A. Keen (1992, 204) wrote that the narrow column of swirling winds descended from a sunny sky, appearing as a "black spiral, easily one-half mile high." The funnel tore a brick veneer off the side of a school building, uprooted trees, and downed power lines over a 0.2-mile path.

Early Pennsylvania Tornadoes

The earliest recorded Pennsylvania tornado was described in the *American Mercury* of Philadelphia in August 1724. The tornado struck northwest of Philadelphia, near Paoli and Valley Forge, and followed an east-northeasterly track through Chester and Bucks Counties in the early afternoon of August 14, 1724 (Ludlum 1970, 37).

Trees were uprooted, fences blown down, and roofs torn off houses and barns. A mill was destroyed in the path of the storm. Fallen trees blocked roads and hindered travel for days afterward. A report described it: "On the third instant [August 14, 1724, New Style], about the hour of 12 (at New Garden in Chester) there began a most terrible and surprizing Whirl-wind; which took the roof of a barn and carried it into the air and scattered it about 2 miles off, also a mill that had a large quantity of wheat in it, and has thrown it down and removed the millstones, and took a lath of the barn, and carried it into the air; it also carried a plough into the air" (*American Mercury,* August 13 [24], 1724).

The first waterspout reported in Pennsylvania was witnessed over the Delaware River on June 4, 1754, in the midst of a "violent gale of wind with rain and hail," as reported in the *Pennsylvania Journal and Weekly Advertiser* on June 6, 1754. The account noted "considerable damage in the country" as the storm "broke in the Jerseys."

A squall line with embedded small tornadoes raced through parts of Maryland, Pennsylvania, New Jersey, and New York on June 22, 1756 (Ludlum 1970, 39). One person was killed and several others seriously injured at Moyamensing, near Philadelphia, where a barn sought out for shelter collapsed. Two other deaths may have occurred at Gloucester.

The public library on Fifth Street in Philadelphia was one of a number of buildings damaged in the storm, according to the *Pennsylvania Gazette.* Elsewhere, two hundred homes were "blown down" in a large tornado that hit St. Mary's County, Maryland, on June 22, 1756. Storms also struck Jamaica on Long Island and Essex County, New Jersey (Ludlum 1984, 22), the same day.

One of the earliest known descriptions of a tornado over the Pennsylvania interior appeared in Heverling's *History and Geography of Bradford County, Pennsylvania* (1926, 71): "In [June 1794], a tornado swept through the southwestern part of Bradford county, extending into Sullivan county, and in its path of a mile in width, almost every tree was uprooted or broken."

Alexander Wilson sailed from Scotland to America in May 1794. Wilson, a renowned ornithologist and nature-lover, would hold a number of positions as a schoolmaster in western New Jersey and eastern Pennsylvania in his early years in the United States. In October 1804, Wilson and a companion set out from Philadelphia to walk to Niagara Falls and back. Along his journey, which included a trip up the Susquehanna River, he composed a poetic travelogue called *The Foresters,* in which he recounted a pattern of storm damage.

The tornado occurred sometime before 1800 in the Great Pine Swamp, near the present site of Long Pond in western Monroe County (Lesh 1945). Wilson concluded, "These tornadoes are frequent in the different regions of the United States. The one we allude to had been extremely violent, and for many miles had leveled the woods in its way. It extended nearly 20 miles."

Local residents continued to gather pine knots for firewood for another hundred years along the path of the whirlwind that originated near the Lehigh River and the small town of Stoddartsville and continued along the brow of the ridge north of Effort.

Major Pennsylvania Tornadoes

Nineteenth Century

Many tornadoes undoubtedly went unrecorded in the nineteenth century, so a complete account of early storms is not possible. Several storms left an unmistakable path of destruction clearly the work of a tornado. Rural storms were not always reported in detail, however, and press reports are being reviewed in order to ascertain whether the damage was likely the work of a tornado or straight-line winds.

May 18, 1825: Butler Tornado

A family of violent tornadoes ripped through northern and central Ohio during the afternoon of May 18, 1825, wiping out the new community of Burlington, about twenty-five miles northeast of Columbus, Ohio (Ludlum 1970, 103). At least one tornado developed over western Pennsylvania on May 18, 1825, blasting through the small town of Butler.

A detailed description of the storm from the local press appeared in the *National Intelligencer* (Washington, D.C.) on June 1, 1825, reporting that "houses, barns, fences, orchards, and woods, were levelled to the ground."

> On Wednesday, the 18th instant, a part of this county was visited by one of the most violent and destructive tornadoes that has ever passed through it. The storm came from the southwest, and passed in a northeast direction. We have not yet learned where it commenced, nor how far it continued its destructive march. It passed diagonally through this county, and its ravages are about a mile in width. It had a huge volume of smoke, arising from a tremendous fire, which, with the vivid and continued flashes of lightning, the loud peaks of thunder, the rattling of hail, and the crash of timber, with which it was accompanied, gave to it an awful and terrible appearance, that baffles description. (*Butler Repository* in *National Intelligencer,* May 21, 1825)

March 22, 1830: Allegheny County Tornado

Southern Allegheny County was hit by a powerful tornado on March 22, 1830, soon after a squall line crossed the Pennsylvania border. Damaging tornadoes had already occurred over central and eastern Ohio earlier in the day. Around 1:30 P.M. on March 22, 1830, the small town of Urbana, Ohio (about thirty miles northwest of Columbus), was devastated by a twister that killed four persons and seriously injured many others, while damaging seventy homes (Schmidlin and Schmidlin 1996, 231).

A notice of the storm in the *Pittsburg Gazette* that later appeared in the *National Intelligencer* (April 2, 1830) reported the town of Elizabeth (then Elizabethtown) in Allegheny County was hit by fearful winds around 7:00 P.M. on March 22, 1830: "Fourteen houses are blown down and unroofed; five barns and stables, one boat-house, one mill and one wool-carding establishment, completely crushed, with many other houses much damaged. Many families are turned out, without a roof to shelter them from the pitiless storm. Beds, bedding, and household furniture, are to be seen hanging amongst the broken timber, and strewn along the road."

Boats were tossed about and broken to pieces along the banks of the Monongahela River. The press account added, "Thanks to that Providence, who watches over and Protects us amid such calamitous visitations, no human lives are lost, though many have received slight wounds."

July 3, 1834: Razorville (Scranton) Tornado

A powerful tornado plowed through the Lackawanna Valley on July 3, 1834, hitting the community of Razorville with its full fury, destroying virtually every building, including a Methodist church that was under construction (Grazulis 1993, 559).

In a *History of Wilkes-Barre,* Oscar J. Harvey (1909, 4:2159–2160) outlined the path of the storm, which worked its way around the base of "Wilkes-Barre Mountain" at Ashley, where "several barns and other outbuildings were torn to pieces" and wreckage was strewn "as far north as Laurel Run."

> The path of the tornado, or by whatever name it might be called, seemed to be in the direct line up the valley along its eastern side, passing back of Pittston and entering Lackawanna Valley at about the mouth of Spring Brook, touching lightly on its way further north, nor striking Hyde Park at all, but exerting its expiring force on ill-fated Razorville, now a portion of Scranton City. Hyde Park and Razorville were at that time bustling villages on the stage route between Wilkes-Barre and Carbondale. Scranton proper was only Slocum Hollow and of little consequence.

July 8, 1840: York County Tornadoes

Two tornadoes cut a swath of destruction across York County on the evening of July 8, 1840. The *York Gazette* (July 14, 1840) reported, "We have been visited by one of the greatest whirlwinds that has ever been witnessed in Pennsylvania —Yesterday [July 8, 1840], between three and four o'clock, P.M., a tremendously large and dense cloud arose in a direction about South West from the village of Newberry. . . . Instantly, hundreds of thousands of the largest forest trees were hurled to the ground. . . . Those at a distance of two miles could see the tops of trees and grain in the sheath whirled along high in the air."

The storm narrowly missed Newberry, traveling "within half a mile" of the town, which explains the absence of injuries or fatalities, considering the fury of the storm winds. The path length was estimated at two miles (Grazulis 1993, 560).

A few hours later, a second tornado took a lethal course through the town of Shrewsbury, causing "great destruction of property, personal injury, and loss of life." The storm struck around 8:30 P.M., according to a letter published in the *York Gazette*. One person was killed and several children were gravely injured as the tornado tore through Shrewsbury, tearing up buildings and barns: "In a few minutes the whole town was thrown into confusion and uproar. . . . Nearly every house in the place was submerged, and a number entirely destroyed."

August 5, 1843: Cloudburst Tornadoes in Chester and Delaware Counties

At least five tornadoes, and perhaps more, accompanied an active frontal boundary extending from the Maryland-Pennsylvania border northeastward to Long

Island on August 5, 1843. The biggest weather story was a terrible cloudburst in the southeast corner of Pennsylvania that triggered a flash flood, killing at least nineteen persons west and southwest of Philadelphia (Ludlum 1970, 61–64). A storm survey undertaken by the Delaware Institute of Science reviewed the damage:

> In the township of Bethel, not far from the line of the State of Delaware, a hurricane of great violence occurred about four or five o'clock in the afternoon. The wind blew from different points at different places in the neighborhood, as is manifest from the position of uprooted trees, &c. . . . The wind came from the south east, and tore up a large quantity of timber (said to be about two hundred cords) all in a narrow strip, not more than two hundred yards in width. A valley of woodland, bounded by pretty high hills, had nearly all of its timber blown down, and what is very remarkable, the trees are not generally laid lengthwise of the valley, but across it, with their tops toward the north-east, while on the adjacent hills but few trees were uprooted. (Y. S. Walter, 1844, Delaware Institute of Science)

April 13, 1856: Philadelphia Tornado

High winds and a probable tornado struck Philadelphia on the night of April 12, 1856. A late dispatch from Philadelphia reported that the storm "unroofed 150 houses in different sections of the city" but remarkably did not cause any serious injuries. Much of the damage was the work of straight-line winds, but an embedded tornado was the likely cause of a vein of major damage in northeast Philadelphia, where fifty buildings were unroofed. As reported in the *New York Times,* "About 10 o'clock last evening our City was visited by a most violent gale of wind, unroofing an immense number of buildings, demolishing fences. . . . In the northeast section of the City, comprising the former district of Kensington, the damage was most serious."

The most serious damage occurred on Frankford Road above Franklin Street, where a Presbyterian church was "partially destroyed" after the roof was stripped from the structure. A "large fragment of the roof was carried about 100 feet, and completely demolished a frame building, two stories high" a short distance away. Another scene of damage suggestive of a tornado was the Franklin Iron Works, where a boiler house 150 feet long and 50 feet wide was "leveled to the ground."

May 30, 1860: Clarion Tornado

The spring of 1860 brought two death-dealing storms to Pennsylvania. The first struck the northwestern highlands on May 30, tracking twenty miles through Armstrong, Clarion, and Jefferson Counties and killing seven persons and injuring thirty others. Tornado historian Thomas P. Grazulis (1993, 566) wrote, "Where the funnel was narrowest its force was greatest, and it plowed up the earth to the depth of two feet, hurled large stones through the air, forcing smaller ones into trees and wood to such a depth that they could not be extricated."

A full report of the storm in *Vincent's Register* (Philadelphia) stated, "In fact in a radius of ten or twelve miles heard from, thirty or forty houses and barns were torn down." A local dispatch from the *Brookville Republican* traced the "southwest to northeast" course of "an inverted cone, in color like smoke, and well defined in its outlines." The storm was aptly described as "a whirlwind of fire and smoke."

The tornado first touched down near Adams, along the border of Armstrong and Clarion Counties, and would eventually lift into the clouds about three miles south of Brookville in Jefferson County. The village of Mayville, near Clarion and about sixteen miles south of Brookville, was the scene of terrible destruction. Twenty-five buildings were demolished, taking the lives of four residents and injuring another "twenty-five or thirty." Elsewhere, three people died north of New Bethlehem. On May 30, 1860, another tornado struck southwestern New York in Cattaraugus County, killing one person near Waverly.

June 19, 1860: Lancaster County Tornado

On the evening of June 19, 1860, another violent Pennsylvania windstorm whirled across western Lancaster County, in the southeastern section of the state. An account of the tornado in the *Lancaster City Express* defined the storm track: "Last evening [June 19, 1860] between 5 and 6 o'clock, one of the most destructive hailstorms and tornadoes which has ever visited this vicinity, passed over the townships of Mount Joy, Rapho, West Hempfield, Manor, and Conestoga, doing great damage to property and crops."

Large hail pelted Mount Joy, about fifteen miles northwest of Lancaster, breaking windows and damaging yards and gardens. Hail covered the ground to the depth of 3 inches in places as the storm traveled southeast. At Mountville, there was also evidence of a tornado, where crops were sheared or stripped off the ground. A description of the storm at Safe Harbor, in the western part of the county, reported the storm's "destructiveness to property and crops is incalculable." Another dispatch report from Conestoga stated that the storm "completely lifted the entire body of water from its bed, so that those who were on the banks of the creek at the time could see the bottom."

Substantial storm damage to property and crops occurred as the large tornado tore through several small islands while crossing the Susquehanna River, where the funnel reportedly attained a width of three-quarters of a mile. By the time the squall line had reached the Maryland border, the fierce winds left behind a path of structural and crop damage, though no serious injuries were mentioned in any of the reports.

May 11, 1865: Philadelphia Tornado

A squall line developed over eastern Pennsylvania during the late afternoon on May 11, 1865, accompanied by downburst winds and a few tornadoes, causing extensive damage in pockets from Philadelphia to New York City. While most of the damage was probably due to straight-line winds, there were areas of destruction probably associated with short-lived funnel clouds.

One apparent tornado emerged from roiling clouds over Philadelphia around 6:00 P.M. on May 11, damaging or destroying twenty-three homes in the Fairmount Park section in the northwest part of the city. The storm traveled northeast, wreaking havoc that covered several city blocks. The roof of a water tank at the Reading Railroad Depot, weighing several tons, was lifted and deposited onto the tracks 150 feet away.

The storm reached the Delaware River and crossed into North Camden, New Jersey, before dissipating. A fifteen-year-old boy was killed, and another woman may have drowned crossing from the west side of the Schuylkill River. The *Philadelphia Inquirer* reported "a number of miraculous escapes" from serious injury: "The tornado seemed to confine its worst ravages to a circumscribed space, for while a number of trees were blown down, fences carried away and awnings shivered to pieces in the most populous portion of the city, the Nineteenth Ward presents a scene of terrible destruction. The worst effects of the unwelcome visitor are visible from the corner of Cumberland and Sepviva streets, and extending from there in a northeastern direction to the Delaware River."

Local press accounts suggest a few tornadoes were likely embedded in broader pattern of downburst damage in sections of Newark, New Jersey, and southeast Brooklyn, New York.

July 4, 1874: Lewistown Tornado

On the Fourth of July, 1874, tragedy struck Lewiston in Mifflin County in south-central Pennsylvania. Heavy weather had hit Pennsylvania on July 2, causing localized flooding in the community of Chickies. However, a Fourth of July squall line accompanied by pockets of damaging winds would make headlines from Washington, D.C., and Baltimore northward across eastern Pennsylvania.

A singular tragedy unfolded on the Lewistown bridge over the Juniata River when a tornado blew the bridge to pieces, taking the lives of three boys and injuring three others seeking shelter from the storm on or under the bridge. Three workers at the Glamorgan Iron Company were also killed when a furnace was nearly destroyed in the storm.

The total death toll from the storm was put at seven, with a number of injuries. More than fifty buildings in Lewistown suffered serious damage or were destroyed in the tornado, and losses were estimated beyond $100,000 (Grazulis 1993, 580). A nineteen-car freight train was blown off the tracks a few miles west of Lewistown, probably by a downburst out of the side of the storm.

June/July 1877: Severe Storms Hit Southeastern Pennsylvania

The early days of summer in 1877 brought several rounds of severe weather to the Northeast that caused pockets of wind damage.

On June 21, 1877, a tornado touched down eleven miles northeast of Reading near Fleetwood, traveling six miles in a northeasterly direction. The F2 storm caused property damage in the vicinity of Lyons and Topton (Grazulis 1993, 590). The *New York Times* reported, "Three large barns were completely destroyed, houses were unroofed, shedding demolished, trees uprooted, and fences blown down. The roads were very much obstructed by the debris of fences, trees, & etc."

Tornadoes struck the Midwest on June 25 and the Ohio Valley on June 30. The stormy pattern progressed eastward on July 1, spawning tornadoes in Pennsylvania, New York, and New Hampshire during the late afternoon and early evening hours.

A large tornado that was "widely viewed" moved southeast across Lancaster County into Chester County, damaging ten homes and taking one life near Parkesburg. The tornado passed north of Atglen, traveling through the western and southern parts of Parkesburg in western Chester County, remaining on the ground for nineteen miles before lifting eight miles southeast of Ercildoun. Two persons were killed near Ercildoun, three miles south of Coatesville. Twenty buildings were destroyed, along with the new seminary, which had only recently been vacated by students leaving for summer vacation. The storm injured twenty-five persons.

July 4, 1878: Sunday School Tragedy

Another weather disaster struck on the Fourth of July, four years to the day after the Lewistown tornado. The storm swept over the city of Pittsburgh, causing localized flooding. A number of buildings were struck by vicious lightning, resulting in "great damage" but no fatalities. Twelve miles above Pittsburgh, a flash flood claimed three lives at Sandy Creek Village, where a house was washed away in the storm runoff.

Another tragedy developed at a picnic in the community of Ross Grove, about seven miles northeast of Pittsburgh. Either a tornado or possibly a downburst struck the area where a Sunday School picnic was under way around 3:00 P.M. A large tree smashed into a wagon, killing seven children and adults (Grazulis 1993, 596–597). Press accounts indicated sixteen others were injured, some seriously. Flash floods several miles away took another five lives.

June 30, 1882: Coaltown Tornado

The spring of 1882 was unusually chilly, indicating a strong northwesterly component to the jet stream pattern over Pennsylvania. On April 19, a tornado developed over Fayette County, one mile west of Pennsville, cutting a 200-yard damage path through the northwest part of town along an eight-mile track. The F2 storm killed one person in the community of Mount Vernon and damaged fifty buildings, causing $75,000 of damage (Gazulis 1993, 614).

A second deadly twister hit in the opening days of the summer season. A tornado touched down on June 30 two miles west of Coaltown, Lawrence County, in the northwest part of the state near the Ohio line. The twister promptly moved through the heart of the small western Pennsylvania community, killing three persons and injuring nearly three dozen more. Fifteen homes were damaged, along with a dozen businesses. The F3 storm was 400 yards wide and traveled along a ten-mile track (Grazulis 1993, 617).

April 2, 1884: Pittsburgh Tornado

A powerful cold front raced through the upper Ohio River valley on the morning of April 2, 1884. Six persons died at Oakville, Indiana, five miles south of Muncie, and fifty others were injured on the evening of April 1 as a series of twisters ripped through Indiana and western and central Ohio.

A squall line blasted through the Monongahela Valley around 9:30 A.M. on April 2, striking Homestead on the outskirts of Pittsburgh, where windows were blown in, trees knocked down, and outbuildings overturned. A home under construction was blown down, injuring six workers. Another home atop a nearby hill was "displaced from its foundations," and injuries resulted from flying debris.

The storm was almost certainly a tornado as it struck the south side of Pittsburgh, blowing down a new wire mill at the bottom of Ninth Street, where about a hundred workers were toiling. Several workers narrowly escaped death, and six were injured. The *Pittsburgh Commercial Advertiser* reported: "The girders and iron work were bent and twisted, and nearly all of the columns were knocked off their foundations." Several homes in the vicinity were damaged by high winds. The roof of a home on Wylie Avenue was torn off, causing serious injuries for three occupants. In all, about twenty-one Pittsburgh-area residents were injured in the storm, and four were thought to have life-threatening injuries.

August 3, 1885: Camden-Philadelphia Tornado

A tornado outbreak in the mid-Atlantic region on the afternoon of August 3, 1885, spawned a deadly F2 tornado that swept eight miles up the Delaware River valley, killing six persons and injuring fifty-eight others (Grazulis 1993, 636).

The August 3 tornado outbreak began around 11:30 A.M. in Montgomery County. Three hours later a severe thunderstorm spawned a tornado in Juniata County. Less than an hour later, a writhing funnel cloud over the south side of Philadelphia touched down at Greenwich Point, killing a child and a railroad worker.

The whirling funnel crossed the Delaware River into Camden, New Jersey, following a course that straddled both sides of the river for two miles before swerving into Camden. Three people died in Camden, and a fourth was killed aboard the steamer *Major Reybold,* which was torn apart by fierce winds in the river.

The *Monthly Weather Review* reported that the storm touched down around 3:20 P.M. in Philadelphia and commenced a north-northeast track for eight miles, crossing back and forth over the Delaware River into Camden, New Jersey. The damage path in places was reportedly 1,200 yards, though the storm was not as wide as it crossed Philadelphia:

> The rush of the cyclone was estimated to be 500 feet wide. Its appearance was that of a dense black cloud revolving at a terrific rate. In the heart of it the gloom was like the darkness of midnight, and eye witnesses describe the air as so black that they could not see their hands before their faces. The bottom of it moved over the river like a rolling ball of smoke. The phenomenal force of the wind can only be imagined from the visible evidence of its destruction, and its power seemed to be almost supernatural. In recollection of no one in this city has a phenomenon of such character and ruinous results ever visited the neighborhood of Philadelphia, and by those who were the victims of its work it will never be forgotten. After the cyclone passed, a heavy rain storm set in, which lasted during the early part of the evening, with frequent sharp flashes of lightning. (*Philadelphia Inquirer,* August 4, 1885)

In addition to the six fatalities, one hundred people were injured, and storm damage was estimated at around $500,000. Damage in the Philadelphia area totaled $150,000, and in Camden three hundred homes were damaged with losses put at $200,000.

Tornadoes were later sighted around 4:00 P.M. north of Landsdale in Montgomery County and north of Feasterville in Bucks County. The Bucks County storm was judged to be the strongest tornado (F3) of the group, traveling north-northwest for eleven miles to Solebury, damaging two homes and several barns. Grazulis (1993, 636) noted two additional veins of tornado damage, suggesting that possibly two more funnels were spawned by a supercell thunderstorm over Bucks County. The damage was substantial, with reports of sixteen homes demolished by the roaring winds. A tombstone traveled one hundred yards in the whirlwind.

Around 5:00 and 5:30 P.M., two tornadoes were later sighted at Chester County west of Unionville and in East Nanteal Township. The path length of the first storm was one and a half miles, and the second storm that struck near Pocopson traveled two miles. Several barns suffered damage in both instances. Another storm was reported in Berks County, though no time was noted. No injuries were reported with these storms.

Tornadoes were also reported in Maryland (4) and Delaware (1) on the afternoon of August 3, 1885, according to the *Monthly Weather Review*. A storm that hit New Castle County, Delaware, around 4:45 P.M. damaged two homes and three barns.

July 16–17, 1887: Tornadoes in Easton and Carlisle

During the midst of an oppressive heat wave in a blistering summer, the boundary between hot, humid air over Pennsylvania and cooler, drier air to the north became the focus of severe thunderstorms on successive days in the middle of July 1887.

On July 16, 1887, between 6:00 and 7:00 P.M., a localized storm struck Easton, causing about $500,000 in property damage (Flora 1953, 161). A small tornado blew a railroad car down an embankment in Easton, and several homes were unroofed. Another tornado was sighted at Mechanicsburg, which slammed into a wagon and carriage factory and blew down a steeple in front of the Methodist church. One serious injury was reported in the press account. In neighboring Phillipsburg, New Jersey, lightning felled the Delaware Rolling Mill's brick smokestack, which fell into another and crashed through the roof.

A stronger squall line developed out ahead of a cold front on the afternoon of July 17, spawning a tornado that struck Carlisle around 3:00 P.M. and caused considerable damage to several schools and homes. Buildings were reportedly twisted or demolished, and roofs were blown off buildings at Dickinson College. Widespread damage and property losses included a number of dwellings, crops, and livestock in the area. Strong thunderstorms blasted parts of Pennsylvania again on July 23–24, 1887, dropping 3.98 inches of rain on Philadelphia.

January 9, 1889: Great Wind Rush and Tragedy

A powerful winter cyclone over the Great Lakes and southeastern Canada triggered a rare midwinter outbreak of severe weather on January 9, 1889. Heavy snow accompanied by winds caused considerable damage around the Great Lakes on January 9–10, while high winds battered Ohio, New York, and Pennsylvania southeast of the storm track, where unseasonably warm and humid air collided with cold air from the northwest.

An apparent squall line developed along the leading edge of much colder air on the morning of January 9. Strong winds aloft, reflecting a sharp temperature contrast in the atmosphere over the Northeast, mixed down to the surface as clusters of storms raced northeast across Pennsylvania. Powerful straight-line winds, representing a downward transfer of momentum from strong upper-level currents, developed in the warm sector of the cyclone across Ohio, Pennsylvania, and New York.

Tragedy struck just south of Pittsburgh shortly after noon when high winds caused an unfinished seven-story building to collapse, taking down adjoining structures. Fifteen people died and forty-nine others suffered injuries. One fatality occurred when another unfinished building collapsed farther along in the storm's path. Twelve buildings in Pittsburgh and Allegheny City were hit hard by the storm, and the total damage reported in the *Monthly Weather Review* was put at $165,000.

According to an account in the *New York Times,* "The storm had many of the characteristics of a tornado. Its path was about two miles wide and its centre passed a little south of the city. So depressed was the condition of the atmosphere that the wind rushed down upon the city as water would run down a declivity."

Another disaster occurred later in the day on the north side of Reading in the southeast. High winds blew down the Reading Silk Mill, where 275 employees were working at the time. The mill caved in under the force of the powerful blast of winds. Twenty-three workers were killed as the walls collapsed, and dozens more suffered serious injuries (Grazulis 1993, 116). Witnesses at the silk mill calamity watched helplessly as "the building went down all in a heap as if a huge weight had dropped upon and smashed it." Another related storm tragedy occurred at the Philadelphia and Reading Company paint shop, which was blown down and caught fire, killing five trapped workers.

A dispatch from East Brady in Clarion County that appeared in the Pittsburgh *Leader* stated that "a terrific hail storm passed over this place at 2 o'clock." Farther east, high winds at Harrisburg at 4:18 P.M., estimated around 100 miles per hour, carried away a portion of the wind speed indicator at the weather bureau office. Extensive property damage associated with straight-line winds was reported around the capital city.

A strong wind shift to the northwest occurred at Philadelphia at 6:40 P.M., marking the passage of a cold front. A "whirlwind" hit the eastern side of Camden, New Jersey, stripping the roof off an icehouse and tossing it against a row of brick homes, which crushed the front of another building. Wind damage was widespread over Pennsylvania, New Jersey, and New York City on January 11, 1889.

The Stroudsburg *Jeffersonian* provided an account of the storm in eastern Monroe County, Pennsylvania, near the Delaware River: "Prior to the storm reaching this neighborhood the day was stormy. Occasionally it rained very hard and then it could come down moderately, when towards evening it cleared away and the sun shone for a few minutes, when it clouded up again, the clouds coming from the southwest, and about 5 minutes after 6 o'clock, the gale or tornado struck this place or vicinity, accompanied by a roar similar to running cars, and began to tumble things around."

Downburst winds, possibly accompanied by an embedded small tornado, hit Snydersville, southwest of Stroudsburg, blowing out the windows of a home. Following a northeasterly course, high winds damaged a farm in Stroud Township and the fairgrounds nearby. A home in the vicinity had "a large hole torn into it" and roof damage, and a cemetery had monuments blown down. Damage in southwest Stroudsburg was confined to mostly rooftops, trees, and fences, suggesting straight-line winds.

A press dispatch from Sunbury reported that at the Sunbury Nail Mill winds toppled two stacks, which smashed through a roof, killing two workers and injuring at ten others, with four reported missing. Reports of wind damage came from Williamsport, Carlisle, and York. At Easton, twenty-five men on a suspension bridge had a harrowing experience when the heavy wire guy rope broke, causing the bridge to "sway and shake heavily." One man was thrown eight feet into the river but was able to swim safely to shore. Two others clung to the railing, while the rest lay down until all were able to depart the bridge after the winds subsided.

A report filed by a correspondent in the *Monthly Weather Review* (January 1889) described an apparent tornado that struck Brooklyn, New York City, at 7:40 P.M. and had a path width of 500 to 600 feet and traveled a two-mile course, lifting "here and there a roof" and blowing down fences. Upon reaching the Citizens' Gas Company, the storm clearly resembled a tornado, lifting a gas tank that caused a major explosion. "The iron pillars not less than two feet in diameter and perhaps forty feet high, were thrown principally in a northerly direction, one or two of those nearest the tornado track being thrown in a westerly direction, thus showing clearly enough the whirl of the tornado."

The Signal Service officer at New York City reported the storm in South Brooklyn destroyed several homes moving from "south to northeast; its path was well-defined and houses were unroofed over its entire cost. The damage will probably reach $500,000."

The editor of the Stroudsburg *Jeffersonian* commented on the abnormal winter: "The East is rapidly taking on the peculiar traits and fashions of the West. Last winter [1887–88] we beat the West on snow, while this winter we are beating it on tornadoes. It is about time to call a halt."

May 10, 1890: Venango County Tornado

A severe thunderstorm spawned a powerful F3 tornado on the south side of Akron, Ohio, in the late afternoon of May 10, 1890. An hour later, around 5:30 P.M., a killer F3 tornado would rip through Mercer and Venango Counties in the northwestern Pennsylvania.

The twister traveled fifteen miles before lifting four miles southeast of Franklin. More than a dozen houses and a hundred oil derricks were damaged or destroyed. A Venango County couple milking cows in a barn were killed when the structure collapsed. The storm uprooted "hundreds of acres of timber, mostly oak." Seventeen persons were injured (Grazulis 1993, 651–652). A Franklin dispatch in the *New York Times* reported that the funnel was 300 feet wide, and "everything in its path was demolished." The storm ended at the Allegheny River.

Another severe windstorm was reported later in the month at Johnstown on May 25, 1890, causing "great damage" mostly from flooded streets and cellars (*Monthly Weather Review*).

July 17, 1890: Lehigh Valley Tornadoes

The *Philadelphia Inquirer* described a squall line that crossed eastern Pennsylvania and western New Jersey in the middle of the afternoon of July 17, 1890, as a "storm of extraordinary severity." High winds, torrential downpours, and large hail pounded many communities, causing considerable property damage.

A tornado descended on Ashland, about ten miles northwest of Pottsville, where "every building was wrecked, and the hailstones broke nearly every window pane." Extensive wind damage was also reported at Uniontown and Mauch Chunk (now Jim Thorpe).

A rotating thunderstorm continued southeast from Schuylkill County over the mountains into the Allentown/Bethlehem area, continuing a pattern of downburst wind damage before spawning another funnel cloud. In Allentown, a probable tornado blew over a 229-foot-tall brick stack, which landed on an engine house at the Barbour Thread Mill, partially destroying the structure. A brick home was partly destroyed and another frame home was overturned, and many others were unroofed. Several injuries were attributed to flying debris.

The storm continued southeast, lifting for a short time before making another appearance at Hellertown, several miles south of the city of Bethlehem. A press dispatch strongly suggested a tornado developed over the Lehigh Valley: "About 4 o'clock an inky black cloud was noticed coming over the Lehigh Mountains, whirling and tossing in fury. It came with terrific speed, sweeping everything before it, cutting a path about a mile in width" (*Philadelphia Inquirer,* July 18, 1890). The tornado blasted a brick building under construction into pieces, and falling debris killed a thirteen-year-old. Small buildings were demolished and trees were blown down over a distance of several miles.

Wind damage was also reported at Trenton, New Jersey, where more homes were unroofed and two men died after being struck by lightning. Another storm fatality was reported down the river at Camden, New Jersey. Wind and lightning damage were reported throughout southeastern Pennsylvania. At Norristown there was "a terrific hail and rain storm" that lasted fifteen minutes, beginning around 6:00 P.M. The hail accumulated sufficiently that "the streets were whiter than at any time last winter."

A number of small boats were flipped over in the onslaught of high winds that cut a swath through northeast Philadelphia and Port Richmond. At Five Mile Point in the Delaware River, the steamboat *Columbia,* en route to Bristol, was broadsided by a downburst that seriously damaged the ship and frightened the passengers. Lightning damage and heavy rain struck Altoona around 7:00 P.M., showing a very widespread storm pattern, or a broad thunderstorm system.

August 19, 1890: Wilkes-Barre Tornado

A major tornado outbreak hit eastern Pennsylvania during the late afternoon of August 19, 1890. The first significant damage occurred around 4:30 P.M. in Berks County northwest of Reading, where an F2 tornado destroyed several barns along a five-mile course traveling east-northeast (Grazulis 1993, 651).

The action shifted to northeastern Pennsylvania around 5:00 P.M., when a tornado struck north of Shickshinny and traveled ten miles to near Silkworth. Grazulis (1993, 653) wrote that "probably a family of small but intense tornadoes" were responsible for the havoc that ensued in Luzerne County. Several persons died and at least ten more were injured as the storm struck several barns and homes along a ten-mile journey. The press reported the damage totaled $25,000 at Harveyville.

The probable supercell moved on toward Wilkes-Barre, spawning a violent F3 storm around 5:30 P.M., first appearing as "a column of smoke" on the south side of town. The storm, packing winds estimated in excess of 157 miles per hour, tracked to the northeast along the "north edge of South Wilkes-Barre." The tornado destroyed four hundred buildings, killing sixteen people and causing $400,000 of damage. The storm continued on a northeasterly course, striking the community of Sugar Notch three miles east of the city.

A dispatch in the *Philadelphia Inquirer* described the awful storm in chilling detail: "The first premonition of danger was a sudden darkening of the heavens which made it black as night. Then the wind increased in velocity and in a few minutes it was blowing a terrific gale. The sound of crashing thunder and falling walls, added to the wind's fury, made a noise which resembled the cannonading of a great fort by a mighty artillery. In half an hour everything was quiet and then the stillness of death fell on the stricken city."

Grazulis (1993, 654) noted several other significant tornadoes in eastern Pennsylvania on August 19, 1890. Another violent F3 tornado struck Susquehanna County around 6:00 P.M., touching down several miles west of New Milford and tracking five miles to a point two miles east of Summerfield. Two children died as "at least two homes were levelled."

Two days later, on August 21, 1890, storms hit Fryburg (Clarion County) and near Richland (Lebanon County), the latter storm injuring four people as "a barn and two homes were unroofed and torn apart" on the west side of the community of Sheridan.

May 28, 1896: Tornado Swarm Hits Southeastern Pennsylvania and New Jersey

A major tornado outbreak in the Midwest on successive days from May 24 to 27, 1896, spawned at least two dozen significant (F2 or greater) tornadoes (Grazulis 1993, 676–677). The most notorious storm was a violent F4 tornado that barreled through the St. Louis area on May 27, 1896, killing 255 people and injuring about a thousand more, certainly one of the worst single tornado disasters in American weather history. The path width of the tornado was estimated around a thousand yards.

The following day turned stormy in the East as a cold front advanced into humid air. A tornado was spotted in Adams County around 2:00 P.M. on May 28, several miles east of Gettysburg. The storm traveled thirteen miles into York County, causing "considerable damage" northeast of Hanover (*Climate and Crops*). Four injuries were reported as barns were blown down, and "one home was leveled, and its furniture was carried for over a half mile" (Grazulis 1993, 677). The path width was about five hundred yards.

Around 2:30 P.M. a second funnel, probably from the same rotating thunderstorm, touched down in eastern York County just west of Wrightsville. According to *Climate and Crops,* the storm "unroofed barns, uprooted trees, and demolished fences" in Hillam Township and then proceeded to damage several buildings in Wrightsville.

The storm continued east-northeast into Lancaster County, crossing the Susquehanna River before hitting Columbia, about ten miles west of Lancaster. The powerful storm destroyed a planing mill and a part of the Columbia Rolling Mills, killing one person. Fifteen workers were trapped in the ruins of the rolling mill, accounting for most of the twenty injuries. Damage was also reported at Mountville and Rohrerstown to the east, and minor damage associated with this storm extended all the way to Montgomery County, though likely the work of straight-line winds.

Three homes were severely damaged in Columbia, resulting in a second fatality, according to an account in the *Philadelphia Inquirer.* One interesting footnote to this storm was a report of water being drawn into the core of the funnel as it crossed the river, "leaving the bed of the river visible nearly its entire width."

Another killer tornado appeared south of Ambler in Montgomery County around 2:55 P.M. on May 28. The F3 storm continued northeast, striking Jarrettstown, Horsham, and Hatboro into Bucks County. The tornado passed near Langhorne and then hopped over the Delaware River, ending four miles south of Trenton, New Jersey. The storm path was "marked by demolished and damaged buildings, uprooted trees, together with the usual wind damages and characteristics found in the path of tornadoes."

Grazulis suspected that "a family of two or three small tornadoes" was responsible for the wide swath of damage over thirty-five miles that was estimated at around $200,000. The tornado, or series of storms, killed two persons in Montgomery County and two others in Bucks County, along with reports of at least fifteen injuries. Grazulis noted, "At least sixteen barns were destroyed and all of the deaths may have been in barns or stables." A story in the *Philadelphia Inquirer* also reported damage at Jarrettstown that was inflicted on a schoolhouse, church, and several buildings.

Farther north, heavy downpours accompanied the violent thunderstorms. Flooding was reported at Hamburg, Reading, and throughout the Lehigh Valley, where forty residences sustained water damage in Bethlehem. To the east, another vein of tornado damage developed east of Philadelphia near Bordentown, New Jersey, where a barn was blown down, killing one person.

The storm followed an east-northeast path, damaging several homes and ripping many trees out of the ground at Rutherford, New Jersey. The same storm may have spawned another tornado at Allentown, New Jersey, which killed two men and caused $100,000 of damage. Small tornadoes were also sighted near Littletown in Adams County before a storm crossed the Pennsylvania border into Maryland (Grazulis 1993, 678) and at Nutley, New Jersey, where damage was confined to a little less than a mile. A funnel cloud was later viewed over Perth Amboy that turned into a waterspout over the bay and may have been the storm responsible for wind damage around Asbury Park.

High winds ripped through Washington, D.C., toppling tress on the White House grounds. A press dispatch noted the damage path as "a space less than 100 yards wide [that] marked the progress of its fury." The roof of a church at Vermont Avenue and Fourteenth Street was blown off, and young boy died after being struck by debris from a chimney that was blown down. Considerable straight-line wind damage was reported, consisting of fallen trees and branches.

September 6, 1898: Bradford County Tornado

A protracted heat wave in early September 1898 was brought to a halt by a series of squall lines on September 6–7 across New York, Pennsylvania, and New Jersey. The first of two deadly twisters on September 6 struck western New York near Geneva, killing three persons at Phelps. One man was carried several hundred feet in the air over an orchard before landing on a pile of debris.

The storms raced eastward and developed farther south into northern Pennsylvania during the evening and early nighttime hours. Northern Bradford County was hit by a tornado later in the evening of September 6. A Stroudsburg *Jeffersonian* story reported that one man died when the roof of a barn caved in near Springfield Centre, and two Mansfield residents were killed in another barn that collapsed in the strong winds.

The storm reportedly came from the northwest, ripping through the community of Springfield Centre, demolishing several buildings and barns. Based on damage to orchards and fields, it is estimated that the path width was about a quarter-mile and the storm lasted about fifteen minutes.

High winds raked the Northeast from Vermont to New Jersey on September 7, 1898, causing several storm-related deaths.

March 27, 1911: Philadelphia Tornado

A violent thunderstorm moved through Philadelphia around 6:00 P.M. on March 27, 1911, killing one person, injuring more than one hundred others, and causing about $100,000 of damage (Flora 1953, 161). The storm hit Overbrook, Germantown, and West Philadelphia before wreaking havoc in the northeast section of the city, suggesting a southwest to northeast path that managed to skirt Center City. The whirling winds almost certainly took the form of a tornado, filling the air with debris as the sky turned black as night, according to press accounts.

Hundreds of injuries, many serious, were attributed to a combination of flying debris, falling trees and telephone poles, and lightning strikes that destroyed a number of buildings. One direct fatality occurred at the Tacony Station of the Pennsylvania Railroad where the roof was blown off and carried for a distance of a city block, landing on a Pittsburgh man who was traveling through town.

> Never before perhaps in the history of the city has a more violent storm been experienced here. Great steel signal towers stationed along the New York division of the Pennsylvania Railroad were torn from their concrete foundations and swept away like sapling trees, while telegraph poles were blown down in rows. Frame and even brick dwellings failed to withstand the fury of the gale, which swept over the section like a tornado. Hardly a building of any kind in Tacony and the upper portion of Port Richmond escaped damage, while everything movable along the highways was carried away by the gale. (*Philadelphia Inquirer,* March 28, 1911)

April 2, 1912: Philadelphia–Camden Tornado

A cluster or line of severe thunderstorms spawned one or more tornadoes as it crossed northeastern Delaware, southeastern Pennsylvania, and southwestern New Jersey during the early evening hours on April 2, 1912. The storm struck

Philadelphia at 7:00 P.M. and shortly thereafter crossed the Delaware River, wreaking havoc in neighboring Camden, New Jersey, where the damage was described as even worse than that caused by the 1885 tornado.

A vivid account of the storm appeared in the *Philadelphia Inquirer:* "Traveling at a terrific velocity, a miniature cyclone of seven minutes' duration encircled the city last evening, leaving in its wake a path of destruction and injury." Streets were littered with shattered glass. The storm damage was tracked by the weather bureau in downtown Philadelphia, "starting in the vicinity of Delaware avenue and Market street and traveling south along Delaware avenue to South Philadelphia, round West Philadelphia to Frankford and Manayunk, where it crossed the river again and continued southward into New Jersey."

The storm initially "came up the Delaware" from the southwest, making it likely that the circuitous damage path was part of a broader downburst pattern, since no mention of a funnel cloud on the ground in Philadelphia has been uncovered. A wind gust of 32 miles per hour (corrected) was measured on the roof of the Federal Building downtown, but it was estimated to have been "doubled this in the sections where the damage was wrought."

The storm had probably spawned a tornado by the time the high winds rushed through Camden, New Jersey, where "the northwest section of the city was laid in ruins." Two nurses were crushed when debris landed on a trolley car they were riding, and one died from her injuries. At that point, they were caught in "the center of a maelstrom of flying roofs, falling telegraph poles and trees and odds and ends of debris."

The *Monthly Weather Review* (April 1912) reported a total of two hundred buildings were damaged in the storm, leaving a hundred people homeless northeast of downtown Philadelphia and in Camden. There were several severe injuries in addition to those caused by the trolley accident.

August 21, 1914: Wilkes-Barre Tornado

History repeated itself almost to the date of the anniversary of the August 19, 1890, killer tornado that struck Wilkes-Barre. On August 21, 1914, seven persons died and fifty more were injured when a tornado struck the southwestern side of the city, destroying twenty buildings. According to the Stroudsburg *Morning Press,* "Shortly after 6 o'clock, while an electrical storm swept the entire valley, the tornado came out of the southwest. It struck in the Blackman patch and Blackman and New Empire Streets. A row of twenty dwelling houses, of the type occupied by miners, was first struck by the wind. They were torn from their foundations of concrete like so many card houses."

Next in line was the Laurel silk mill, where fourteen young women were preparing to leave work. Two were killed and twelve persons were injured, left in the ruins of the mill. The storm managed to skip the densely populated New Empire neighborhood before slamming into the hill section, ripping up trees and tearing off a portion of the Welsh Congregational Church on Hillside Avenue. The state police at Wyoming, across the Lackawanna River, joined local law enforcement officials to aid in the rescue work.

August 22, 1915: Hanover Tornado

The Second Galveston Hurricane slammed into the southeast Texas coastline on the night of August 16, 1915, accompanied by 120-mile-per-hour winds, dumping up to nineteen inches of rain, and killing 275 persons (Longshore 1998, 303). The remnants of the storm spun northeast across the middle Mississippi Valley, crossing northwestern Ohio and over the eastern Great Lakes on the afternoon of August 21.

Torrential downpours swamped St. Louis on August 19–20 and triggered rounds of heavy thunderstorms across southern New York and Pennsylvania on August 21–22. The circulation center spawned a twister in southeastern Pennsylvania at Hanover in York County, according to an account in the *New York Times:* "Hundreds of houses were unroofed and scores of structures and manufacturing plants were wrecked, while trees were uprooted and many poles blown over."

Twelve homes were demolished by the storm as two funnels may have merged over the city of Hanover. Wind damage likely associated with straight-line winds blew over streetcars. Flash floods, damaging winds, and possible tornadoes were also reported in southern New York, mostly in Sullivan and Ulster Counties.

November 17, 1918: Harrisburg Tornado

A tornado swirled through the Riverside section of Harrisburg shortly before midnight on November 17, 1918, causing extensive damage but, miraculously, only two minor injuries.

Tornadoes in the late autumn are a rare occurrence in Pennsylvania, though occasionally the ingredients for severe weather, notably a strong wind field associated with the passage of a vigorous storm, come together to spawn a short-lived tornado. The storm was described in the Harrisburg *Patriot:* "Riverside is in ruins. Caught in the swirl of the terrific wind an electrical storm that swept across the Susquehanna at 11:50 o'clock last night, the little suburban section to the north of the city is a wreck. More than a score of houses are almost completely wrecked. Dozens more are unroofed. One house was completely turned over. Others were swept from their foundations. Scarcely one of the picturesque little homes of the suburb but has not been damaged to the extent of hundreds of dollars."

One report mentioned a street car entangled "in the network of fallen wires and tangled debris on North Sixth street," and another stated that a "granite stew pan was blown through a parlor window of a house on Lewis street into the midst of a family which had huddled before the fireplace during the storm." Huge trees were uprooted across different parts of the capital city, signs were blown down, and fallen wires led to widespread outages. Grazulis (1993, 761) listed a storm path width of two hundred yards over a 0.5-mile course, resulting in the two known injuries.

July 10, 1919: Bradford Tornado

Rugged McKean County in northwestern Pennsylvania, where the terrain rises more than two thousand feet above mean sea level, is normally a safe haven from destructive storms. Yet on May 25, 1918, an F2 storm formed southeast of Aiken in the late evening hours and tracked southeast for seven miles before ending west of Smethport. A barn was destroyed, along with "timber, oil drilling equipment, part of the Poor Farm, and the roof of a factory," amounting to $150,000 of damage (Grazulis 1993, 761).

A singular occurrence of a strong tornado on the high Allegheny Plateau near the New York border would have been noteworthy enough, but another powerful storm struck the county a little over a year later. On July 10, 1919, a tornado touched down a mile southwest of Bradford, traveling east-northeast for six miles through the south side of town (Grazulis 1993, 765). The storm was judged to be severe (F3): "Eight homes and a warehouse were destroyed, and 30 others were damaged as the tornado periodically lifted and touched down again."

June 28, 1924: Meadville Tornado

The first week of summer in 1924 took a stormy turn in parts of Pennsylvania. Damaging winds blasted areas around Erie on June 20, causing significant property damage. Five days later, on June 25, an F2 tornado formed northwest of Gettysburg and traveled over the northern fringe of town for a distance of nine miles before ending near New Oxford. Six barns were destroyed and several homes were unroofed, with reports of furniture being lifted from the upper stories (Grazulis 1993, 790).

A few days later, a line of violent thunderstorms formed in the sultry air over northern Ohio on the evening of June 28, 1924, spawning several deadly twisters. A devastating tornado formed near Sandusky, Ohio, around 4:35 P.M. on that day, tearing through the lakeshore city with deadly swiftness as it carved a path of death and destruction nearly 0.5 mile wide.

The storm crossed over Lake Erie around Cedar Point for about twenty-five miles before blasting into the city of Lorain around 5:15 P.M. Eight persons died in Sandusky and sixty-four were killed in Lorain. The final death toll for the Sandusky-Lorain tornado was eighty-five persons. The large tornado, or possibly two funnels, destroyed nearly two hundred businesses and five hundred homes, with damage reported to about a thousand more homes (Flora 1953, 106).

As the line of storms advanced southeastward into northwestern Pennsylvania, a strong tornado (F3) struck Meadville, Crawford County, around 6:30 P.M. The storm track was along a line from two mile south of Geneva to a little south of Frenchtown. One person was killed as two homes were destroyed near the beginning of the tornado's ten-mile path (Grazulis 1993, 790). Five others died in the aftermath of downburst winds, and a train derailment was attributed to the tornado, as reported in the *Monthly Weather Review* (June 1924).

Shortly after 7:00 P.M., another tornado (F2), on the ground about one mile, caused extensive wind damage to about thirty-seven homes near Erie in the Lawrence Park area. Farther south, a terrific cluster of thunderstorms lashed the Pittsburgh area, bringing a heavy loss of life from a combination of flash flooding, collapsed buildings, and electrocutions as wires were toppled by high winds. The storms claimed eleven lives in the Pittsburgh area, the greatest loss of life attributable to a violent thunderstorm without a confirmed tornado in Pennsylvania since 1889.

Two family members died and six others were injured in a single home that caved in at North Braddock after the foundation was loosened in a landslide. A Pittsburgh dispatch summarized the disaster: "Eleven lives were lost, many persons were injured, heavy property damage was inflicted, trolley and railroad schedules were demoralized and telephone and telegraph service were crippled as the result of the terrific rain, wind, and electrical storm that swept this region late last night and early today. Almost four inches of rain fell during the few hours of the storm's duration" (*Philadelphia Inquirer,* June 30, 1924).

April 1, 1929: Portland Storm

A powerful tornado described as "sweeping down from almost an almost clear sky" appeared out of a "peculiar, milky-white haze" about a mile southwest of Portland on the afternoon of April 1, 1929, reported the East Stroudsburg *Morning Sun.*

The storm struck around 4:30 P.M. and promptly destroyed the historic Portland–Columbia bridge as it whirled up the Delaware River valley before turning northeast across New Jersey. The F2 tornado traveled along a northeasterly path before dissipating near Blaristown, New Jersey, a distance of about ten miles. The press account stated: "Houses were torn to bits. . . . Barns and lighter buildings were destroyed. Thousands of trees and poles were strewn about."

A New Jersey farmer was killed instantly by flying timber after being caught out in the open on his farm, three miles north of Polkville, New Jersey. Two other injuries were judged to be serious, which may account for the death toll listed as three by Snowden D. Flora (1953, 154). The storm damage was put at $50,000.

May 20, 1933: Berks County Tornado

Grazulis (1993, 852) described a "complex tornado/downburst combination" of F3 intensity that tracked east-northeast through a part of Reading in the late afternoon of May 20, 1933. Thirty-five injuries were reported in the storm, though most of the $750,000 of damage and some of the injuries were attributed to downburst winds rather than the funnel that briefly touched down.

July/August 1941: Southeastern Tornadoes

Several tornadoes hit Pennsylvania in late summer of 1941. On July 18, "an apparently intense path was cut through eight miles of forest" over Clinton and Potter Counties in the northwest as a storm passed several miles east of Cross Forks (Grazulis 1993, 895). There were no injuries, even though the storm had a wide damage path of eight hundred yards through largely uninhabited terrain.

Another large funnel struck on July 30 at Mechanicsburg in Bucks County, a little north of Philadelphia, with a path width a quarter of a mile. The storm destroyed several small buildings while causing some property and crop damage.

On August 25, 1941, a hit-skip tornado caught a section of southeastern Chester County, where it unroofed fifteen homes near Kemblesville along a four-mile path. Damage was reported to be $75,000, and there was one injury. The storm churned east-northeast across the northwest portion of Wilmington, Delaware, where damage reached $150,000 and seven people were injured.

One person died at Swedesboro, New Jersey, as the storm rolled into the south-westpart of that state before lifting. The tristate storm traveled a path of thirty-two miles, though not always in contact with the ground, and was three hundred yards wide at times.

June 23, 1944: Deadly Tornadoes Hit Southwestern Pennsylvania

A family of tornadoes followed nearly parallel paths during early evening hours of June 23, 1944, developing over hilly terrain in eastern Ohio, western Pennsylvania, and northern West Virginia. The storm rampage ultimately killed forty-five people in southwestern Pennsylvania, and five more died in western Maryland (Flora 1953, 117). Violent tornadoes also took a terrible toll in West Virginia, killing 104 people (NOAA). There were 846 serious injuries, and property losses exceeded $5 million.

Four violent tornadoes were on the ground at almost the same time between 6:30 and 9:30 P.M., moving southeast at speeds of thirty to forty miles per hour. A review of the June 1944 tornado outbreak (Grazulis 1993, 915) places the first in a series of devastating tornadoes in Armstrong County in southwestern Pennsylvania around 5:30 P.M. The twister traveled southeast from Rural Valley to Twin Rocks, damaging fifty homes and farms and causing three injuries.

As the storm progressed into Indiana County, another fifteen homes were destroyed and two people died. Damage extended into Cambria County, though was possibly due to a downburst by that time. The F3 storm had a damage path that extended thirty miles, causing nineteen injuries. Around 6:00 P.M., a smaller storm touched down in northeastern Ohio and was responsible for eight injuries as it passed south of Palmyra.

Another supercell thunderstorm near Wellsburg, West Virginia, spawned a deadly family of tornadoes beginning at 6:11 P.M. One death occurred at Wellsburg, West Virginia, where twenty homes were unroofed. The storm continued southeast into Pennsylvania, killing four people in Washington County and twenty-two more in Greene County, where the tornado reached F4 strength, with winds in excess of 206 miles per hour. The storm passed eight miles southeast of Uniontown in Fayette County and then lifted briefly before reentering West Virginia.

Ten injuries were reported after four homes were destroyed during another touchdown in northern West Virginia. In all, some eighty-six homes were destroyed in Pennsylvania. Yet another tornado skipped across northwestern Maryland, killing three persons and injuring twenty-five others two miles north of Oakland, Maryland.

At about 6:30 P.M., a deadly F4 tornado formed eight miles south of Pittsburgh in Allegheny County and traveled fifty miles through Westmoreland and Somerset Counties. Eighty-eight homes were destroyed and 306 were damaged south of McKeesport in Allegheny County. Homes either "collapsed or were blown apart" by the ferocity of the winds. Seventeen Pennsylvanians died and two hundred were injured as the storm roared southeast parallel to the turnpike, inflicting serious damage near Donegal and northwest of Somerset.

Death-dealing tornadoes continued to develop farther southeast across northeastern West Virginia at the same time southwestern Pennsylvania was raked by violent twisters. A powerful F4 storm struck at 6:30 P.M. northwest of Wyatt, killing a hundred people. The remarkable aspect of the storm was its sixty-mile path over rugged terrain while maintaining continuous contact with the ground. The last major tornado of the evening (F3) hit Tucker, West Virginia, at 10:25 P.M. and took three more lives.

When the horrible evening ended, the storms of June 23, 1944, had claimed 154 lives and injured nearly 1,000 persons in Pennsylvania, West Virginia, western Maryland, and Delaware. More than 400 homes were destroyed and 1,456 buildings, 691 of which were homes, were damaged (Flora 1953, 117).

June 7, 1947: Sharon Tornado

The 1947 tornado season was quite active in Pennsylvania, especially in the late springtime. On May 21, a tornado (F1) developed south of Centerport in Berks County around 4:45 P.M., tracking six miles. The storm killed one boy and injured his brother when it demolished the garage they were in. The damage path was judged to be seven hundred yards (Grazulis 1993, 930). Another storm hit Berks County on May 25, causing minor damage between Hamburg and Lenhartsville.

On May 29, a second tornado fatality of the month occurred at Pine Grove in Schuylkill County around 4:30 P.M., when a man died in a barn that was hit by a tornado. However, the major tornado of the 1947 season developed over the northeast corner of Ohio in Trumbull County around 3:30 P.M. on the afternoon of June 7, 1947 (Grazulis 1993, 931).

The tornado formed a few miles southeast of Warren, Ohio, and tracked east over a long forty-mile course, plowing into Sharon, Pennsylvania, about 3:55 P.M. (Flora 1953, 121). The F4 tornado, with winds in excess of 206 miles per hour, had already killed three people and injured forty others in a residential area south of Vienna, Ohio, damaging or destroying 150 buildings before exiting the state.

The storm continued on into Sharon and Farrell in Mercer County, Pennsylvania, causing a substantial $1 million in property damage. Seventy homes were destroyed, and three Pennsylvanians lost their lives in the storm. Homes and factories collapsed under the force of 200-mile-per-hour winds. The violent tornado injured about three hundred persons in northwestern Pennsylvania. Damage was also reported at Mercer and Grove City.

On September 2, 1947, a powerful F3 tornado struck western Pennsylvania in Washington County at the unusual hour of 2:15 A.M. The storm crossed Eldersville-Burgettstown Road traveling east-northeast along nine-mile path between Eldersville and Racoon. Five houses and forty buildings, including a number of barns, were damaged or destroyed. Two persons died in their homes, and forty others were injured, with the worst damage around South Burgettstown. A roof was flung a mile from its original location, and boards landed as far as four miles away (Grazulis 1993, 932).

April 5, 1952: York and Lancaster County Tornadoes

Four tornadoes touched down in eastern Pennsylvania in a little more than two hours in the early afternoon of April 5, 1952. The first storm (F2) touched down between Hanover and Spring Grove in York County at 1:15 P.M. and followed a discontinuous twenty-mile track past York to Wrightsville. A crane that weighed several tons was moved a distance of forty feet across a plant yard, and a greenhouse frame was twisted off its foundation, shattering more than a thousand panes of glass.

In one home, the wind "rolled up a linoleum runner in a hallway and blew a thirteen-year-old girl standing in the hallway off her feet" (Flora 1953, 130–131). The storm caused $1.5 million of damage, destroying a factory, unroofing several buildings, and damaging a number of barns and garages in the countryside. There were four storm-related injuries.

A half-hour later, about 1:45 P.M., a Lancaster County twister (F2) hit north of Lititz, injuring six more persons, and one was carried sixty-five feet. Several buildings were damaged and a 420-foot tower was blown, with a total damage estimate of $75,000 (Grazulis 1993, 964).Weaker storms hit Dauphin County (2:00 P.M.) and Monroe County (3:30 P.M.). The Monroe County storm came down briefly near Mountainhome and again in Paradise Valley.

May 12–13, 1956: Western Storms

Severe thunderstorms accompanied by tornadoes and torrential downpours blasted parts of southwestern Pennsylvania on May 12–13, 1956, causing an estimated $1 million in property damage. A twister (F2) embedded in a downburst pattern struck Beaver County shortly after midnight on May 13 about twenty miles northwest of downtown Pittsburgh.

The storm moved in a southeasterly direction after touching down about two miles north of Midland. Along a six-mile path, an elementary school and five barns were destroyed and several homes were damaged. Four persons were injured at a drive-in theater by flying glass. Downburst damage in Aliquippa totaled $200,000, including losses sustained at the Aliquippa-Hopewell Airport (Grazulis 1993, 997).

A second F2 tornado traveled southeast from the southeastern portion of West Mifflin in Allegheny County passing through Duquesne less than ten minutes after the Beaver County storm touched down to the northwest. Five persons were injured, which was remarkable considering that extensive damage occurred in Duquesne over twelve city blocks. Seventy-five buildings sustained serious damage, and two hundred others had comparatively minor losses. A third tornado (F2) tracked from north of Windber in Cambria County into Somerset County. The storm traveled five miles but caused only minor damage.

July 5–6, 1984: Eastern Pennsylvania Tornadoes and Downbursts

A stormy pattern developed across the Keystone State on the afternoon of July 5, 1984. An early-afternoon tornado touched down in the Laurel Highlands in Somerset County at High Point Lake. The storm followed a ten-mile track that destroyed a barn and two mobile homes. This was only a prelude to a larger outbreak of tornadoes and downburst winds in northern Berks County during the evening hours.

Grazulis (1993, 1261), who reviewed damage surveys published in *Storm Data,* described the stormy events that took place between 6:30 and 9:15 P.M. on July 5,

1984. He concluded that "six homes were destroyed and 40 homes were severely damaged" by four tornadoes bounded by an area seven miles long and three miles wide in northern Berks County.

An intense F3 twister touched down near Pricetown, about ten miles northeast of Reading, around 6:30 P.M., passing a little north of New Jerusalem and damaging several homes and uprooting or twisting off hundreds of trees along a seven-mile trek. Two injuries were reported in the storm. At 6:45 P.M. on July 5, a second tornado traveled three miles between Lyons and New Jerusalem.

A third storm developed two miles south of Topton and tracked eight miles into Lehigh County shortly before 7:00 P.M. The fourth identifiable twister unroofed homes along a five-mile course southwest of Macungie about 7:15 P.M., also tracking from Berks County into Lehigh County.

The following day, July 6, 1984, a tornado in eastern Pennsylvania was reported at Sweet Valley in Luzerne County around 5:15 P.M. The F2 storm was only on the ground a fraction of a mile but managed to destroy six homes and ten farm buildings, and it also damaged fifty-five houses plus forty-five cars. Three injuries occurred when a car was tossed into a pond.

May 31, 1985: Pennsylvania's Deadliest Tornado Outbreak

The deadliest tornado outbreak in Pennsylvania history occurred in the early evening hours of May 31, 1985. Sixty-three Pennsylvanians died on Friday, May 31, as a series of tornado families tore through western and central Pennsylvania in a five-hour reign of terror. This was the deadliest national tornado outbreak since 1974. Twelve persons died in Ohio on the same day, bringing the United States death toll to seventy-five (Schmidlin 1996, 292–295).

The meteorological setting on May 31 was regarded as potentially explosive as early as 4:00 A.M., when the National Weather Service put out a statement forecasting a risk of severe weather over northeastern Ohio and western Pennsylvania. The parameters included hot, humid air in place over Ohio and western Pennsylvania and a strong jet stream disturbance moving south from Canada.

The weather was surprisingly calm across Ohio and Pennsylvania through the middle of the afternoon, as temperatures soared into the eighties with hardly a cloud in the sky. The catalyst for severe weather would be a 140-mile-per-hour jet stream dipping down from the north across the Great Lakes into northeastern Ohio. Powerful winds ten miles above the surface would soon draw air upward very rapidly, breaking the "cap" that allowed a layer of warm, moist air to build up in the lower levels.

Over a period of several hours starting around 3:00 P.M., thirteen tornadoes formed over southeastern Ontario, Canada, killing twelve (eight at Barrie). The first killer tornado (F4) to hit northwestern Pennsylvania in the late afternoon of May 31, 1985, formed two miles west of the Ohio border around 5:00 P.M. The storm roared through Albion and Cranesville in Erie County, Pennsylvania, following a northeasterly track that covered twelve miles. The vicious 1,200-foot-wide tornado destroyed twenty square blocks of Albion, killing twelve and injuring eighty-two people.

Another violent (F4) storm developed around 5:17 P.M. just west of the Ohio border east of Kinsman, Ohio, traveling fifty-six miles across the rugged hills of northwestern Pennsylvania before ending four miles south of Tionesta. The storm first crossed Crawford County, hitting Jamestown, Atlantic, and Cochranton. The twister would continue east through Venango County before lifting in Forest County. The human toll was considerable (16 killed, 125 injured), and the path width covered 350 yards.

Another strong tornado (F3) formed near Saegertown in northern Crawford County at 5:23 P.M. that killed two persons at Centreville along a twenty-three-mile path. Seven more Pennsylvanians died along the path of another violent F4 storm that developed northwest of Tionesta in Venango County around 6:30 P.M. and tracked a distance of twenty-nine miles to near Pigeon in Forest County. The fatalities occurred at German Hill.

The strongest (F5) and deadliest tornado on May 31, 1985, first appeared about thirty miles west of Youngstown, Ohio, about 6:30 P.M., striking hard at Newton Falls and Niles, Ohio, before crossing into Pennsylvania. Police Captain Clayton Reakes was credited with saving lives in Newton Falls by climbing atop the municipal building and ordering the sounding of the town's siren (Witten 1985, 193–198).

The storm tore through the heart of Newton Falls before proceeding toward Niles, Ohio, where nine people ultimately died. The tornado entered Pennsylvania one mile west of Wheatland, taking seven lives before striking Hermitage and ending near Mercer, a path of forty-seven miles. The devastating storm packed winds of more than 260 miles per hour, killing 18 people (8 in Pennsylvania) and injuring 310 others (Grazulis 1991, 1267–1268).

Four persons died and forty were injured as another violent F4 storm rolled through Warren, McKean, and Elk Counties beginning around 8:00 P.M., doing considerable damage at Kane, where several schools suffered losses totaling $3 million. Four deaths occurred in trailers and frame homes, and the damage was put at $15 million (Grazulis 1993, 1269).

Another powerful (F3) storm began in Beaver County two miles west of Darlington at 8:10 P.M. and tracked thirty-nine miles across Beaver and Butler Counties, claiming 9 lives, injuring 120 people, and causing $10 million in Beaver County alone.

At 9:25 P.M., the last major tornado on May 31 was sighted one mile west of Bastress in Lycoming County. It traveled nineteen miles through Union and Northumberland Counties, killing six and injuring sixty persons. At one point the F4 funnel was nearly 1.5 miles wide as it crossed the Susquehanna River. Damage was estimated at $16 million, with the greatest losses reported in Northumberland County ($10 million). Two persons were killed in each of the three counties, where a number of trailer homes and campers were destroyed. A total of 190 structures were either damaged or destroyed, along with fifty vehicles. Thousands of trees were snapped off or uprooted by 200-mile-per-hour winds.

The last tornado touched down in the northeastern corner of Pennsylvania in Monroe County, between Tobyhanna and Mount Pocono, five minutes past midnight on June 1, 1985. The storm caused minor damage ($5,000), bringing the tornado count to twenty-one for the outbreak of May 31–June 1, 1985.

At the time, this was the single greatest tornado swarm in Pennsylvania history. Seven of the Pennsylvania storms on May 31 were rated F4 (winds greater than 206 miles per hour), and one was classified F5 (winds greater than 260 miles per hour). The 1985 tornado tally in Pennsylvania (34) was a state record until 1998.

November 16, 1989: Late Autumn Squall Line

During the midday hours of November 16, 1989, a powerful squall line accompanied by tornadoes and damaging straight-line winds raced across eastern Pennsylvania and New York. November is not a time normally associated with severe weather, but on occasion a strong storm draws tropical moisture northward into Pennsylvania, where it collides with a strong cold front approaching from the west.

The collision between tropical and polar airstreams turned deadly around noontime on November 16. A series of tornadoes touched down in southeastern New York and southeastern Pennsylvania. A great tragedy occurred in Coldenham when an elementary school cafeteria wall collapsed under the force of a downburst, killing seven children and injuring dozens more.

In southeastern Pennsylvania, a tornado came out of the clouds over Montgomery County, where winds gusted to nearly 100 miles per hour. Additional tornado sightings were called in over Montgomery and Bucks Counties. High winds shattered windows in several of Philadelphia's tall skyscrapers. In the northeast, high winds struck shortly before 11:00 A.M. on November 16, causing widespread power outages in the Poconos as trees landed on power lines. A trailer was pulled off its foundation and spun around ninety degrees at McMichaels in southwestern Monroe County. Winds gusted to 61 miles per hour at the Lehigh Valley International Airport, and a funnel cloud that did not touch down was sighted overhead at 10:43 A.M.

July 1992: Active Storm Season

July 1992 brought a series of stormy periods in Pennsylvania, beginning with a July 10 squall line that caused wind damage in the southeastern part of the state.

On July 15, the atmosphere turned more turbulent. Five twisters touched down over the eastern half of the state over a four-hour period during the afternoon hours. The first storm was sited in Clinton County (F1), and the next at Columbia, east of Berwick, along the Susquehanna River. A third tornado came down over Northampton County, two miles north of Chapman, and a fourth briefly touched down in a parking lot in downtown Bethlehem. A fifth storm was reported near Philadelphia in Delaware County. Numerous reports of straight-line wind damage came in from other sections of eastern Pennsylvania.

Two days later, on July 17, another outbreak of tornadoes saw eight funnels touch down in the eastern counties, starting in Snyder County and continuing east to near Philadelphia. The strongest storm (F2) struck near Unionville in Chester County.

On the last day of the month, a funnel cloud lowered to the ground east of Levittown in Bucks County, north of Philadelphia, and was witnessed again east of Trenton on the other side of the Delaware River. A total of twenty-six tornadoes touched down in Pennsylvania in July 1992, besting the previous July record of ten (1976).

July 27, 1994: Limerick Tornado

A stationary front stretching across the mid-Atlantic region became the focus of a severe weather event during the afternoon of July 27, 1994, affecting a wide area from North Carolina to Pennsylvania. Clusters of severe thunderstorms spawned five tornadoes in northern Virginia, three in Delaware, and fourteen in Maryland (state record).

The focus of severe weather shifted north into southeastern Pennsylvania after sunset. A powerful F3 tornado was spotted at 10:55 P.M. south of Avondale that would soon destroy six homes and damage twenty-three others, injuring eleven people. One critical injury resulted when a resident was thrown from a second-story window. Downburst winds hit sections of Chester County, causing significant damage. Total losses in Chester County were assessed at $3.5 million.

A smaller F1 tornado came down south of Downingtown before the parent storm apparently split into two cells exiting Chester County. The western cell went on to spawn a deadly F3 tornado in Montgomery County at Limerick at 11:52 P.M., which leveled four homes and severely damaged sixteen more. One man survived being thrown fifty feet through a second-story window and landing in a neighbor's family room. An infant was tossed onto the front lawn of another property and also lived, but three family members who were sleeping when the storm struck were killed.

July 19, 1996: A Dozen Tornadoes Touch Down in the Southwest

A large tornado outbreak for so late in the season occurred during the evening of July 19, 1996, in western Pennsylvania. A dozen funnels touched down, destroying a total of 92 homes and causing major damage to 311 homes and minor damage to another 792 dwellings. Most of the tornadoes were small in stature, but a storm in Clarion County killed one person and caused the most damage of any single storm ($100 million). Another twister in Franklin County was responsible for $500 million of damage.

Flash floods hit a number of western counties following a 4.00- to 6.00-inch rainfall, resulting in $100 million of damage in Jefferson County. The hardest-hit areas were the towns of Punxsutawney and Brookville. Severe weather caused more storm damage on July 29–31, 1996.

May 31 and June 2, 1998: Twin Tornado Outbreaks

Two record-breaking tornado outbreaks in three days in the late spring of 1998 established a single-day record for touchdowns in Pennsylvania (21) and contributed to a record annual number of confirmed tornadoes (59) in 1998 in the Keystone State (NOAA data).

The month of May 1998 was a stormy one in Pennsylvania. A cluster of thunderstorms raked the state on May 29, causing widespread wind damage and one confirmed tornado in Centre County. On May 31, thirteen years after the anniversary of Pennsylvania's deadliest tornado outbreak, another tornado rampage would leave its mark on Pennsylvania.

The weather pattern on the last day of May 1998 featured an unusually robust jet stream that would provide plenty of energy for a series of potent disturbances diving southeast from Canada into northern Pennsylvania. An unseasonably powerful storm turned northeast across southern Quebec on the morning of the thirty-first, pushing a warm front through Pennsylvania. This placed the state in the warm sector of the storm.

Southerly winds imported warm, tropical air northward into Pennsylvania, while daytime heating generated considerable instability in advance of an approaching disturbance from the northwest. Shifting winds with height generated powerful updrafts that helped to build a few storms into rotating supercell thunderstorms.

The first tornado reported in Pennsylvania on May 31, 1998, was spotted west of Buttonwood in Lycoming County (F1) at 5:20 P.M., causing minor property damage as it traveled east across Route 15 over a distance of a half-mile. The atmosphere soon become highly energized, setting the stage for the development of nineteen confirmed tornadoes in a three-hour span from 7:00 to 10:00 P.M. across parts of northern and western Pennsylvania, areas not accustomed to severe storms.

In the northeast, rotating thunderstorms accompanied by large hail and damaging winds spun off several tornadoes east of Scranton/Wilkes-Barre. The first of four tornadoes sighted in Pike County on the evening of May 31, 1998, was spotted at 8:08 P.M. three miles southwest of Blooming Grove. The F2 tornado came down around Promised Land and proceeded to carve a path of destruction up to 550 yards wide and two miles long through Promised Land State Park. Hundreds of trees were mowed down, and the damage was estimated at $200,000. No

Fig. 8.1. May 31, 1998. Tornado damage on Cody Street, one block east of Route 219, in Salisbury. (Photo by V.W.H. Campbell; *Pittsburgh Post-Gazette* Photo Archives, copyright 1998, all rights reserved)

serious injuries were reported in the storm, which passed through a rural section of Blooming Grove Township.

A second tornado came down from the roiling skies over Pike County around 8:20 P.M. near Blooming Grove, just south of Interstate 84, cutting a swath of damage three miles long and two hundred yards wide before lifting east of Route 739 near Cranberry Ridge. Again, there were no injuries reported, and damage was confined mostly to wooded areas, totaling $400,000.

The rotating thunderstorm that spawned the Promised Land tornado was soon linked with another strong tornado (F2) near Pecks Pond. This storm had staying power, cutting a continuous damage path twenty miles long, based on an aerial survey, before lifting one mile northeast of Dingmans Ferry. Virtually every tree was leveled along the 200-yard-wide path of the storm, blocking roads and driveways.

Routes 402 and 390 would be closed for several days after the storm, which briefly attained F3 intensity around the vacation community of Blue Heron Lake. An estimated one thousand trees were either toppled or sheared off bordering both sides of the lake, and several homes and campers were also damaged. The storm caused only two minor injuries, but the damage estimate was a substantial $1 million. Remarkably, near Greentown at 9:53 P.M. a fourth tornado on May 31, 1998, would touch down briefly in Pike County.

Northwest of the Pike County activity, two smaller tornadoes associated with another supercell developed over southern Lackawanna County near Old Forge and Elmhurst around 8:20 P.M.. The north side of Scranton, along with the communities of Waverly and Taylor, suffered tree and power line damage between 9:45 and 10:00 P.M.

In the Laurel Highlands, an extremely strong tornado formed over rugged terrain near Mount Davis in Somerset County around 8:50 P.M. The F2 tornado traveled east-southeast for fifteen miles, quickly reaching downtown Salisbury. Ten to fifteen businesses and a number of homes suffered storm damage, forcing 150 people to move to overnight shelter. A thirteen-year-old girl died in a van when a tree landed on the vehicle, and fifteen others in the Salisbury area sustained mostly minor injuries. The storm continued east for another eight miles, demolishing a barn at Pocohontas, where the storm may have briefly reached F3 intensity. Storm damage was estimated around $4 million, which would be the greatest single storm loss on the night of May 31, 1998, in the state.

Later in the evening, the action shifted southeast as clusters of severe storms formed in the juiciest air. A powerful F3 vortex emerged from a cluster of severe storms near Evansville in northern Berks County around 9:00 P.M., just to the east of Lake Ontelaunee. Crossing over Route 222 in Maiden Creek Township, the whirling storm traveled eight miles through the northern portion of Lyons, which suffered a direct blow. More than forty homes were damaged or destroyed, injuring seven persons. The path width of the storm was relatively narrow—120 yards —but still caused $1.4 million of damage.

The final two twisters in the May 31 outbreak developed after midnight in Chester County. A tornado that appeared at 12:43 A.M. on June 1 in Londonderry Township trekked six miles before vanishing five miles north of Avondale. Many trees were blown down in the narrow 100-yard path of the storm. A second twister followed a three-mile course through eastern Pocopson Township after touching down around 12:52 A.M. just east of the Brandywine River. The storm damaged hundreds of trees and tore the roofs off of five homes along a three-mile path that ended just west of the Dilworthtown Inn. Vehicles were damaged by falling trees, and storm damage in Chester County from the twin funnels and straight-line gusts was close to $1 million.

The outbreak of May 31–June 1, 1998, yielded twenty-two tornadoes (twenty-one on May 31). The total storm count for May 1998, including the Centre County storm on May 29, was twenty-three, setting a record for the month.

Remarkably, as the cleanup from the May 31, 1998, tornado outbreak continued, a second round of violent storms would strike some of the same areas two days later. On June 2, 1998, a widespread outbreak of severe weather from southern New England to the Middle Atlantic states killed two persons in Pennsylvania and injured at least fifty more persons in the region.

Two squall lines developed over northwestern Pennsylvania during the late-afternoon hours of June 2. The first twister (F1) in western Pennsylvania was sighted at 5:30 P.M. in Beaver County near Shippingport, which damaged four homes and overturned a trailer. The storm moved into Raccoon Township, causing minor damage to nineteen houses, resulting in $400,000 of damage. A weaker F0 storm would visit the same area two hours later, blowing down fifty to one hundred cherry trees and damaging a home.

Weather forecasters watched with alarm as a series of funnels developed from a number of storms over the western part of Pennsylvania. At 5:45 P.M., a storm touched down four miles west of Custer City in McKean County, traveling eight miles through the Allegheny National Forest and crossing over Route 219.

Farther southeast, around 5:55 P.M., a tornado (F1) formed five miles northwest of Carnagie in Allegheny County and passed through a heavily populated area, causing sporadic damage. The twister covered a distance of a little more than thirty-two miles, passing through the southern and eastern suburbs of Pittsburgh.

The urban twister with a path width of up to 800 yards moved through heavily populated areas, including Mount Washington, Hazlewood, Irwin, and Manor. Fifty-one injuries, mostly minor, occurred, mainly in and around Mount Washington. More than a thousand homes suffered slight to moderate damage, and trees were snapped in two. The funnel cloud passed over Three Rivers Stadium, interrupting the baseball game between the Pittsburgh Pirates and New York Mets. The storm dissipated over Westmoreland County at 6:28 P.M. after causing $3 million of damage.

In Somerset County a tornado (F2) touched down around 7:00 P.M. about four miles southeast of Markelton, traveling in a southeasterly direction for twelve miles through Boynton before dissipating in Pocahontas. The tornado crossed the path of a twister that had struck Salisbury only two days earlier. Tornadoes rarely strike twice in one location, but a Pocahantas carpentry shop under repair after being demolished in the storm two days earlier lost its new frame structure under construction when it was toppled by high winds on June 2.

Remarkably, a stronger tornado would hit southern Somerset County around 8:00 P.M., following a path about 0.75 mile to the north of that of the storm that had passed through the region only two hours earlier. The tornado traveled twenty-six miles to the Maryland border, five miles southeast of Salisbury, and continued

Fig. 8.2. June 2, 1998. Twin funnels moving northeast along the Ohio River approaching
Mount Washington, photographed by a KDKA-TV cameraman. (*Pittsburgh Post-Gazette*
Photo Archives, copyright 1998, all rights reserved)

for on five more miles to Frostburg, Maryland, before lifting. Boynton residents
were outside at work with chainsaws and front-end loaders, cleaning up debris
from the early evening twister, when they were warned by firefighters to seek
shelter.

The F3 tornado at one point was about a mile wide, destroying several farms
in rural southern Somerset County. A Laurel Falls family watched from the basement shelter as their three-story dwelling and eight rows of foundation blocks were
lifted above their heads. Fortunately, there were no injuries in the second Somerset County storm, considering its intensity and path width.

Thirty to forty properties reported damage in Somerset County from the twin
tornadoes on the evening of June 2, 1998. A hundred cattle died in one barn, and
many more died in other barns struck by the tornadoes.

Another strong tornado (F2) formed around 9:35 P.M. about a mile southwest of
Elliotsville in southern Fayette County, carving a twelve-mile path east-southeast
across the northeastern tip of Preston County, West Virginia, before dissipating
over Garrett County, Maryland. A dairy barn and two house trailers suffered damage, but again, no injuries occurred in this tristate storm.

Thunderstorms with hail and high winds raked central and northeastern Pennsylvania all evening long. One intensifying supercell over eastern Bradford County
became tornadic in southwest Susquehanna County around 9:05 P.M., damaging
several structures and mobile homes and shearing trees as it moved up and down
the ridges over a discontinuous path of twelve miles.

At 9:45 P.M., a storm touched down east of Robinwood Mountain near the community of Terrytown, Bradford County, blasting a trailer off its foundation a distance of eight feet. Luckily for the two occupants inside the trailer, a farm vehicle,
pickup truck, and storage shed prevented the trailer from rolling down a steep hill.

The tornado tracked six miles, on and off the ground, flattening a barn and shearing off trees.

The violent cell went on to spawn a much stronger F3 tornado as it moved in northern Wyoming County, hitting the small vacation community of Lake Carey, where two fatalities occurred. Forty-two homes were damaged in the Lake Carey area as the storm attained F3 intensity and carved a damage path a third of a mile wide. The storm weakened near Factoryville and the Lackawanna County line. In all, the storm was responsible for $2 million of property damage to fifty homes and caused fifteen injuries.

The same storm dropped another weaker F1 tornado in Lackawanna County around 10:40 P.M., causing minor damage at Keystone Junior College before crossing Routes 6 and 11 and entering the Lackawanna State Park. No injuries were reported along the storm's three-mile path.

A total of twenty tornadoes touched down across Pennsylvania in a little more than five hours between 5:30 and 10:45 P.M. on June 2, 1998, contributing to an all-time monthly record for tornadoes in Pennsylvania (27) in June 1998.

Winter Tornadoes

While the vast majority of severe storms that strike Pennsylvania communities occur during the spring, summer, and late fall, a powerful winter cyclone is capable of spinning off an isolated damaging twister on rare occasion.

In the nineteenth century, a possible tornado struck the Pottsville area in January 1839 when a vigorous disturbance passed over eastern Pennsylvania and northern New Jersey. Charles Peirce (1847, 30) mentioned the storm in his Philadelphia weather book: "On January 26th Pottsville was visited by a tremendous hurricane which swept away almost everything before it." Great floods also attended the passage of this massive winter storm. At Allentown, "the Lehigh river perhaps was never so high," and floodwaters swept several people away in a boat near Norristown (*New York Evening Post,* January 29, 1839).

A violent squall line moved across Indiana, Ohio, and western Pennsylvania on the afternoon of January 20, 1854, causing widespread wind damage and several strong tornadoes of unprecedented intensity in the Ohio Valley in the middle of winter. Unseasonably warm and humid air had pushed the thermometer to near 70 degrees ahead of a strong cold front across southern Ohio, triggering the severe weather. One especially violent tornado tore through Knox County, Ohio, about thirty-five miles northeast of Columbus, part of a family of storms that touched down again farther northeast. A damaging windstorm that was probably a tornado later struck near Cannonsburg, Pennsylvania (Ludlum 1970, 115).

The greatest winter tornado outbreak in Pennsylvania weather history occurred on February 11, 1887. The *Monthly Weather Review* listed several possible tornado touchdowns in southwestern Pennsylvania, though it is probable that some of the damage was caused by straight-line winds. During the morning hours of February 11, 1887, a series of winter twisters touched down briefly in eastern Ohio, causing substantial damage at Louisville and Wooster.

Farther east, a press dispatch reported "a terrible rain and wind storm" between

10:00 and 11:00 A.M. at Greensburg, Pennsylvania, that unroofed homes and blew down trees and fences: "The new jail smokestack was cracked for at least twenty feet from the base, a portion of the roof of the new Lutheran church was blown off, as well as roofs of private dwellings. The court house windows were blown in on the west side. A large derrick on the Sisters of Charity farm was blown down, telegraph wires were disabled and damage generally done" (*Philadelphia Inquirer,* February 12, 1887). A tragedy occurred at Tyrone as the high winds accompanying a squall line advanced east into central Pennsylvania. Four Hungarian laborers were killed when a tree was blown down where they were sheltered.

On the evening of November 26, 1998, a late-autumn tornado swirled through Honey Brook, a small farming community about fifty miles northwest of Philadelphia. Ten persons were injured in the storm, which destroyed two barns and four homes. A total of twenty-five homes were damaged in the storm. About six thousand persons were without power during the height of the storm in parts of western Chester County.

The strongest January tornado (F2) on record in the state of Pennsylvania descended on the northwestern highlands on January 17, 1952, and traveled one mile through a rural section of Crawford County. The path was 1,200 yards wide, and property damage was estimated at $500,000.

On January 14, 1992, a tornado briefly touched down near Moosic, west of Scranton, spawned by a rare January squall line that brought wind gusts of 73 miles per hour at Scranton/Wilkes-Barre and 74 miles per hour at Philadelphia. Earlier in the afternoon of January 14, 1992, a weak F0 tornado briefly touched down in Bedford at 1:20 P.M., with minimal damage reported. Severe storms accompanied by high winds caused 35,000 residents of southeastern Pennsylvania to lose power during the stormy January afternoon. A peak wind gust of 55 miles per hour was recorded at the Philadelphia International Airport.

More recently, a rare midwinter tornado (F0) with a narrow path width of twenty yards descended on south Philadelphia on January 18, 1999, at 4:36 P.M., blowing across Oregon Avenue and onto Marconi Plaza at 10th Street. Eighteen persons were injured around the plaza, one critically, by flying debris and falling trees.

The month of February has on rare occasion brought a small twister in Pennsylvania. Heavy thunderstorms containing torrential downpours attended the passage of a strong cold front across eastern Pennsylvania during the afternoon of February 15, 1939, spawning at least two tornadoes. High winds "unroofed homes, collapsed farm buildings, leveled wires, telephone poles and trees" north of Ephrata in northeastern Lancaster County on that day, according to the *Philadelphia Inquirer.*

The February 1939 issue of *Climatological Data* stated that although no funnel was witnessed, the storm damage appeared to be the work of a small tornado. Farther north, a "funnel-shaped formation" touched down in Bath, in Northampton County, demolishing a two-and-a-half-story frame garage. Three automobiles were lost in the ensuing fire. A two-story frame barn "collapsed like a matchbox" at the Keystone Portland Cement Company, and two other buildings and a dozen homes were unroofed by the storm. Wind damage was also reported at Belvidere and Washington, New Jersey.

At Philadelphia the temperature shot up to 66 degrees at 11:15 A.M. on February 15, 1939. A cold front crossed the city at 4:50 P.M., and by 8:00 P.M. the temperature had fallen to 34 degrees in Philadelphia as the rain changed to sleet and snow. Winds gusted past 65 miles per hour, with a five-minute average velocity of 50 miles per hour just after noontime, knocking down trees and signs all around the city.

A February twister (F1) with winds estimated at 110 miles per hour touched down in Centre County near Oak Hall around 7:30 P.M. on February 16, 1990. The storm formed over an open field near an elementary school and traveled three miles through a rural section of the county. The damage path was 1,050 yards, evident as twisted trees, flattened grass, and minor property damage. The thunderstorm that spawned the tornado passed 0.5 mile from the Pennsylvania State University weather station and was surveyed by a university team headed up by Professor Gregory Forbes, now a severe weather analyst with the Weather Channel in Atlanta, Georgia.

9 Floods and Droughts

We have had years and periods of drought and plenteous rainfall, and
will have them again. Nothing new in the weather line has occurred in
historic times, and nothing new can occur until the order of our solar
system is changed.

—*Monthly Weather Review,* May 1907

Water weighs 62.4 pounds per cubic foot, and only two feet of moving water will
exert enough force to displace a passenger vehicle weighing 1,500 pounds. One
of the greatest dangers posed by floodwaters is that motorists cannot accurately
gauge the depth of the water spilling over a highway or beneath an underpass. No
one should ever attempt to cross a roadway if the surface is not clearly visible.

In an average year, floods claim more lives (127) in the United States than any
other weather phenomenon except heat waves. Some floods are classified as *flash
floods* due to their sudden nature, and others are *river floods,* which may develop
over a period of hours or even days.

If you live in a flood-prone area, have a battery-powered radio, lights, and flash-
lights, and be prepared to evacuate your home on short notice in the event of rapidly rising water levels. Each year, about a week before the advent of spring, the
National Weather Service and Emergency Management officials distribute flood
safety information to local schools during Weather Emergency Preparedness
Week. Flood warnings are broadcast to the public through NOAA weather radio
stations and the media.

Flash Floods

Flash floods seem to be increasing in the United States, due in part to urban development that has altered the natural terrain and drainage patterns but also as a
result of more frequent one-day heavy precipitation events.

Flash floods develop quickly, usually during a stormy pattern accompanied by
torrential rainfalls that are not absorbed by saturated soils. In the warmer months,
clusters of thunderstorms sometimes line up like freight trains moving along the
same track. Narrow valleys are vulnerable to flooding from heavy runoff pouring
down steep hillsides.

Moisture convergence is a requisite for heavy precipitation that develops along
a boundary where damp winds collide. A pocket of upper-level energy interacts
with a stream of Gulf moisture, and diverging air currents lift warm, wet air to high

altitudes, generating substantial rainfalls. A plume of tropical moisture evident on satellite imagery provides a forecaster with an important clue on the rainfall potential of large storms.

River Floods

River floods usually occur in the cooler months following a prolonged period of moderate to heavy rain that falling on saturated ground. Winter and early spring floods typically follow a cold, snowy pattern followed by a thaw and heavy rain. The surface is still frozen, and there is little vegetation to absorb the heavy runoff.

Huge blocks of ice that formed during a protracted cold spell begin to break up as the weather warms, and they subsequently become ensnared in narrow passages and under bridges. The ice acts as a temporary dam that suddenly gives way, unleashing a massive volume of water downstream.

Spring floods along Pennsylvania rivers are commonly associated with slow-moving cold fronts and large upper-air storms. Heavy rain is focused along boundaries separating warm and cold air masses, forcing moist air to rise and condense into clouds and bands of steady rain. Further lifting of humid air over the Pennsylvania ridges increases the potential for heavy rain and widespread river and stream flooding.

Late-summer and early-autumn floods historically have accompanied the passage of the remnants of a tropical storm moving northward along the eastern seaboard, or the Appalachian foothills. Copious rains develop as when tropical moisture is forced to rise over a dome of cool, dry air near the surface.

Pennsylvania Drainage Patterns

Pennsylvania has 83,261 miles of flowing water, along with thousands of scenic lakes, ponds, and reservoirs. Streams transport runoff from rain and melting snow through a variety of channels, irrigating croplands, filling reservoirs, and helping to preserve nature's moisture balance through a recycling process of evaporation and condensation.

Several hundred million years ago, most of Pennsylvania east of Pittsburgh rested at the bottom of an ancient, shallow sea. Shifting plates beneath the earth's surface placed immense pressure on a four-mile-deep layer of sedimentary rock that had accumulated on the ocean floor east of Pennsylvania, causing the land to fold like an accordion and giving rise to the Appalachian Mountains.

Subsequent erosion from rainwater and wind planed down the folded rock over millions of years to nearly sea level. The Pennsylvania landscape would be periodically uplifted, worn down, and thrust upward again, causing the land to tilt upward to form the high plateaus in western Pennsylvania. Over time, rivers and streams cut through softer layers of sedimentary rock to carve deep mountain valleys that traverse the northern and western portions of the state.

In the past few million years, several waves of glaciers swept down from the north, rearranging the drainage patterns of northern Pennsylvania streams. Rivers that flowed northwest to the Great Lakes changed course and drained southward.

A dip in the surface of southwestern Pennsylvania to the west and north reversed the southward flow of the Monongahela River, which instead drains north to join the Allegheny River at Pittsburgh.

As the ice sheets retreated from most of Pennsylvania about 15,000 years ago, glacial debris impounded the many scenic mountain lakes that dot northern Pennsylvania. Water from melting ice forged new outlets to the lakes and sea.

Major Pennsylvania Rivers

The eastern boundary of Pennsylvania is formed by the Delaware River, which rises up in the Catskill Mountains of New York. Two branches of the river merge in southeastern New York before tracing a southeasterly course along the border between Pennsylvania and New York. The Delaware River turns southwest then southeast in the direction of the Atlantic Ocean by way of the mouth of Delaware Bay along its 330-mile course. The Lehigh and Schuylkill Rivers are the two main tributaries of the Delaware River.

Farther west, the Susquehanna River and its tributaries drain about half of Pennsylvania en route to Chesapeake Bay in Maryland. The entire Susquehanna drainage system covers 27,510 square miles of New York, Pennsylvania, and Maryland. The North Branch of the Susquehanna River rises near Cooperstown, New York, and follows a winding course over a distance of some 444 miles through central and eastern Pennsylvania before emptying into Chesapeake Bay at Havre de Grace, Maryland.

The West Branch of the Susquehanna River forms over the Allegheny Mountains in western Pennsylvania and follows an easterly course before turning south to merge with the North Branch above Sunbury. In south-central Pennsylvania, the Juniata River flows eastward from the mountains to join up with the Susquehanna River north of Harrisburg.

Western Pennsylvania is drained by the Ohio River system, which forms at Pittsburgh at the junction of the Allegheny and Monongahela Rivers and their tributaries. The Allegheny River rises over the plateau region of southwestern New York, while the Monongahela River forms over the mountains of West Virginia.

Other major tributaries of the Ohio River include the Youghiogheny River, which empties into the Monongahela, and the Beaver River, which flows south to join the Ohio. Westward-flowing streams joining the Allegheny River include the Clarion and Conemaugh Rivers, whereas the Genesee River in Potter County drains into the St. Lawrence River by way of Lake Erie.

Waterfalls

There are seventy-five named waterfalls in Pennsylvania. In the northeastern part of the state, thirty waterfalls draw visitors annually to enjoy the scenic wonderment of water tumbling hundreds of feet to the forest floor (Oplinger and Halma 1988, 27). The perpetual motions of running water created the spectacular falls that grace the Poconos.

The largest waterfall in the state is Bushkill Falls, plunging in spectacular fashion hundreds of feet over the rock shelf before winding a southeasterly course to the Delaware River valley. Other waterfalls in northeastern Pennsylvania include Dingmans and Silver Thread, which are part of the Delaware group, and Buttermilk, Buck Hill, Paradise, Raymondskill, Swiftwater, and Winona, which tumble over the Pocono Front.

Historic Pennsylvania Floods

Early settlers documented historic floods along the Delaware River and its tributaries as early as 1687. A report by the United States Geological Survey compared the magnitude of a great river flood on February 27, 1692, to the catastrophic flooding in the Delaware Valley in August 1955 (Ludlum 1983, 182).

Two early destructive floods along the Susquehanna River in the spring of 1771 and near the end of the snowy winter of 1783–84 ("Great Ice Flood") were described by Bradford County historian Clement Heverling (1926, 70):

> On May 28th [1771], the Susquehanna river rose to an unprecedented height, inundating both the towns of Sheshequannunk (Ulster) and Wyalusing. At the latter place great damage was done by the water sweeping off fences and stock. The inhabitants of Sheshequannunk were compelled to take to their canoes and retire to the wooded heights back of the town.
>
> The breaking up of the Susquehanna river on the 15th of March 1784, greatly distressed the inhabitants who had built their houses on the lowlands near the banks of the river. The uncommon rain and large quantities of snow on the mountains together with the amazing quantity of ice in the river . . . swelled the streams to an unusual height—ten and in many places twenty feet higher than had ever been known since the settlement of the country.

October 6, 1786: Pumpkin Flood

The wet autumn of 1786 culminated in a flood of vast proportions in Pennsylvania, known as the Pumpkin Flood. In the Susquehanna River valley, the flooding was severe. Heverling (1926, 70–71) wrote: "Crops were swept away and the bosom of the river was covered with floating pumpkins. The loss was severely felt and many cattle died the following winter for want of sustenance. For years this freshet was designated by the old inhabitants as the Pumpkin Flood."

Another account of the Pumpkin Flood of 1786 appeared in the *History of Lehigh, Northampton, Monroe, Schuylkill, & Carbon Counties* (Rupp 1845, 218–219). A major flood along the Lehigh River swamped the village of Weissport, a Moravian missionary station settled on the edge of the river about 1746. In one tragic account, the Tippey family was carried downstream in their house, which eventually caught in a clump of trees. The parents survived by clinging to tree limbs and were eventually rescued by canoe, but two children were swept to their deaths in the raging waters.

February 10, 1832: Pittsburgh Flood

After the Pittsburgh flood of March 1907, the meteorologist-in-charge at the city weather bureau sent press clippings from the *Pittsburg Gazette* of another great flood, that of February 1832. Weatherman Henry Pennywitt forwarded the historic material to the *Monthly Weather Review* (March 1907) in Washington, D.C.

Tuesday morning, February 14 [1832]. . . . The winter commenced several weeks earlier than usual. On the 9th of January the ice broke up and navigation opened. On the 5th of February it began to rain, and continued to rain with slight interruptions until the night of the 9th. On the 9th the rivers commenced to rise, and continued rising rapidly and regularly until 9 p.m. of Friday the 10th, "when they were higher than had been known by any living inhabitant of this city or neighborhood." The whole of the low ground of the boroughs of the Northern Liberties and Allegheny and the greater part of the city of Pittsburg north of Liberty street were inundated.

January 8, 1841: Bridges Freshet

A deep snowstorm blanketed eastern Pennsylvania on December 4–6, 1840, with 12 to 18 inches of snow. A major thaw in early January, accompanied by heavy rain, swelled the Delaware River, causing large blocks of ice to break off and soon become trapped in the bridges downstream. As the chunks of ice would work free, torrents of water that had been backed up by the ice jam rushed downstream, resulting in mass destruction.

The Bridges Freshet of January 1841 along the Delaware River earned its name from the destruction of nine bridges by turbulent waters (Dale 1996, 103–104). Farms and villages along the river basin were swept away by powerful currents that reached a flood stage of 35 feet at Easton. The local press filled in the meteorological details leading up to the flood: "The weather which had been for three days previous intensely cold, began to moderate, and early on Tuesday morning [January 5] it commenced raining. . . . It continued raining without intermission until about eleven o'clock Thursday night. . . . The great body of snow which had fallen, speedily dissolved, and together with the rain, produced the greatest freshet ever in this section" (*Jeffersonian Republican* [East Stroudsburg], January 8, 1841).

I. Daniel Rupp (1845, 155–157) described the terrible damage done by the Bridges Freshet of January 1841 in Monroe County, noting that 90 percent of the bridges were washed away. Widespread damage was reported along eastern Pennsylvania rivers, where property was inundated by rising waters. A number of mills, tanneries, barns, shops, and homes were damaged beyond repair. A young New Jersey man drowned attempting to salvage his property along the Delaware River.

A paper presented at the Bucks County Historical Society in 1927 entitled "Floods and Freshets in the Delaware and Lehigh Rivers" (in Ludlum 1983, 182–183) compared the Bridges Freshet to earlier floods. The information was copied from the family Bible of George Wyker, who resided in Upper Tinicum Township in Bucks County, providing an indispensable summary of historic Delaware River floods:

On Friday and Saturday, the 8th and 9th of January, 1841, the river Delaware was higher than it has been for 107 years before, for in 1734 [June 4] it covered what is now called the Erwinna flats or lowlands from one to five feet deep and the inhabitants had to flee to the hills, but this fresh [January 8] was not by three feet as high, so that families could stay in their houses, but the fresh carried away four bridges on the Delaware and five on the Lehigh, besides doing a great deal of damage to property of every description; and on the Lehigh it carried away several houses, with all their furniture, and several lives were lost.

March 14–15, 1846: River Floods

Sixty-two years to the date following the Great Ice Flood of March 1784 came another pattern of widespread flooding resulting from heavy rain and melting snows in eastern Pennsylvania. Heverling (1926, 571) wrote that there was a "great freshet in the Susquehanna; nearly all the river bridges and those on the larger creeks, swept away."

Bucks County resident George Wyker noted in his Bible on March 15, 1846: "Quite a high flood in the river, but not by 2 or 3 feet as high as that of 1841. The above I have written on the 8th day of April, 1846, being now in my 80th year."

September 2, 1850: Southeastern Floods

Two episodes of serious flooding occurred in southeastern Pennsylvania in the summer of 1850. A tropical storm moving north from Virginia soaked the region overnight on July 18–19, causing flash floods that killed at least twenty along the Schuylkill River (Ludlum 1963, 96–99). Great destruction to crops and roads was reported throughout the eastern Pennsylvania countryside.

Less than two months after the July 1850 floodwaters receded, on September 2, 1850, another great rainstorm sparked more flooding in southeastern Pennsylvania. A number of lives were lost when rivers spilled out of their banks in the scenic valleys nestled in the foothills of the Appalachians in east-central Pennsylvania.

The *Pennsylvania Inquirer* in Philadelphia recalled that a "heavy and incessant rain—the unusual amount of 3.80 inches—is recorded as having fallen in one day." A dispatch from Easton described the widespread flooding: "The heavy rain on Sunday and Monday [September 1–2] caused the Lehigh to rise to a fearful height. At the mouth of the river it was about twenty inches higher than July last [July 18–19]. On Monday afternoon [September 2] between two and four o'clock the water rose at that place about five feet, filling many cellars in the lower part of the town, and destroying considerable property by its sudden and rapid movement" (*Easton Argus* in *Jeffersonian Republican,* September 12, 1850).

The situation was called "one of the most destructive floods ever known upon the waters of the Lehigh and Schyulkill." At Mauch Chunk (now Jim Thorpe), a dam gave way, unleashing torrents of water that carried away several bridges. No loss of life was reported at Mauch Chunk, but thirty-one people "swept away and drowned" in the surging waters downstream at Tamaqua. The loss of life at Pottsville was put at "fifteen or twenty," where "about 30 or 40 houses were swept away."

Along the length of the Schuylkill River "numerous bridges were destroyed" and "vast damage was done." The Schuylkill River crested at a 23.3 feet at Reading on September 2, 1850, which exceeded the peak crest of 19.7 feet observed in August 1933, according to the summary in *Climatological Data—Pennsylvania Section.*

June 4–5, 1862: Great Flood of '62

In *A History of Bethlehem, Pennsylvania, 1741–1892,* Joseph Levering called the Great Flood of '62 "the most disastrous flood on record in the valley." A publication called "Incidents of the freshet on the Lehigh River" (Weiss 1863, 56) estimated the loss of life to be about 150 persons, the worst disaster to ever affect the region. Eighteen bridges over the Lehigh River were destroyed by the floodwaters from White Haven to the Delaware River, leaving only three bridges (Lehigh Gap, Bethlehem, and Easton) that survived the onslaught of water and floating debris.

The Lehigh River rose more rapidly than had ever been known before on the afternoon of June 4, 1862. Dams that were a power source for lumbermen and grist mill operators burst along the many streams feeding into the Lehigh and Delaware Rivers. Historian Thomas D. Eckhart, in the first of a three-volume series entitled *The History of Carbon County* (1992, 161–163) described the extensive flooding along the Lehigh River in Carbon County that claimed more than thirty lives. He explained that a network of twenty dams operated by the Lehigh Coal and Navigation Company "supplied the canal locks and provided depots for logs to be sawed or transported." The first dam break (Dam No. 4) occurred at White Haven after the pounding water caused booms holding sawed lumber and logs to break up. The upper Lehigh River became choked with logs and debris as successive dams gave way, inundating low-lying communities downstream.

Seven lives were lost at Penn Haven in the flood. At Mauch Chunk, the swollen Lehigh River tore through the center of town, sweeping away more than fifty buildings and killing four persons. Two young women later drowned when their boat capsized at East Mauch Chunk. Another nineteen people drowned at Burlington, and four more died at Weissport on the east side of the river across from Lehighton.

Joseph M. Levering (1903, 736) compared the Great Flood of '62 with its predecessor in 1841: "The water rose only a little higher at this point than in 1841, but the ruin was very much greater, not only because there was more property and a larger population to be imperiled, but because the chief flood was occasioned by the breaking of a succession of great dams far up the river, and the unprecedented rise of the water came with appalling suddenness."

Citing records maintained by the Bethlehem Bridge Company, Levering noted that the water gauge on the Lehigh River reached 20.5 feet in June 1862, slightly above that of the Great Flood of January 1841 (20 feet). The Lehigh River eventually crested around noon on June 5, 1862, although the Delaware continued to rise, swelled by the very heavy runoff from tributaries entering the river basin.

Total property damage was enormous, estimated at $2 to $3 million, by far the greatest weather-related disaster ever known in the area. The terrible destruction was also noted in the *New York Times.* A report from Easton described water reaching the second story of homes in Glendon, one mile above town: "All the bridges between this and Mauch Chunk are swept away. The Lehigh Bridge is partly gone, and will probably be totally demolished. All the canals are under water. The iron works have stopped, and the railroads are submerged. Many people were drowned in their houses, so sudden was the rise."

A dispatch from Delaware Water Gap, about twenty-five miles northeast of Easton, reported "quantities of furniture, store goods, bridges, houses, cattle . . . all going down the river." The Delaware, Lackawanna, and Western Railroad suffered severe damage along the Delaware River. At Stroudsburg the Pocono Creek rose through the early morning hours of June 5, 1862, "carrying away many houses and bridges. The damage done was very great." A story carried on June 19 in Stroudsburg's *Monroe Democrat* described the terrible destruction:

> It commenced raining on Tuesday evening [June 3], and kept steadily on through the whole of Wednesday day and night. The water poured down without intermission, and every body expected that there would be a respectable freshet in our streams, but no one dreamed that such a terrific and destructive flood was about to sweep over the land. It came so sudden that many families in lower portions of our town were obliged to leave their houses in boats, and the water rushed into the lower stories of their dwellings before they could remove their furniture to the upper stories.

Property damage in the Stroudsburg area was estimated at $75,000, according to local historian and former chief burgess Dr. Jackson Lantz (1897, 15).

March 17–18, 1865: Barrel Flood

Heavy snow over the highlands of New York and Pennsylvania during the winter of 1864–65 contributed to Pennsylvania's St. Patrick's Day Flood of 1865. Heavy rain fell on March 16–17, 1865, which combined with melting snow and ice jams to push central and western Pennsylvania rivers and their tributaries out of their banks.

In a *History and Geography of Bradford County, Pennsylvania,* Heverling (1926, 574) noted "the highest water, twenty-eight feet, ever known in the Susquehanna" on March 17. In northwestern Pennsylvania, the flood of March 1865 was called the Barrel Flood after thousands of oil barrels waiting to be shipped were carried away in the rising waters (Shank 1988, 15). A press dispatch from Franklin told the story: "We are having the greatest flood ever known in this region. The bridge at Oil City and the French Creek bridge, at Franklin, are swept away. Miles of the railroad track are gone and the telegraph lines are washed away, houses, tanks and barrels, full and empty, cover the river. The loss is estimated by millions" (*Philadelphia Inquirer,* March 18, 1865).

The "Great Freshet" did considerable damage along the West Branch of the Susquehanna River in north-central Pennsylvania. Raging waters took out all the bridges between Williamsport and Danville. The report stated that about half of Danville was under water. The high water fed into the main branch of the Susquehanna River, causing "unprecedented" flooding at Harrisburg as it rose two and a half feet above the "destructive freshet of 1846." A later dispatch from Harrisburg reported that a "larger portion of the lower and eastern end of town" had been inundated by rising waters. Paxton Creek, on the eastern edge of the city, "backed up" and submerged a number of homes.

Floodwaters swept "thousands of timber logs, with millions of feet of sawed lumber" downstream past Harrisburg on March 17, 1865, and the lower portion of the city was under water. The press reported, "Much suffering has been created among many poor families who live at Middletown and in the villages along the shore, clear to Columbia."

October 3–4, 1869: Saxby's Gale

An offshore hurricane, predicted a year in advance by British naval officer Lieutenant S. M. Saxby, interacted with an upper-level low-pressure trough to dump copious amounts of rain along the eastern seaboard on October 2–4, 1869. Rainfall at New Jersey weather stations averaged 5.00 inches, sending rivers in the northern part of the Garden State into high flood (Ludlum 1983, 78). The heaviest official rainfall measurement was 12.35 inches at Canton, Connecticut.

In southeastern Pennsylvania a rain gauge in Lancaster County at Mount Joy measured 8.00 inches of water on October 2–3. A weather station in northeastern Pennsylvania near Honesdale caught 4.50 inches of rain. Observer Marcus Corson at Plymouth Meeting, northwest of Philadelphia, recorded 6.00 inches. He added in his observational notes: "Disastrous freshet on the Schyulkill. Water 16 feet above ordinary level, higher than the great flood of January 26, 1839." Corson noted in his report that four people drowned along the Schuylkill River between Norristown and Philadelphia, adding, "much property damaged."

During the evening hours of October 2, 1869, light rain began falling over eastern Pennsylvania that would gradually become a steady downpour by the evening of the third. Flood waters in the Poconos broke through the cribbing of a dam below South Stroudsburg around 7:00 A.M. on October 4, then swirled into town and took out a bridge to Main Street.

In a flood retrospective published on February 13, 1896, the *Stroudsburg Times* described the Flood of '69: "The great volume of dark, angry waters soon swept away the old grist mill, with all its machinery, swirled down on the woolen mill and Wallace's saw mill, past J. O. Saylor's building, carrying ruin with its fearful march."

Historian Thomas Eckhart (1996, 437) compared the flood of 1869 farther south in Carbon County to the high water levels in 1862: "Overall damage to the [Lehigh Valley Railroad] line as a result [of] this flood was comparable to losses sustained in the June 1862 flood."

The rainstorm of June 1869 had a peculiarity—snail shells reportedly mingled with a light shower at Chester and were later sent to the Academy of Natural Sciences in Philadelphia (Watson 1993, 233).

August 12, 1873: Lehigh Valley Flash Flood

An account in the *Allentown Chronicle* that later appeared in the Stroudsburg *Jeffersonian* described a torrential rainfall that swamped the town of Guthsville, five miles southeast of Allentown, in the late afternoon of August 12, 1873. Streets and cellars were swamped, and water rose as high as the first floors of several homes. Roads were washed out and property damage to homes and yards was considerable.

The report continued, "Of all the severe rains known to the oldest inhabitants in Lehigh County, that of Tuesday afternoon [August 12] from about a quarter past three o'clock till a quarter past five, was the most copious. . . . It is somewhat remarkable that the very hard rain only visited a semi circular belt of territory about a mile and a half wide, from four to six miles to the southeast of this city, leaving Allentown with only a usual summer rain."

A singular occurrence, probably spawned by downburst, occurred between 5:00 and 6:00 P.M. at the headwaters of Cedar Creek. Hiram J. Schantz, Esq., "noticed a body of water five or six feet high rushing towards the mill from above, coming from a direction where no creek ran." The storm was thought to be "a waterspout which it is said descended near Crackersport, and rushed across the fields carrying fences before it." About one-half of Schantz's saw mill, including the water wheel, was destroyed, causing $5,000 of damage.

The trigger for the heavy downpours was a cold front that might have merged with the offshore tropical system moving northward along the eastern seaboard on August 12–14. On August 13–14, copious rains accompanied by a raw northeasterly wind pelted the coastal plain. On August 13, a chilly rain turned into a downpour in Philadelphia that totaled 5.21 inches, which was followed by another 1.15 inches the next day.

The August 1873 storm was included in a listing of Atlantic tropical storms that were featured in the August 1915 issue of the *Monthly Weather Review* (405). Measurable rain totaling nearly ten inches (9.96 inches) fell on eleven consecutive days in Philadelphia from August 12 to 22.

July 26, 1874: Pittsburgh Flash Flood

The city of Pittsburgh (then Pittsburg) suffered through its worst weather disaster in terms of loss of life on a humid summer evening in July 1874. Heavy downpours associated with a cluster of slow-moving thunderstorms pounded the Pittsburgh area, and the subsequent runoff from the hilly terrain in the northern and western suburbs channeled a deadly torrent of water into unsuspecting neighborhoods. As was reported in the *New York Times,* "At about 8 o'clock on a Sunday evening a storm set in which, as far as the destruction of human life is concerned, was the greatest calamity which has ever visited our city, and, in some degree of horror, rivals the recent Mill Run disaster in Massachusetts."

The awful destruction was attributed to "the sudden down-pouring of immense volumes of water." The storm account mentioned "copious showers during the earlier part of the day" that saturated the soils before a heavy evening thunderstorm set in. Damage in the city of Pittsburgh was termed "comparatively light," being mainly to streets, curbing stones, and shade trees, which were washed out by heavy drainage from the hillsides.

The greatest disaster commenced two miles north of an area called Allegheny City along the north bank of the Allegheny River, which flows from the northeast into the city of Pittsburgh before merging with the northward-flowing Monongahela River. The junction of the two rivers gives rise to the Ohio River, which travels northwest to eventually form the boundary between Ohio and West Virginia.

The community of Allegheny City just outside of Pittsburgh was vulnerable to flash floods because "the avenues ran through narrow valleys, hemmed in by great hills." The runoff rate from the hills was so enormous that water swept into second-story frame houses before some residents realized what was happening. Homes along formerly quiet, narrow streams were swept away by torrents of water. Severe losses occurred along streams known as Butcher's Run, Wood's Run, Plummer Run, and Saw Mill Run.

A stream that ran parallel to Saw Mill Run in a town called Charter Valley before emptying into the Ohio River "three miles below" was the scene of many fatalities. There were heart-rending accounts of entire families being swept away: "All the little runs, emptying into Charter's Creek, became rushing rivers. The loss of human life has been frightful," according to a graphic account in the *New York Times.*

Although no significant wind damage was reported during the storms, an observer a few miles downstream from the scene of the flooding could make out a "huge, inky, black funnel-shaped cloud which overhung the city, the narrow end being lowest, while the dark parts emitted almost continuous flashes of lightning." It is unknown whether this funnel cloud actually touched down on the western edge of the storm.

Local newspapers gave widely varying death tolls, which is understandable considering the nature of the disaster and overlapping reports. Grazulis (1993, 195) cited 134 fatalities in the flood, correcting an erroneous item in another government publication that had attributed the loss of life to a tornado at Erie, Pennsylvania.

December 10–11, 1878: River Floods

Heavy rain overspread eastern Pennsylvania early on December 9, 1878, emptying into creeks and rivers that were higher than normal after a heavy rainfall at the beginning of the month. Torrential rains fell over the headwaters of the Delaware River in southeastern New York, causing the river to spill over its banks along the New York border southward to Delaware Water Gap. Swollen creeks caused damage over interior portions of northeastern Pennsylvania, washing away railroad tracks, bursting dams, and causing several small bridges to crumble in the rushing waters.

> The heavy rain which commenced Monday morning [December 9, 1878] ceased at 10 o'clock last night, changing suddenly into a gale. The Delaware and Lackawaxen Rivers at noon to-day were higher than they have been since 1836 [January 1839?] when millions of feet of lumber and other valuable property swept away. The Delaware, between this place and the Delaware Water Gap, overflowed its banks in many places, and thousands of acres of flat lands are submerged between Milford and Stroudsburg, a distance of 33 miles. (*New York Times,* December 12, 1878)

A dispatch from Scranton reported flooding in low-lying areas along the Susquehanna River, engulfing several homes in Kingston Flats, near Wilkes-Barre, and covering the Lackawanna and Bloomsburg railroad track in the lower Wyoming Valley. The city of Harrisburg was surrounded by floodwaters that covered low-lying areas a little northwest of the city and swamped homes and railroad lines.

The intense early winter storm was centered over Arkansas on Sunday morning, December 8. The storm tracked northeast, reaching the New York City area on the tenth. At 6:00 P.M. on December 10, the barometer at New York City registered an extremely low reading of 28.80 inches as the temperature rose to 56 degrees. A strong wind ensued by midnight, suggesting the storm passed very close to New York City, placing eastern Pennsylvania, southeastern New York, and southern New England on the northwest semicircle of the storm where the heaviest rainfalls typically occur.

High winds battered the East Coast, and heavy rains resulted in more serious flooding in parts of New England, eastern New York, and northern New Jersey. Heavy flooding was reported at Paterson, New Jersey, where the Passaic River was higher than it had been since the snowmelt floods of April 1854.

February 6–7, 1884: Snowmelt Floods

A soggy February in 1884 followed a stormy January, triggering serious floods resulting from a combination of heavy rainfall and the break-up of ice. The Ohio River at Pittsburgh crested at 33.3 feet around 11:00 P.M. on February 6, which was the highest stage since February 1832 (35 feet) and well above the level reached on February 8, 1883 (27.5 feet), when flooding was less serious.

The February 1884 flood was confined mostly to lower sections of Pittsburgh and nearby Allegheny City. Railroad communications and gas lines were cut off for several days until waters receded. More than five thousand residents were left temporarily homeless. Flood damage was listed as $2 million in the *Monthly Weather Review.*

In the northeastern part of the state, an ice jam broke along the Susquehanna River, which rose 17 feet in twelve hours on February 7, flooding low-lying areas around Wilkes-Barre and Kingston, which were buried under up to 12 feet of caked ice. The monthly rainfall accumulation was quite substantial for February around the state, with top totals of 7.40 inches at Millville Depot in southwestern Wayne County and 7.29 inches at West Chester in the southeast.

May 31, 1889: Great Johnstown Flood

The weather on Memorial Day, Thursday, May 30, 1889, in western Pennsylvania was gray, giving way to a fine mist that began to fall during the evening hours. After tapering off for a short while, rain commenced to fall again shortly before midnight, only with much greater intensity and accompanied by strong winds.

The weather scenario that ultimately led to the disastrous Johnstown Flood of 1889 featured a trough of low pressure extending from the Great Lakes to the Gulf of Mexico (Ludlum 1989). The confluence of chilly Canadian air colliding with moisture-laden tropical air flowing northward along the Atlantic coastal plain turned a light rain into a heavy downpour that would trigger Pennsylvania's greatest human catastrophe.

An earthen dam built in 1852 at the junction of South Fork Creek and the Little Conemaugh River, fourteen miles northeast of Johnstown, was designed to furnish water to the Pennsylvania Canal. A railroad line would eventually render the dam obsolete, and a group of wealthy Pittsburgh investors, including Andrew Carnegie and Andrew Mellon, purchased the site in 1879, establishing the South Fork Hunting and Fishing Club.

The seeds of tragedy were sown by complete indifference to engineering concerns regarding the integrity of the dam. The South Fork Dam stood 50 feet high, about 450 feet above the elevation of a stone-arch bridge in the middle of Johnstown eighteen miles downstream. The dam did not have a solid central foundation, and for ten years Conemaugh Valley residents had voiced concerns about the potential dangers of the neglected dam to no avail.

The great reservoir, Lake Conemaugh, was 2.5 miles long, 1.5 miles wide, and as deep as 100 feet. As heavy rain pelted down on western Pennsylvania throughout the morning hours of Friday, May 31, 1889, the waters rose at the rate of an inch per hour. As early as 11:30 A.M., engineers were alarmed that the dam was in trouble, as many worked feverishly to open the sluiceway to release pent-up pressure. Floodwaters from runoff were already knee-deep in Johnstown from the heavy rains, but when messengers arrived shortly after noon warning of a grave danger, few chose to evacuate their homes and flee for the hills. One Pennsylvania Railroad engineer reportedly rode eighteen miles frantically sounding his whistle and "crying out that the dam was bound go to."

As the afternoon wore on, it became apparent that the dam was showing signs of imminent collapse. Residents in the area frantically attempted to shore up the

Fig. 9.1. May 31, 1889. Stereoscopic views of the Great Johnstown Flood at Main and Franklin Streets (*top*), and near the junction of Conemaugh and Stony Creeks (*bottom*), where the Woodvale prison had floated to from one mile away. (Courtesy Pennsylvania State Archives)

Fig. 9.2. May 31, 1889. Stereoscopic views of the Great Johnstown Flood at Main and Clinton Streets (*top*), and from the Pennsylvania Railroad Depot (*bottom*) near the Club House and large iron bridge. (Courtesy Pennsylvania State Archives)

crumbling earthen structure, but at about 3:15 P.M. the middle of the dam gave way, creating a breach of 300 feet, which sent a thunderous wall of water 35 feet high and a half-mile wide down the narrow valley at a rate of 40 miles per hour.

Twenty million tons of water raced through the river valley "like a cannon ball," stated a press account. The wall of water tore through the villages of South Fork, Mineral Point, and East Conemaugh, wiping out everything in its path. Debris turned into "battering rams" and twenty-ton railroad engines parked at the Pennsylvania Railroad yard "were tossed like chips of wood." The towns of Franklin and Woodvale disintegrated under the rush of water and debris that was headed for the city of Johnstown, a vital manufacturing town home to 28,000 residents and the Cambria Iron Works. The force of the water against the hillside caused a backwash up the valley of Stony Creek, wiping out the center of town in ten minutes (Watson 1993, 126).

The mass of debris borne by the flood was checked by the bridge of the Pennsylvania Railroad, and an effective dam was made. The water recoiled upon the city,

Fig. 9.3. May 31, 1889. Great Johnstown Flood damage near the center of town. (Courtesy Pennsylvania State Archives)

meeting there the wing that had been diverted and had flowed around the city. The result was a gigantic whirlpool which ground to pieces any building that escaped the first onset. The noise of the destruction was maddening to the survivors. ("Johnstown Flood; Other Disasters," *New York Times,* October 1, 1911)

An ominous rumble was all the warning Johnstown residents would receive before a tall dark spray became visible above the deadly wave of water heading for the city. By then it was too late to for many to seek higher ground. The merciless torrent swept locomotives and railroad cars, homes and factories, trees and furniture downstream. Thirty acres of water-logged debris careened into the stone arch railroad bridge, which ignited a horrible conflagration. The rampaging waters and subsequent fires that broke out in the city left 2,209 known dead and 979 more missing, who were certainly lost (Shank 1988, 33). Property damage was estimated at $17 million.

The terrible destruction wrought by the Johnstown Flood was conveyed by eyewitness accounts in *The Johnstown Flood* (1968, 145) by historian David G. McCullough:

It began as a deep, steady rumble, they would say; then it grew louder and louder, until it had become an avalanche of sound, "a roar like thunder" was how they generally described it. But one man said he thought the sound was more like the rush of an oncoming train, while another said, "And the sound, I will never forget the sound of that. It sounded to me just like a lot of horses grinding oats."

Everyone heard shouting and screaming, the earsplitting crash of buildings going down, glass shattering, and the sides of houses ripping apart. Some people would later swear they heard factory whistles screeching frantically and church bells ringing.

Hundreds of desperate souls were swept off rooftops and buildings, and those unfortunate souls who clung to the remnants of the railroad bridge suffered a terrible fate when the mass of debris became engulfed in flames. Ruptured oil tanks ignited and burned flood refugees alive, despite valiant rescue efforts that were clearly hampered by the loss of fire-fighting equipment. After the floodwaters receded, 25,000 residents were left homeless and disease took even more lives.

We will never know how much rain fell in Johnstown on May 30–31, 1889, because the weather observer perished in the flood. An observer at Wellsborough (now Wellsboro), in north-central Pennsylvania, logged 1.70 inches early on the thirty-first, and then added another 7.45 inches, ending at 4:20 A.M. on June 1, 1889. The three-day storm total at Wellsboro tallied 9.80 inches. In the south-central part of the state, the official Harrisburg rain gauge caught 7.56 inches in the storm.

Major flooding also occurred along the West Branch of the Susquehanna River at Renovo and Clearfield, which would be relayed by telegraph to the city of Williamsport on the morning of May 31, 1889. However, it would be another twenty-four hours before the full impact of the heavy rain upstream would be felt in the city. Around noontime, Saturday, June 1, floodwaters had topped the Pennsylvania Railroad line in downtown Williamsport and flooded areas north of the tracks. By the time the water reached its maximum depth around 9:00 P.M., 75 percent of the city was under water, which was six feet deep in the buildings on Market Square (Shank 1988, 20).

Williamsport was then a "prosperous lumber town," and losses would include "about 200 million feet of logs and about 40 million board feet of lumber" (Eckhart 1996, 437–438). The Susquehanna River crested at Williamsport at 32.4 feet, 12.4 feet above flood stage and almost 7 feet higher than the record 1865 flood.

Fig. 9.4. May 31, 1889. The Great Johnstown Flood reduced homes to rubble. (Courtesy Pennsylvania State Archives)

Many lives were reportedly lost when people were swept away in the unexpected surge of water.

Twenty persons drowned in the Nittany Valley, and seven more lost their lives in Wayne Township, west of Lock Haven in Clinton County. Only one person drowned in Lock Haven, since residents wisely took precautions after receiving news that Renovo had been hit hard by flooding. William Shank (1988, 22–23), author of *Great Floods of Pennsylvania,* wrote, "The millions of board-feet of logs and sawed lumber which had been swept down the Susquehanna and its tributaries by the great floods of 1889 did great damage as they went downstream. Like a tremendous army of battering rams, the heavy logs and lumber destroyed everything in their path-bridges, factories, houses. They razed the whole town of Milton and swept on. Eventually, they came to rest at tidewater in Chesapeake Bay."

Floodwaters rampaged through the Juniata River valley in south-central Pennsylvania between Tyrone and Lewistown, with the worst damage at the junction of the Raystown Branch and the Juniata River. Again, there was loss of life, and the flood was reportedly 8 feet above the record 1846 flood in the region. Only one bridge survived the flood in Huntingdon County, and the town of Huntingdon was completely isolated by floodwaters that were 35 feet above low-water mark.

The floods of 1889 were the most widespread and severe in state history until 1936. The Pennsylvania Railroad reported that 172 bridges were damaged or carried away by the surging waters and that fifty miles of track were damaged or destroyed. In the decade following the floods of 1889, a series of river gauges were constructed to develop an accurate system of stream flow readings to improve on early river flood warnings.

May 20–22, 1894: Eastern Floods

Light rain that had been falling for about twenty-four hours over central and eastern Pennsylvania turned into a downpour on the night of May 19–20, 1894. Saturated soils could no longer hold the heavy runoff, causing Pennsylvania creeks to overflow their banks. Serious flooding was reported at Williamsport, where water from the West Branch of the Susquehanna overflowed, covering city streets with up to eight feet of water.

In the central mountains, the water on May 20–21, 1894, was reportedly higher than during the flood of 1889. Serious flooding occurred along the Conemaugh, Juniata, and Susquehanna Rivers in the south-central mountains. At Harrisburg, the Susquehanna River crested at 25.7 feet, close to the crest attained in 1889.

In Wilkes-Barre, two children drowned in high water. Along the Delaware River at Easton, the flooding was the worst since October 1869. Floodwaters surged along the Lehigh, Little Lehigh, and Jordan Rivers in the Allentown area, where waters were the highest since June 1862. The heaviest official rainfall total was 8.66 inches in twenty-four hours at Mauch Chunk (Jim Thorpe) in eastern Carbon County. This rain emptied into the Schuylkill River and neighboring tributaries, where flooding was severe.

The average rainfall in May 1894 of 8.88 inches set a state record that stood until June 1972, when a new monthly mean rainfall total of 11.23 inches was recorded in Pennsylvania, mostly associated with the passage of Tropical Storm Agnes.

February 6–7, 1896: Winter Flood in East

February 1896 opened on a cold and snowy note, with a heavy snowfall on February 2–3. Then came several days of rain and a general thaw that melted the snow. The ground was still frozen, however, so when heavy rains pelted Pennsylvania on February 6–7 there was no room for moisture.

Flooded basements were common, and roads resembled "a regular sea" along area creeks. Dams were overrun by high water, causing flooding at Effort and Kellersville. The *Stroudsburg Times* described the scene: "Never in the recollection of the oldest inhabitant has such a steady volume of water Poured down upon this county, as commenced about 1 o'clock of the above morning [February 7]. The center of the attraction seemed to be McMichael's Creek, which at the South Stroudsburg falls was a miniature Niagara. The water rushed over the dam with a boom-like cannon, dashing up a wave fully 40 feet high. Damage to the railroads running through the Stroudsburgs was estimated to be $100,000."

August 24, 1901: Carbon County Flash Flood

Two heavy rainstorms in late August 1901 led to a flash flood that took four lives in Mauch Chunk (Jim Thorpe). Eastern Pennsylvania was swamped with 3.00 to 6.00 inches of rain on August 18–19, with large totals at Philadelphia (4.71 inches) and Hamburg (6.10 inches). Another wet period from August 22–24 deposited 1.00 to 3.00 inches of rain on areas saturated from the previous storm. Hamlinton in Wayne County had rain every day from August 17 to 24.

The Lehigh River, already swollen by the previous rainfall, raged through Mauch Chunk, pouring down Broadway with great force, flooding stores and basements. The boilers at the Mauch Chunk Electric Company went out, plunging the town into darkness (Eckhart 1996, 438–439). The torrent of water created deep gullies in the middle of town and washed out roads and trolley tracks.

December 13–14, 1901: Widespread Floods

The *Philadelphia Inquirer* described the breadth of flooding triggered by a powerful disturbance along the eastern seaboard, accompanied by high winds and torrential rainfalls on December 14–15, 1901: "Floods, such as have rarely devastated the State of Pennsylvania, are reported from all points between Altoona and Easton. West and East, and from the northern state line to as far south as Lancaster. Millions of dollars' damages have resulted from a storm of wind with little less violence than a tornado, and a downpour of rain characterized by some as almost a continuous cloudburst."

Heavy flooding occurred on many eastern Pennsylvania rivers, including the Susquehanna, Lackawanna, Lehigh, and Schuylkill. There were many reports of railroad tracks and roads being washed out and bridges torn from their foundations as rivers and creeks overflowed their banks. Houses along river basins were undermined by loosened soils from the high water. Damage along the Schuylkill

River was estimated at not less than $1.5 million. In southeastern Pennsylvania high winds tore the roofs off an opera house and several hotels in Lancaster, and there was considerable property damage suggestive of a small tornado.

Fifteen miles north of Reading, country roads were submerged under six feet of water and homes along creeks and streams were badly flooded. Local residents could not recall a time when waterways had risen so rapidly as they did on the afternoon of December 15, 1901. In the east-central hills, the Mahanoy Creek at Ashland was described as a "raging torrent" that ripped up railroad tracks and washed away outbuildings and bridges.

A tragic railway accident occurred when a portion of the Pennsylvania Railroad Bridge over Lycoming Creek between Williamsport and Newberry collapsed. The engine and nine freight cars of the westbound Oyster Express plunged into twenty feet of water, killing an engineer, a breakman, and a fireman, who were in the cab of the engine. More than twenty township and railway bridges were destroyed in Schuylkill County alone. Large mudslides damaged sections of the Pennsylvania Railroad at Rock Station east of Auburn.

In the Lehigh Valley communities of Easton, Allentown, and Bethlehem, the December 1901 flood was thought to be the worst to hit the region since June 1862. Extensive flooding occurred around Easton as the rising water of the Delaware River backed up into some of the swollen tributaries. The Lehigh Valley Traction Company, which furnished electricity to Allentown, was flooded. The Lehigh River was so high at 10:00 P.M. on December 15 that the Allentown Gas Company turned off the gas, darkening much of the city. Backwater flooding occurred along the Little Lehigh River and Jordan Creek, cutting off South Allentown from the rest of the city.

A dam along a privately owned two-mile lake at Naomi Pines in the Poconos burst, sending even more water spilling into the Little Lehigh River, which aggravated the situation. In neighboring Carbon County, the pounding waters tore out a span of a new steel railroad bridge and destroyed a railroad bridge at Penn Haven. The Lehigh River rose five feet higher than it had during the August 1901 flood. The county was darkened again by the loss of electricity. Damage to the canal and railroad lines paralleling the river was extensive.

The town of Weissport, on the east side of the river from Lehighton, was covered by four feet of water (Eckhart 1996, 439–445). The storm lashed Tamaqua for twenty-four hours before abating early on December 15, causing "awful damage." The Wabush Creek spilled over its banks, flooding the business district. At Pottsville about four feet of water poured down Railroad Street, flooding basements and extinguishing the town's steam-heating plant fires.

Farther north, in Bradford County, the Susquehanna River inundated Monroeton, sweeping one woman to her death. In Wayne County near Honesdale, the Penwarden Pond dam broke in Dyberry, and a courier was dispatched to alert residents downstream as the water rushed toward the Delaware River. Streets were flooded in Scranton, and there was "a great deal of damage" in and around Wilkes-Barre.

The rains ushered in a cold wave, suggesting a powerful collision of polar and tropical air that contributed to the twenty-four-hour deluge. The powerful winds were associated with a large temperature drop accompanied by a vigorous depression moving through the region.

February 28, 1902: Ice Jam Flood

The latter half of February 1902 brought two major winter storms, followed by heavy rain and a thaw. In eastern Pennsylvania, heavy snow averaging 8 to 12 inches blanketed the region on February 16–17. A second storm brought a substantial load of snow and ice on February 21–22, and mixed precipitation at Philadelphia totaled 1.96 inches.

As the weather thawed, rain began to fall on February 25, saturating the heavy snowpack that covered Pennsylvania while loosening great masses of ice that were lodged in the waterways. The *Philadelphia Inquirer* described the breakup of ice that unleashed a large quantity of water into eastern Pennsylvania rivers: "Bearing masses of ice, logs, debris of every description, and even tearing tugs and scows from their anchorage, the usually placid Schuylkill River tore its way over its course yesterday with terrific vehemence, wreaking ruin in many places and incapacitating works along its entire banks."

The ice freshet that followed in February 1902 was much like the one in February 1896. In southeastern Pennsylvania, high water caused major flooding along the Susquehanna River and on some tributaries, causing widespread flooding at Chambersburg, Shippensburg, Lancaster, and York. Significant flooding occurred along the Schuylkill River at Pottstown and Norristown. A large dam owned by the Glasgow Iron Company was swept away in a rush of water and debris. In western Pennsylvania, flooding was extensive around Waynesboro, involving "all the streams in this vicinity."

Another heavy rainfall on February 28, 1902, deposited 1.40 inches at Philadelphia, aggravating the already serious problem of high water in the eastern part of the state. The latest rainstorm, combined with melting snow and ice, pushed rivers and creeks beyond their banks again in eastern Pennsylvania, including the Lehigh and Delaware Rivers.

The *Wayne Independent* in Honesdale, in an account of the flood that appeared in the *Bicentennial Edition* (February 4, 1978), told how the Lackawaxen River overflowed its banks on February 28. Huge chunks of ice swept through Honesdale, and Main Street resembled an ice floe. Dynamite was used to break up the ice jam at Park Lake, but the effort was in vain. The Main Street bridge was swept away, and before long one-third of Honesdale below Park Lake was under water.

North of the Lackawaxen River, floodwaters backed up to High Street, filling cellars with water. More bridges were taken out over the ensuing days as the ice and water pressed on. A week later, a weakened stone arch bridge over Wallenpaupack Creek went out with another round of high water. In neighboring communities, floodwaters reached almost to the second floor of homes in Milanville, and significant flood damage to homes and businesses occurred in Damascus and Cochecton.

The new $250,000 Lehigh Valley Railroad Bridge at Bridgeport in Carbon County was destroyed in the February 1902 flood, and two crewmen lost their lives as the bridge gave way (Eckhart 1996, 445–454). The Lehigh River went into high flood, causing widespread damage at Mauch Chunk (Jim Thorpe) and at Weissport, across the river from Lehighton. The water at Allentown was reportedly 2 feet higher than it was during the previous record flood in June 1862, and water levels at Easton reached 33 feet. The river flood stage of 16 feet at Bethlehem was exceeded by 10 feet, and was reportedly nearly 3 feet above the June 1862 flood mark.

Extensive flooding was reported at Pittsburgh, Philadelphia, Reading, Allentown, and Wilkes-Barre. The Susquehanna achieved its highest level at Wilkes-Barre about 10:00 A.M. on March 2, 1902, where "all flood records were broken," and "three or four feet of water" filled the "lower end of the city." West Nanticoke was flooded, and the electric railroad system in Wyoming County was washed out. A report stated: "In Pittsburg there has been no parallel for the flood at that point since 1832. The waters in the Susquehanna, Lehigh, and Delaware rivers on this side of the Alleghenies have not been so high before in the last forty years. The destruction of life has not been large, but the destruction of property was never greater" (*Climate and Crops—Pennsylvania Section,* February 1902).

October 9–10, 1903: Pumpkin Freshet of 1903

Weather historian David Ludlum (1983, 176–177) described the storm of October 8–10, 1903, as the "greatest rainstorm in the history of the New York metropolitan and northern New Jersey areas." The remnants of a tropical storm drifting up the Atlantic coast caused light rain to overspread Pennsylvania on October 7–8, which soon turned into a driving rainstorm. The rain finally tapered off to mostly drizzle on October 10, but runoff from tropical downpours continued to swell creeks and rivers in eastern Pennsylvania and New Jersey.

Water levels along the Delaware River at Portland rose 8.7 feet above flood stage, exceeding the high marks reached during the Bridges Freshet of January 1841. By the time the Delaware River had crested in the early evening of October 10, a vast swath of the river valley was immersed in muddy waters. Pumpkins bobbed in the water, carried away by the roiling floodwaters that consumed the vulnerable croplands.

Bridges collapsed along the way, taking the lives of unsuspecting onlookers, starting with a 651-foot span between Matamoras and Port Jervis, New York. Severe flooding occurred in Easton at the junction of the Bushkill and Lehigh Rivers, which feed into the Delaware. The aftermath of the flood was described in detail by Dale (1996, 108): "The city lost hotels, trolleys, gas and electric plants, and its sewer plants, as well as most businesses. Homes along the Lehigh, Bushkill, and Delaware rivers lay underwater. The Mineral Springs and Salts Eddy hotels were swamped. Phillipsburg [New Jersey] received similar devastation."

In Pike County, farther north, tributaries feeding into the Delaware River also went into high flood. Several fatalities were reported along the Manunka Creek near Milford. Damage was estimated to be in excess of $200,000 along the upper Delaware Valley, including $60,000 in the eastern Poconos. Rainfall totals were exceptionally heavy in the northeastern corner of Pennsylvania. Stroudsburg drugstore proprietor J. Clyde LaBar, who, prior to becoming the official government observer in 1910, kept daily weather observations and provided weather records to the local press, measured a storm total of 8.00 inches of rain.

Farther north along the Delaware River, Alla K. Doughty, the government observer in Milford, logged a remarkable 9.90 inches of rain from October 7 to 10, 1903, with a twenty-four-hour total of 7.70 inches on October 8–9. On the Pocono Plateau, a weather station at Pocono Lake received a storm total of 6.90 inches. North of Honesdale the measurement at Dyberry was 7.63 inches.

The rain was even heavier near the coast, closer to the track of the tropical storm. In northeastern New Jersey, a total of 15.04 inches at Paterson came close to the totals of the great rainstorm of September 1882, also occurring with the passage of an offshore tropical storm. The New York City (Central Park) measurement of 11.17 inches established an all-time twenty-four-hour rainfall record for the city.

March 14–15, 1907: Pittsburgh Flood

On March 10–11, 1907, 4 to 8 inches of wet snow fell on much of western Pennsylvania, which would set the stage for flooding when heavy rains and thawing temperatures set in on March 12–14. This was the second flood to hit the area in the winter of 1906–7, as high water had caused problems two months earlier.

The flood stage on the Ohio River reached 35.5 feet on March 14, surpassing the record stage of 30 feet recorded back on February 10, 1832. A summary of the conditions and watershed discharge that contributed to the March 1907 flood in the Pittsburgh area appeared in the *Monthly Weather Review:* "An inspection of the weather maps and special reports shows that the flood at Pittsburg can be attributed mainly to the enormous volumes of flood water caused by the excessive rains and melting snows from march 12 to 14 over the Kiskiminetas and Youghiogheny watersheds. The Monongahela, of course, contributed largely, but not so much as in the January [1907] flood, when the stages above the mouth of the Youghiogheny were from 3 to 5 feet higher."

The Ohio River would eventually crest at 38.4 feet, which was supposed to be the highest flood stage since that of March 9, 1763 (adjusted to 41.1 feet), according to Shank (1988, 35). Telegraph and telephone services were wiped out in the aftermath of heavy rains and electrical storms on March 13, 1907, limiting the transmission of flood warnings. Ice jams broke free in various places, releasing huge quantities of water that coursed through the Kiskiminetas, Allegheny, Monongahela, and Youghiogheny Rivers toward Pittsburgh. The Ohio River surpassed flood stage between 6:00 and 7:00 P.M. on the thirteenth, reaching 31.1 feet (8.1 feet above flood stage) at 8:00 A.M. on March 14.

On the evening of March 13, the Conemaugh-Kiskiminetas River had already reached an elevation of 18 feet, some 11 feet above flood stage and the highest level since that of the Johnstown Flood on May 31, 1889. South of Pittsburgh, the Youghiogheny River crested at a record height of 28.2 feet at West Newton, 5.2 feet above flood stage and 6.2 feet above all previous high-water marks. The flood damage at Pittsburgh was estimated at $5.6 million, hitting the industrial and manufacturing districts the hardest. Nine lives were lost in the area, including three when a railroad bridge collapsed.

September 30, 1911: Austin Flood

In a rainy conclusion to the hot summer of 1911, the Philadelphia weather bureau rain gauge picked up 9.99 inches of rain from August 23 to 30, with maximum daily falls of 2.32 inches on the thirtieth and 3.41 inches on the thirty-first.

Another week of heavy rain in late September 1911 in the northern mountains of Pennsylvania caused many streams to overflow. After a soggy day on the twenty-ninth, the morning of the thirtieth offered the promise of a drier day. However, the pleasant turn in the weather belied an impending disaster that would afflict the small town of Austin, between St. Mary's and Coudersport in Potter County, on the fateful afternoon of September 30, 1911.

A huge dam had been built on a hill about a half-mile above Austin in 1909 that spanned the valley of Freeman Run. The dam was built to supply reserve power for the Bayless Pulp and Paper Mill that provided financial opportunities for the industrial town of 3,200 in the southwestern part of Potter County.

The concrete dam was a structural marvel for its breadth—530 feet long, 49 feet high, and 32 feet wide at the base. The dam was supposedly constructed on modern engineering principles. However, in the middle of January 1910 after a series of heavy snowfalls that were followed by a thaw and heavy rain, the Bayless Dam bulged thirty-six feet, flooding a small portion of town and raising serious concerns and protests over the integrity of the dam and subsequent concrete reinforcements.

Most residents were satisfied that the dam was safe in the fall of 1911, with the exception of a diligent resident named William Nelson, who continued to take daily measurements and warn of the potential for disaster (Nuschke 1960, 6–7). On September 30, 1911, the reservoir was full for the first time and spilling over the top while holding 4.5 million gallons of water. Suddenly, a small hole developed in the western end of the dam a little past 2:30 P.M., and the pressure caused the dam to burst.

Skies were sunny in Austin on the afternoon of September 30, and no one could have anticipated that the loud roar was a wall of water heading directly for the town. The disaster struck quickly, whisking away homes and unsuspecting residents, who felt their homes lifted in the churning, raging waters. The wall of water continued past Austin, swallowing up the small communities of Costello and Wharton a short distance away.

The death toll from the Austin dam was initially estimated in the hundreds, but apparently many were able to make a narrow escape and the figure was later put at seventy-eight (Shank 1988, 35). Author Marie Kathern Nuschke (1960, 6–7) further described the horrible event in *The Dam That Could Not Break:* "No person who witnessed the flood wants to remember the night that followed it. It continued to rain hard. A heavy mist settled over the Valley and through it streaked billowing black smoke while the bright red lights from the flames that came from burning debris pierced it now and then, giving a ghastly color to the faces of the people who continued to walk aimlessly on all the streets."

August 3, 1915: Mill Creek Disaster

A tropical system came ashore along the northeastern coast of Florida on August 1, 1915, and then followed a northerly track along the eastern seaboard. Remnants of the disturbance crossed central Pennsylvania early on the fourth, before curving northeastward across southern New England. Tropical moisture streamed along the eastern flank of the Appalachians into Pennsylvania and New Jersey on August 3–4, generating heavy downpours that led to pockets of flash flooding.

Heavy rains pounded northwestern Pennsylvania on the afternoon and evening of August 3, 1915, causing Mill Creek in Erie to overflow. The press account labeled the storm a "cloudburst" that swamped parts of Erie with five feet of water. The official city rain gauge caught 5.40 inches on August 3, and a total of 5.77 inches in twenty-four hours (August 3–4), triggering a deadly flash flood along Mill Creek that claimed thirty lives. Other parts of town were swamped with an estimated 20.00 inches of rain.

As a narrow channel of water gushed through Mill Creek, residents along the normally peaceful watercourse were caught without warning. A disaster ensued along the pathway of the creek, where thirty persons were swept away to their deaths in the city's worst natural disaster. Houses were washed from their foundations as water rose to the second story of some dwellings. The entire city of Erie was plunged into darkness as water swirled around power plants and lines of communications were cut off in all directions. Damage was estimated at $3 million (*Monthly Weather Review*).

Floods and Droughts

195

August 22–23, 1933: Hurricane Floods

Heavy rains attended the passage of the Chesapeake-Potomac Hurricane on August 22–23, 1933, over southeastern Pennsylvania, causing serious flooding that was described to be the worst in the state since 1889. The Pennsylvania Highway Department estimated the damage to bridges and roads alone on the order of $800,000 (*Climatological Data*). Crop losses were heavy southeast of the mountains.

Forty-three weather stations in Pennsylvania reported in excess of 6.00 inches of rain on August 21–23, 1933. The heaviest rainfall was 13.82 inches at York (8.48 inches fell in twenty-four hours on August 22–23, 1933). The storm established a new rainfall record for the state, eclipsing the previous mark of 11.00 inches on June 25–26, 1884, which also occurred at York! The monthly rainfall at York in August 1933 also set a state record (17.70 inches) at that time.

The Schuylkill River reached a stage of 19.7 feet at Reading, near the all-time record crest of 23.2 feet observed on September 2, 1850. Much of the south side of Reading was heavily flooded. Basements filled with water, and in some cases floodwaters rose as high as the first floor of dwellings. Flooding was widespread over southeastern Pennsylvania, including the lower Delaware Valley.

Mauch Chunk Creek in Carbon County spilled out of its banks on the afternoon of August 23, 1933, sending water pouring down Broadway in Mauch Chunk (Jim Thorpe). The rushing water caused considerable damage through the center of town, isolating residents in some parts of town. The gas company, which was owned by the Pennsylvania Power and Light Company, laid temporary lines while repairing the damage estimated at $50,000. The Big Creek at Weissport lived up to its name, flooding numerous properties, and a bridge at Nesquehoning was swept away, isolating residents of New Columbus (Eckhart 1997, 540–545).

Two weeks later, on September 3, 1933, another flash flood brought on by a cloudburst struck Carbon County and lasted about twelve hours. A dam broke in East Mauch Chunk that aggravated the flooding and damage to the Lehigh Valley Railroad, including two railroad bridges. A seventeen-year-old boy averted disaster by warning a train engineer along the Central Railroad of New Jersey shortly after midnight of a washout near Nesquehoning (Eckhart 1997, 546–547). Torrential rains sent the Codorus Creek roaring out of its banks, cresting at a record height of 24 feet at York, which exceeded the June 1884 flood record (Shank 1988, 35).

July 9–10, 1935: Northeastern Floods

A period of wet weather commencing on July 7, 1935, turned into a tropical downpour over parts of eastern Pennsylvania on July 8–9. In southern Wayne County, the weather station at Gouldsboro received 6.47 inches of rain on July 9–10 and a storm total of 7.26 inches over four days. In eastern Monroe County, 6.94 inches of rain fell at Stroudsburg during the same period, including a record July twenty-four-hour total of 4.70 inches. The weather station at Bethlehem's Lehigh University measured 5.10 inches in twenty-four hours on the ninth.

Heavy rains also hit central and southern New York on July 7–8, overfilling the Susquehanna watershed, which worked its way south into Pennsylvania. Ithaca, New York, received 7.90 inches of rain on July 7–8, contributing to major flooding in the region that took forty lives in New York State. Farther south a swollen Susquehanna River caused extensive property damage along with flash floods that claimed the lives of twelve Pennsylvania residents. Storm damage in the upper Susquehanna Valley was estimated around $25 million (Ludlum 1982, 81).

Rounds of heavy rain in eastern Pennsylvania on July 9, 1935, also brought the Delaware and Schuylkill Rivers and their tributaries out of their banks in some areas. Nine inches of rain reportedly fell in the Pottsville area at the headwaters of the Schuylkill River on July 8–9. The Perkiomen Creek, one of the tributaries of the Schuylkill, rose to a height of 20 feet (*Climatological Data*).

March 17–20, 1936: St. Patrick's Day Floods

The cold, snowy winter of 1935–36 brought a heavy accumulation of snow in January and February, which coupled with periods of intensely cold weather. The snowpack began to recede by late February and early March, though a considerable quantity of snow remained over the northern mountains of Pennsylvania. A series of heavy rainstorms falling on mostly frozen ground during the middle of March combined with melting snow over the higher elevations to bring serious flooding to much of Pennsylvania and the Ohio Valley.

A wet weather pattern developed over Pennsylvania on March 9–10, with heavier rain falling on the eleventh and twelfth. A heavy winter snowfall left a considerable quantity of snow in the higher elevations, which combined with a steady rain to produce a heavy runoff. Ice jams developed along many Pennsylvania rivers, compounding flooding in lowland areas. Many places in the state received an inch of rain or more, with up to 2.50 inches falling at Gouldsboro on the high Pocono Plateau in the northeast. The Susquehanna River at Harrisburg flooded areas north of downtown and the West Shore suburbs on March 13, 1936.

Light rain commenced again in western Pennsylvania on March 15–16, which became locally heavy statewide on the seventeenth and eighteenth and continued intermittently to the twentieth. In the northwestern corner of the state, heavy rain changed to wet snow on March 17, accumulating to a depth of 20 inches at Corry in Erie County. Rain pelted the remainder of the state, and the amounts were

Fig. 9.5. March 18, 1936. The St. Patrick's Day Flood in Harrisburg along the Susquehanna River. (Courtesy Pennsylvania State Archives)

heavy. The greatest twenty-four hour rainfall was 4.50 inches at Buffalo Mills on March 17–18.

Rivers were already running high in Pennsylvania from constant rains and melting snow, which had caused minor flooding a week earlier. There was no room in the soils and waterways for additional heavy rains that came on March 16–17, 1936.

Shank (1988, 44) described the terrible plight of Pittsburgh residents who lived in the Triangle district:

> Unconfirmed rumors of a dam break at Johnstown had Pittsburgh citizens jittery on Tuesday, March 17, 1936. Water had been rising all day, reached 27.1 feet at noon, and by late afternoon was invading the Golden Triangle. A fire which broke out in the Crucible Steel Plant, on the lower north side, added to the confusion and apprehension as streets became clogged with traffic leaving the flood area. Forecasters were still predicting a maximum crest of only 33 feet. By Wednesday morning terror gripped the city as water swirled around office buildings downtown and homes on the north side. Power went off all over Pittsburgh. Phone lines went down. More fires broke out.

Floodwaters in downtown Pittsburgh crested at an all-time record level of 46 feet at 7:00 P.M. on March 18, 1936, which was 21 feet above flood stage, and 7.5 feet above the previous high water mark on March 15, 1907. Fifteen feet of water covered the Triangle, forcing thousands to flee for their lives.

Boats maneuvered through flooded city streets that resembled canals in an attempt to rescue trapped victims, as fires and gas explosions rocked the downtown area. The National Guard and state police struggled to maintain order and prevent looting in downtown Pittsburgh, which was sealed off to the public.

Stefan Lorant (1964, 354–355) reported that 3,000 residents were injured and more than 100,000 lost their homes in the Pittsburgh area alone. The March 1936 edition of *Climatological Data* called the losses along Pennsylvania watersheds

Fig. 9.6. March 18, 1936. The St. Patrick's Day Flood left high water on this residential street in Harrisburg. (Courtesy Pennsylvania State Archives)

"appalling and unprecedented." Sixty-seven persons were confirmed dead in Pittsburgh, another twenty-two in Johnstown, and many others reported missing were almost certainly lost in the flood, which conservatively put loss of life in Pennsylvania at "upwards of 100."

Property losses were estimated at about $9 million in Wilkes-Barre and the Wyoming Valley and more than $28 million downstream along the Susquehanna River. The Pittsburgh area suffered incalculable destruction, estimated by government engineers around $250 million, raising total losses in the state of Pennsylvania to about $300 million (Shank 1988, 46). Damage in the greater Pittsburgh area was estimated at $250 million in 1936 dollars, and it would be several months before the city began to recover from the terrible losses inflicted by the St. Patrick's Day Flood.

In the northeastern part of the state, Stroudsburg was drenched with 6.92 inches of rain on March 17–18, 1936, and Mount Pocono received 5.20 inches in twenty-four hours. Pocono tributaries feeding into the Delaware River raised water levels at Easton to the highest point since October 1903. The river crested 10 feet above flood stage, sending water pouring into downtown Easton and other low-lying communities.

The flooding along the Delaware River in March 1936 was not as severe as in October 1903, mainly because the tributaries farther north did not reach flood stage at the same time, as they did in 1903. Back-channel flooding slowed the discharge into the main river but managed to cover up rail lines and roads. When the river peaked during the evening of March 18, many of the islands, including Island Park, were submerged.

The Stroudsburg *Record* described the flooding in the lower Pocono region: "The swirling, roaring waters, which last week pounded down the river, hurling huge cakes of ice, now poured the fullest vengeance against banks, homes, and bungalows and swept everything before them as they rushed along. Banks were eaten out, transportation stopped, homes were flooded, bungalows and garages were washed away and lives were endangered, although there were no fatalities up until noon today."

Serious flooding was widespread in Pennsylvania along every major river. The West Branch of the Susquehanna River emptied into the streets of Williamsport, cresting 11 feet above flood stage on March 19, 1936, at a height of 33.07 feet. The town of Sunbury, at the confluence of the West and North branches of the Susquehanna River, was swamped with six to twelve feet of water, as the river crested at a record height of 34.65 feet, 11 feet above flood stage.

On the Susquehanna North Branch, Wilkes-Barre suffered major flood damage as the river rose 11 feet above flood stage, within inches of the record height attained on March 18, 1865 (Shank 1986, 41). Some four thousand residents were marooned by the high waters that caused extensive damage and suffering. Above Wilkes-Barre, the river level at Towanda reached 25.03 feet, slightly above the 1865 previous record flood stage.

In south-central Pennsylvania, heavy flooding carried away bridges and homes at Mount Union, where the Raystown branch joined the Juniata River. Heavy property losses also occurred at Huntingdon. Farther downstream, at Newport, the river gauge read 34.34 feet, only slightly below the crest of 35.9 feet in the flood of 1889 (Shank 1988, 42).

Surging waters from the Juniata fed into the lower Susquehanna, adding to the rising waters around Harrisburg on March 17. Over the next two days, water from four to fifteen feet deep would cover almost a third of the city. Maximum flood stage was recorded at 6:00 P.M., Thursday, March 19, at 29.23 feet at the official Nagle Street gauge and 30.33 feet a little upstream at the Walnut Street site (Shank 1988, 37).

Fig. 9.7. March 18, 1936. Flooding at the Point near downtown Pittsburgh, where the Allegheny and Monongahela Rivers meet to form the Ohio River. (*Pittsburgh Post-Gazette* Photo Archives, copyright 1999, all rights reserved)

Fig. 9.8. March 18, 1936. Flooding on Liberty Avenue, Pittsburgh. (*Pittsburgh Post-Gazette* Photo Archives, copyright 1986, all rights reserved)

Reservoirs were built to provide better flood control after the Great March Floods of 1936 in the Northeast and Ohio Valley. Widespread flooding killed at least 107 people, with many more missing and presumed lost. The Flood Control Act of 1938, which gave Army engineers the right to obtain property for the sake of flood control and to construct high flood walls, was an outgrowth of the March 1936 floods.

May 22–23, 1942: Northeastern Floods

Heavy rain drenched northeastern Pennsylvania on May 20–23, 1942, sending rivers and creeks out of their banks beginning late on the twenty-second. A weather observer at Carbondale reported 7.00 inches of rain between 4:00 P.M. and midnight on May 22, and another rain gauge at Tanner's Falls, north of Honesdale, collected 4.96 inches between 6:00 P.M. and midnight, with a storm total in excess of 7.00 inches.

In the hills of eastern Carbon County, the observer at Mauch Chunk (Jim Thorpe) measured 6.14 inches in twenty-four hours (May 22–23). A storm total of 8.00 inches fell at Hickory Run on May 20–22.

A wooden bridge over Robinson's Creek between Coalport and East Mauch Chunk collapsed around midnight on May 22–23, stranding Coalport residents. Down in Weissport, floodwaters inundated the Lehigh Canal, submerging homes under eight feet of water. Damage to the Lehigh Coal and Navigation Company between White Haven and Easton reached $5.7 million (Eckhart 1997, 547–550).

Records maintained by the Department of Forests and Waters showed a rapid rise on the Lackawaxen River near Hawley between the 10:00 P.M. observation on May 22 and 4:00 A.M. on May 23 to a height of 17.4 feet. This total was 6.23 feet

Fig. 9.9. May 23, 1942. Heavy thunderstorms sent the Lackawaxen River out of its banks in a deadly flash flood. This view is looking north from Willow Avenue in Honesdale. (Courtesy Elizabeth [Korb] Schuman)

higher than the peak discharge in March 1936. Flooding also occurred farther south along the Lehigh and Schuylkill Rivers.

Tragedy struck in Wayne County, where twenty-four people drowned along a fifteen-mile stretch of the Lackawaxen River between Prompton and Hawley. The disaster occurred after water spilled over a dam around 9:30 P.M. on the twenty-second. The only alarm was a fire gong that sounded at 11:30 P.M. Darkness and loss of communications prevented a reasonable transmission of high water warnings.

The death toll in eastern Pennsylvania mounted to thirty-three persons as high waters continued to sweep through the region until early on the twenty-third. Flooding was also reported along the Delaware and Susquehanna Rivers. The *Climatological Data* report noted, "Property damage, conservatively estimated, amounted to $13,000,000."

July 17–18, 1942: North-Central Floods

The summer of 1942 was unusually stormy. A series of cloudbursts associated with a slow-moving thunderstorm complex drenched central Pennsylvania on July 17–18. Excessive rainfall turned quiet mountain streams into raging torrents that were channeled through narrow mountain passes. Rainfall estimates ran as high as 15.00 inches in less than twenty-four hours in Cameron, Potter, McKean, and Elk Counties.

Communications were cut off from Emporium, a town of 4,500 that was especially hard hit. Flooding at Port Allegany in McKean County claimed six lives. On July 23, highway department chief engineer T. C. Frame reported that damage to Pennsylvania highways and bridges was estimated at $500,000, noting, "We lost about 16 bridges ranging from 75 to 250 feet."

The death toll in northern Pennsylvania and southern New York rose to sixteen, according to the press. The July *Climatological Data* report listed a maximum twenty-four-hour rainfall total of 8.48 inches at Coudersport. The rain gauge at the Smethport Highway Shed registered 6.68 inches before the gauge was lost in the flood. The 1942 *Annual Summary* for Pennsylvania noted unofficial rain gauge readings as high as 15.00 inches in the north-central mountains on July 17–18, 1942.

A bucket survey undertaken after the storm estimated that Smethport had received a world-record rainfall of 30.60 inches in six hours on July 17 and a storm total of 34.50 inches on the seventeenth and eighteenth. This figure has traditionally been accepted as the official state record (Ludlum 1983, 185), along with a monthly total of 40.90 inches. However, the extraordinary rainfall total was only an estimate, so the author believes that the state July rainfall record actually belongs to Park Place in July 1947 (19.81 inches).

July 1947: Record Soggy July

The spring and summer of 1947 were cool and unusually stormy. The United States Soil Conservation Service reported soil and crop losses in excess of $900 million in May and June. A persistent and unseasonably strong jet stream was the likely source of trouble, providing energy and pathway for frequent storms that tracked from the Midwest across the Great Lakes into Pennsylvania. A weather modification experiment in New Mexico involving a silver-iodide generator used for rainmaking studies in 1947 was implicated in the unusually stormy pattern in the Midwest (Petterrsen 2001, 293–294).

July 1947 was an unusually wet and cool month in Pennsylvania. Measurable rain fell on sixteen days across the state, and the month tied with July 1920 for the coolest seventh month in over fifty years of state records. The heaviest monthly total—19.81 inches—was measured at a weather station (Park Place) on top of a ridge in northern Schuylkill County (el. 1,900 feet), five miles northwest of Mahanoy City. The nearly-twenty-inch total is the heaviest monthly rainfall ever recorded in July in Pennsylvania, and the second greatest single-month total, which has been exceeded only in August 1955 at Mount Pocono (23.66 inches). Record July rainfall totals in northern Pennsylvania included 15.32 inches at Freeland, 13.27 inches at Erie, and 12.94 inches at Hawley.

A slow-moving front on July 7–8, 1947, stagnated over the mountains of northern Pennsylvania, creating an upslope condition that forced warm, moist Atlantic air to ascend over a shallow layer of cooler air over hilly eastern Pennsylvania. Waves of severe thunderstorms contributed to torrential rainfalls and flash flooding. At Freeland 5.86 inches of rain came down in twenty-four hours. The maximum rainfall was measured at a weather station at Park Place—7.83 inches fell in twenty-four hours. Five-inch rain totals were common in southern Wayne County.

A week later a vigorous summertime low-pressure system brought heavy downpours to the Keystone State on July 16–17, 1947, totaling 4.29 inches of rain at Hawley, 3.29 inches at Park Place, and 3.10 inches at Reading. However, the greatest rainfall event in the stormy month was yet to come.

On July 21–22, a cluster of thunderstorms dumped 6.32 inches of rain on the city of Erie in three hours on the twenty-first, and a storm total of 10.42 inches fell in twenty-four hours. As much as 20.00 inches were estimated to have fallen in other parts of the city, though the airport received a little less than 4.00 inches.

High water forced the evacuation of sixty-six residents, and a state of emergency was declared in the city. Basement flooding and damage to homes and businesses primarily south and east of the downtown area was conservatively estimated at $250,000.

August 1955: Hurricane Floods and a Campground Tragedy

Eastern Pennsylvania suffered through the most destructive flood in the region's history in August 1955, ironically, after the driest July in Pennsylvania since 1909. Two ex-hurricanes unloaded wave after wave of heavy rain on eastern Pennsylvania in quick succession, resulting in severe flooding that took at least one hundred lives in Pennsylvania.

The first storm to hit the eastern seaboard was Hurricane Connie, which brought drought-busting rains to the Middle Atlantic states on August 12–13. Ex-Hurricane Connie weakened over North Carolina after making landfall on the twelfth, but it was still a prolific rainmaker. Ex-Hurricane Connie crossed the Chesapeake Bay before heading into south-central Pennsylvania during the mid-day hours of August 13.

A tropical deluge pelted eastern Pennsylvania as the remains of Connie traveled northwest to a position near Erie, in the northwestern part of the state, around 7:30 P.M. During the soggy period of August 10–14, 1955, 6.00 to 10.00 inches of rain pelted the rugged hills of Monroe County and portions of Montgomery and Chester Counties in the southeast. Stroudsburg received 6.82 inches from August 11 to 13 (6.17 inches in twenty-four hours on the twelfth and thirteenth), and Mount Pocono had a storm total of 9.84 inches from those days.

Fig. 9.10. August 19, 1955. The swollen Delaware cut the passageway from Easton to Phillipsburg, New Jersey, through the Delaware River free bridge. (Courtesy *Easton Express-Times*)

Two persons, one in Lancaster County and the other near Coatesville, west of Philadelphia, drowned in flooding caused by ex-Hurricane Connie, according to the August 1955 edition of *Climatological Data*. Both fatalities happened in automobiles that were swept away in swift currents. Flooding also occurred along the Perkiomen Creek in Bucks County and the Brandywine Creek in Chester County, inundating roads, industrial plants, and homes in low-lying areas. Basement flooding was widespread in southern Allegheny County near Pittsburgh. River flooding was not a problem during the onslaught of Connie's rains, because the stream flow was low after a summer drought.

As the remnants of Connie disintegrated over Ontario, Canada, weather forecasters were already keeping a wary eye on Hurricane Diane, centered several hundred miles off the Georgia coast. Diane made landfall near Wilmington, North Carolina, early on August 17, 1955, packing 85-mile-per-hour winds. Diane then took a northwest trajectory into the foothills of the Appalachians before curving north in the direction of Pennsylvania. Ten inches of rain soaked the Blue Ridge Mountains of Virginia on August 17–18.

The weather bureau in Washington, D.C., issued their final storm bulletin at 11:00 P.M. on the seventeenth, apparently believing the worst was over. But a trough of low pressure over eastern Pennsylvania set up a convergence line for moisture-laden tropical air, which collided with cooler air along the Appalachian foothills.

Stream levels rose to dangerously high levels in the evening hours of August 18, as Diane made a right turn across southeastern Pennsylvania. Heavy rains pelted

Fig. 9.11. August 19, 1955. Flooding in downtown Easton, accurately depicted as the world's fastest car wash, where the Delaware River rose to a height of 43 feet. (Courtesy *Easton Express-Times*)

Fig. 9.12. August 19, 1955. Flooding in downtown Easton at Northampton and Front
Streets, where the waters ignored the one-way street sign. (Courtesy *Easton Express-Times*)

the eastern portion of the state, falling on wet ground saturated by Connie's rainfall less than a week earlier. The main streams were already running high, so there
was little room for the ensuing heavy runoff from the hills.

Rainfall estimates on the order of 7.00 to 9.00 inches were reported in a six-
hour period during the night of August 18–19. In northeastern Pennsylvania storm
totals ranged from 6.00 to 12.00 inches in thirty hours. The heaviest amounts were
reported in southeastern Lackawanna and southwestern Wayne Counties.

Northeastern Pennsylvania received the brunt of the rainfall. At Tamaqua,
8.00 inches fell between 2:00 and 6:00 P.M. on the nineteenth (Shank 1988, 50).
Mount Pocono Airport measured a record 10.75 inches (10.63 inches in twenty-
four hours), and, fifteen miles southeast, 6.15 inches of rain fell at Stroudsburg in
twenty-four hours.

Heavy runoff from mountain streams feeding northeastern Pennsylvania rivers
led to the most destructive flooding since the region was settled in the late eighteenth century. Normally placid Pocono creeks (Brodhead, Pocono, Bushkill, Mc-
Michaels, and Scioto) would become raging torrents of water channeled through
narrow passages.

During the late-evening hours of August 18, 1955, a succession of dam failures
released pent-up water and debris, sending the Brodhead on a rampage of death
and destruction.

Forty-seven unsuspecting vacationers at Camp Davis, situated on the banks of
the Brodhead Creek five miles north of East Stroudsburg, were huddled in fourteen cottages waiting out the heavy rain. A swirling wall of water thirty feet high
filled with uprooted pine trees, boulders, and debris was sweeping through the

normally tranquil watercourse. In a few horrifying seconds, the cottages, housing mostly children and their mothers, were torn from their foundations and swept away. Thirty-eight people were killed.

As the waters rose, the campers left their cabins and gathered in the main building, a two-story frame structure. Another camp, Pine Brook, lay on higher ground a mere hundred yards distant, but the Camp Davis people underestimated their danger and stayed put. The turbulent waters continued to mount and the terrified campers were forced up to the second floor and then finally to the attic, where they huddled in the dark and prayed. . . . Then the building disintegrated in a thirty-foot wall of water and all forty-six campers, most of them children, were swept away. Nine were later found alive, clinging to tree limbs or debris, or having been miraculously swept ashore. Some bodies were never recovered. (Dale 1996, 133)

Water and debris tore through the Stroudsburg with little warning during the late-evening hours of August 18. Unsuspecting bingo players in the Day Street fire hall were swept away as water tore the building apart, killing six people. A number of homes were also carried away in the thundering waters.

The Civil Defense estimate of seventy-eight lives lost in Monroe and Pike Counties along and near the Delaware River makes it the single worst tragedy to strike the region. Twenty bridges were destroyed in Monroe County, including the bridge connecting Stroudsburg and East Stroudsburg. Portions of both towns were isolated by swirling waters that quickly overtook the "flats" section along Brodhead Creek, which would expand in width to nearly a mile across.

Southeast of Stroudsburg where the Brodhead joins the Delaware River, a ma-

Fig. 9.13. August 19, 1955. Floodwaters along Brodhead Creek, Stroudsburg, rampage through the twin boroughs, taking scores of lives. (Courtesy Monroe County Historical Association)

jor tragedy was averted, as noted in William H. Shank's *Great Floods of Pennsylvania:* "A miracle saved a number of campers and cottagers on Shawnee Island in the Delaware, who had watched the Delaware rise all day on August 18, until by ten o'clock that night it was too turbulent to escape to the mainland. Suddenly the rain stopped and the waters smoothed. The campers could hardly believe their eyes —the Delaware had reversed its direction and was placidly running *upstream!*"

South of Shawnee Island, two tributaries of the Delaware—one flowing from the west (Brodhead) and the other from the east (Binnekill)—created a "huge water barrier" that temporarily halted and actually reversed the flow of the main stream, just long enough for island residents to escape by boat. In a scene reminiscent of the parting of the Red Sea in the Bible, the waters resumed their rapid and destructive course once the refugees had made their way to safety.

In Wayne County near Hawley, rising water consumed a dam where the Lackawaxen River merged with Middle Creek, taking two lives. A weather station two miles northwest of Paupack in southern Wayne County caught 9.07 inches of rain in less than twenty-four hours. The Lackawanna River overflowed in southern Wayne, Lackawanna, and Luzerne Counties, due to rapid runoff from muddy hillsides, causing the worst flooding in Scranton's history. The weather station at Avoca, midway between the cities of Scranton and Wilkes-Barre, recorded 4.58 inches of rain in twenty-four hours, which is the third heaviest total on record (after 1924 and 1985).

Severe flooding spread downstream along the Delaware River to Easton. The Portland-Columbia (New Jersey) covered bridge, started in 1831 and completed in 1869, spanned 725 feet and was the longest wooden bridge of its kind in the country. The bridge had withstood the Pumpkin Freshet of 1903 and all other previous floods, but the historic structure collapsed when it was nearly submerged on August 19, 1955 (Ludlum 1983, 185). A little farther downstream, the sixty-year-old Phillipsburg-Easton free bridge was ripped from its foundation by the force of the water. Four bridges spanning the Delaware River were severely damaged or destroyed.

The Lehigh Valley was hard-hit by the upstream runoff from Diane's deluge. Homes and businesses in the Easton area in low-lying areas suffered heavy damage in Easton's worst flood. An unofficial gauge reading put the crest at 43.7 feet on August 19, 1955, about 5.6 feet higher than that of the October 1903 flood (Shank 1988, 51). Floodwaters lapped every town along the Lehigh River, though no fatalities were reported.

The state storm summary reported that the Hurricane Flood of 1955, which affected 6,600 square miles, was "the most disastrous flood ever to strike eastern Pennsylvania." Many homes, bridges, and telephone poles were swept away by turbulent waters racing through narrow channels that spilled across roads and railroad lines. Navy and Marine helicopters manned by government and volunteer pilots airlifted hundreds of trapped victims to safety, saving countless lives.

Despite many heroic efforts, the death toll from flooding in Pennsylvania was estimated around one hundred victims, including ten persons missing and presumed drowned. Additional deaths attributed to electrocutions, automobile accidents, and other flood-related calamities pushed the death toll to 113 in Pennsylvania (Longshore 1998, 95). Six deaths occurred in New Jersey as the remnants

Fig. 9.14. August 19, 1955. Raging waters tore down the Canadensis Bridge north of
Stroudsburg. (Courtesy Monroe County Historical Association)

of the circulation center passed over central New Jersey in the early morning of
August 19, before crossing Long Island.

Flooding along the Delaware River reached historic proportions, as waters rose
more than 10 feet above flood stage. The peak discharge at Riegelsville, in Warren
County, New Jersey, near the site of the Stroudsburg disaster, was 340,000 cubic
feet per second, 1.2 times greater than that of the Great Flood of 1903. The flood
stage in August 1955 was 3 feet higher than in October 1903 (Ludlum 1983, 187).
Serious flooding occurred along the Lackawanna River from the Scranton area
southward on the night of August 18–19, 1955. The river stage at Old Forge, five
miles southwest of Scranton, reached 20.05 feet early on August 19.

More than a foot of rain fell on parts of Connecticut, and nearly 20.00 inches
came down in the hills of Massachusetts, causing devastating New England floods.
The total loss of life attributed to Diane was 191 victims, and flood damage has
been estimated at about $4 billion in modern dollars—the costliest hurricane in
United States history at the time.

Not surprisingly, August 1955 was the wettest August in Pennsylvania weather
history, with a state average rainfall of 8.42 inches, and was surpassed only by
May 1894 (8.88 inches) until June 1972 (11.23 inches). In the northeastern corner
of the state, which took the brunt of the rain from the twin ex-hurricanes, Connie
and Diane, August 1955 was the wettest month on record at Stroudsburg (15.09
inches) and Mount Pocono (23.66 inches)—the latter total also setting a state rainfall record.

June 22–25, 1972: Agnes Floods

The most costly weather-related disaster in Pennsylvania history was wrought by the remnants of an early-season hurricane in June 1972. Agnes was an early-season Gulf hurricane born east of the Yucatan Peninsula on June 16.

Hurricane Agnes lashed Cuba with high winds and torrential rain before crashing into the Florida panhandle on June 19, 1972, near Valparaiso. The storm weakened as it tracked north over Georgia and the Carolinas, but it regained energy over the Virginia Capes. A broad upper-level trough over the East and an area of high pressure off the coast of New England worked in tandem to slow the forward progress of the storm, which would veer to the northwest across northern Pennsylvania and southern New York.

On Monday, June 20, the first plume of moisture reached Pennsylvania, accompanied by pockets of heavy rain. Over the ensuing five days, however, the remnants of Agnes looped across north-central Pennsylvania and south-central New York and would in the end settle over the mountains of western Pennsylvania. A prolonged heavy rainfall exceeded the carrying capacity of rivers and streams from southern New York to Virginia, pushing waters to all-time high levels that caused widespread flooding.

Pennsylvania Governor Milton Shapp declared a state of emergency early on Thursday, June 22. Meanwhile, the Susquehanna River continued to rise, threatening low-lying areas around the state capital. An average of 7.00 inches of rain fell in twenty-four hours on June 21–22, and some areas received more than a foot. Raging floodwaters poured over embankments, forcing nearly 250,000 Pennsylvanians to flee their homes, reaching levels 3 to 6 feet higher than those recorded in the great March 1936 floods.

A watershed research site operated by the United States Department of Agriculture in extreme western Schuylkill County measured a state record twenty-four-hour rainfall of 14.50 inches of rain on June 21–22, 1972, and an estimated storm total of 19.00 inches (*Storm Data*). A York gauge collected 13.50 inches in twenty-four hours.

The daily rainfall totals at Harrisburg on June 21 (5.81 inches) and 22 (9.13 inches) tell the story, together with a record twenty-four-hour catch (12.55 inches) on June 21–22 and a storm total of 15.26 inches through the twenty-sixth. By early on the twenty-third, floodwaters swamped the south side of the city known as the Riverside section and also covered the north side up to four blocks from the river (Shank 1988, 64). Water surrounded the governor's mansion on North Front Street, pouring into the first floor. Nearly half of the city of Harrisburg was partially under water.

On Saturday morning, June 24, 1972, the Susquehanna River would eventually crest at 32.57 feet, some 3.34 feet higher than the March 1936 record flood stage. The stream flow at Harrisburg during peak discharge was a little over a million cubic feet per second!

At 10:00 P.M. on June 24, the North Branch of the Susquehanna River crested at 33.25 feet at Towanda, more than 17 feet above flood stage (16 feet). Along the West Branch, the town of Clearfield was spared a major disaster, thanks to a

Fig. 9.15. June 25, 1972. The Susquehanna River roars through downtown York, depositing tons of water and mud at the Dauphin Deposit Bank. (One of a series of photographs appearing in the *York Daily Record;* courtesy Pennsylvania State Archives)

dam built by the Army Corps of Engineers that was completed in 1965. The river crested a mere foot below flood stage.

Dams prevented more serious flooding in northern Pennsylvania, though Shank (1988, 60–61) described some close calls: "The City of Williamsport owes its escape from the 1972 Flood completely to the work of the Corps of Engineers. The 1955 flood levees, plus the three major upstream dams . . . effectively kept all major flood water out of the city."

The towns of Muncy, Milton, and Lewisburg, however, were hit hard by flooding along tributaries of the main stem of the Susquehanna River. At the confluence of the North and West Branches, Sunbury had been the scene of major flooding in March 1936 and June 1972. However, a system of floodwalls, levees, and five pumping stations erected by the Army Corps of Engineers and completed in 1948 saved Sunbury in June 1972 from a calamity similar to that caused by the March 1936 flood.

In northeastern Pennsylvania, flooding was widely anticipated in the Wyoming Valley, but the extent far exceeded what anyone could have imagined based on past experience. As early as 6:00 A.M. on Friday, June 23, 1972, the Civil Defense reported that the river level had exceeded the previous high-water mark of 33.07 feet attained on March 20, 1936 (Shank 1988, 55–56).

Wyoming Valley residents listened to a steady stream of information on the radio and television warning of imminent flooding and urging them to go to local disaster shelters. Evacuations began in and around Wilkes-Barre and Kingston, while residents hoped dikes constructed after the March 1936 floods to withstand water levels up to 37 feet above flood stage would hold back the steadily rising waters.

By mid-morning on June 23, it was evident to river forecasters that water levels would reach 40 feet, requiring the evacuation of Wilkes-Barre residents in harm's way. Ten thousand volunteers applied sandbags to weaker links in the dikes and openings in the bridges in a desperate attempt to stave off the inevitable. The bad news came at 1:12 P.M., when the first dike at Forty Fort gave way near a cemetery. The National Guard was charged with the gruesome task of retrieving the bodies and caskets afterward.

A succession of dike failures prompted an endless string of dire warnings for residents downstream along the Susquehanna River. At 2:37 P.M. the large Wyoming Dike failed at the Midway Shopping Center. With catastrophic flooding imminent, 100,000 residents of Wilkes-Barre and Kingston were forced to move to high ground, congregating in public buildings and schools designated as refuges for flood victims.

Around 7:00 P.M. on June 24, the river crested 18.9 feet above flood stage at Wilkes-Barre at a height of 40.91 feet, nearly 8 feet above the previous high-water

Fig. 9.16. June 25, 1972. Floodwaters swamp the city of York after the passage of Agnes dumped more than a foot of rain on the valley. (Courtesy Pennsylvania State Archives)

Fig. 9.17. June 25, 1972. The Susquehanna River fans out over a mile in width near York.
(Courtesy Pennsylvania State Archives)

mark in March 1936. The floodwaters had topped the levees by 4 feet, ruining over
25,000 homes and businesses and taking seventeen lives. The incredible damage
was estimated around $1 billion. Another 2,278 homes were damaged by water
9 feet deep in downtown Wilkes-Barre. In nearby Kingston nearly every home suffered water damage. Many dwellings were deemed uninhabitable when residents
returned to survey the destruction as the waters receded several days later.

Floodwaters along the North Branch of the Susquehanna River brought record
high-water marks at Sunbury, Bloomsburg, and Danville. The waters at Sunbury
reached 12 feet above flood stage at noon on Saturday, June 24, a foot higher than
in March 1936. Flash flooding was widespread on June 22 even before the Susquehanna swallowed up the central section of Danville under 5 feet of water (Shank
1988, 8). The river crested at 32.32 feet at 7:00 P.M. on June 24, more than 4 feet
above the March 1936 level at Danville.

Record flooding also hit Reading when the Schuylkill River rose 8.5 feet above flood stage (31.5 feet), well above the previous record height of 23.3 feet (September 2, 1850). Flood damage was extensive at Pottstown and Norristown. Three persons died in the flooding in the Philadelphia area.

Heavy flooding was also reported along the Codorus Creek at York following a round of torrential tropical downpours on June 22. An average storm total of 16.00 inches fell over the watershed, pushing the normally placid creek to a height of 26.4 feet in the late afternoon, 2.4 feet above the 1933 record crest, "cutting the city in two" (Shank 1988, 66). Nonetheless, the Indian Rock Dam prevented a greater disaster, holding back "nine billion gallons of water at the height of the flood."

In western Pennsylvania, Pittsburgh suffered $45 million of flood damage when the Ohio River crested 11 feet above flood stage (35.85 feet), though it was nearly 10 feet below the record 1936 stage. Dams built by the Corps of Engineers along upstream tributaries saved the city of Johnstown from a repeat of the disastrous 1936 flood. Flood protection included the enlargement of portions of the Little Conemaugh River, and the construction of a reservoir south of the city.

The death toll mounted as floodwaters receded and more bodies were discovered. An estimated 250,000 residents in the region afflicted by high waters were forced to leave their homes as floodwaters ravaged scores of communities. The largest monthly rainfall total in Pennsylvania in June 1972 from an official reporting station (York Pump Station 3 SSW) was 20.45 inches. The previous rainfall record for the entire month of June was 13.74 inches at Gettysburg (1951). Harrisburg measured a record 18.55 inches of rain in June 1972.

The loss of life from flooding in June 1972 was greatest in Pennsylvania (48) and New York (25), and Pennsylvania suffered the greatest economic losses ($2.8 billion). In northern Virginia, at least 10.00 inches of rain caused $222 million of damage and flooding claimed thirteen lives.

The death toll from Agnes in the eastern United States (112), coupled with massive economic losses ($4 billion), place the event among the nation's greatest storm disasters. In fact, in 1990 dollars the cost of Agnes would have been about $6.4 billion—the second costliest storm in United States history after Andrew ($26.5 billion), which lashed south Florida in August 1992.

September 25–26, 1975: Hurricane Eloise

Only three years and three months after being inundated by tropical moisture unleashed by ex-Hurricane Agnes, the Susquehanna Valley would be struck with another deluge, the remnants of Hurricane Eloise, resulting in serious flooding.

Eloise made landfall on September 23, 1975, near Fort Walton Beach, Florida, only ten miles to the west of where Agnes came ashore in June 1972. Eloise took a different path, tracking west of the Appalachians and losing some moisture before reaching Pennsylvania. A stalled front over the Middle Atlantic states, however, provided a substantial lifting mechanism, forcing warm, moist tropical air to rise over cooler air lying over Pennsylvania.

As in June 1972, a blocking upper-air pattern over Pennsylvania greatly enhanced rainfall totals. At Harrisburg, 7.22 inches of rain came down in twenty-four hours on September 25–26, 1975, helping to set a September rainfall record of 14.97 inches. Extensive flooding developed along the Susquehanna River and many of its tributaries in central and northeastern Pennsylvania on September 26–27, forcing nearly 20,000 persons to evacuate their homes. In north-central Pennsylvania, floodwaters in Tioga County at Westfield and Lawrenceville exceeded the June 1972 levels, sending residents fleeing for safety.

The earlier addition of the Raystown Dam northwest of Harrisburg controlled flooding along the Juniata River, one of the major tributaries of the Susquehanna River. The Susquehanna crested an average of 10 feet above flood stage along the west branch at Milton, Lewisburg, and Muncy and downstream at Harrisburg. Two Pennsylvanians lost their lives in south-central Pennsylvania, at York and in Franklin County.

In the northeast, an area along the Susquehanna River from about Williamsport to Sunbury and continuing south through the Wyoming Valley was protected by levees and dikes that were built after the Agnes flood. Nonetheless, precautionary evacuations continued until the water began to recede.

July 19–20, 1977: Another Johnstown Tragedy

The city of Johnstown in Cambria County has a long history of devastating floods, most notably the Great Johnstown Flood of May 1889, which took more than 2,200 lives. History would sadly be repeated on a steamy July night in 1977, when a small cluster of thunderstorms seemed to stall, or essentially regenerate over the Conemaugh Valley and the surrounding mountains above Johnstown on the night of July 19.

The thunderstorm complex brought heavy rain commencing around 8:30 P.M. on the nineteenth, according to a flood survivor, and did not let up until around 4:30 A.M. in the morning of the twentieth. Rainfall totals as high as 12.00 inches were measured in West Taylor Township northwest of Johnstown. Torrents of water poured off the deep hillsides of Cambria County into the Little Conemaugh River, which meets the Conemaugh River just above Johnstown. A break in the Laurel Run Dam sent an angry wall of rushing water 10 feet high through the valley into Johnstown without warning, sweeping away unsuspecting residents in their homes and cars.

Flood controls in the Little Conemaugh Valley that completed in 1943 averted disaster in June 1972, but this time they were unable to handle the volume of rain that fell on the night of July 19–20, 1977, according to the Army Corps of Engineers. The flash flood that struck Johnstown in July 1977 took at least seventy-seven lives and caused $424 million of damage. The greatest monthly rainfall in Pennsylvania in July 1977, 15.29 inches, was recorded at Marion Center.

January 1996: Snowmelt Floods

Record snow depths amassed in eastern Pennsylvania during the first two weeks of January 1996 following several major snowstorms, including the Blizzard of '96 on January 7–8. Snowbound residents in the northeastern and Middle Atlantic states hoped for a gradual thaw, but a series of heavy rainstorms brought inevitable disaster.

The water content of the snow by the middle of January was very high. The first batch of heavy rain to fall on Pennsylvania in January 1996 accompanied a cold front on January 18–19. A total of 3.03 inches of rain fell on Williamsport in twenty-four hours on the nineteenth, setting a January record. Winds gusted to 67 miles per hour in a thunderstorm at Philadelphia.

The combination of melting snow and heavy rain falling into a dense snowpack set the stage for massive runoff into Pennsylvania creeks and streams that would result in near-record flooding in many areas. Rivers packed with chunks of ice backed up until the temporary blockage collapsed, cutting loose torrents of water. A tragedy occurred when an ice jam broke loose along the Lycoming Creek, unleashing a wall of water that roared through several small communities and killed six residents. Hundreds were forced to flee their homes as water rose suddenly downstream.

At Wilkes-Barre the Susquehanna River rose to a height of 34.4 feet (12.4 feet above flood stage), and at Harrisburg the river crested 7.7 feet above flood stage, causing extensive damage. Ice floes along the Delaware River dammed up a large volume of water, which flooded riverfront property at Shawnee and Price's Landing on January 19. One to 2.00 inches of rain pelted the frozen surface and promptly drained into streams and creeks, inundating roads and highways. Heavy damage was done to the ninety-year-old Shawnee Inn and Country Club and along the Delaware Water Gap National Recreation Area. Flood damage in Monroe County alone reached $25 million.

Widespread flooding caused damage in the millions of dollars along the Delaware River and smaller creeks throughout Monroe, Northampton, Lehigh, Berks, Bucks, Chester, and Delaware Counties. Flooding along the Perkiomen Creek in Montgomery County resulted in two deaths, and another person died in a storm-related incident. As many as five thousand residents were evacuated in Bucks County, mainly from Riegelsville to Yardley along the Delaware River, which reached its highest level since August 1955. Flood damage in eastern Pennsylvania was estimated at $50 million.

In western Pennsylvania, the slow-moving weather system generated rainfall totals of 2.00 to 4.00 inches or more in twenty-four hours, resulting in the worst flooding downstream from Pittsburgh since Agnes struck in June 1972. The Allegheny River crested 10 feet above flood stage on January 20, 1996, reaching a level of 34.6 feet, which was only slightly lower than the high-water mark recorded in June 1972 (35.8 feet).

More heavy rain on January 27–28, pushed eastern Pennsylvania rivers to flood levels all over again. One to 2.00 inches of rain accompanied a cold front for the second weekend in a row, taking another life in Bucks County along the Delaware River. Water rescues were required as some people attempted to drive past barricades through high water and became trapped.

The stream flow of the Susquehanna River at Harrisburg in January 1996 reached 570,000 cubic feet per second, though this was not as high as the rate of a million cubic feet per second recorded in June 1972 during the Agnes floods. Total financial losses in Pennsylvania incurred during January 1996 from the blizzard and floods were estimated at $1 billion.

The January 1996 Snowmelt Floods took nineteen lives in Pennsylvania. Floodwaters damaged 52,000 homes, and 11,000 suffered irreparable damage. Fifty-seven of Pennsylvania's sixty-seven counties were affected by flooding, which resulted in 200,000 evacuations. Storm surveys reported that 2,000 businesses were damaged in the floods, plus 1,500 bridges and 78 parks. The cost of the water damage to Pennsylvania highways and bridges totaled nearly $500 million.

August 20, 1999: Bradford Flood

A stalled upper-air storm over the Northeast and a series of disturbances pivoting around the low-pressure system led to pockets of rain and thunderstorms that culminated in serious flooding in Bradford, McKean County, on August 20, 1999, the worst the area had seen since 1947.

A burst of heavy rain mainly between 2:00 and 5:00 A.M. dropped 3.42 inches of rain at the Bradford Central Fire Station. A second round of slow-moving storms dumped torrential rains on the city of Bradford and surrounding townships between 1:00 and 4:00 P.M., totaling another 5.56 inches at the fire station weather site for a storm total of 8.98 inches.

Streets turned into rivers and water poured off the hillsides with nowhere else to go. The flooding situation became serious in the city of Bradford by 3:00 P.M. on August 20. At least ten water rescues were required to pull trapped residents and motorists from dangerous situations, though only one injury was reported. As many as 211 homes and 53 businesses incurred water damage. Twenty-two homes reported major losses, and eight were destroyed. The damage toll in Bradford was put at $25 million.

Other areas hard-hit by heavy rainfall and localized flooding included Richfield in eastern Juniata County, where an estimated 8.00 to 9.00 inches of rain were reported, causing $500,000 damage. Thirty homes and four businesses suffered flood damage. Flooding was also reported in Union County at Lewisburg, where another 8.00 to 9.00 inches of rain were estimated to have fallen by late evening, resulting in $100,000 of damage.

Droughts

The National Drought Mitigation Center at the University of Nebraska estimated that cost of drought in the United States averages $6 to $8 billion annually, which is considerably higher than that of floods ($2.4 billion) and hurricanes ($1.2 to $4.8 billion). The economic toll for the drought of 1988 has been figured at nearly $40 billion, even greater than that of the Mississippi Valley floods of 1993 ($28 billion) and Hurricane Andrew in 1992 ($25 to $33 billion).

The worst drought to plague the nation in the twentieth century lasted through the entire 1930s, known as the Dust Bowl years in the breadbasket of Middle America. In 1934 drought conditions prevailed over 65 percent of the contiguous United States. Another protracted drought from 1952 to 1957 affected 42 percent of the nation at its peak in 1954. The searing heat and withering drought of 1988 was felt across 34 percent of the country and ruined about half of the crops in the Great Plains.

Pennsylvania Droughts

Dry spells that develop in the autumn and persist through the winter months become problematic if moisture is not replenished in early spring. Groundwater is recharged between October and April, provided an adequate amount of moisture percolates through the upper soil layers. By late spring, as the sun climbs higher in the sky, evaporation rates are already high. The demand for water from residential, agricultural, and commercial users peaks in midsummer, and wells and reservoirs may fall to alarmingly low levels during a drought.

A prolonged dry pattern in the Northeast arises when the predominant circulation limits the transport of moist air into the region. A short-term drought is not uncommon in Pennsylvania. However, the formation of a blocking pattern, involving an expansive cell of high pressure that consistently deflects storms away from Pennsylvania, promotes dryness.

Droughts are perpetuated by parched soils that offer up little moisture to the atmosphere through evaporation. Historic droughts in Pennsylvania have occurred at intervals of about twenty to thirty years over the past two centuries, possibly in tune with sea-surface temperature cycles in the Atlantic and Pacific Oceans, which play a role in the position of the jet stream.

The driest years at Pittsburgh since records commenced in 1836 came in clusters: 1839–40, 1851, 1854, 1856, 1862, 1894–95, and 1900. A weather chronology of Bradford County by Heverling (1926, 568–594) noted a "severe June drought" in 1853, and "weeks without rain" that caused "a terrible Autumn drought" in 1854. In 1881, "a drought prevailed from the first week of July till the 13th of October; a water famine ensued; the Susquehanna river the lowest in 41 years; much suffering and damage, corn and buckwheat ruined."

Palmer Hydrological Drought Index (PHDI)

The Palmer Hydrological Drought Index (PHDI) weighs rainfall and ground moisture storage against evaporative losses, which factor in absorption and transpiration of plants and evaporative losses from soils, lakes, and rivers.

Near-normal temperature and rainfall patterns register close to zero on the index. The PHDI may reach +4 or higher when conditions are very wet, or −4 or lower during an extremely dry period. Abnormally dry periods in Pennsylvania, based on various drought indices, occurred in 1894–95, 1908–11, 1914–16, 1921–26, 1929–32, 1953–55, 1962–69, and 1998–99.

The lowest PHDI values in Pennsylvania, which reflect the cumulative effects of a prolonged drought, show up in calculations for January 1896 (−4.21), November 1909 (−4.81), November 1914 (−3.36), December 1922 (−4.60), January 1931 (−7.26), February 1954 (−2.62 inches), and August 1966 (−3.37).

A string of hot summers (1980, 1983, 1988, 1991, 1993, and 1999) contributed to serious short-term drought conditions in Pennsylvania that were generally relieved by late-summer or autumn rains. Two particularly severe dry spells in the summers of 1988 and 1999 were generally attributed to a persistent pool of chilly water in the eastern tropical Pacific Ocean (La Niña). The interaction of cooler waters with the overlying atmosphere is thought to nudge the jet stream farther north, deflecting storms away from Pennsylvania during the warmer months, when the sun is high in the sky and evaporation rates are greatest.

The weather maps in the summers of 1988 and 1999 shared similar features. A trio of high-pressure cells over the eastern Pacific Ocean, the High Plains, and the western Atlantic Ocean shunted potential rainstorms north of Pennsylvania. Once dry conditions became established, weather systems had little moisture to work with, which prolonged the droughts in 1989 and 1999 across much of Pennsylvania.

A southward shift in the jet stream in late July 1988 brought torrential rains to parts of the state. Even so, Pittsburgh received only 27.09 inches of rain in 1988, though ample rains in 1989 and a record wet year in 1990 (52.24 inches) ended the drought. The drought of 1998–99 came to an abrupt end when the remnants of Dennis and Floyd swamped the Keystone State in September, bringing more than a foot of rain in places.

1929–1932: Severe Drought

Dry conditions developed over Pennsylvania in the fall of 1928 and recurred in the summer of 1929. Adequate moisture in the autumn of 1929 offset moisture short-falls temporarily, but a serious drought developed in 1930, which became the driest year in the state (25.37 inches) since records began in 1895.

Precipitation averaged below normal in Pennsylvania from December 1929 through March 1931. Near- or above-normal rainfall in the summer of 1931 eased the extreme drought, but dry weather returned in the autumn and continued through September 1932, with only a few months recording above-normal precipitation.

The 1930–32 drought was especially harsh in western Pennsylvania, where crops suffered severely. Pittsburgh had its driest year in 1930 (22.65 inches) and its fourth driest year in 1932 (25.89 inches), compared with the contemporary normal precipitation of 36.85 inches. Heavy rain in early October 1932 eased the situation in Pennsylvania, though moderate drought persisted before a hurricane blew in from the south in August 1933.

The nation's worst drought in modern times still plagued the agricultural heartland of the United States through the middle and late 1930s during a period known as the Dust Bowl years. On May 12, 1934, the Great Dust Bowl Storm circulated enough dust to darken skies from Oklahoma to the Atlantic coast.

As midwestern soils turned to dust and blew away, farmers in the nation's midsection were financially ruined, and many chose to migrate westward in search of a new livelihood. Fifty million acres of farmland were affected by the Dust Bowl drought, which did not officially end until 1940–41.

1962–1966: Great Drought of the Early 1960s

The driest periods of the twentieth century in Pennsylvania, with some remissions, occurred during the years of 1908–1917 and 1962–1969. The Great Drought of the early 1960s was more severe than the dry pattern in the 1910s. Moisture deficits were more severe in the 1960s in Pennsylvania, because there was virtually no break in the pattern.

The long 1960s drought was concentrated during the warm season (June through October), when evaporation rates are high and water usage reaches its highest levels. The upper-air circulation pattern through much of the 1960s featured a dry northwesterly flow that favored cold winters and hot, dry summers. The disappearance of an active hurricane track along the eastern seaboard during the late summer and autumn prevented serious replenishment of ground moisture, causing reservoirs to remain at alarmingly low levels entering the growing season.

As the drought worsened, the Department of Agriculture placed twenty-two counties on drought emergency status on July 13, 1962, the first of many drought declarations that put into effect various levels of water usage restrictions as reservoirs dipped to record low levels. As corn and hay shriveled in parched fields, Governor William W. Scranton sought drought aid for Pennsylvania in 1963–64 in the face of mounting agricultural losses.

The driest year in the state was 1963, when precipitation averaged below normal during ten of twelve months. October 1963 is the driest month in state history, averaging a scant 0.24 inch. Twenty-four southeastern Pennsylvania weather stations recorded no rain during October 1963.

The drought worsened in the summer and fall of 1964 across the Northeast. A dry winter in 1964–65 heralded another year with major moisture deficits. Extremely dry conditions continued through 1965 across Pennsylvania. In the southwest, Breezewood recorded only 15.71 inches of rain in all of 1965, establishing a record for the driest year at a Pennsylvania observing site.

The worst of the twentieth century in the Northeast did not abate in 1966. Searing heat aggravated water shortages in late June and July 1966. Finally, heavy rainfall in September 1966 signaled an partial end to the protracted drought, and the winter of 1966–67 brought ample precipitation and heavy snowfall to much of the Keystone State. However, the moisture shortages were not fully balanced until 1969.

1998–1999: La Niña Drought Pattern

The emergence of La Niña, a cool pool of water in the eastern tropical Pacific Ocean, in the early summer of 1998 coincided with the beginning of a prolonged drought in the eastern United States. Precipitation was below normal in five of the last six months of 1998, with especially dry conditions in the fall and early winter.

A stormy January 1999 and near-normal precipitation in February and March seemed to signal a break from the dry pattern, but the relief was temporary. Very dry conditions developed over Pennsylvania and much of the mid-Atlantic region in April and May 1999, worsening during the summer months, when evaporation rates are highest.

Ground wells dried up by mid-summer in eastern Pennsylvania, where the drought was most severe, notably in Monroe, Pike, and Northampton Counties, with average rainfall 7.00 to 8.00 inches below normal since January 1, 1999. Over a thirteen-month span back to July 1998, precipitation totals were close to 15.00 inches below normal in parts of eastern Pennsylvania.

On July 20, 1999, Pennsylvania became the first state to issue mandatory water restrictions. Governor Tom Ridge declared a drought emergency in fifty-five of sixty-seven counties in the commonwealth. The only area excluded from water regulations was the northwestern corner of Pennsylvania. Similar water usage rules were mandated in all of Maryland and New Jersey, much of Delaware, and parts of New York and Virginia.

There were a few noteworthy storms during the height of the drought that provided local relief. A heavy thunderstorm on July 22 brought more than 2.00 inches of rain to Harrisburg/Middletown. The following week Pittsburgh was doused with an all-time record twenty-four-hour rainfall of 4.14 inches on July 27–28, creating a veritable oasis in a sea of drought.

Although eastern sections of the state were still classified as severe or extreme drought status in early September, the remnants of Tropical Storm Dennis dropped up to 7.00 inches of rain on parts of western and central Pennsylvania on September 6–7, 1999.

An active cold front brought additional heavy rains to some eastern counties on the ninth, but the real drought-buster was the remnants of Hurricane Floyd arriving on September 15–16. Floyd unloaded frequent tropical downpours on the Middle Atlantic and northeastern states east of the Appalachians, on the order of 4.00 to 12.00 inches over the drought-stricken eastern counties of Pennsylvania.

Drought conditions developed along the Eastern Seaboard during the fall of 2001, and drought emergencies were declared in parts of eastern Pennsylvania and New Jersey before the end of February 2002.

10 Tropical Storms and Hurricanes

Hurricanes have played an awesome role in the American panorama. They have touched the lives of Americans great and small and, at times, changed the course of our destiny—as well as the shape of our coastline.

—Patrick Hughes, "Hurricanes Haunt Our History"

The power of a hurricane was displayed when Hurricane Andrew devastated south Florida on the night of August 24–25, 1992, resulting in an incomprehensible $26.5 billion of damage. The sheer force of winds gusting as high as 175 miles per hour drove two-by-fours into palm trees and wedged pieces of straw into concrete sidewalks.

Tropical storms affect Pennsylvania an average of once every few years, though winds are sharply diminished during overland transit as the storm encounters rough terrain. The greatest threat from tropical disturbances is flash flooding, as the blustery remnants of a weakening storm unload a vast store of tropical moisture along the eastern slopes of the Appalachians.

During the course of the Atlantic hurricane season, which runs from June 1 through November 30, about a hundred tropical disturbance traverse the tropical Atlantic Ocean, traveling in a westerly direction at an average speed of 10 to 15 miles per hour. In a typical year nine or ten waves will grow into tropical storms, attaining wind speeds of at least 39 miles per hour, and about six will become full-fledged hurricanes, with sustained winds of at least 74 miles per hour (Table 10.1).

Hurricane Tracks

Early-season tropical systems are more likely to develop over the warm waters (80 degrees or higher) of the Gulf of Mexico or western Caribbean Sea. Gulf storms often drift northwest, making landfall along the western Gulf coast. During August and September, the eastern Atlantic basin becomes more active in the vicinity of the Cape Verde Islands.

Disturbances originating over northern Africa move steadily westward across the Atlantic, guided by the vast Central Atlantic high-pressure area. Clockwise winds generally steer a slowly organizing cluster of thunderstorms around the southern periphery of high pressure in a westerly direction, unless a stronger feature or fast high-altitude westerly winds change the course of the storm, or tear it apart.

Table 10.1. The Saffir-Simpson Scale for Rating Hurricanes

Category	Central pressure (millibars/inches)	Winds (mph)	Surge (feet)	Potential damage
1	980+/28.94+	74–95	4–5	minimal
2	965–979/28.50–28.91	96–110	6–8	moderate
3	945–964/27.91–28.47	111–130	9–12	extensive
4	920–944/27.17–27.88	131–155	13–18	extreme
5	919–less/27.16 or less	156+	18+	catastrophic

Some years, the Central Atlantic high is anchored a little farther east, paving the way for an upper-level trough of low pressure over the eastern United States to draw a tropical storm or hurricane northward along the eastern seaboard. Heavy rain, high winds, and powerful waves typically lash the shoreline, while torrential downpours cause flooding along the coastal plain. Occasionally, a storm will make landfall somewhere along the southeast or mid-Atlantic coast and track northward into Pennsylvania and New Jersey, bringing heavy rain west to the Appalachian foothills.

Storms forming or regenerating in the northern Gulf of Mexico have a tendency to turn north and come ashore between the Florida panhandle and the southeast coast of Texas. More than a few weakening tropical systems have tracked up the Mississippi and Ohio Valleys or along the western flank of the Appalachians, dropping prodigious rain resulting in widespread flooding.

Atlantic hurricane activity seems to run in cycles, which may be related to changes in tropical sea-surface temperatures. Active storm periods were observed during a warm-water phase from about 1930 to 1970, and more recently, since 1994. More Atlantic storms were reported in the six-year period from 1995 to 2001 than during any other time in the past one hundred years.

Hurricane Names

Once a tropical disturbance attains sustained winds of at least 39 miles per hour, the storm is given a name by the National Hurricane Center in Coral Gables, Florida. Atlantic storms have been formally named since 1950, initially by the letters of the alphabet, following military practices. A few years later, tropical storms were given female appellations, such as Carol, Edna, and Hazel in 1954—three names that will be long remembered for the devastation wrought by three major hurricanes that slammed into the northeastern United States. In 1977 the National Hurricane Center agreed to incorporate a naming scheme alternating between male and female, paying heed to gender equality.

Historic East Coast Hurricanes

1740–1785

The majority of storms that affect the East Coast have occurred in the late summer and early autumn months—August, September, and October. The storm that affected the eastern seaboard earliest in the season traveled northward from Florida

Table 10.2. Most Powerful Atlantic/Caribbean Hurricanes

Rank	Name	Year	Central pressure (millibars/ inches)	Category 5 (hours)	Maximum winds (mph)
1	Gilbert	1988	888/26.23	18	185
2	Florida Keys	1935	892/26.35	6	175+ (estimated)
3	Allen	1980	899/26.55	24	195
4	Camille	1969	905/26.73	24	195
5	Mitch	1998	905/26.73	33	180

to New England during June 2–5, 1825. The latest full-fledged hurricane to menace the East Coast hit Cape Cod, Massachusetts, on November 27, 1888, before dissipating in the northwestern Atlantic on December 2, 1888.

One of the first hurricanes to affect Pennsylvania and receive notice occurred on Friday evening, October 22, 1743 (November 2, 1743, New Style), when the city of Philadelphia was on the western fringe of an offshore hurricane. The *Pennsylvania Gazette* reported that the storm brought "a violent Gust of Wind and Rain attended with Thunder and Lightning." The hurricane, referred to as "Franklin's Storm," prevented Benjamin Franklin from viewing a lunar eclipse, which he later discovered had been visible at Boston before the clouds arrived four hours later.

Another East Coast hurricane in October 1749, studied by Benjamin Franklin, affected the Middle Atlantic states and southeastern New England on October 18–19, 1749 (New Style). Franklin's notion that coastal disturbances traveled from the southwest, though accompanied by surface winds blowing from the northeast, represented an early understanding of the nature of rotary storms.

A number of powerful hurricanes lashed southeastern Pennsylvania in the late eighteenth century (Ludlum 1963, 24–30). A coastal hurricane on September 7–8, 1769, uprooted trees and sent rivers out of their banks in southeastern Pennsylvania. The Independence Hurricane crossed eastern Pennsylvania on September 3, 1775, and was logged by Philadelphia observer Phineas Pemberton: "Stormy & showery. A violent gale from NE to SE the preceding night with heavy rain, lightning and thunder—a remarkably high tide in the Delaware this morning. Flying clouds & wind with sunshine at times P.M." The *Pennsylvania Gazette* reported that the storm brought the highest tide ever recorded.

Two storms affected extreme eastern Pennsylvania and New Jersey in October 1783, providing a good blast of rain and wind on the eighth and eighteenth. The Equinoctial Storm that blasted the Carolinas on September 23–24, 1785, caused storm damage from Baltimore northward to Philadelphia and New York City.

August 18–19, 1788: Compact Hurricane

A small but intense tropical disturbance affected southeastern Pennsylvania on August 18–19, 1788, leaving a path of significant wind damage fifty miles wide from Cape May, New Jersey, to New York City. David M. Ludlum wrote, "It is probable that the area of high winds did not exceed 100 miles in breadth, but in about a fifty-mile-wide path the speeds must have been well in excess of 75 mph to cause such destruction, especially in the forests" (1963, 340). On the western edge of the "compact hurricane" as much as 7.00 inches of rain pelted Philadelphia (Ludlum 1983, 232).

October 9, 1804: Snow Hurricane

The October Snow Hurricane in 1804 brought strong winds and heavy rain to Philadelphia on the morning of the ninth. The interesting feature of the storm was the arrival of cold Canadian air into the circulation of the storm, bringing heavy snow to parts of New England and upstate New York. Ludlum (1963, 37) placed the storm track "between Philadelphia and Atlantic City" and continuing northward "very close to New York City."

September 3, 1821: Cape May Hurricane

The Cape May Hurricane of September 1821 is the only storm to have a tropical eye structure over New Jersey as it traveled north close to the present path of the Garden State Parkway (Ludlum 1983, 92–93). The storm made landfall just west of Cape May, New Jersey, on the afternoon of September 3, 1821, and then raced north-northeast to western Long Island by evening. The storm caused extensive wind damage over New Jersey as it brushed past eastern Pennsylvania, dropping 7.00 inches of rain on Philadelphia (Ludlum 1983, 74). A brief note on the storm in Philadelphia appeared in John F. Watson's *Annals of Philadelphia and Pennsylvania, in the Olden Time* (1868, 368): "A great storm of rain and wind from the north-east destroyed many trees, blew down many chimneys, and unroofed the bridge at the Upper ferry. The Schuylkill dam rose much."

June 4, 1825: Earliest East Coast Hurricane

The earliest hurricane in the past two centuries to make the journey up the East Coast traveled from St. Augustine, Florida, to New England on June 2–5, 1825 (Ludlum 1963, 87–88). The storm ruined crops, flattened trees, and caused extensive property damage in the neighborhood of Washington, D.C., northward to Philadelphia on the morning of June 4, 1825. Shipping fleets also suffered severely in the storm, and many sailors were lost at sea.

September 11–12, 1838: Hurricane Brushes Pennsylvania

A dry pattern developed over eastern Pennsylvania and New Jersey from August 12 through September 11, 1838, resulting in "probably the largest [forest] fire in the first half of the nineteenth century" in Burlington and Monmouth Counties, New Jersey (Ludlum 1983, 198). Weather records taken by Dr. John Conrad at the Pennsylvania Hospital in downtown Philadelphia reported nary a cloud in the sky from September 3 to 8. However, on the night of September 11–12, the tinder-dry conditions would be relieved by the passage of an offshore hurricane, which dropped 6.01 inches of rain at Philadelphia—4.19 inches in eight hours. The strongest winds remained offshore, minimizing the threat of any serious storm damage.

October 13, 1846: Great Hurricane of 1846

A large hurricane raked the mid-Atlantic coast and inland areas from Washington, D.C., northward to Philadelphia and New York during the early morning hours of October 13, 1846 (Ludlum 1963, 94–95). The winds at Philadelphia were deemed "the most destructive storm in 30 years," causing a backup of the Delaware River that flooded the wharves, according to an account in the *North American.*

The records of Pennsylvania Hospital observer John Conrad reported "a tremendous gale" from the southeast during the early afternoon of October 13, though the rainfall totaled only 1.25 inches.

July 18–19, 1850: Early Hurricane

A heat wave in July 1850 ended with the arrival of a tropical disturbance that struck the Carolinas and Virginia on July 18. The storm blasted Delaware and the Chesapeake Bay region during the afternoon of the eighteenth. High winds and heavy rain swept over southeastern Pennsylvania and western New Jersey overnight on July 18–19.

Major damage occurred during the night as streams and rivers went out of their banks in southeastern Pennsylvania, inundating fields and roads. Tropical downpours reached east-central Pennsylvania, causing the worst flooding on the Lehigh River since 1841. At least twenty lives were lost as boats capsized and sank in the Schuylkill River (Ludlum 1963, 96–99).

A dispatch from Philadelphia provided a chronology of the storm: "After a week or two of hot and scorching weather, we were favored with a refreshing shower on Monday [July 15, 1850]. . . . Then for nearly three days every cloud dropped down more or less rain. On Thursday [July 18] we had heavy and quickly succeeding falls of rain, which soaked the ground thoroughly. In the evening the wind shifted from the South-east, and throughout the night blew a perfect hurricane, accompanied by a very heavy fall of rain" (*Jeffersonian Republican* [East Stroudsburg], July 25, 1850).

Agricultural losses were substantial. Corn was "blown down" and "oats and grain were leveled to the ground, and the wheat and rye ungathered in much the same condition." The high winds took down trees and branches, and the torrential rainfall flooded creeks and rivers in eastern Pennsylvania. A dam break at Mauch Chunk (Jim Thorpe) resulted in heavy damage to the Delaware Canal.

Press accounts from throughout eastern Pennsylvania described widespread damage to trees, fences, roofs, and small buildings. Rising floodwaters swept away houses and bridges and sunk small craft along the Delaware and Schuylkill Rivers. The Schuylkill River "was never known higher," resulting in substantial damage at Pottsville and Reading. The event was described as a "terrible storm . . . uprooting trees, wrecking vessels, and carrying away houses and bridges in every direction. It is thought more damage has been done by this storm than by any other for very many years. The freshet appeared to be *universal*" (*Pennsylvania Inquirer,* March 18, 1851).

October 3–4, 1869: Saxby's Gale

A British naval officer, Lieutenant S. M. Saxby, achieved notoriety by predicting a hurricane would strike the East Coast of the United States and Canada a year in advance. The storm eventually crashed into Maine and Nova Scotia on the morning of October 4, 1869, after drenching the eastern seaboard with torrential rain.

The storm came under the influence of an upper-level trough of low pressure over the eastern United States, which accounted for the torrential rains that unloaded on the Northeastern states on October 3–4 (Ludlum 1983, 176). In New Jersey, heavy rains averaging 4.00 to 5.00 inches or more sent Garden State rivers into high flood. In southern New England, 12.35 inches of rain fell at Canton, Connecticut.

The shield of heavy rain extended west across eastern Pennsylvania. In Lancaster County, the Mount Joy observer recorded an 8.00-inch deluge. Northwest of Philadelphia, the observer at Plymouth Meeting measured 6.00 inches of rain in about twenty-four hours, contributing to a "disastrous freshet on the Schuylkill" that caused extensive damage from Norristown to Philadelphia and claimed a number of lives.

In the northeastern highlands, the Dyberry rainfall total was 4.50 inches. Heavier rains fell to the south over the Pocono Plateau. Around daybreak on October 4, 1869, water breached a dam below South Stroudsburg, flooding the lower portion of town, which resulted in major damage.

August 12–13, 1873: Offshore Storm Brings Wind and Rain

A tropical system moving northward some distance off the East Coast brought an onslaught of winds and driving rains to the Middle Atlantic states on August 12–13, 1873. Heavy thunderstorms rolled across parts of eastern Pennsylvania southward to Washington, D.C., on the morning and afternoon of the twelfth, suggesting the arrival of a cold front or trough that would eventually interact with the coastal disturbance.

The main effect of the storm on eastern Pennsylvania was the ensuing deluge. Several small bridges were washed away by heavy rain and high water at Lancaster when a dam burst. On the thirteenth, Philadelphia was inundated with a record rainfall of 7.32 inches, recorded by a government rain gauge, resulting in widespread urban flooding and damage to railroad tracks. No storm damage was reported north of the Delaware Valley.

Measurable rain fell every day in Philadelphia from August 12 to 22, 1873—eleven consecutive days—to set a mark that would later be tied May 15 to 25, 1894. In the wet spring of 1894, a little over a foot of water fell in the official city gauge during the month of May.

September 17, 1876: Philadelphia Hurricane

The remnants of a hurricane blew into eastern Pennsylvania on September 17, 1876, at the end of a long, hot, and dry summer in Pennsylvania. As the storm disintegrated over the interior Middle Atlantic states, high winds and heavy rains pelted eastern sections of the state, resulting in considerable property damage around Philadelphia.

The *Philadelphia Inquirer* reported, "All over the city trees were blown down, and travel by horse cars was greatly interrupted. Chimneys toppled over and the roofs of houses came down without ceremony." Farther north a dispatch from Milford called it a "severe northeast rainstorm," adding that the storm brought the first significant rain since June.

At New York City the wind was "blowing fearfully" and accompanied by "torrents of rain." The signal service observer reported a peak wind speed of 40 miles per hour (corrected) at New York City at 7:15 P.M. on September 18, 1876. In western Pennsylvania, Pittsburgh received 3.38 inches.

October 23, 1878: Gale of '78

The Gale of '78 caused more damage in the Philadelphia area than any other inland tropical storm. A hurricane made landfall on October 22–23, 1878, over southeastern North Carolina, hitting Wilmington and Morehead City hardest. The storm's center tracked inland near Richmond, Virginia, and Washington, D.C., with a low barometric pressure of 28.78 inches.

The storm continued north into central Pennsylvania during the morning of October 23, wreaking havoc over the eastern and central counties. Extensive wind damage occurred in the southeastern counties, and Philadelphia suffered the greatest blow with seven hundred homes damaged by high winds (Ludlum 1971, 90). The local press reported eight people dead and seventy-five injured, mostly as a result of flying debris or the collapse of small buildings.

The incessant winds and rain battered Philadelphia for six hours, according to the following press notice:

> A tempestuous gale of unprecedented severity swept over this city early this morning, commencing about 2:30 o'clock, and reaching its height between 6 and 7:30 A.M., subsiding with a heavy rainfall toward 9 o'clock. The velocity of the gale at 2:45 was 25 miles an hour, blowing in a westerly direction. Its fury gradually increased, and from 7:25 until 7:55 A.M. it attained a velocity of 72 miles an hour [corrected to 58 miles per hour]. Not in many years, if ever before, has there been so much damage done in the streets, the public squares, and along the river fronts. Many of the public school buildings are damaged, and the public squares devastated. Over 40 churches are more or less damaged by the demolition of their steeples, &c., several of which are expected to fall at any moment. (*New York Times,* October 24, 1878)

A press dispatch from Reading reported, "The city is strewn with broken and uprooted trees, fences, and awnings. The damage to private dwellings, and business houses is very great." A report from Harrisburg noted the onset of the storm around midnight, October 23, 1878, lasting until the forenoon hours. The rain "descended in torrents, flooding streets, cellars, and sewers."

One or more tornadoes may have been spawned by the weakening tropical storm, based on dispatches from Scranton and Wilkes-Barre in the northeastern part of the state. At Wilkes-Barre, "a tornado inflicted great damage. . . . Houses were unroofed, trees uprooted, windows broken, and fences and mine-drilling apparatus demolished." In Scranton, "a whirlwind with the force of a cyclone" demolished a pudding mill. About sixty trees were uprooted in Dunmore. The storm brought stiff southeasterly winds and a "drenching torrent of water" to the Lackawanna Valley.

It is difficult to ascertain at this late date whether buildings "destroyed all along the valley" were the work of a tornado. Reports of roofs being lifted high into the air and stacks blown down indicate a combination of very low pressure and wind shear associated with the circulation center of the tropical disturbance, though surface friction could have spawned localized tornadoes.

Southeast of Scranton, the Stroudsburg *Jeffersonian* reported, "In this place it blew violently, but fortunately it did not do much damage," though it was "one of the worst storms we have had for years."

September 22–23, 1882: Equinoctial Storm

A tropical storm passed a short distance off the New Jersey coast on the night of September 22–23, 1882, bringing a tremendous volume of rain and high winds to southeastern Pennsylvania. Philadelphia received its greatest rainstorm in modern history, which began on September 21, when 1.72 inches of rain fell in advance of the storm. The rain intensified the next day, when city records showed 4.65 inches falling during the calendar day. Heavy rain continued to fall on the twenty-third, adding up to another 3.72 inches, for a storm total of 10.09 inches.

Tropical downpours swamped the Passaic River valley in northeastern New Jersey, dropping a state-record 17.90 inches at Paterson over a three-day period. The weather bureau in New York City's Central Park location received 10.62 inches, the second greatest rainfall ever recorded in the metropolitan area.

As reported in the *Philadelphia Inquirer,* "The equinoctial storm . . . was the heaviest on record in this region. In some places the rainfall measured thirteen inches. The floods that were caused by the rain did great damage, but the loss was lessened by the absence of high winds. The heaviest rainfall was in New Jersey, and Philadelphia bore the brunt of the storm."

August 21, 1888: Gulf Hurricane Curves Northeast

A powerful hurricane lashed the western Gulf Coast during the night of August 19–20, 1888, before coming ashore near the Louisiana/Texas coast. The storm quickly weakened as it moved rapidly northeast, curving across the lower Ohio Valley on the twenty-first. Soaking rains reached southwestern Pennsylvania around midnight, August 21, becoming heavy at times in the eastern part of the state by daybreak.

The tropical disturbance caused pockets of flooding, along with high winds and a few tornadoes as it tracked across the northwestern half of Ohio on the twenty-first. After 3.57 inches of rain fell on the twenty-first, the Ohio River rose 18 feet in twenty-four hours at Pittsburgh on August 22, achieving its highest level since February 6, 1884.

More than 5.00 inches of rain fell west of Pittsburgh, where the flooding was more severe. High water was reported in low-lying sections of Pittsburgh and the "flats" section of McKeesport. Twenty miles west of downtown Pittsburgh, the Washington County community of Burgettstown was submerged when the Racoon Creek overflowed. The heaviest official rainfall totals averaged close to 5.00 inches: Girardville, 5.65 inches; Selinsgrove, 5.25 inches; and Johnstown, 4.49 inches.

Destructive flash floods were reported at Washington, Uniontown, Altoona, Reading, and in parts of Philadelphia. The worst tornado outbreak in the history of the Chesapeake Bay area occurred in association with the passage of the circulation center of the storm. Grazulis (1993, 645) believed that upwards of two dozen funnels and waterspouts were sighted in the region. Eleven fatalities occurred in Kent County, Maryland.

A tornado developed six miles southwest of Wilmington, Delaware, and tracked into the south side of the city. The damage path was 200 yards wide and 5 miles in length. One person was killed and twenty-two others were injured. Forty buildings were damaged or destroyed, and the damage was estimated at $200,000, according to the *Monthly Weather Review*. A dispatch in the *New York Times* also mentioned a "cyclone" at Salem, New Jersey, likely the scene of another tornado, and reported extensive flooding in Maryland that claimed twelve lives. Urban flooding in Philadelphia reportedly caused more than $100,000 in damage.

August and October 1893: Record Number of East Coast Hurricanes

The hurricane season in the late summer and early autumn of 1893 was unusually active along the eastern seaboard of the United States. On August 22, 1893, no less than four tropical storms or hurricanes were evident on the weather map in the western Atlantic basin, establishing a record for tropical storm activity in the region that would not be equaled until September 24–26, 1998.

The first in a series of five tropical disturbances tracked in the western Atlantic region in late August 1893 was first spotted on August 15 and would pass by Newfoundland on the eighteenth. About the same time, a new tropical disturbance was developing over the eastern Caribbean Sea, which would later take a swipe at the eastern tip of Long Island on August 20–21, bringing rain and gusty winds.

On August 19, 1893, a third disturbance appeared over the western Atlantic Ocean, which eventually curved northwest and then northward along the eastern seaboard. Wind damage was widespread along coastal sections of New Jersey and over New York City on the night of August 23–24. An ocean tug named *Panther* sank off the coast of New Jersey, taking the lives of sixteen crewmen—only one of a number of vessels damaged or lost in the storm.

The rain gauge at Central Park in New York City caught 3.82 inches of water between 8:00 P.M. on the twenty-third and 8:00 A.M. on the twenty-fourth. Hundreds of trees were felled by high winds in Central Park and around the city, and many homes and buildings were unroofed, especially in Brooklyn. The storm passed just east of New York City at 7:00 A.M. on the twenty-fourth, when the lowest pressure (29.23 inches) was recorded, crossing western Long Island before heading northeast into New England.

The fourth tropical system to affect the East Coast in late August 1893, which was first plotted on August 21 in the western Atlantic Ocean, turned out to be the most destructive of the series. A full-fledged hurricane pounded the South Carolina coast on August 27–28, where an estimated one thousand people drowned in the storm surge and tidal flooding. The remnants of the storm traveled northward across Pennsylvania on the twenty-eighth, reaching Lake Ontario before curving northeastward to the Maine-Quebec border early on the twenty-ninth.

The hurricane season of 1893 in the western Atlantic remained active well into the autumn. A mighty hurricane plowed into Louisiana on October 1, 1893, causing horrific flooding that took 2,000 lives. The storm finally exited the coast of North Carolina on the fourth. A second October storm formed over the central

Atlantic on October 5, taking a slow westward track that brought it ashore in South Carolina on October 13. The disturbance turned northward along the Appalachian highlands, reaching the mountains of western Maryland on the evening of the thirteenth before passing over western Pennsylvania early of the fourteenth.

Winds gusted to 48 miles per hour (corrected) at Philadelphia, knocking down trees and telegraph lines, unroofing some homes, and disrupting railroad traffic. The storm traveled all the way to Ontario by late on the fourteenth as a windy rainstorm. Sixty years later, in October 1954, a powerful mid-October hurricane named Hazel would take a similar path from North Carolina to eastern Ontario, also causing extensive wind damage in eastern Pennsylvania.

Yet another tropical disturbance affected Pennsylvania on October 23, 1893. The storm was tracked near the Bahamas on the twenty-first before making landfall over North Carolina on the twenty-second. The remnants of this disturbance traveled north, reaching south-central Pennsylvania on October 23 accompanied by wind and rain, but causing much less damage than had occurred ten days earlier.

September 29, 1896: Another Gulf Hurricane

A powerful hurricane swept ashore along the west coast of Florida, making landfall near Cedar Keys on September 28, 1896, and then traveling north-northeast across Florida and Georgia. Extensive wind damage occurred in the Southeast as the ex-hurricane headed up the eastern seaboard, passing a little west of Washington, D.C., where a barometric pressure reading of 29.14 inches was recorded on the twenty-ninth.

Widespread damage was reported from eastern and central Virginia northward to Pennsylvania. The long span of the Pennsylvania Railroad Bridge over the Susquehanna River was destroyed as the storm battered the southeastern part of the state on the twenty-ninth with heavy winds and torrential rains. The local observer in York, near the Maryland border, made the following remarks on the tropical storm in his monthly summary: "Terrible hurricane with cyclonic conditions at midnight between the 29th and 30th [September 1896]. Damage in York County estimated at $200,000—probably more. Greatest storm in the history of [York] county."

October 8–9, 1903: Tropical Storm Brings
Record Rainfalls and Terrible Floods

Two tropical systems took aim on the Middle Atlantic coast in 1903. An ex-hurricane scored a direct hit on Atlantic City on September 16, bringing 50-mile-per-hour winds and up to 6.00 inches of rain, resulting in extensive wind damage over the southeastern half of the Garden State. This is the only instance of a tropical system actually making landfall over the state of New Jersey by way of the Atlantic coast.

Eastern Pennsylvania experienced strong winds and heavy rainfall on the fringes of the storm as it moved across southern New Jersey on September 16. The *Philadelphia Inquirer* reported, "With the first sweep of the wind, borne with driving rain at a velocity of eighty miles an hour [corrected to 64 miles per hour], telegraph poles and wires were blown down and communication with the city from almost all points was cut off." Damage was estimated in the thousands of dollars.

Another tropical storm would leave a lasting impression on the residents of eastern Pennsylvania and northern New Jersey in the chilly, wet autumn of 1903. A light rainfall that began on October 7 turned into a deluge over the next twenty-four hours. The upper Delaware Valley received 4.00 to 10.00 inches of rain, causing some of the worst flooding ever experienced along the upper Delaware Valley.

In northeastern Pennsylvania, Milford logged 9.90 inches over a four-day period, with 7.70 inches falling in twenty-four hours on October 8–9. Extensive flooding was reported in the Passaic River valley in northern New Jersey after Paterson received a record 15.51 inches of rain—11.45 inches coming on the ninth. Total losses from flooding in the region exceeded $7 million (Ludlum 1983, 177).

September 19, 1928: Lake Okeechobee Hurricane Affects Pennsylvania

A massive hurricane first struck Guadeloupe on September 12, 1928, a week after forming over the eastern Atlantic Ocean. The storm roared onto the coast of Puerto Rico just after dawn on September 13, packing winds of at least 150 miles per hour and causing catastrophic damage that claimed 1,498 lives on the island. The storm was later dubbed the San Felipe Hurricane, so named for the storm's Saint's Day visitation (Longshore 1998, 281).

The storm continued on a treacherous course northwestward past Hispaniola and the Bahamas before raging ashore over central Florida near West Palm Beach on the evening of September 16. The hurricane packed 148-mile-per-hour winds, which was reflected in the very low central pressure of 27.43 inches. A towering 20-foot storm surge swept hundreds to their deaths. High winds churned up Lake Okeechobee, driving deadly floodwaters in all directions.

The Lake Okeechobee Hurricane claimed the lives of 1,836 Floridians, the third worst death toll from a storm in the United States, after the Great Galveston (Texas) Hurricane of 1900 and the Grand Isle (Louisiana) Hurricane of 1893. The death toll from the hurricane, including its passage through the Caribbean Islands, was estimated at 3,336.

The storm tore across central Florida to near Orlando before turning north. The circulation center continued north across Georgia, depositing 11.44 inches of rain on Savannah on September 16–17, 1928. The remains of the circulation center headed northward up the eastern seaboard, reaching eastern Pennsylvania early on September 19, 1928. Although the storm was a shell of its former self, high winds flattened crops in eastern Pennsylvania. Rainfall totals were relatively light, and no flooding was reported.

August 22–23, 1933: Chesapeake-Potomac Hurricane

The hurricane season of 1933 was the most active for Atlantic storms in the twentieth century, spawning twenty-one named storms. Developing on August 17 in the western Atlantic, the Chesapeake-Potomac Hurricane was the most infamous of that year.

The storm intensified into a Category 3 hurricane, packing winds of up to 113 miles per hour shortly before slamming into Cape Hatteras, North Carolina, during the early morning hours of August 23. The central pressure of the storm dipped to 27.98 inches as the center made landfall. The eye of the storm passed thirty miles west of Norfolk, Virginia, tracking north over Washington, D.C., into central Pennsylvania by early evening.

Winds gusted to 82 miles per hour at Cape Henry, Virginia, and extensive tidal flooding occurred along the Virginia coast northward to the western shore of the Chesapeake Bay. Damages were estimated at $11 million in Virginia, and fifteen people died in the storm surge that sent waves 5 to 8 feet higher than all previous records at Newport News. High winds lashed coastal sections of Maryland and Delaware, swamping low-lying areas under many feet of water.

At high tide the Philadelphia airport was inundated as a ten-square-mile area on the southwest side of the city was submerged. A wind gust of 88 miles per hour was recorded at Wildwood, New Jersey, while southern New Jersey was being battered by wind and rain. Winds reached 60 miles per hour over Long Island, knocking down trees and overturning small buildings.

Shortly before midnight on August 23, 1933, the weakening storm was located over central Pennsylvania, where flooding followed a second day of heavy rainfall. "The damage was estimated as high as fifty percent in some sections, and seems to have averaged nearly thirty percent for the eastern half of the State. This loss was partly balanced by the improvement that moderate rains caused at most places in the western half of the State. The storm covered practically all of the tobacco growing regions, and nearly ruined the crop" (*Climatological Data—Pennsylvania Section,* August 1933).

Tropical moisture resulted in excessive, record-breaking rainfall in parts of southeastern Pennsylvania. The heaviest storm total was 13.82 inches at York over a three-day period from August 22 to 24, with a maximum twenty-four-hour measurement of 8.48 inches on the twenty-second and twenty-third. The monthly rainfall at York totaled 17.70 inches, also a state record at the time.

Flooding was widespread in the Delaware River drainage area. The Schuylkill River at Reading crested at 19.7 feet on August 24, causing extensive flooding on the south side of the city. A conservative estimate put the damage in southeastern Pennsylvania in the neighborhood of several million dollars. Total damage to Pennsylvania highways and bridges was estimated by engineers to be about $800,000.

A storm report in the August issue of *Climatological Data* added, "The crop damage undoubtedly exceeded the total flood damage by a wide margin," calling the storm "the most destructive that Pennsylvania has experienced during the 45 years of the State Weather Service."

September 13–14, 1944: Great Atlantic Hurricane

A powerful hurricane packing 140-mile-per-hour winds swept the eastern seaboard in September 1944, accompanied by an assault of heavy rain and very high winds. New Jersey state climatologist A. E. White commented that the hurricane was the most destructive to hit the Garden State since the Civil War (*Climatological Data—New Jersey Section*).

The damage from the offshore storm was confined mostly to the coastal plain. Winds at Philadelphia were clocked at 60 miles per hour. The storm caused minor flooding in parts of eastern Pennsylvania, where on September 13–14 up to 4.00 inches of rain fell – on ground already saturated from several days of wet weather.

Along the coast, winds gusted to 82 miles per hour at Atlantic City, New Jersey, as the storm passed about fifty miles east of the shoreline on the evening of September 13. Two navy ships were lost in the storm near the coast, taking the lives of 300 sailors. Rahway, New Jersey, received 11.40 inches of rain during the storm passage.

The Great Atlantic Hurricane eventually made landfall near Port Judith, Rhode Island, on the evening of September 14, 1944, with a central pressure of 28.34 inches. Twenty-six lives were lost in New England and storm damage exceeded $100 million.

October 15, 1954: Hazel Blows through Pennsylvania

The hurricane seasons of 1954 and 1955 were two of the most active ever experienced along the East Coast. Hurricane Carol struck central Long Island on August 31, 1954, with winds of 125 miles per hour, causing considerable damage over the island.

A week and a half later, on September 10, Hurricane Edna nipped at the Outer Banks of North Carolina before coming ashore over Martha's Vineyard, Massachusetts, just after daybreak on the eleventh. Edna packed 115-mile-per-hour winds that increased to 145 miles per hour in the northeastern semicircle of the storm, where the storm's forward motion augmented wind velocities.

The third major hurricane to hit the East Coast in the 1954 season arrived in the middle of October. Hurricane Hazel developed into a dangerous Category 4 hurricane over the southeastern Caribbean Sea on October 5, blasting Hispaniola on October 12. Ninety-eight died in western Haiti, where winds gusted to 100 miles per hour.

After wreaking havoc in the islands, Hazel took aim on the United States' eastern seaboard, striking the North Carolina–South Carolina border shortly after daybreak on October 15. Sustained winds reached 106 miles per hour, and the central barometric pressure at landfall fell to 27.70 inches.

Hazel's rapid forward movement (45 miles per hour) increased the force of the winds that buffeted the North Carolina coast, which reached 130 miles per hour. Hazel was expected to weaken rapidly over the foothills of the Appalachians, but swift steering currents helped maintain very powerful winds near the surface, even after the circulation center had weakened over eastern Virginia.

The storm crossed into south-central Pennsylvania around 9:00 P.M. on October 15, 1954, still packing hurricane-force winds that knocked down about one billion bushels of fruit in eastern and central Pennsylvania. Hazel was centered north of Coudersport along the New York–Pennsylvania border, where the storm joined up with an eastward-moving cold front. The rain diminished over most of Pennsylvania by 10:00 P.M. As reported in *Climatological Data—Pennsylvania,* "Wind damage was apparently most general and severe in the eastern half of Pennsylvania. Peak gusts shaded from 94 miles per hour at Philadelphia to 86 miles per hour at Reading to 80 miles per hour at Harrisburg to 58 miles per hour at Philipsburg. Major damage was spotty, but more or less general. Rail traffic was delayed or halted by downed trees, wires and poles. Many highways were blocked by fallen trees and downed wires. Ships and small craft were torn loose from their moorings in the Delaware River." The Weather Bureau in Philadelphia reported eleven fatalities and two persons missing in the aftermath of the storm in eastern Pennsylvania. The Weather Bureau estimated the damage to have reached $1.88 million in Philadelphia and $2 million in east-central sections, based on newspaper reports. An additional $1 million in damage was projected in surrounding sections of eastern Pennsylvania.

In the western part of the state, the meteorologist-in-charge at the Weather Bureau Office in Pittsburgh, Jacob T. B. Beard, described the flood damage in the greater Pittsburgh area, where thirteen people lost their lives: "Hardest hit in Allegheny County was Turtle Creek, where high waters invaded stores, homes, churches, and the East Pittsburgh Westinghouse Plant. In many Monongahela and Youghiogheny River communities, hundreds of persons were reported left home-less due to the high water."

At the Point in Pittsburgh, where the Monongahela and Allegheny Rivers join to form the Ohio River, the Ohio River was pushed 7.4 feet above flood stage on October 16, 1954. Low-lying areas and cellars were flooded in downtown Pitts-burgh, and ten feet of water covered the B&O railroad yard. The official rainfall at Pittsburgh on October 15 totaled 3.56 inches.

In West Newton, five feet of water flooded covered streets as the Youghio-gheny River reached a level 2 feet above the March 1936 flood level, judged to be the worst flooding ever known in the borough. Newspaper reports estimated flood damage in western Pennsylvania to be upwards of $15 million. The Ohio River exceeded flood stage in every community from Pittsburgh to the West Vir-ginia panhandle.

The remnants of Hazel continued northwestward with unusual ferocity all the way into Ontario, Canada, early on October 16, 1954. Torrential downpours and extensive flooding in Ontario were deemed the worst such weather disaster in Ca-nadian history. With a record low barometric pressure of 28.96 inches, thunder-storm winds gusted as high as 100 miles per hour at Toronto, and flash flooding took the lives of sixty-nine people, with damage estimated around $100 million.

August 1955: Twin Hurricanes Trigger Destructive Floods in the East

The remnants of two hurricanes lashed Pennsylvania with gusty winds and heavy rainfall in the middle of August 1955, breaking a searing heat wave and prolonged drought. However, the passage of two ex-hurricanes in rapid succession did not give the ground enough opportunity to absorb the copious rainfall, which resulted in catastrophic flooding in eastern Pennsylvania.

Hurricane Connie arrived on the shores of North Carolina on August 12, 1955, packing 83-mile-per-hour winds. The storm traveled inland before turning north along the Appalachian foothills into south-central Pennsylvania during the late-morning hours of the thirteenth. The storm center continued northwest to a posi-tion near Erie at 7:30 P.M. The most forceful winds and heavy rainfall affected southeastern Pennsylvania. A peak wind gust of 67 miles per hour was recorded at Philadelphia, knocking down some trees and power lines. Extensive damage to fruit trees occurred in Erie County in the northwest, and a large fair tent was blown over in York County.

Ex-Hurricane Connie was a prolific rain-producer in eastern Pennsylvania, which would lay the seeds for the terrible floods wrought by Diane less than a week later. Rain totals exceeded 9.00 inches in parts of Monroe, Montgomery, and Chester Counties on August 10–14, 1955. Along the coast, New York City's La Guardia Airport reported an estimated rainfall of 12.20 inches, resulting in heavy flooding in parts of New York City and on Long Island.

A number of creeks in eastern Pennsylvania flooded, but the larger rivers stayed within their banks, because water levels had been so low during the hot, dry summer of 1955. Meanwhile, forecasters were already concerned about a new storm named Diane, which was approaching the southeastern coastline of the United States. Hurricane Diane, accompanied by 85-mile-per-hour winds, made landfall during the morning of August 18, near Wilmington, North Carolina.

Early forecasts were hopeful that the storm would turn northeastward and head out to sea, passing entirely to the south of Pennsylvania. Instead the storm followed a northerly path through western Virginia and eastern West Virginia. The remnants of Diane eventually curved northeast into southern Pennsylvania a little before midnight on August 18 before spinning eastward to the Atlantic coast and Long Island.

Streams and river were still running high from Connie's heavy rainfall a few days earlier, and there was little room for Diane's tropical deluges falling on still-saturated ground. Over a thirty-hour period on August 18–19, 1955, eastern Pennsylvania was pelted with 4.00 to 10.00 inches of rain. The heaviest amounts centered in southeastern Lackawanna and southwestern Wayne Counties. The run-off pouring down water-logged hillsides brought Scranton's worst flood to date, as the Lackawanna River overflowed its banks in southern Wayne, Lackawanna, and Luzerne Counties.

Over southern Pike and northern Monroe Counties, 6.00 to 10.00 inches of rain fell which poured into tributaries feeding the Delaware and Lehigh Rivers. Ten inches of rain or more also fell on parts of Schuylkill, Carbon, and Luzerne Counties. Widespread flooding occurred along the length of the Lehigh River and along the Delaware River from Wayne County south to Easton and all the way to Philadelphia.

The usually placid Brodhead Creek in southeastern Monroe County, one of the premier trout-fishing streams in the Northeast, was transformed into a thunderous wall of water thirty feet high, fed by excessive runoff from mountain streams and waterfalls. The torrent of water swept through Camp Davis, which was along the Brodhead Creek at Analomink, a few miles north of Stroudsburg, taking the lives of thirty-eight campers, most of them youngsters.

Stroudsburg and East Stroudsburg residents were largely unaware that a wall of water was heading for the twin boroughs. Raging Pocono creeks quickly clogged with debris as runoff poured off the hillsides and then burst forth with a torrent of deadly water. The Stroudsburg area and surrounding communities would suffer the severest blow, with seventy-eight flood-related fatalities tallied by the Civil Defense. The *Climatological Data* summary for the state reported that at least ninety Pennsylvanians died in the August 1955 hurricane flood, and ten more were unaccounted for and presumed lost. Additional storm-related deaths from electrocution and accidents pushed the Flood of '55 state death toll to more than one hundred.

The remnants of Diane passed lengthwise over Long Island before heading out into the open Atlantic. In the Berkshires of western Massachusetts, several state rainfall records were set at Westfield: 18.15 inches in twenty-four hours; a storm total of 19.76 inches and 26.85 inches for the month. Hartford, Connecticut, measured 12.50 inches. Flooding rains in southern New England capped off one of the most destructive storms in United States history.

Diane claimed 191 lives in the Northeast and displaced 35,000 families (Longshore 1998, 94). Storm damage was estimated at $4.2 billion in 1990 dollars.

August 27–28, 1971: Hurricane Doria

Hurricane Doria had weakened slightly and was downgraded to a tropical storm by the time the system made landfall close to Kennedy International Airport on the western tip of Long Island, on the evening of August 27, 1971. Winds gusted to 80 miles per hour along the coast, as hard rains pounded New Jersey and eastern Pennsylvania all day long and into the night of August 27–28.

Streets and subways were flooded around New York City by morning on the twenty-eighth as the storm passed just offshore. The damage was heaviest in New Jersey ($138 million), primarily due to flooding of central and northeastern sections of the Garden State. The heaviest rainfalls occurred in southeastern Pennsylvania and caused serious flooding in low-lying areas.

The greatest twenty-four-hour rainfall was a substantial 11.42 inches at Neshaminy Falls. Philadelphia's second heaviest August rainstorm brought 5.68 inches, which came close to the monthly record of 5.98 inches (August 3, 1898). Farther north, 4.19 inches of rain fell at Stroudsburg.

June 20–25, 1972: Tropical Storm Agnes

An early-season hurricane born in the warm Gulf waters to the east of the Yucatan Peninsula on June 16, 1972, will be forever remembered for causing catastrophic flooding from Virginia to New York State that took 105 lives and caused a record $4 billion of damage.

Hurricane Agnes struck Cuba en route to a rendezvous with the Gulf Coast. The storm crashed ashore near Valparaiso, Florida, early on June 19. Agnes promptly weakened over land, tracking north-northeast through Georgia and the Carolinas, but it would gain a second wind as the storm center emerged over the Virginia capes.

Meanwhile, due to low pressure in the upper levels, conditions were favorable for a slow migration northward parallel to the Atlantic coast. An area of high pressure off the coast of New England slowed the northward progress of Agnes, setting the stage for catastrophic flooding in the Middle Atlantic and northeastern states.

Bands of heavy rain developed across eastern Pennsylvania on Monday, June 20, 1972. The remnants of Agnes veered to the northwest from near New York City across southern New York State. Caught in a cyclonic flow aloft, Agnes drifted to the southwest into the mountains of northern Pennsylvania, prolonging the period of drenching rains from south-central New York to northern Virginia.

A rain gauge monitored by the United States Department of Agriculture in far western Schuylkill County recorded 14.50 inches of rain in twenty-four hours on June 21–22, where an estimated rainfall of 19.00 inches occurred, according to *Storm Data.* Also in that twenty-four-hour period, 6.00 to 9.00 inches fell over the Susquehanna River basin from just north of Williamsport southward to Harrisburg and the Pennsylvania-Maryland border.

The capital city of Harrisburg was engulfed in floodwaters that swamped about half of the city by June 23, 1972. On Saturday morning, June 24, the Susquehanna River would eventually crest at an all-time record stage of 32.57 feet, 3.34 feet higher than the March 1936 record flood stage. The stream flow observed at Harrisburg at peak discharge was an incredible 1 million cubic feet per second. A record total of 18.55 inches of rain fell at Harrisburg in June 1972.

September 26–27, 1975: Eloise

Hurricane Eloise lashed Puerto Rico on September 17, 1975, before moving on to blast Haiti and the Dominican Republic. Taking a westward track, the storm would hit Mexico's Yucatan Peninsula and then veer northwestward into the Gulf of Mexico.

Just before daybreak on September 23, Eloise made landfall in the United States near Fort Walton Beach, Florida, as a Category 3 hurricane accompanied by 130-mile-per-hour winds. Over the next few days the remnants of Eloise would head northward to the west of the Appalachians, following a course farther west than Agnes's in June 1972.

Copious downpours developed around the nation's capital on the twenty-sixth as tropical moisture surged northward. Major flooding occurred for the second time in four years in eastern Pennsylvania on September 25–26, 1975, resulting in the evacuation of nearly 20,000 Pennsylvanians.

Six to 12.00 inches of rain resulted in serious flooding along the Susquehanna and Juniata Rivers, which claimed the lives of four in Pennsylvania. Ten persons died in the northeastern United States in the flooding triggered by Eloise, and property damage was estimated at $50 million.

September 5–6, 1979: Hurricane David

Hurricane David formed west of Africa on August 28, 1979, then traveled west on the wings of the easterly trade winds through the islands of Dominica, Guadeloupe, Martinique, and the Bahamas. Sustained winds reached 150 miles per hour as David pushed on to the northwest into the Dominican Republic on the thirty-first. The staggering death toll of 2,052 in the Caribbean attested to the storm's ferocity.

A weakening David finally made landfall over southeastern Florida on September 3, then moved briefly back over water along the coast before making a rare second landfall on the South Carolina coast on the fourth. On September 5–6, the storm turned inland and headed north through Virginia and Maryland into Pennsylvania, accompanied by tropical downpours, strong winds, and a few tornadoes

Rainfall totals in eastern Pennsylvania ranged from 4.22 inches at Stroudsburg to 5.24 inches at Tobyhanna in the northeast, to as much as 6.32 inches at South Mountain near the Maryland border. Flash flooding and power outages were reported in southeastern Pennsylvania.

One week later, Hurricane Frederic slammed into the west side of Mobile Bay, Alabama, shortly after daybreak on September 12, 1979, accompanied by wind gusts of 145 miles per hour. The remains of Frederic journeyed northward along the western side of the Appalachians, pelting eastern Ohio and western Pennsylvania with more than 5.00 inches of rain in some places. The storm passed over northwestern Pennsylvania on September 14 and continued into Canada, causing $2.3 billion damage.

September 26–27, 1985: Hurricane Gloria

Hurricane Gloria raced up the eastern seaboard with sustained winds of 130 miles per hour on September 26, 1985, after grazing the Outer Banks of North Carolina. Gloria sped northward, threatening the New York City area with the prospect of being struck by a major hurricane. Gloria made landfall over Jones Inlet in central Long Island during the forenoon of the twenty-seventh, fortunately at low tide, sparing the metropolitan area from a serious threat. Winds, which had diminished to 90 miles per hour, uprooted trees and caused damage over parts of eastern Long Island.

Eastern Pennsylvania was on the left side of the storm track, bringing waves of tropical downpours that dropped an average of 6.00 to 9.00 inches of rain over the eastern hills. Several eastern cities established record twenty-four rainfall totals for any storm, including Allentown/Bethlehem (7.85 inches) and Scranton/Wilkes-Barre (6.52 inches). Stroudsburg (6.59 inches) established a local September twenty-four-hour rainfall mark. Several rain gauges in Carbon County topped out at a little more than 9.00 inches.

September 15–17, 1999: Hurricane Floyd

The Drought of '99 had left Pennsylvania soils parched by the end of August, but two tropical systems would bring a swift end to the drought over much of the state in early September. On September 4, 1999, a weakening Hurricane Dennis would make landfall along the North Carolina coast and was later swept northwestward by high-level winds across western Pennsylvania.

The remains of Dennis collided with an eastward-moving cold front, generating heavy rain in central Pennsylvania. Williamsport was deluged with 6.29 inches on the seventh, which was the second heaviest single-day rainfall in city history. (The record daily rainstorm—8.66 inches—occurred on June 22, 1972, with the passage of Agnes.)

As Dennis fell apart over eastern Pennsylvania, Hurricane Floyd was already strengthening in the eastern Atlantic. Floyd made its appearance on September 2, 1999, in the vicinity of the Cape Verde Islands. Floyd would grow into a monster Category 5 hurricane with sustained winds of 155 miles per hour by the time the eye of the storm passed over the Bahamas on September 13–14.

As the storm pressed on to the west, the eye widened to a diameter of 50 miles, and the expansive storm now covered an amazing 700 miles. Floyd was deemed the largest Atlantic storm of the century—four times the aerial size of Hurricane Andrew (1992).

The largest peacetime evacuation in United States history occurred along the East Coast as Floyd veered to the northwest, though the storm ultimately bypassed Florida and Georgia. Floyd eventually crashed into the Carolinas with more devastating force than had 1996's Hurricane Fran, a formidable hurricane that had caused $6 billion of damage.

Floyd arrived at Cape Fear, North Carolina, at about 3:20 A.M. on September 16, packing sustained winds of 110 miles per hour. Over the succeeding hours, Floyd crossed eastern North Carolina before reemerging along the coast at Virginia Beach. Wilmington, North Carolina, was swamped with a record 19.06 inches of rain, including 13.38 inches in twenty-four hours.

Floyd accelerated to the northeast at thirty miles per hour, caught up in an upper-level trough of low pressure over the eastern states. The center of the tropical storm passed just east of Atlantic City in the early afternoon of the sixteenth, making landfall over western Long Island in the evening. The storm passed twenty-five miles east of Hartford, Connecticut, just before midnight on September 16, continued on to near Worcester, Massachusetts, and later visited Portland, Maine.

Bands of torrential rains pelted the coastline from the Carolinas to Maine. The rains of Dennis, which averaged 10.00 to 20.00 inches in eastern North Carolina ten days earlier, combined with the Floyd's rain to result in the worst flooding in North Carolina history, with damage running into the billions of dollars.

Eastern Pennsylvania and New Jersey lay in the northwestern semicircle of the storm path, which is normally the area that receives the heaviest rainfall. A cool, dry Canadian air mass wedged in against the Appalachians was denoted on the weather map by a stalled cold front. Tropical moisture was forced to rise along the stalled frontal boundary, generating torrential rainfalls.

Some of the heaviest totals reported to the weather service were 14.00 inches at Chestertown, Maryland, 13.70 inches at Brewster, New York, 13.34 inches at Somerville, New Jersey, and 12.36 inches at Vernon, Delaware. The urban centers from Washington, D.C., northward to New York City were swamped with more than 6.00 inches of rain. Wilmington, Delaware, had a record twenty-four-hour rainfall of 8.79 inches on September 15–16, 1999.

The storm total at the Philadelphia International Airport of 6.98 inches was the heaviest on record in the city in the twentieth century. The twenty-four-hour measurement of 6.70 inches at Philadelphia ending at 8:00 P.M. on the sixteenth exceeded the previous record of 5.98 inches on August 3, 1898.

More than 10.00 inches of rain fell in Delaware County, with official figures of 10.66 inches at Newton Square and 10.52 inches at Radnor. Northwest of Philadelphia, rainfall amounts reported to the weather service at Mount Holly, New Jersey, were as high as 10.07 inches at Doylestown (Bucks County), 10.04 inches at Valley Forge Park (Chester County), and 9.25 inches at King of Prussia (Montgomery County).

Farther north an average of 6.00 to 9.00 inches of rain fell over eastern portions of the Lehigh Valley and the southeastern Poconos. In Lehigh County, 9.05 inches of rain fell at Coopersburg. The rainfall of 7.61 inches at the Lehigh

Valley International Airport in a little over twenty-four hours was 0.24 inch shy of the record storm total accompanying Hurricane Gloria on September 26–27, 1985.

In Monroe County, the East Stroudsburg observer measured 7.12 inches of rain, including 6.56 inches in twenty-four hours (0.03 inch shy of the September 1985 record). In the higher elevations, 6.87 inches of rain filled the gauge at Tobyhanna. Farther west, rainfall totals were generally in the 3.00- to 6.00-inch range over the Susquehanna and Lackawanna Valleys.

Fortunately, due to the recent drought, a low stream flow provided room for much of the runoff in eastern Pennsylvania, though flash flooding along creeks and streams and in urban areas was widespread in the southeastern counties. Eight Pennsylvanians died in storm-related accidents and flooding as Floyd moved up the coast on September 16, 1999. The storm toll included more than two thousand homes and businesses suffering major damage. Operations along the Southeast Pennsylvania Transportation Authority rail service were brought to a halt by heavy flooding. More than 410,000 Pennsylvania residences and businesses were without power at one time or another during the storm.

Conditions were much worse in eastern New Jersey, where the United States Geological Survey reported that the flooding along the Raritan River basin was the worst in more than two hundred years. At Manville the river reached a height of 27.5 feet, surpassing the high-water mark of 23.8 feet attained during the passage of Tropical Storm Doria on August 28, 1971. At Bound Brook, where eight hundred families were trapped in the upper stories of their homes by swirling floodwaters, a level of 42.13 feet (20 feet above flood stage) broke the 1971 record stage of 37.5 feet.

The death toll in the United States attributed to Floyd reached fifty-six, which was the heaviest loss of a life from a tropical system since Agnes (112) in June 1972.

June 16–17, 2001: Remnants of Allison

Tropical storm Allison formed in the western Gulf of Mexico on June 5, 2001, and proceeded to swamp portions of southeast Texas and southwest Louisiana with 1 to 3 feet of rain.

The weakened remains of the storm tracked across the Gulf states before turning up the eastern seaboard on the weekend of June 16–17. A cold front approaching from the west intercepted the remnant circulation features of Allison near the Atlantic coast, producing copious rains from the Carolinas to Rhode Island. Rainfall rates in excess of 3.00 inches per hour were observed in a few places.

In southeastern Pennsylvania, 4.00 to 10.00 inches of rain triggered local floods, particularly in Bucks and Montgomery Counties. Four residents of the Village Green apartment complex in Upper Moreland Township, Montgomery County, died in a natural gas explosion triggered by high water. Top rainfall totals included 10.16 inches at Willow Grove and 10.17 inches at Chalfont, north of Philadelphia. As much as 9.30 inches fell in twenty-four hours at Doylestown.

11 Other Natural Events

There are a few other natural events worthy of inclusion that do not directly fit into one particular weather category, such as "dark days," smog disasters, earthquakes, and the infamous "Year without a Summer."

1816: Year without a Summer

Pleasantly warm summer weather in early June 1816 gave Pennsylvania farmers renewed hope for crops damaged by a hard interior freeze on May 29, 1816. Yet, despite the seeming advent of summer, a pool of wintry air must have lingered to the north near Hudson Bay.

Although we don't have access to weather maps of 1816, a vigorous upper-air disturbance likely plunged southward from eastern Canada on June 5, setting the stage for a remarkable series of wintry events in the Northeast. Snowflakes swirled over the Pennsylvania mountains, and widespread damaging frosts occurred on the mornings of June 7 to 12.

An interesting item on the summer of 1816 in the *Bethlehem Daily Times* (March 14, 1888) suggested snow may have reached the highlands of northeastern Pennsylvania: "From 'a record of unseasonable snows' in this part of Pennsylvania, being extracts from old diaries and note books, dating as far back as 1774, we extract the following: 'In 1816, the memorable "year without a summer," heavy snows fell on several days in June.'"

A good summary of the anomalous weather conditions in Pennsylvania in 1816 is found in W. J. McKnight's (1905, 366) *A Pioneer Outline History of Northwestern Pennsylvania:* "In 1816, of the year without a summer, frost occurred in every month. Ice formed half an inch thick in May. Snow fell to the depth of three inches in June. Ice was formed to the thickness of a common window-glass on July 5. Indian corn was so frozen that the greater part was cut in August and dried for fodder; and the pioneers supplied from the corn of 1815 for the seeding of the spring of 1817."

The *Philadelphia Inquirer* (June 30, 1924) came upon a clipping about the cold summer of 1816 from an old Bible in the possession of Mrs. Joseph Mitchell of Lansdale, recalling "heavy frosts from the middle of May to June 12 [1816], resulting in several crop losses." At nearby Downington, "severe frosts" on the mornings of June 10 and 11 killed the beans and "destroyed whole fields of corn" (Watson 1868, 362). The latest modern frost on June 11, 1972, was less severe.

The source of the unseasonable weather conditions in 1816 was the violent eruption of Mount Tambora in Indonesia in early April. This explosion was one of several major volcanic events during the years of 1812 to 1815 that may have been responsible for a series of cold years in the northern United States and Europe. Tambora ejected billions of cubic yards of ash and dust that reached the stratosphere about fifteen miles above the earth's surface, where high-level winds circulated the dust around the globe in a little less than a month. A veil of dust and haze no doubt filtered solar rays over the middle latitudes of the Northern Hemisphere, lowering global temperatures.

On August 10, 1816, the editor of *Niles' Weekly Register* took notice of the unusual weather in "Climate of the United States," reporting that snow had reached "the neighborhood of Pittsburg" in June, but added that there was "very little in Pennsylvania east of the mountains." Corn and hay were badly stunted in the northern highlands of Pennsylvania in the dry summer of 1816, though vegetables planted in late June did reasonably well in the southern part of the state.

A letter from a correspondent in Erie, dated June 14, 1816, did not mention snow, but observed: "The season has been dry and frosty for weeks together. It appears as if we should have no crops in these parts—the corn has been all killed by the frost of the 9th [June 1816], and until very lately lake Erie was not navigable for the ice." An interior freeze struck the Northeast on August 22, 1816.

The last straw for farmers in the Northeast in 1816 would be a killing freeze on September 27, which put an early end to an otherwise miserable growing season. Serious food shortages in the winter of 1816–17 led to a westward migration that became known as "Ohio Fever."

October 25, 1823: Dark Day

The unusual thickness of the moisture-bearing clouds hovering over the Northeast on October 25, 1823, caught the attention of the local press and was described by Philadelphia historian John F. Watson (1868, 353): "There was a great darkness at 9 o'clock A.M., so as to make candlelight desirable. At Norristown they were obliged to use candles. The darkness at New York came on at about 11 o'clock, and compelled the printers to print by candlelight. It was stormy there at an earlier hour. At Philadelphia there was thunder and some rain. At Albany, 8 A.M., it snowed fast all day, forming a fall of twelve inches, but melted very fast."

January 26–27, 1927: Highest Pressures

A massive high-pressure system settled over Pennsylvania in late January 1927, bringing record high atmospheric pressure readings in central and eastern Pennsylvania on January 26–27. New records were established at Scranton/Wilkes-Barre (31.08 inches), Harrisburg (31.04 inches), Erie (31.02), and Philadelphia (31.02 inches). In the southwest, a record high atmospheric pressure was recorded at Pittsburgh seven years later, on February 9, 1934 (30.97 inches). In recent times, a large bubble of dry Canadian air brought a record atmospheric pressure reading of 31.08 inches at Philadelphia on February 13, 1981.

October 26–30, 1948: Donora Smog Disaster

The Pennsylvania State Bureau of Industrial Hygiene recently created a new division of air pollution and launched a mobile laboratory attached to a truck that will sample air and water pollution, as well as monitor local weather conditions. The goal is to provide important air quality information and to prevent another episode like the one that afflicted Donora, Pennsylvania, in the late autumn of 1948.

The Monongahela River valley in southwestern Pennsylvania was susceptible to smog problems throughout the early twentieth century, due to the prominence of steel mills and heavy industry. Two lengthy pollution episodes occurred at Donora on October 14–18, 1923, and October 7–18, 1938.

The reason for the clustering of smog events in October in southwestern Pennsylvania is not coincidental. High pressure frequently stalls over the central Appalachians in early autumn, becalming the weather for days on end. Light winds prevent proper mixing of the atmosphere, allowing pollutants to become trapped above an area for days.

A serious air stagnation problem developed in southwestern Pennsylvania on October 26, 1948. An accumulation of sulfur dioxide and other particles hung over the heavily industrialized Monongahela Valley (Ruffner and Bair 1977, 167). Before a cold front arrived to clear the air, a toxic shroud would claim twenty-two lives, with all but two deaths occurring on the thirtieth (Ludlum 1982, 239). During the last week of October 1948, nearly half of Donora's population of 14,000 reported upper respiratory symptoms directly attributable to the poor air quality.

September 25, 1998: Sharon (Pymatuning) Earthquake

At 3:53 P.M. on September 25, 1998, portions of western Pennsylvania and eastern Ohio were rattled by an earthquake that measured 5.2 on the Richter scale and was centered twenty miles west of Sharon, a little south of the Pymatuning Reservoir.

The Sharon (Pymatuning) Earthquake may have been the strongest quake ever felt in the Keystone State. The only significant damage occurred in Mercer County, where the concussion knocked store items from shelves, rattled dishes, loosened ceiling tiles, and shook the county courthouse enough to scatter books from shelves. The range of the quake extended to downtown Pittsburgh and was felt in parts of Venango, Butler, and Beaver Counties. The earthquake shook the earth as far away southern Ontario, Detroit, Cleveland, and Columbus, Ohio.

Earthquakes in the eastern United States are not well understood but are generally thought to occur along ancient faults left over from previous continental collisions. Most of these faults are not readily visible and may extend several miles below the surface. Eastern Seaboard earthquakes are triggered by the release of stress from the spreading Atlantic Ocean sea floor.

About two dozen earthquakes have been strong enough to be widely felt in Pennsylvania since the region was settled in 1682. The New Madrid (Missouri) Shocks in the very early hours of December 16, 1811, rattled pioneer cabins in northwestern Pennsylvania. In the eastern part of the state, a strong jolt on August 10, 1884, rattled furniture and overturned chimneys. The shock was felt for as long as ten seconds.

Appendixes

Weather extremes for the state of Pennsylvania are taken from National Weather Service records on file at the National Climatic Data Center in Asheville, North Carolina. Government data has fallen under a series of different headings, including the *Monthly Weather Review* and *Climatological Data—Pennsylvania.*

A compilation of records has been produced and authenticated by the office of the State Climatologist of Pennsylvania at the Pennsylvania State University. Monthly and seasonal state averages are available through the Northeast Regional Climatic Center in Ithaca, New York. Some stations are listed with an additional notation in reference to distance in miles and compass direction from the post office, i.e., Clermont 4 NW is a location four miles northwest of the Clermont Post Office.

Temperatures are in degrees Fahrenheit, and precipitation is in inches, following the conventions of the previous chapters.

Pennsylvania Weather Stations

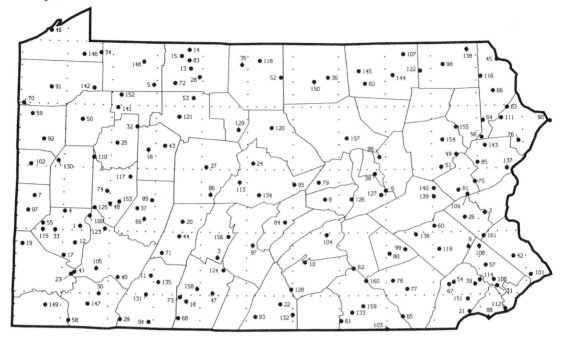

Source: National Climatic Data Center

No.	Station Name	Latitude Deg/Min	Longitude Deg/Min	Elev	No.	Station Name	Latitude Deg/Min	Longitude Deg/Min	Elev
1	Acmetonia Lock 3	4032N	07949W	748	27	Clearfield	4101N	07827W	1140
2	Allentown WSO AP	4039N	07526W	388	28	Clermont 4 NW	4144N	07832W	1620
3	Altoona FAA AP	4018N	07819W	1476	29	Confluence 1 SW Dam	3948N	07922W	1490
4	Bakerstown 3 WNW	4039N	07959W	1230	30	Connellsville 2 SSW	4000N	07936W	900
5	Barnes	4140N	07902W	1360	31	Conshohocken	4004N	07519W	70
6	Bear Gap	4050N	07630W	900	32	Cooksburg	4120N	07913W	1180
7	Beaver Falls 1 NE	4046N	08019W	760	33	Coraopolis Neville Island	4030N	08005W	720
8	Beavertown 1 NE	4046N	07709W	540	34	Corry	4155N	07938W	1440
9	Betchtelsville 1 ENE	4023N	07537W	460	35	Coudersport 4 NW	4150N	07804W	2300
10	Bloserville 1 N	4016N	07722W	650	36	Covington 2 WSW	4144N	07707W	1745
11	Boswell 1 SW	4009N	07902W	1830	37	Creekside	4041N	07912W	1050
12	Braddock Lock 2	4024N	07952W	730	38	Danville	4058N	07637W	460
13	Bradford FAA AP	4148N	07838W	2142	39	Devault 1 W	4005N	07533W	360
14	Bradford Central F S	4157N	07839W	1500	40	Donegal 2 NW	4008N	07924W	1800
15	Bradford 5 SW Res 5	4154N	07844W	1693	41	Donora 1 SW	4010N	07952W	762
16	Brookville Sewage Plt	4109N	07905W	1210	42	Doylestown	4018N	07508W	360
17	Bruceton 1 S	4018N	07959W	1040	43	Du Bois FAA AP	4111N	07854W	1814
18	Buffalo Mills	3957N	07839W	1310	44	Ebensburg Sewage Plt	4028N	07844W	1940
19	Burgettstown 2 W	4023N	08026W	980	45	Equinunk 2 WNW	4152N	07516W	890
20	Carrolltown 2 SSE	4035N	07842W	2040	46	Erie WSO AP	4205N	08011W	732
21	Chadds Ford	3952N	07537W	170	47	Everett	4001N	07822W	1000
22	Chambersburg 1 ESE	3956N	07738W	640	48	Ford City 4 S Dam	4043N	07930W	930
23	Charleroi Lock 4	4009N	07954W	749	49	Francis E. Walter Dam	4107N	07544W	1509
24	Clarence	4103N	07756W	1390	50	Franklin	4123N	07949W	990
25	Clarion 3 SW	4112N	07926W	1114	51	Freeland	4101N	07554W	1900
26	Claussville	4037N	07539W	670	52	Galeton	4144N	07738W	1365

No.	Station Name	Latitude Deg/Min	Longitude Deg/Min	Elev	No.	Station Name	Latitude Deg/Min	Longitude Deg/Min	Elev
53	Glen Hazel 2 NE Dam	4134N	07836W	1725	108	Palm 3 SE	4023N	07530W	302
54	Glenmoore	4006N	07547W	440	109	Palmerton	4048N	07537W	410
55	Glenwillard Dash Dam	4033N	08013W	707	110	Parker	4105N	07941W	1060
56	Gouldsboro	4115N	07527W	1890	111	Paupack 2 WNW	4124N	07514W	1360
57	Graterford 1 E	4014N	07526W	240	112	Philadelphia WSCMO AP	3953N	07514W	10
58	Greensboro Lock 7	3947N	07955W	788	113	Philipsburg 8 E	4054N	07805W	2000
59	Greenville 2 NE	4125N	08022W	1130	114	Phoenixville 1 E	4007N	07530W	105
60	Hamburg	4033N	07559W	350	115	Pittsburgh WSCMO2 AP	4030N	08013W	1150
61	Hanover	3948N	07659W	600	116	Pleasant Mount 1 W	4144N	07527W	1800
62	Harrisburg FAA AP	4013N	07651W	338	117	Putneyville 2 SE Dam	4056N	07917W	1270
63	Hawley 1 E	4129N	07510W	890	118	Raymond	4152N	07752W	2220
64	Hollisterville	4123N	07526W	1365	119	Reading 3 N	4022N	07556W	270
65	Holtwood	3950N	07620W	200	120	Renovo	4120N	07744W	660
66	Honesdale 4 NW	4137N	07519W	1410	121	Ridgway	4125N	07845W	1360
67	Honey Brook 1 S	4005N	07550W	665	122	Rushville	4147N	07607W	870
68	Hyndman	3949N	07844W	960	123	Salina 3 W	4031N	07933W	1109
69	Indiana 3 SE	4036N	07907W	1102	124	Saxton	4012N	07815W	780
70	Jamestown 2 NW	4130N	08028W	1040	125	Schenley Lock 5	4041N	07940W	783
71	Johnstown	4020N	07855W	1214	126	Selinsgrove 2 S	4046N	07652W	420
72	Kane 1 NNE	4141N	07848W	1750	127	Shamokin	4048N	07633W	770
73	Kegg	3959N	07843W	1280	128	Shippensburg	4003N	07731W	680
74	Kittanning Lock 7	4049N	07932W	790	129	Sinnemahoning	4119N	07806W	820
75	Kresgeville 2 W	4054N	07532W	830	130	Slippery Rock 1 SSW	4103N	08004W	1250
76	Lake Minisink	4113N	07503W	1360	131	Somerset	4000N	07905W	2100
77	Lancaster 2 NE	4003N	07617W	270	132	South Mountain	3951N	07730W	1520
78	Landisville 2 NW	4007N	07626W	360	133	Spring Grove	3952N	07652W	450
79	Laurelton St Village	4054N	07713W	800	134	State College	4048N	07752W	1170
80	Lebanon 2 W	4020N	07628W	450	135	Stoystown	4006N	07857W	1800
81	Lehighton	4050N	07543W	580	136	Strausstown	4029N	07611W	600
82	Le Roy	4141N	07643W	1040	137	Stroudsburg	4100N	07511W	480
83	Lewis Run	4152N	07839W	1560	138	Susquehanna	4157N	07536W	910
84	Lewistown	4035N	07735W	460	139	Tamaqua	4047N	07559W	925
85	Long Pond 2 W	4103N	07530W	1860	140	Tamaqua 4 N Dam	4051N	07559W	1120
86	Madera 2 SE	4048N	07824W	1600	141	Tionesta 2 SE Lake	4129N	07926W	1200
87	Mapleton Depot	4024N	07756W	580	142	Titusville Waterworks	4138N	07942W	1220
88	Marcus Hook	3949N	07525W	10	143	Tobyhanna	4111N	07525W	1935
89	Marion Center 2 SE	4045N	07902W	1610	144	Towanda 1 ESE	4145N	07625W	745
90	Matamoras	4122N	07442W	400	145	Troy 1 NE	4147N	07647W	1110
91	Meadville 1 S	4138N	08010W	1065	146	Union City Filt Plant	4154N	07949W	1400
92	Mercer	4113N	08014W	1220	147	Uniontown 1 NE	3955N	07943W	956
93	Mercersburg 1 E	3950N	07754W	540	148	Warren	4151N	07909W	1210
94	Meyersdale 2 SSW	3947N	07903W	2000	149	Waynesburg 1 E	3954N	08010W	940
95	Millheim	4053N	07729W	1070	150	Wellsboro 3 S	4142N	07716W	1860
96	Millville 2 SW	4106N	07634W	860	151	West Chester 1 W	3958N	07538W	450
97	Montgomery L and D	4039N	08023W	690	152	West Hickory	4135N	07924W	1140
98	Montrose	4150N	07552W	1560	153	Whitesburg	4044N	07924W	1320
99	Myerstown	4022N	07618W	480	154	Wilkes Barre	4114N	07553W	660
100	Natrona Lock 4	4037N	07943W	760	155	Wilkes Barre-Scranton WSO AP	4120N	07544W	930
101	Neshaminy Falls	4009N	07457W	60					
102	New Castle 1 N	4101N	08022W	825	156	Williamsburg	4028N	07812W	840
103	New Park	3944N	07630W	780	157	Williamsport WSO AP	4115N	07655W	524
104	Newport	4029N	07708W	380	158	Wolfsburg	4003N	07832W	1200
105	New Stanton 1 SW	4012N	07938W	950	159	York 3 SSW Pump Stn	3955N	07645W	390
106	Norristown	4007N	07521W	70	160	York Haven	4007N	07643W	310
107	Orwell 2 NW	4155N	07618W	1600	161	Zionsville 3 SE	4028N	07527W	680

Appendix A. Pennsylvania Monthly Extremes

January

Warmest (*maximum temperature, in degrees Fahrenheit*)	85	Freeport	22/1906	Coldest (*minimum temperature, in degrees Fahrenheit*)	−34	Smethport	5/1904
Wettest (*total monthly precipitation, in inches*)	12.81	Laporte	1996	Driest (*total monthly precipitation, in inches*)	0.06	Everett	1981

February

Warmest	83	Hyndman	11/1932	Coldest	−39	Lawrenceville	11/1899
Wettest	11.60	Tioga (Hammond Dam)	1981	Driest	Trace	Huntingdon	1968

March

Warmest	92	Everett	23/1907	Coldest	−31	West Bingham	18/1916
Wettest	11.60	Galeton	1936	Driest	0.00	Skidmore (New Castle)	1910

April

Warmest	98	Bloserville Punxsutawney Norristown Port Clinton	25/1915 26/1915 19/1976 19/1976	Coldest	−5	Corry Saegerstown	1/1923
Wettest	14.92	Ephrata	1874	Driest	0.19	Austinburg 2 W	1950

May

Warmest	102	Lock Haven Marcus Hook	30/1895 27/1941	Coldest	10	Clermont 4 NW	10/1966
Wettest	15.02	Quakertown	1894	Driest	0.06	Bethlehem	1964

June

Warmest	107	Sharon	8/1933	Coldest	20	Somerset	10/1913
Wettest	20.45	York 3 SSW	1972	Driest	0.02	Gettysburg	1966

July

Warmest	111	Phoenixville	9–10/1936	Coldest	28	Clermont 4NW	9/1963
Wettest	19.81	Park Place	1947	Driest	Trace	Myerstown Middletown	1955 1955

August

Warmest	108	Claysville	6/1918	Coldest	23	Clermont 4 NW	29/1982
Wettest	23.66	Mount Pocono	1955	Driest	0.01	Strausstown	1995

September

Warmest	106	Stroudsburg	2/1953	Coldest	17	Hawley 1 S (Wallenpau- pack Dam)	28/1947
Wettest	16.13	Marcus Hook	1999	Driest	0.00	Loyalhanna Lake	1985
						Honesdale	1985

October

Warmest	100	Phoenixville	5/1941	Coldest	7	Coudersport	21/1952
Wettest	13.30	Pimple Hill	1955	Driest	0.00	Beavertown	1963
						Berne	1963
						Breezewood	1963
						Chadds Ford	1963
						Huntingdon	1963
						Lebanon 4 WNW	1963
						Virginville	1963

November

Warmest	88	Claysville 3 W	3/1961	Coldest	−15	Somerset	29/1930
Wettest	13.93	Chalk Hill 3 ENE	1985	Driest	0.12	Centre Hall	1917

December

Warmest	82	Washington 3 N	4/1982	Coldest	−29	Clermont 4 NW	25/1980
Wettest	13.39	Joliett	1996	Driest	0.05	Carlisle	1877

Source: Pennsylvania State University, State Climatologist.

Appendix B. Pennsylvania Weather Extremes

Temperatures (in degrees Farenheit)

Highest	111	Phoenixville	July 9–10, 1936
Lowest	−42	Smethport	January 5, 1904
Coldest month	4.3	Bradford FAA	January 1977
Warmest month	84.1	Philadelphia (Franklin Institute)	July 1999

Precipitation (in inches)

Greatest in twenty-four hours	14.50	Schuylkill Co.	June 21–22, 1972
Greatest monthly	23.66	Mount Pocono	August 1955
Greatest annual	81.64	Mount Pocono	1952
Least annual	15.71	Breezewood	1965

Snowfall (in inches)

Greatest in twenty-four hours	40	Seven Springs	March 13–14, 1993
Greatest snowstorm	50	Morgantown	March 19–21, 1958
Greatest monthly snowfall	96	Blue Knob	December 1890

Appendix C. Pennsylvania Monthly Climate Averages and Extremes

	Temperature (degrees Farenheit)			Precipitation (inches)		
	Mean	*Warmest*	*Coldest*	*Mean*	*Wettest*	*Driest*
January	24.6	39.1 (1932)	13.4 (1977)	2.65	6.41 (1978)	0.74 (1981)
February	26.9	35.5 (1998)	16.5 (1934)	2.69	5.32 (1981)	0.62 (1968)
March	36.8	47.2 (1945)	25.4 (1960)	3.24	7.01 (1936)	0.54 (1910)
April	47.2	53.8 (1921)	41.6 (1943)	3.42	6.47 (1943)	1.22 (1946)
May	57.4	64.8 (1944)	51.0 (1967)	4.01	7.69 (1989)	1.43 (1903)
June	65.9	72.2 (1943)	62.4 (1958)	4.23	11.23 (1972)	1.24 (1966)
July	70.3	75.6 (1955)	67.4 (2000)	4.11	7.27 (1992)	1.82 (1909)
August	68.7	73.9 (1900)	64.4 (1927)	3.82	8.42 (1955)	1.29 (1930)
September	61.7	67.8 (1931)	57.5 (1918)	3.68	7.64 (1975)	0.79 (1943)
October	50.0	57.8 (1947)	44.9 (1925)	3.10	6.59 (1976)	0.24 (1936)
November	40.9	48.0 (1931)	33.8 (1976)	3.54	8.28 (1985)	0.53 (1917)
December	29.9	38.4 (1923)	17.8 (1989)	3.13	6.23 (1990)	0.58 (1955)
Annual	48.4	51.9 (1921)	46.1 (1917)	41.39	56.08 (1966)	25.37 (1930)

Source: Northeast Regional Climate Center.

Appendix D. Seasonal Averages and Extremes

	Temperature (degrees Farenheit)			Precipitation (inches)		
	Mean	*Warmest*	*Coldest*	*Mean*	*Wettest*	*Driest*
Winter	27.0	36.7 (1931–32)	20.7 (1917–18)	8.21	13.83 (1978–79)	4.53 (1979–80)
Spring	47.1	53.0 (1921)	43.6 (1984)	10.67	15.49 (1983)	4.89 (1926)
Summer	68.3	72.0 (1900)	66.0 (1927)	12.06	16.94 (1972)	6.42 (1966)
Autumn	51.0	56.8 (1931)	46.3 (1976)	10.36	15.92 (1996)	4.03 (1908)

Source: Northeast Regional Climate Center.

Appendix E. Climate Extremes for Selected Cities

Philadelphia

Temperature (in degrees Fahrenheit)

Highest	106	August 7, 1918
Lowest	−11	February 9, 1934
Warmest month	82.1	July 1994
Coldest month	20.0	January 1977

Precipitation (in inches)

Greatest in tweny-four hours	6.63	September 16, 1999
Greatest monthly	13.07	September 1999
Least monthly	0.0	October 1963 and October 1924
Greatest annual	56.47	1996
Least annual	29.3	1922

Snowfall (in inches)

Greatest in twenty-four hours	27.6	January 7, 1996
Greatest in a snowstorm	30.0	January 7–8, 1996
Greatest monthly	33.8	January 1996
Greatest in a season	65.5	1995–96
Least in a season	Trace	1972–73
Greatest depth	28.0	January 9, 1996

Allentown

Temperature (in degrees Fahrenheit)

Highest	105	July 3, 1966
Lowest	−15	January 21, 1994
Warmest month	79.0	July 1955
Coldest month	16.4	February 1934

Precipitation (in inches)

Greatest in twenty-four hours	7.85	September 26–27, 1985
Greatest monthly	12.10	August 1955
Least monthly	0.00	October 1924
Greatest annual	67.69	1952
Least annual	28.76	1941

Snowfall (in inches)

Greatest in twenty-four hours	25.2	February 11–12, 1983
Greatest in a snowstorm	25.6	January 7–8, 1996

(*continued*)

Appendix E. Climate Extremes for Selected Cities (*continued*)

Greatest in a month	43.2	January 1925
Greatest in a season	75.2	1993–94
Least in a season	5.0	1931–32
Greatest depth	28.0	February 12, 1983

Wilkes-Barre/Scranton

Temperature (in degrees Fahrenheit)		
Highest	103	July 9, 1936
Lowest	−21	January 21, 1994
Warmest month	77.4	July 1955
Coldest month	15.0	January 1977
Precipitation (in inches)		
Greatest in twenty-four hours	6.52	September 26–27, 1985
Greatest monthly	11.76	August 1955
Least monthly	0.03	October 1963
Greatest annual	53.72	1945
Least annual	26.12	1930
Snowfall (in inches)		
Greatest in twenty-four hours	21.0	January 7–8, 1996
Greatest in a snowstorm	21.4	March 13–14, 1993
Greatest in a month	42.3	January 1994
Greatest in a season	98.3	1995–96
Least in a season	7.3	1988–89
Greatest depth	29.0	January 13, 1996

Harrisburg

Temperature (in degrees Fahrenheit)		
Highest	107	July 3, 1966
Lowest	−22	Jan. 21, 1994
Warmest month	81.9	July 1999
Coldest month	19.1	January 1918
Precipitation (in inches)		
Greatest in twenty-four hours	12.55	June 21–22, 1972
Greatest monthly	18.55	June 1972
Least monthly	0.02	October 1924
Greatest annual	59.27	1972
Least annual	26.02	1895
Snowfall (in inches)		
Greatest in twenty-four hours	25.0	February 11–12, 1983
Greatest in a snowstorm	25.0	February 11–12, 1983
Greatest in a month	38.9	January 1996
Greatest in a season	81.3	1960–61
Least in a season	9.5	1937–38
Greatest depth	32.0	January 13, 1996

Williamsport

Temperature (in degrees Fahrenheit)		
Highest	106	July 9, 1936
Lowest	−20	January 21, 1994

Warmest month	79.6	July 1901
Coldest month	14.9	January 1977
Precipitation (in inches)		
Greatest in twenty-four hours	8.66	June 22, 1972
Greatest monthly	16.80	June 1972
Least monthly	0.16	September 1943
Greatest annual	61.27	1972
Least annual	25.98	1895
Snowfall (in inches)		
Greatest in twenty-four hours	23.1	January 12–13, 1964
Greatest in a snowstorm	24.1	January 12–13, 1964
Greatest in a month	40.1	January 1987
Greatest in a season	87.7	1995–96
Least in a season	7.0	1988–89
Greatest depth	29.0	February 23, 1902

Pittsburgh

Temperature (in degrees Fahrenheit)		
Highest	103	July 16, 1988
Lowest	−22	January 19, 1994
Warmest month	80.3	July 1887
Coldest month	11.4	January 1977
Precipitation (in inches)		
Greatest in twenty-four hours	3.57	August 21, 1888
Greatest monthly	11.05	November 1985
Least monthly	0.06	October 1874
Greatest annual	52.24	1990
Least annual	22.65	1930
Snowfall (in inches)		
Greatest in twenty-four hours	23.6	March 13, 1993
Greatest in a snowstorm	27.4	November 24–26, 1950
Greatest in a month	41.3	December 1890
Greatest in a season	82.0	1950–51
Least in a season	8.8	1918–19
Greatest depth	26	January 22, 1978

Erie

Temperature (in degrees Fahrenheit)		
Highest	100	June 25, 1988
Lowest	−18	January 19, 1994
Warmest month	77.6	July 1921
Coldest month	12.5	January 1977
Precipitation (in inches)		
Greatest in twenty-four hours	10.42	July 22–23, 1947
Greatest monthly	13.27	July 1947
Least monthly	0.02	October 1924
Greatest annual	61.70	1977
Least annual	23.84	1934

(*continued*)

Appendix E. Climate Extremes for Selected Cities (*continued*)

Snowfall (in inches)		
Greatest in twenty-four hours	26.5	December 11–12, 1944
Greatest in a snowstorm	30.2	December 11–14, 1944
Greatest in a month	66.9	December 1989
Greatest in a season	149.1	2000–2001
Least in a season	19.6	1932–33
Greatest depth	39	December 21, 1989

Largest Snowstorms (in inches)

Philadelphia	
January 7–8, 1996	30.7
February 11–12, 1983	21.3
December 25–26, 1909	21.0
April 3–4, 1915	19.4
February 12–14, 1899	18.9
Allentown	
January 7–8, 1996	25.6
February 11–12, 1983	25.2
March 19–21, 1958	20.3
January 2, 1925	20.2
March 13–14, 1993	17.6
Wilkes-Barre/Scranton	
March 13–14, 1993	21.4
January 12–13, 1964	21.1
January 7–8, 1996	21.0
November 24–25, 1971	20.5
January 18–20, 1936	20.0
Harrisburg	
February 11–12, 1983	25.0
January 7–8, 1996	22.2
January 15–16, 1945	21.0
February 18–20, 1964	20.8
March 13–14, 1993	20.4
Pittsburgh	
November 24–26, 1950	27.4
December 16–18, 1890	25.9
March 12–14, 1993	25.3
January 8–9, 1886	18.5
January 8–9, 1884	18.0

Snowiest Winters (in inches)

Philadelphia (Average: 20)	
1995–96	65.5
1898–99	55.4
1977–78	54.9
1960–61	49.1
1966–67	44.3
Allentown (Average: 32)	
1993–94	75.2
1995–96	71.8

1966–67	67.2
1960–61	65.1
1957–58	63.6
Wilkes-Barre/Scranton (Average: 49)	
1995–96	98.3
1993–94	90.4
1904–05	88.6
1915–16	82.8
1969–70	76.8
Harrisburg (Average: 35)	
1960–61	81.3
1995–96	77.6
1993–94	75.9
1963–64	74.7
1977–78	70.6
Williamsport (Average: 42)	
1995–96	85.9
1977–78	83.6
1969–70	82.6
1993–94	81.2
Pittsburgh (Average: 44)	
1950–51	82.0
1913–14	78.5
1993–94	76.8
1960–61	76.0
1995–96	74.5
Erie (Average: 86)	
2000–2001	149.1
1977–78	142.8
1993–94	131.3
1995–96	129.2
1985–86	124.9

Bibliography

Newspapers

Albany, N.Y.: *Cultivator and County Gentleman*
Allentown: *Allentown Chronicle*
Baltimore, Md.: *Niles' Weekly (National) Register, Baltimore Sun*
Bellefonte: *Central Press*
Belvidere, N.J.: *Belvidere Apollo, Warren Journal*
Bethlehem: *Bethlehem Daily Times*
Bloomsburg: *Bloomsburg Register*
Boston, Mass.: *Boston Gazette, Daily Evening Transcript*
Bradford: *Bradford Era*
Brookville: *Brookville Repository*
Carlisle: *Carlisle Volunteer*
Centre Hall: *Centre Reporter*
Cleveland, Ohio: *Plain Dealer*
Columbia: *Columbia Spy*
Columbus, Ohio: *Ohio State Journal*
Doylestown: *Doylestown Intelligencer*
Easton: *Easton Argus, Sentinel and Argus, Easton Democrat and Argus, Easton Sentinel, Easton Express*
East Stroudsburg: *Jeffersonian Republican, Morning Sun*
Elizabethtown, N.J.: *New Jersey Journal*
Erie: *Erie Observer*
Fishkill, N.Y.: *New York Packet*
Germantown: *Germantown Zeitung*
Gettysburg: *Gettysburg Sentinel*
Hanover: *Hanover Gazette*
Harrisburg: *Hazard's Register of Pennsylvania, Patriot Daily Union, Patriot*
Hazleton: *Hazleton Standard-Speaker*
Hempstead, N.Y.: *New York Chronicle Advertiser*
Honesdale: *Wayne Independent*
Lancaster: *Lancaster Journal, Lancaster City Express*
Lewistown: *Lewistown Eagle*
Mauch Chunk (Jim Thorpe): *Mauch Chunk Courier*
Milford: *Pike County Press, Milford Herald*
Montrose: *Independent Volunteer*
Mount Vernon, Ohio: *Mount Vernon Democratic Banner*
Newark, N.J.: *Newark Daily Advertiser, Sentinel of Freedom*
New York, N.Y.: *(New York) Evening Post, New York Herald, New York Times*
Philadelphia: *American Mercury, Pennsylvania Advertiser and Weekly Journal, North American, Philadelphia Gazette, Democratic Press, Franklin Gazette, United States Gazette, Evening Traveller, Public Ledger, Evening Bulletin, Vincent's Register Pennsylvania Inquirer, Philadelphia Inquirer*
Pittsburgh: *Pittsburgh (Commercial) Gazette, Pittsburgh Chronicle Telegraph, Leader*

Pottsville: *Miners' Journal*
Reading: *Reading Eagle*
Rochester, N.Y.: *Genessee Farmer*
Savannah, Ga.: *Savannah Republican*
State College: *Centre Daily Times*
Stroudsburg: *Jeffersonian, Stroudsburg (Daily) Times, Monroe Record, Morning Press, Daily Record, Record, Pocono Record*
Sussex, N.J.: *Sussex Register*
Toledo, Ohio: *Blade*
Washington, D.C.: *National Intelligencer, Washington Post*
West Chester: *Republican*
Wilkes-Barre: *Times-Leader*
Williamsport: *Williamsport Bulletin, Williamsport Sun*
York: *York Gazette*

Books and Periodicals

Barnes, John. H., and W. D. Sevon. 1996. *The Geological Story of Pennsylvania.* Harrisburg: Pennsylvania Geological Survey (4th series).

Bausman, Joseph H. 1904. *History of Beaver County, Pennsylvania.* New York: Knickerbocker Press.

Brodhead, Col. Daniel. 1780. Letter to Gen. George Washington, Fort Pitt. *Pennsylvania Archives,* 12 (1855): 206.

Clayton, H. H. 1944. *World Weather Records.* Washington, D.C.: Smithsonian Miscellaneous Collection 79:891.

Creigh, Alfred. 1870. *History of Washington County, Pennsylvania.* Washington, Pennsylvania: A. Creigh.

Crowther, Hugh G. 1995. "Tornadoes: Philadelphia Story." *Weatherwise* 48(1): 50.

Dale, Frank. 1996. *Delaware Diary.* New Brunswick: Rutgers University Press.

Eckhart, Thomas D. 1992, 1996, 1997. *The History of Carbon County.* 3 vols. Allentown: Thomas D. Eckhart and The Carbon History Project.

Fitch, John. "Accounts 1784–91." *John Fitch Papers II–35–D–4* (Library of Congress).

Flora, Snowden D. 1953. *Tornadoes of the United States.* Norman: University of Oklahoma Press.

Fulks, J. R. 1954. "The Early November Snowstorm of 1953." *Weatherwise* 7(1): 12–16.

Gaine, Hugh. *The Journals of Hugh Gaine.* 1902. Edited by Paul L. Ford. New York: Dodd, Mead & Company.

Garriott, Edward B. 1906. *Cold Waves and Frosts in the United States, Bulletin P.* Washington, D.C.: U.S. Department of Agriculture.

Gelber, Benjamin D. 1998. *Pocono Weather.* Stroudsburg, Pa.: Uriel Publishing.

Grazulis, Thomas P. 1993. *Significant Tornadoes 1680–1991.* St. Johnsbury, Vt.: Tornado Project of Environmental Films.

Hall, Jonathon P. 1858. "Register of the Thermometer for 36 Years, from 1821 to 1856" (Boston). *Mem. American Academy* 6(2): 233.

Hanes, Benjamin F. 1902. *Illustrated Wayne County.* Honesdale, Pa.: B. F. Haines.

Harvey, Oscar J. 1909. *A History of Wilkes-Barre.* Vol. 2. Wilkes-Barre, Pa.: Raedor.

Hazard, Samuel. 1828. "Effect of Climate on Navigation [Delaware River, 1681–1828]." *Register of Pennsylvania* 2: 23–26 (July); 2: 379–386 (December).

Henry, A. J. 1907. "The Cold Spring of 1907." *Monthly Weather Review* 35(5): 223–225.

Heverling, Clement F. 1926. *History and Geography of Bradford County, Pennsylvania, 1614–1924.* Towanda, Pa.: Bradford County Historical Society.

Hildreth, Samuel. 1826. *American Journal of Science* 11(2): 232.

Hoffman, Luther S. "Historical Notes of Luther S. Hoffman on the History of Smithfield Township and Monroe County, Pennsylvania."

Hughes, Patrick. 1987. "Hurricanes Haunt Our History." *Weatherwise* 40(3): 134–140 (revised version of an article that appeared in *American Weather Stories,* Government Printing Office, 1976).

Johnson, Kirk. 2000. "Not Complaining about the Weather, Doing Something about It." *New York Times,* June 30, A23.

Karl, Thomas R., Laura K.Metcalf, M. K. Nicodemus, and Robert Quayle. 1983. *Statewide Average Climatic History—Pennsylvania, 1888–1982, Series 6–1.* Asheville, N.C.: National Climatic Data Center.

Keen, Richard A. 1992. *Skywatch East: A Weather Guide.* Golden, Colo.: Fulcrum Publishing.

Kocin, Paul J., and Louis W. Uccellini. 1990. *Snowstorms along the Northeastern Coast of the United States: 1955 to 1985.* Boston: American Meteorological Society.

Kocin, Paul, Alan D. Weiss, and Joseph J. Wagner. 1988. "The Great Arctic Outbreak and East Coast Blizzard of February 1899." *Weather and Forecasting* 3: 305–318.

Lantz, Jackson. 1897. *Picturesque Monroe County, Pennsylvania.* Stroudsburg, Pa.: Morris Evans.

Laskin, David. 1996. *Braving the Elements: A Stormy History of American Weather.* New York: Doubleday.

Lesh, William S. 1945. "Landmarks of Monroe County." *Record* (Stroudsburg), August 23.

Levering, Joseph M. 1903. *A History of Bethlehem, 1741–1892.* Bethlehem, Pa.: Times Publishing.

Lewis, Joseph. 1941, 1943. "Diary of Joseph Lewis." *Proceedings of the New Jersey Historical Society* 59(3): 159–61; 61(1): 49, 51.

Linn, John B. 1877. *Annals of Buffalo Valley, Pennsylvania, 1755–1855.* Harrisburg, Pa.: Lane S. Hart.

Longshore, David. 1998. *Encyclopedia of Hurricanes, Typhoons, and Cyclones.* New York: Facts on File.

Lorant, Stefan. 1964. *Pittsburgh: The Story of an American City.* Garden City, N.Y.: Doubleday & Company.

Ludlum, David M. 1960. "The Weather at Gettysburg." Weatherwise 13(3): 101–105.

———. 1960. "Big Snow of 1836." *Weatherwise* 13(6): 248–252.

———. 1961. "New York City Weather Highlights." *Weatherwise* 14(2): 66.

———. 1963. *Early American Hurricanes, 1492–1870.* Boston: American Meteorological Society.

———. 1966. *Early American Winters, 1604–1820.* Boston: American Meteorological Society.

——— 1968. *Early American Winters, 1821–70.* Boston: American Meteorological Society.

———. 1970. *Early American Tornadoes, 1586–1870.* Boston: American Meteorological Society.

———. 1971. *Outstanding Weather Events.* Princeton: Weatherwise.

———. 1982. *The American Weather Book.* Boston: Houghton Mifflin Company.

———. 1983. *The New Jersey Weather Book.* New Brunswick, N.J.: Rutgers University Press.

———. 1984. *The Weather Factor.* Boston: Houghton Mifflin Company.

———. 1985. *The Vermont Weather Book.* Montpelier: Vermont Historical Society.

———. 1988. "New York City Icebound: The Hard Winter of 1780." *Weatherwise* 41(6): 334–336.

———. 1989. "The Johnstown Flood." *Weatherwise* 42(3): 88–92.

Mason, Charles.1899. "Charles Mason's Daily Journal" (National Archives), quoted in Maryland Weather Service. Baltimore: Johns Hopkins Press 1: 343–334.

McCullough, David G. 1968. *The Johnstown Flood.* New York: Simon and Schuster.

McKnight, W. J. 1905. *A Pioneer Outline History of Northwestern Pennsylvania.* Philadelphia: J. B. Lippincott.

Mellick, Andrew Jr. 1889. "The Story of an Old Farm; or, Life in New Jersey in the Eighteenth Century." *Unionist Gazette* (Somerville), 514.

Monmonier, Mark. 1999. *Air Apparent.* Chicago: University of Chicago Press.

Muhlenberg, Henry M. 1945. *The Journals of Henry Muhlenburg.* 3 vols. Philadelphia: Muhlenberg Press.

Musgrove, William. 1831. "Comments on January 1831 Snow Depth." *Hazard's Register of Pennsylvania,* February 12, 104.

Nuschke, Marie Kathern. 1960. *The Dam That Could Not Break.* Coudersport, Pa.: The Potter Enterprise.

Nutting, Wallace. 1924. *Pennsylvania Beautiful: Eastern.* New York: Bonanza Books.

Oplinger, Carl. S., and Robert Halma. 1988. *The Poconos: An Illustrated Natural History.* New Brunswick, N.J.: Rutgers University Press.

Owenby, James. R., and D. S. Enzell. 1992. *Monthly Station Normals of Temperature, Precipitation, and Heating and Cooling Degree Days, 1961–90–Pennsylvania.* Climatography of the United States, No. 81. Asheville, N.C.: U.S. Department of Commerce, National Oceanic and Atmospheric Administration, National Climatic Data Center.

Peirce, Charles. 1847. *A Meteorological Account of the Weather in Philadelphia, January 1, 1790, to January 1, 1847.* Philadelphia: Lindsay and Blakistan.

Pemberton, Phineas. Meteorological Observations in Philadelphia. American Philosophical Society Library.

Pershing, Benjamin H. 1924. "Winthrop Sargent." *Ohio Archeological and Historical Quarterly* 33(3): 237–281.

Petterssen, Sverre. 2001. *Weathering the Storm: Sverre Petterssen, the D-Day Forecast, and the Rise of Modern Meteorology.* Edited by James R. Fleming. Boston: American Meteorological Society.

Rittenhouse, David. 1780. "Height of Fahrenheit's Thermometer at Philadelphia, 1780." Pennsylvania Historical Society (Philadelphia).

Rosenfeld, Jeffrey. 1999. *Eye of the Storm.* New York: Plenum Trade.

Ruffner, James A., and Frank E. Bair. 1977. *The Weather Almanac.* Detroit: Gale Research Company.

Rupp, I. Daniel. 1845. *History of Northampton, Lehigh Monroe, Carbon, & Schuylkill Counties.* Lancaster, Pa.: G. Hills.

Schmidlin, Thomas, and Jeanne A. Schmidlin. 1996. *Thunder in the Heartland.* Kent, Ohio: Kent State University Press.

Schott, Charles A. 1876. *Tables, Distribution, and Variations of the Atmospheric Temperature in the United States, and Some Adjacent Parts of America.* Washington, D.C.: Smithsonian Institution.

Sevon, W. D., and Gary. M. Fleeger. 1999. *Pennsylvania and the Ice Age.* Harrisburg: Pennsylvania Geological Survey (4th series).

Shank, William H. 1988. *Great Floods of Pennsylvania: A Two-Century History.* York, Pa.: American Canal and Transportation Center.

Sloane, Eric. 1963. *Folklore of American Weather.* New York: Duell, Sloan, and Pearce.

Stevens, William K. 2000. "Persistent and Severe, Drought Strikes Again." *New York Times,* April 25, D1, D4.

U.S. Department of Agriculture, Weather Bureau. 1934. *Climatic Summary of the United States, Sections 87–89: Pennsylvania.* Washington, D.C.: U.S. Government Printing Office.

Walter, Y. S. 1844. Report of a committee of the Delaware Institute of Science on the Great Rain Storm and Flood of August 1843. Chester: Delaware Institute of Science.

Walters, Mrs. Horace G. 1965. *Stodgell Stokes Ledger-C.* Monroe County Historical Society. (Additional source for this material was taken from the Stroudsburg *Jeffersonian,* April 16, 1874; July 15, 1875; December 16, 1886; and the Stroudsburg Census, 1850–60.)

Watson, Benjamin F. 1993. *Acts of God: The Old Farmer's Almanac Unpredictable Guide to Weather and Natural Disasters.* New York: Random House.

Watson, John F. 1868. *Annals of Philadelphia and Pennsylvania, in the Olden Time* 2:347–69. Philadelphia: J. B. Lippincott and Company.

Webster, Noah. 1835. "Notices of Extraordinary Seasons of Cold." *American Journal of Science* 28(1): 186.

Weiss, Webster C. 1863. *Incidents of the Freshet on the Lehigh River.* Philadelphia: Crissy and Markley.

Witten, Donald E. 1985. "May 31, 1985: A Deadly Tornado Outbreak." *Weatherwise* 38(4): 193–199.

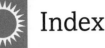

Index

Note: Page numbers in italics indicate illustrations.

 About the Author

Ben Gelber is the author of two books on the weather history of northeastern Pennsylvania and northwestern New Jersey, as well as numerous weather articles in newspapers and science magazines. Gelber earned his degrees in geography and meteorology from the Pennsylvania State University and Northern Illinois University. He has been an on-air meteorologist at NBC 4 (WCMH-TV) in Columbus, Ohio, for more than twenty years, and he lectures on the subject of meteorology and related topics in central Ohio schools.